Peggy J. Kleinplatz, PhD
Charles Moser, PhD, MD
Editors

Sadomasochism: Powerful Pleasures

Sadomasochism: Powerful Pleasures has been co-published simultaneously as *Journal of Homosexuality*, Volume 50, Numbers 2/3 2006.

Pre-publication
REVIEWS,
COMMENTARIES,
EVALUATIONS . . .

" **A** TIMELY AND WELL-CHOSEN COLLECTION! Drawing from academic and other sources, and from commentators outside the United States, it is a fascinating and easy-to-read book. It will be enjoyed by the public and professionals alike."

Colin J. Williams, PhD
Professor, Department of Sociology
Indiana University-Purdue University
at Indianapolis

Martin S. Weinberg, PhD
Professor, Department
of Sociology, Indiana University
(Co-authors of Dual Attraction
and other books)

More pre-publication
REVIEWS, COMMENTARIES, EVALUATIONS . . .

"This mythbreaking collection GOES WHERE MOST SEX RESEARCHERS FEAR TO TREAD. It offers extraordinary insights into a contemporary lifestyle that remains largely invisible despite millions of Web pages devoted to SM behaviors, scripts, and code words. Physicians, social workers, lawyers, and other professionals who dare venture beyond standard judgments and diagnoses can find a rich mine of information here about personal growth, relationships, boundaries, pleasure, pain, clear communication, and the nuances of power."

Gina Ogden, PhD
Author of The Heart and Soul of Sex: Making the ISIS Connection *and* Women Who Love Sex: An Inquiry Into the Expanding Spirit of Women's Erotic Experience

"I WOULD ADVISE ANYONE interested in doing research on this topic or trying to understand this severely stigmatized behavior TO BEGIN WITH THIS COLLECTION.

This is an important addition to the sparse scholarly literature on SM. It includes contributions from many of the names who have written on SM extensively, such as Thomas Wein- berg and the two editors themselves. It also defines SM in its broadest setting, including chapters on spanking, slavery, and fetishism. Also included are chapters on both homosexual and heterosexual SM, and several important contributions on legal aspects."

Vern L. Bullough, PhD, DSci, RN
Visiting Professor Emeritus
State University of New York
Editor of Before Stonewall: Activists for Gay and Lesbian Rights in Historical Context

"A MUST-READ for anyone interested in understanding the complexity of sexuality. . . . A fascinating exploration of a deeply misunderstood phenomenon. Kleinplatz and Moser have pulled together a rich collection which debunks a myriad of myths and challenges us to rethink sadomasochism."

Eli Coleman, PhD
Professor and Director
Program in Human Sexuality
University of Minnesota Medical School

Harrington Park Press

Sadomasochism: Powerful Pleasures

Sadomasochism: Powerful Pleasures has been co-published simultaneously as *Journal of Homosexuality*, Volume 50, Numbers 2/3 2006.

Monographic Separates from the *Journal of Homosexuality*

For additional information on these and other Haworth Press titles, including descriptions, tables of contents, reviews, and prices, use the QuickSearch catalog at http://www.HaworthPress.com.

Sadomasochism: Powerful Pleasures, edited by Peggy J. Kleinplatz, PhD, and Charles Moser, PhD, MD (Vol. 50, No. 2/3, 2006). *"I would advise anyone interested in doing research on this topic or trying to understand this severely stigmatized behavior to begin with this collection."* (Vern L. Bullough, PhD, DSci, RN, Visiting Professor Emeritus, State University of New York; Editor of Before Stonewall: Activists for Gay and Lesbian Rights in Historical Context)

Same-Sex Desire and Love in Greco-Roman Antiquity and in the Classical Tradition of the West, edited by Beert C. Verstraete and Vernon Provencal (Vol. 49, No. 3/4, 2005). *"This wide-ranging collection engages with the existing scholarship in the history of sexuality and the uses of the classical tradition and opens up exciting new areas of study. The book is an important addition to queer theory."* (Stephen Guy-Bray, PhD, Associate Professor, University of British Columbia)

Sexuality and Human Rights: A Global Overview, edited by Helmut Graupner and Philip Tahmindjis (Vol. 48, No. 3/4, 2005). *"An important resource for anybody concerned about the status of legal protection for the human rights of sexual minorities, especially for those concerned with attaining a comparative perspective. The chapters are all of high quality and are written in a straightforward manner that will be accessible to the non-specialist while containing much detail of interest to specialists in the area."* (Arthur S. Leonard, JD, Professor of Law, New York Law School)

Eclectic Views on Gay Male Pornography: Pornucopia, edited by Todd G. Morrison, PhD (Vol. 47, No. 3/4, 2004). "An instant classic. . . . Lively and readable." *(Jerry Zientara, EdD, Librarian, Institute for Advanced Study of Human Sexuality)*

The Drag Queen Anthology: The Absolutely Fabulous but Flawlessly Customary World of Female Impersonators, edited by Steven P. Schacht, PhD, with Lisa Underwood (Vol. 46, No. 3/4, 2004). *"Indispensable. . . . For more than a decade, Steven P. Schacht has been one of the social sciences' most reliable guides to the world of drag queens and female impersonators. . . . This book assembles an impressive cast of scholars who are as theoretically astute, methodologically careful, and conceptually playful as the drag queens themselves."* (Michael Kimmel, author of The Gendered Society; Professor of Sociology, SUNY Stony Brook)

Queer Theory and Communication: From Disciplining Queers to Queering the Discipline(s), edited by Gust A. Yep, PhD, Karen E. Lovaas, PhD, and John P. Elia, PhD (Vol. 45, Nov. 2/3/4, 2003). *"Sheds light on how sexual orientation and identity are socially produced–and how they can be challenged and changed–through everyday practices and institutional activities, as well as academic research and teaching. . . . Illuminates the theoretical and practical significance of queer theory–not only as a specific area of inquiry, but also as a productive challenge to the heteronormativity of mainstream communication theory, research, and pedagogy."* (Julia T. Wood, PhD, Lineberger Professor of Humanities, Professor of Communication Studies, The University of North Carolina at Chapel Hill)

Gay Bathhouses and Public Health Policy, edited by William J. Woods, PhD, and Diane Binson, PhD (Vol. 44, No. 3/4, 2003). *"Important. . . . Long overdue. . . . A unique and valuable contribution to the social science and public health literature. The inclusion of detailed historical descriptions of public policy debates about the place of bathhouses in urban gay communities, together with summaries of the legal controversies about bathhouses, insightful examinations of patrons' behaviors and reviews of successful programs for HIV/STD education and testing programs in bathhouses provides. A well rounded and informative overview."* (Richard Tewksbury, PhD, Professor of Justice Administration, University of Louisville)

Icelandic Lives: The Queer Experience, edited by Voon Chin Phua (Vol. 44, No. 2, 2002). *"The first of its kind, this book shows the emergence of gay and lesbian visibility through the biographical narratives of a dozen Icelanders. Through their lives can be seen a small nation's transition, in just a few decades, from a pervasive silence concealing its queer citizens to widespread acknowledgment characterized by some of the most progressive laws in the world."* (Barry D. Adam, PhD, University Professor, Department of Sociology & Anthropology, University of Windsor, Ontario, Canada)

The Drag King Anthology, edited by Donna Jean Troka, PhD (cand.), Kathleen LeBesco, PhD, and Jean Bobby Noble, PhD (Vol. 43, No. 3/4, 2002). *"All university courses on masculinity should use this book . . . challenges preconceptions through the empirical richness of direct experience. The contributors and editors have worked together to produce cultural analysis that enhances our perception of the dynamic uncertainty of gendered experience." (Sally R. Munt, DPhil, Subject Chair, Media Studies, University of Sussex)*

Homosexuality in French History and Culture, edited by Jeffrey Merrick and Michael Sibalis (Vol. 41, No. 3/4, 2001). *"Fascinating. . . . Merrick and Sibalis bring together historians, literary scholars, and political activists from both sides of the Atlantic to examine same-sex sexuality in the past and present." (Bryant T. Ragan, PhD, Associate Professor of History, Fordham University, New York City)*

Gay and Lesbian Asia: Culture, Identity, Community, edited by Gerard Sullivan, PhD, and Peter A. Jackson, PhD (Vol. 40, No. 3/4, 2001). *"Superb. . . . Covers a happily wide range of styles . . . will appeal to both students and educated fans." (Gary Morris, Editor/Publisher, Bright Lights Film Journal)*

Queer Asian Cinema: Shadows in the Shade, edited by Andrew Grossman, MA (Vol. 39, No. 3/4, 2000). *"An extremely rich tapestry of detailed ethnographies and state-of-the-art theorizing. . . . Not only is this a landmark record of queer Asia, but it will certainly also be a seminal, contributive challenge to gender and sexuality studies in general." (Dédé Oetomo, PhD, Coordinator of the Indonesian organization GAYa NUSANTARA; Adjunct Reader in Linguistics and Anthropology, School of Social Sciences, Universitas Airlangga, Surabaya, Indonesia)*

Gay Community Survival in the New Millennium, edited by Michael R. Botnick, PhD (cand.) (Vol. 38, No. 4, 2000). *Examines the notion of community from several different perspectives focusing on the imagined, the structural, and the emotive. You will explore a theoretical overview and you will peek into the moral discourses that frame "gay community," the rift between HIV-positive and HIV-negative gay men, and how Israeli gays seek their place in the public sphere.*

The Ideal Gay Man: The Story of Der Kreis, by Hubert Kennedy, PhD (Vol. 38, No. 1/2, 1999). *"Very profound. . . . Excellent insight into the problems of the early fight for homosexual emancipation in Europe and in the USA. . . . The ideal gay man (high-mindedness, purity, cleanness), as he was imagined by the editor of 'Der Kreis,' is delineated by the fascinating quotations out of the published erotic stories." (Wolfgang Breidert, PhD, Academic Director, Institute of Philosophy, University Karlsruhe, Germany)*

Multicultural Queer: Australian Narratives, edited by Peter A. Jackson, PhD, and Gerard Sullivan, PhD (Vol. 36, No. 3/4, 1999). *Shares the way that people from ethnic minorities in Australia (those who are not of Anglo-Celtic background) view homosexuality, their experiences as homosexual men and women, and their feelings about the lesbian and gay community.*

Scandinavian Homosexualities: Essays on Gay and Lesbian Studies, edited by Jan Löfström, PhD (Vol. 35, No. 3/4, 1998). *"Everybody interested in the formation of lesbian and gay identities and their interaction with the sociopolitical can find something to suit their taste in this volume." (Judith Schuyf, PhD, Assistant Professor of Lesbian and Gay Studies, Center for Gay and Lesbian Studies, Utrecht University, The Netherlands)*

Gay and Lesbian Literature Since World War II: History and Memory, edited by Sonya L. Jones, PhD (Vol. 34, No. 3/4, 1998). *"The authors of these essays manage to gracefully incorporate the latest insights of feminist, postmodernist, and queer theory into solidly grounded readings . . . challenging and moving, informed by the passion that prompts both readers and critics into deeper inquiry." (Diane Griffin Crowder, PhD, Professor of French and Women's Studies, Cornell College, Mt. Vernon, Iowa)*

Reclaiming the Sacred: The Bible in Gay and Lesbian Culture, edited by Raymond-Jean Frontain, PhD (Vol. 33, No. 3/4, 1997). *"Finely wrought, sharply focused, daring, and always dignified. . . . In chapter after chapter, the Bible is shown to be a more sympathetic and humane book in its attitudes toward homosexuality than usually thought and a challenge equally to the straight and gay moral imagination." (Joseph Wittreich, PhD, Distinguished Professor of English, The Graduate School, The City University of New York)*

Activism and Marginalization in the AIDS Crisis, edited by Michael A. Hallett, PhD (Vol. 32, No. 3/4, 1997). *Shows readers how the advent of HIV-disease has brought into question the utility of certain forms of "activism" as they relate to understanding and fighting the social impacts of disease.*

Sadomasochism:
Powerful Pleasures

Peggy J. Kleinplatz, PhD
Charles Moser, PhD, MD
Editors

Sadomasochism: Powerful Pleasures has been co-published simultaneously as *Journal of Homosexuality*, Volume 50, Numbers 2/3 2006.

HPP

Harrington Park Press®
An Imprint of The Haworth Press, Inc.

New York • London • Victoria (AU)
www.HaworthPress.com

Published by

Harrington Park Press®, 10 Alice Street, Binghamton, NY 13904-1580 USA

Harrington Park Press® is an imprint of The Haworth Press, Inc., 10 Alice Street, Binghamton, NY 13904-1580 USA.

Sadomasochism: Powerful Pleasures has been co-published simultaneously as *Journal of Homosexuality*, Volume 50, Numbers 2/3 2006.

The development, preparation, and publication of this work has been undertaken with great care. However, the publisher, employees, editors, and agents of The Haworth Press and all imprints of The Haworth Press, Inc., including The Haworth Medical Press® and Pharmaceutical Products Press®, are not responsible for any errors contained herein or for consequences that may ensue from use of materials or information contained in this work. With regard to case studies, identities and circumstances of individuals discussed herein have been changed to protect confidentiality. Any resemblance to actual persons, living or dead, is entirely coincidental.

The Haworth Press is committed to the dissemination of ideas and information according to the highest standards of intellectual freedom and the free exchange of ideas. Statements made and opinions expressed in this publication do not necessarily reflect the views of the Publisher, Directors, management, or staff of The Haworth Press, Inc., or an endorsement by them.

Cover design by Jennifer M. Gaska

Library of Congress Cataloging-in-Publication Data

Sadomasochism : powerful pleasures / Peggy J. Kleinplatz, Charles Moser, editors.
   p. cm.
   "Co-published simultaneously as Journal of Homosexuality, Volume 50, Numbers 2/3 2006."
   Includes bibliographical references and index.
   ISBN-13: 978-1-56023-639-9 (hard cover : alk. paper)
   ISBN-10: 1-56023-639-6 (hard cover : alk. paper)
   ISBN-13: 978-1-56023-640-5 (soft cover : alk. paper)
   ISBN-10: 1-56023-640-X (soft cover : alk. paper)
 1. Sadomasochism. I. Kleinplatz, Peggy J. II. Moser, Charles A. III. Journal of homosexuality.
HQ79.S2624 2006
306.77'5–dc22

2005028460

Indexing, Abstracting & Website/Internet Coverage

This section provides you with a list of major indexing & abstracting services and other tools for bibliographic access. That is to say, each service began covering this periodical during the year noted in the right column. Most Websites which are listed below have indicated that they will either post, disseminate, compile, archive, cite or alert their own Website users with research-based content from this work. (This list is as current as the copyright date of this publication.)

(continued)

(continued)

(continued)

(continued)

Special Bibliographic Notes related to special journal issues (separates) and indexing/abstracting:

- indexing/abstracting services in this list will also cover material in any "separate" that is co-published simultaneously with Haworth's special thematic journal issue or DocuSerial. Indexing/abstracting usually covers material at the article/chapter level.
- monographic co-editions are intended for either non-subscribers or libraries which intend to purchase a second copy for their circulating collections.
- monographic co-editions are reported to all jobbers/wholesalers/approval plans. The source journal is listed as the "series" to assist the prevention of duplicate purchasing in the same manner utilized for books-in-series.
- to facilitate user/access services all indexing/abstracting services are encouraged to utilize the co-indexing entry note indicated at the bottom of the first page of each article/chapter/contribution.
- this is intended to assist a library user of any reference tool (whether print, electronic, online, or CD-ROM) to locate the monographic version if the library has purchased this version but not a subscription to the source journal.
- individual articles/chapters in any Haworth publication are also available through the Haworth Document Delivery Service (HDDS).

ABOUT THE EDITORS

Peggy J. Kleinplatz, PhD, is a clinical psychologist, certified sex therapist and sex educator. She deals with sexual issues in individual, couple, and group therapy. She is Associate Professor of Medicine at the University of Ottawa, Canada. Dr. Kleinplatz has been teaching human sexuality in the School of Psychology since 1983 and was awarded the Prix d'Excellence by the University of Ottawa in 2000. She also teaches sex therapy at the affiliated, Saint Paul University's Institute of Pastoral Studies. Her work focuses on eroticism and transformation. She is the editor of *New Directions in Sex Therapy: Innovations and Alternatives,* Brunner-Routledge, 2001, a book intended to combat the increasing medicalization of human sexuality. In her own work as well as with Charles Moser, PhD, MD, and as a member of the Working Group for a New View of Women's Sexual Problems, Kleinplatz has critiqued the pathologizing of sexual difficulties in the *DSM* and called for alternate ways of conceptualizing them.

Charles Moser, PhD, MD, received his PhD in 1979 in Human Sexuality from the Institute for Advanced Study of Human Sexuality in San Francisco. He received his MD in 1991 from Hahnemann University in Philadelphia. He is also a Licensed Clinical Social Worker in California and maintained a private psychotherapy practice specializing in the treatment of sexual concerns prior to his medical career. He is board certified in Internal Medicine by the American Board of Internal Medicine. Currently, Dr. Moser is Professor of Sexology and Chair of the Department of Sexual Medicine at the Institute for Advanced Study of Human Sexuality. He also maintains an Internal Medicine private practice focused on Sexual Medicine (the sexual aspects of medical concerns and the medical aspects of sexual concerns). He has authored or co-authored over 40 scientific papers or books.

Sadomasochism: Powerful Pleasures

CONTENTS

Introduction:
The State of Our Knowledge on SM

Charles Moser, PhD, MD

Institute for Advanced Study of Human Sexuality

Peggy J. Kleinplatz, PhD

University of Ottawa

It is with great pleasure that we introduce an entire issue of the *Journal of Homosexuality* devoted to sadomasochism, also known as SM, S/M, BDSM, D/S and Leather; each has a slightly different meaning. For simplicity, we will refer to the concept generically as SM.

It is vitally important that we include the study of SM in order to have a broader understanding of all sexuality. Havelock Ellis' (1903/1936) statement (made before the terms or concepts of sadism and masochism were in common use) remains true:

> The relation of love to pain is one of the most difficult problems, and yet one of the most fundamental, in the whole range of sexual psychology. . . . [I]f we succeed in answering it . . . we shall have

Charles Moser is Professor and Chair of the Department of Sexual Medicine, Institute for Advanced Study of Human Sexuality, San Francisco, CA. Peggy J. Kleinplatz is affiliated with the Faculty of Medicine and School of Psychology, University of Ottawa, Ottawa, ON, Canada.

[Haworth co-indexing entry note]: "Introduction: The State of Our Knowledge on SM." Moser, Charles, and Peggy J. Kleinplatz. Co-published simultaneously in *Journal of Homosexuality* (Harrington Park Press, an imprint of The Haworth Press, Inc.) Vol. 50, No. 2/3, 2006, pp. 1-15; and: *Sadomasochism: Powerful Pleasures* (ed: Peggy J. Kleinplatz, and Charles Moser) Harrington Park Press, an imprint of The Haworth Press, Inc., 2006, pp. 1-15. Single or multiple copies of this article are available for a fee from The Haworth Document Delivery Service [1-800-HAWORTH, 9:00 a.m. - 5:00 p.m. (EST). E-mail address: docdelivery@haworthpress.com].

Available online at http://www.haworthpress.com/web/JH
doi:10.1300/J082v50n02_01

made clear the normal basis on which rest the extreme aberrations of love. (p. 66)

It is not clear why SM has not engendered more attention from researchers. All the large survey studies of sexual behavior have ignored SM behavior almost completely (e.g., Hunt, 1974; Kinsey, Pomeroy, Martin, 1948; Kinsey, Pomeroy, Martin, Christensen, 1953; Laumann, Gagnon, Michael, Michaels, 1994). Thus, our estimates of the incidence and prevalence of SM behavior are rudimentary. Perusing the average adult bookstore or sexually explicit Internet sites, one finds a large variety of SM materials. It is reasonable to assume that this abundance of media would not be produced unless there were a market for it. SM educational, support, and social organizations can be found in every state in the US and in many foreign countries (see Wright, this volume; SM International, this volume). SM is widespread enough so that mainstream movies, television shows, commercials, and magazines refer to it commonly without having to explain it to their audiences (see Weiss, this volume). Yet it is still virtually unstudied scientifically.

The first task of this introduction is to define SM. As indicated below, we asked all the contributors to this volume to define their terms in their articles. This task is actually quite difficult. First, who is to define it? Is it to be the helping professionals (e.g., physicians, psychotherapists, social workers) who work with these people clinically, though not necessarily for the consequences of SM interests? Should it be the lawyers and legislators who define the crimes and determine when the behavior goes "too far"? Should terms be defined by researchers who study SM and, more specifically, by theorists or by those who collect data? Is it to be defined by SM practitioners themselves, and if so, by which subgroup? Not only the obvious SM subgroups are relevant here (e.g., men versus women, heterosexuals versus homosexuals, and Caucasians versus racial minorities), but also other kinds of group/subgroup variations. Should we differentiate between those who seek only occasional SM encounters incorporated into more conventional sexual patterns or those for whom virtually every sexual act has an SM tinge to it? Other taxonomic issues include recognizing the balance between the physical (e.g., pleasure/pain) dimension and the psychological manifestations (e.g., dominance and submission) of SM. Some people have very specific, and even exclusive, erotic interests (e.g., spanking, bondage), while others are more experimental and incorporate a wide variety of SM and other activities. Some are interested in SM as just part of their sexual relationship and others feel it has nonsexual purposes (e.g., spirituality, fulfilling other emotional needs) or is a mix of the two.

So what is SM? It is sometimes easier to say what it is not. It does not entail violence and it is not nonconsensual. That does not mean that an SM practitioner cannot commit a violent or nonconsensual act but that such acts are not part of SM.

To complicate matters, SM is not necessarily what it appears to be on the surface. Many years ago, one of us (CM) was invited to an SM party; it was my first such experience and the first time the participants allowed a researcher to observe them "in action." At the beginning of the party, a man began what seemed like an especially savage beating of a woman. I watched uncomfortably, not knowing why the other, seemingly nice guests were not coming to her aid. Obviously, this severe beating could not be pleasurable and this must be violating all the limits and party rules I had studied beforehand. While deliberating about what to tell the police when asked why I sat by and did nothing as this man savagely beat this woman to death, I decided I had to act. Just as I stood up to intercede, the woman had a magnificent orgasm and I sank back into my chair to ponder my miscalculation. At the end of the evening, the woman asked her partner, "Can we stop on the way home for a drink, before we do this again?" It was amazing that she could still walk, but unbelievable that she was eager for a repeat performance. Obviously, there was much to be learned and a neophyte researcher's fascination with the subject was born.

So what is SM and who are the practitioners? This is actually the subject of great debate among SM practitioners. It is not uncommon to hear one person denigrate the SM style of another. "Wannabes," "novices," "game players," "thrill seekers," "wankers," and "the clueless" are among many labels used to distinguish "real" practitioners from the supposed posers. (Some people feel that SM stands for "stand and model.") There is conflict between those who engage in SM only "online" and those who do it only in "real-life." Some people denigrate those who do not take part in SM "community" life (i.e., a network or networks of support groups, social events, educational classes, and businesses that cater to an SM clientele). There are those who choose to remain anonymous; they feel they "invented" this with their partners and there is no reason to venture out. There are those who proclaim their SM interests loudly and those who deny their desires. Furthermore, some do not regard SM as a set of interests or desires but as an identity, just as some, but not all, individuals who engage in homosexual acts adopt a gay identity. It is obviously easier to study members of community groups, but we do not know if they are different from those more private individuals.

So is SM a set of sexual behaviors comparable to anal or oral sex? Is it a type of sexual orientation? Is it genetically set? Is it culturally determined? At this time, unfortunately, the answer is "yes" and, "we really do not know yet" to all these questions. More research is in process; this volume is just a beginning.

How has SM been defined in the literature? Some 20 years ago, one of the editors co-authored an article which has been cited widely (see Weinberg, William & Moser, 1984). It indicated that there are five components of SM. Not all five must be present in order to constitute SM, but they usually are found together. The five components are:

1. The appearance of dominance and submission; the appearance of rule by one partner over the other.
2. Role playing.
3. Consensuality, that is, voluntary agreement to enter into the interaction.
4. Mutual definition, i.e., a shared understanding that the activities constitute SM or some similar term.
5. A sexual context, though the concept that SM is always sexual is not shared by all participants.

So does this set of components define SM? These components provide description more than explanation and certainly do not constitute a definition. Of course, it is no easier to define heterosexual, homosexual, gay, or queer.

We have researched SM (both together and separately) previously, often to the bemused glances, yawns or, rarely, the outright consternation of other sexologists. We began to notice that audience members who attended our presentations rarely asked any questions or made comments; that is, not until they caught us alone later. We realized gradually that people were following our work. Slowly, our papers began to be cited in textbooks. Foreign colleagues began telling us that our papers were describing SM in their countries. It eventually became obvious that it was not us, but the subject matter that kept people at a distance.

We have estimated privately that approximately 10% of the general population is involved in SM, but there are no studies on which to base that figure. Based on our experiences in conference hallways (where the real exchange of knowledge and learning in academia often transpires), an even greater proportion of sexologists, sex educators, sex researchers, and sex therapists are so involved. Although sexologists are usually quite nonchalant about their personal sexual behavior, those who have confided in us have done so in hushed tones and have requested our undying pledges of discretion. We have even run across partners who each request our secrecy, but cannot bring themselves to tell one another. Simple self-disclosures are not typically sufficient to solve the couple's problem; such are the intricacies of SM. In some instances, both partners are dominant, or submissive, or maybe one yearns for the physical aspects of SM while the other for the psychological aspects, or maybe their familiarity destroys the fantasy, etc.

Since I attended that first SM play party in 1974, the number of SM support groups in the U.S. has increased from one to over one hundred. A Google search of BDSM reveals over 27 million Web pages (performed 11/21/04). Although many participants worry about the effect if their SM interests became known, others now live their lives without attempting to hide their sexual proclivities.

On the other hand, as is evident in this volume, SM participants lose custody of children, security clearances, inheritances, jobs, are disowned, assaulted, and generally are victims of discrimination and persecution/prosecutions. Much of the discrimination is surprisingly overt. A leader of a gay rights organization admitted that her resistance to working with SM groups was because SM "made [her] sick."

In 1969, the Stonewall riots occurred in New York City and the Gay liberation movement was born. Over the years, the name of the parade honoring this event and promoting acceptance of alternative sexual interests has changed, becoming more inclusive. In San Francisco, this event was initially known as Gay Freedom Day Parade (FDP), then as the Lesbian and Gay FDP, then as the Lesbian, Gay and Bisexual FDP, then the Lesbian, Gay, Bisexual, and Transgendered FDP, and currently the Lesbian, Gay, Bisexual, Transgendered, and Intersexed FDP. The SM community (both Gay and Straight) has always marched in the parade, often over the objections of the parade organizers, but has never been recognized formally. In the early years, the crowd often booed the SM contingent.

Leather is a term often used in the Gay and Lesbian community as a synonym for SM. In San Francisco, there is a public flagpole that flies the Gay Pride Rainbow flag. The city agreed to fly the Leather Pride flag during the week before the Folsom Street Fair, an event that draws 400,000 people per year to celebrate their interest in and support of Leather and SM interests. Nevertheless, it is still over the objections of many Gay activists that the Leather Pride flag flies for even that one week.

Although notable progress in visibility has occurred, in some areas, tolerance is lagging. Recently, a sex research organization chose "unusual sexual interests" as a conference theme. A simple listing of the possible topics in the Call for Papers resulted in a number of statements concerning the inadvisability of proceeding with a conference on such a sensitive topic. There were also a few personal exclamations of being "appalled" and "aghast."

These stories demonstrate that even among other sexual minorities, sex researchers, and sexual rights activists, SM still elicits a panoply of negative feelings. Sexual Sadism and Sexual Masochism are still listed as diagnoses in the *DSM*, despite the absence of studies proving that SM practitioners even fit the criteria for definition of a mental disorder (see Moser & Kleinplatz, 2005).

Nonetheless, SM remains a fascinating topic for further study. It involves sexual behavior that is readily observable, which is useful for descriptive researchers. It has taught us an immense amount about all sexuality and communication. We hope this volume gives the reader a flavor of what there is to learn from the SM practitioners.

A PREVIEW OF SM:
POWERFUL PLEASURES

It seems only fitting that this collection should begin with a review of the SM literature by Thomas S. Weinberg, PhD. Weinberg has written the seminal reviews in this field since 1978. It is our privilege to be able to include his update of social science research in this volume. Weinberg chronicles recent theoretical and methodological advances in the study of SM. Research in this field has moved from early clinical, predominantly psychoanalytic perspectives to an emphasis on psychosocial aspects of SM. Correspondingly, there has been an increase in survey research, content analyses, ethnographic research and critiques of traditional assumptions and beliefs regarding SM. Weinberg summarizes the state of our knowledge in the field. He focuses on the symbolic, ritualistic and theatrical aspects of SM roles, socialization into an SM identity and the organization of SM subcultures. Weinberg concludes that with the shift from the study of clinical populations to SM as a complex social phenomenon, current research depicts SM practitioners as "emotionally and psychologically well-balanced, generally comfortable with their sexual orientation, and socially well adjusted." Weinberg's review illuminates the need for further research in this area. We hope this volume will contribute meaningfully to the burgeoning study of SM.

It became apparent as soon as we began to receive manuscripts that there was great variation in how authors conceived of SM. According to Niklas Nordling, PhD, N. Kenneth Sandnabba, PhD, Pekka Santtila, PhD, and Laurence Alison, PhD, similar differences exist among SM practitioners themselves. Nordling et al. stated, "Clearly, [SM] cannot be thought of as unitary phenomenon: People who identified themselves as sadomasochists probably mean different things by these identifications." Nordling et al. used a questionnaire to study SM in gay (N = 91) versus straight (N = 95) SM subcultures in Finland. They found that the themes predominating, particularly among men, vary depending on sexual orientation. Whereas gay men tend to emphasize "hypermasculinity," straight men veer towards pain and "humiliation." Of course, one might question whether even these terms capture precisely what they mean to the individuals involved.

In addition, Nordling et al. provided another valuable contribution. They questioned the commonly held assumption that SM desires are caused by disturbed early relationships. Nordling et al. tested the assumption that the "etiology" of SM is linked to early family dynamics; they have claimed that SM functions as a form of affect regulation among those who come from dysfunctional families. Nordling et al. found no significant differences between gay and versus straight SM subjects in attachment styles, or between their SM participants as compared to published data on general adult samples.

Rebecca Plante, PhD, examines how we conceptualize SM and how participants construct their identities by examining what may be the quintessential SM activity: spanking. The paradox discovered by Plante is that many of those in the spanking scene do not consider their behavior to be sadomasochistic nor do they identify as SM practitioners. Plante employs fieldwork including interview and observational data from heterosexual spanking parties. She discovered that many of those who engage in spanking neutralize the stigma associated with their activities by distinguishing between their behavior and SM. In fact, participants in Plante's study seemed to distance themselves from and expressed disdain for SM players. Others attempted to vitiate/nullify the stigma by normalizing their desires, explaining that such proclivities are "natural" and commonplace, even if not everyone acknowledges them. Plante works within a sexual script perspective and outlines the narratives used by participants to explain, sustain and justify their activities. It is striking and almost comical how rigidly the rules and roles of the spanking scene are delineated to keep within group norms–just as is the case with conventional sex scripts within the "vanilla" world. As Plante concludes, "Social norms are pervasive, even in a sexually radical subculture."

Much of the research on SM focuses on sexual acts or whatever scenes can be observed by researchers. Peter L. Dancer, PhD, Peggy J. Kleinplatz, PhD, and Charles Moser, PhD, MD, have added to the literature in the area by examining full-time owner-slave relationships. This study was conducted via an Internet questionnaire and involved 146 self-identified slaves in 24/7 SM relationships. Dancer et al. investigated what characterizes such relationships and keeps them viable over time. Dancer et al. found that these relationships are sustained by rules and rituals intended to signify, reinforce and heighten the awareness of the status and position of the slave, even when seemingly out of "role," for example, at work. These rules and rituals governed every moment of the slave's life, from waking to sleeping.

For those who think of SM as purely or even primarily "sexual" in nature, this study calls that assumption into question. Here, SM is more about a way of being and a lifestyle than about discrete acts. Indeed, many of the participants reported that SM slavery constituted and defined their identities and even their "orientation(s)." Interestingly, the option of exiting slavery is built into the relationship (e.g., via solo bank accounts); the paradox is that the possibility of leaving ensures that slaves remain in their relationships of their own free will. That choice, however, whether to stay or to leave, may be the only one they retain upon committing to slavery.

What are we to make of the increasing visibility of SM imagery in American pop culture? According to Margot Weiss, PhD, we should be cautious about equating the rising visibility with corresponding levels of acceptance or understanding. Weiss argues that on the contrary, the nature of current depictions, which simultaneously sensationalize and sanitize SM, reinforce our perceptions of SM practitioners as "other." She used focus group and interview data as well as a review of media representations. Weiss suggests that "mainstreaming kink" signifies a paradox: We are drawn to the exotic, enough to make us peer in on all the deviants from a nice, remote distance; alternately, we co-opt what we disdain, turning sexually provocative, intellectually dangerous imagery into pablum. SM has been "commodified" to boost sales of yogurt or furniture. Weiss suggests that viewers disappointed by increasingly bland SM imagery point to a hunger for something darker, more authentic and transgressive. In a time of sociopolitical repressiveness, Weiss is encouraged by this response and hopes that untamed erotic energy will continue to attract those seeking the real thing.

Patricia A. Cross, PhD, and Kim Matheson, PhD, have conducted a series of three important studies on SM. They set out to investigate the mental health, values and motives of self-identified SM participants. Traditionally, psychoanalytic and other mental health practitioners have commonly believed that SM participants are pathological in a myriad of ways, from being antisocial to running away from reality and from themselves. In addition, others have assumed that dominant men are closet misogynists, inclined to use the guise of SM in order to get away with assaulting women. Cross and Matheson tested these assumptions by giving a battery of psychometric tests to 93 SM participants and 61 members of a control group. Their comparisons showed no significant differences in terms of psychopathology or escapist tendencies. Furthermore, dominant men were *more* likely to hold *pro*-feminist attitudes than "normal" control group participants. Cross and Matheson suggest not only that the prevailing beliefs are erroneous but also that "sadomasochism may simply be a form of sex play, providing those individuals with sufficiently adventurous attitudes towards sex with the experience of intense and intimate encounters."

What, then, is SM about and what is at the core of the experience? Cross and Matheson planned to answer this question by studying online SM interaction. However, in order to ensure the validity and generalizability of their findings, Cross and Matheson had to first design a study to verify that online SM players resembled "real life" SM players. Ingeniously, Cross and Matheson compared online SM players with other online fantasy role-play participants (e.g., Dungeons and Dragons players) and with a sample of "real life" SM players. Cross and Matheson found that online and "real life" SM players were comparable but that both were significantly different from control participants. In an age of extensive Internet-based research, this finding alone constitutes a valuable contribution.

Cross and Matheson then went a step further and performed content analyses on eight online SM dialogues involving 16 self-identified SM participants. Their results demonstrated that power exchange is central to and the motivating factor in SM play.

This set of findings, namely that SM participants are "normal" in terms of mental health and values and that it is the desire for power exchange–rather than pain or psychopathology–which fuels SM activity, forces us to reconsider all the conventional "wisdom" on SM.

Chris White, PhD, relates the story of the Spanner case, as well as discussing its origins and implications. The Spanner case remains the most notorious of the criminal trials to date revolving around SM. In 1989, a group of 16 gay men were arrested in the United Kingdom as a result of their SM activities. Curiously, all the men present were charged with assault even though several were presumably the "victims" while others were the "perpetrators." Those who were "assaulted" in the scene were charged with "aiding and abetting" assault or grievous bodily harm upon themselves. The British law under which the participants were charged was interpreted to mean that no one can consent to being assaulted. Exceptions are justified in terms of the public good. Notably, these exceptions include boxing, parental chastisement of children and military combat. Mutual sexual/erotic gratification was not significant enough to join this group of excluded behaviors, notwithstanding the consent of the participants. White explores the rationales of those who would consider boxing to be in the public interest but would not accord the same status to consensual SM play. The conviction of the Spanner defendants led to appeals all the way up to the European Court of Human Rights in 1997, which upheld the right of the state to apply such laws.

White points out that the deliberations involved in the Spanner case highlight the erroneous beliefs and biases within the justice system. The police and judges failed to distinguish between "real" violence and SM play, regardless of the participants' testimony. According to White, the operative word here is, in fact, "play." She cites an unnamed SM practitioner who testified in the course of the Spanner trials and stated, "Sadomasochism is only violence by metaphor: a closer metaphor would be to view sadomasochism as theater." Furthermore, White contrasts the refusal to consider the defendants' perspective in the Spanner case with the judge's lenience in a similar case, in which the defendant was acquitted. The latter case, however, involved a married couple. Apparently, married (heterosexual) couples are accorded legal protections not afforded to gay men. White's account of the Spanner case, the verdict, sentencing and their meanings suggest the need for a fuller public discourse on sexual consent.

Robert Ridinger, MA, MLS, traces the history of legal conceptions and the status of SM. Ridinger explains that Victorian conceptions of SM as degeneracy and 20th century psychiatric classification of SM as psychopathology set the stage for legal regulation of SM conduct, beginning in the 1960s. Early and continuing beliefs that SM was immoral and that anyone who would engage in such practices must be insane led to a curious legal situation; the implication was that SM was a form of assault to which its participants, by definition, could not give informed consent (as in the Spanner case). The criminalization of SM opened the door to overt and legal discrimination against SM practitioners in court. SM practitioners are threatened with loss of child custody and, in fact, consistently lose custody in court. Similarly justified fears surround the threat of employment termination. Over the last decade, with growing polarization in the United States over sexual mores, prosecutions of SM practitioners have increased. Ridinger reviews the complexities of consent, protection, the right to privacy and to sexual freedom within American law. He concludes by describing emerging responses by SM organizations to attempts at persecution.

Susan Wright, MA, is ideally situated to discuss these efforts by SM activists. As spokesperson for the National Coalition for Sexual Freedom (NCSF), she has been in the forefront of the battle for civil rights for members of sexual minorities. Wright details the history of discrimination against SM practitioners since the 1970s. Over the last 30 years or so, SM has become more visible and thus its practitioners have faced more overt condemnation. She explains that SM has been attacked from both the right and the left. Specifically, SM has been targeted as immoral by the American religious right and as degrading and exploitative by sex-negative feminists. Ironically, for a time, even lesbian SM was condemned as patriarchal violence. Wright describes how the work of pro-SM feminists, including herself, led to a turnaround in the policy of the National Organization for Women (NOW), which has retreated from its previous position opposing SM. Nonetheless, SM remains an "orphan" among sexual minorities, conspicuously excluded from the GLBTIQ umbrella. As such, in 1997, the NCSF was formed as an SM advocacy group. Unfortunately, continuing threats to the civil rights of SM practitioners keep the NCSF busy. Wright chronicles discrimination against individuals, parents, private parties and organized SM community events. She argues effectively that it is only through widespread education that SM can be demystified, thereby preventing further persecution of SM participants.

If Ridinger and Wright speak of pervasive threats and oppression of SM practitioners, Marty Klein, PhD, and Charles Moser, PhD, MD, help to bring the reality of such persecution home. Klein and Moser provide a case illustration of a woman who lost physical custody of her son because of her own SM proclivities. What gives this story its power is that it is real; this is not a fictionalized or even a composite account, although identifying details have been changed to protect confidentiality. It is presented with the participants' courageous and informed consent because they wanted others to know just how devastating the accusation of SM activity can be in court.

Despite the lack of evidence that the child had any knowledge of or was exposed to his mother's sexual activities in any way, let alone affected by them, the mother was seen as dangerous to him.

The presence of the diagnostic category of Sexual Masochism in the *DSM* leaves psychologically healthy, good parents (and their partners) liable to being misdiagnosed and pathologized. Notwithstanding some egregious errors by the psychologist who testified against the mother and despite the expert testimony by the first author, who attempted to set the record straight, the outcome was predictable. The mere allegation of SM in child custody disputes is volatile and prejudicial enough to destroy families.

North American clinicians can be somewhat insulated from international perspectives on mental health and psychopathology. Odd Reiersøl, PhD, and Svein Skeid provide much-needed balance by focusing on the F65 section of the *International Classification of Diseases*, 10th edition (*ICD*-10). The *ICD* is published by the World Health Organization and is the international counterpart to the American Psychiatric Association's *DSM*. The *ICD* classifies Sadomasochism as pathological alongside Fetishism and Fetishistic Transvestism in section F65.

Reiersøl and Skeid discuss the manifold reasons for removing F65 from the next edition of the *ICD*. Their objections to the pathologizing of these "Paraphilias" include conceptual weaknesses (e.g., assumptions about norms, clarity, cohesion, organization) and empirical flaws (e.g., methodological and statistical shortcomings plus the lack of convincing research). Reiersøl and Skeid point out that current nosologies of sexual disorders are based in the notion that heterosexual intercourse is the ideal; they argue that this outdated viewpoint is a holdover from a Victorian value system and early, psychoanalytic domination of the mental health professions. They acknowledge that the sexuality of some individuals leads to distress or to committing antisocial acts. Reiersøl and Skeid contend that impulsive and compulsive acts should rightly be classified in the Personality Disorders or Habit and Impulse Disorders sections of the *ICD*. As for crimes, these should be handled by the criminal justice system and not confused with psychopathology. Furthermore, the classification of Paraphilias as psychopathology has clinical and ethical implications. Reiersøl and Skeid describe the deleterious psychological and social effects of being diagnosed with a mental illness and suggest that the current classification system does more harm than good.

Reiersøl and Skeid review the history of opposition to the F65 section in Europe. In 1997, the Revise F65 Forum was founded in Norway, composed of GLBT SM groups and mental health professionals. Skeid was instrumental in the formation of this organization. The authors discuss a variety of influences which helped to mobilize opposition to F65 including the successful campaign to eliminate the diagnosis of sadomasochism in Denmark, the Spanner case in the United Kingdom, and the human rights concerns of the gay pride movement in Europe. Their account provides an important counterpart to similar attempts at reexamining the Paraphilia classification in general and the Sexual Sadism and Sexual Masochism diagnoses in particular in North America. Reiersøl and Skeid conclude that there is much to be gained by working together. The results of their activism to date are inspiring.

The recognition that most of the readily available, English information on SM tends to be American led us to put out a request on numerous listservs and Websites for information on SM internationally. The request called for information on SM oriented groups in the particular country, SM subculture(s), the social and legal status of SM, levels of acceptance, tolerance or stigma, etc. We are grateful to have received information on BDSM in Brazil from Bia Sel, Helio Pachoal, Maria Cristina Martins, Konstantin Gavros, Misty Avalon and Paulo Roberto Ceccarelli; on SM in Germany from Mark-A, Kathrin Passig, and Johannes Jander; on SM in Austria from Robert; on SM in Switzerland from Matthias Leisi and on SM in Norway from Kelly. In addition, we received regional information on SM in Canada from Naughty Nancy and on SM in the United States from Mistress Blair. Their responses give us an inkling of the diversity in social expressions of SM in North and South America and in Europe. Clearly, far more information will be required to obtain a comprehensive picture of SM around the world. We appreciate the authors' contributions in beginning this endeavor.

The field of psychotherapy has been paying more attention in recent years to ethnic and cultural diversity. Increasing literature has been focusing on the need for therapist sensitivity to minority patients' backgrounds. In addition, there has been a growing interest in the concerns of gay and lesbian clients in therapy. However, little has been written about psychotherapy issues involving other sexual minority patients. Margaret Nichols, PhD, helps to fill this gap. She describes the myths and realities of BDSM and then discusses the common issues confronting therapists who work with this population. Nichols is a sex therapist who has specialized in working with queer clients for over 20 years; as such, she is well situated to note the parallels between the clinical concerns in therapy with gay/lesbian clients and those interested in BDSM. Specifically, she highlights the need for therapists to be aware of negative attitudes towards BDSM. Such prejudices can trigger therapists' own countertransference reactions as well as creating internalized shame in clients. Conversely, therapists who are comfortable with BDSM can look beyond it, to see when sex should *not* be the focus of therapy. In addition, Nichols provides a variety of case examples of individual and couples therapy involving BDSM. These illustrations demonstrate the importance of a strong knowledge base in working with sexual minority clients.

Empirical evidence for the need for culturally competent clinicians, attuned to the needs of clients who practice SM, is provided by Keely Kolmes, PsyD, Wendy Stock, PhD, and Charles Moser, PhD, MD. Kolmes et al. argue that as a matter of ethics, clinicians should not be providing services outside their areas of education, training, supervised experience, etc. They contend that BDSM practitioners constitute a discernible subculture and that specialized training is required for ethical treatment of this population. This assertion was supported by the survey of 175 BDSM practitioners regarding their experiences in therapy. Fully one-third of participants reported choosing not to disclose their BDSM proclivities in therapy, many for fear of being judged negatively by their therapists. Participants reported 118 incidents of biased care, including having to educate therapists about SM, being pathologized a priori on the basis of their desires, and being subject to therapists who failed to distinguish between BDSM and abuse. Indeed, their data establish the need for ethical guidelines for provision of clinical services with BDSM-identified individuals.

Peggy J. Kleinplatz, PhD, concludes this volume by turning common assumptions surrounding SM on their ear. Many of the contributors to this collection point out that beliefs about SM are typically unfounded and attempt to separate myth from reality. Fittingly, Kleinplatz starts with a question: What if instead of pathologizing SM practitioners, we attempt instead to learn from them? What lessons can we learn about the farther reaches of human erotic potential by learning from those who engage in extraordinary sex? Kleinplatz is a sex therapist and focuses on optimal sexual development rather than the more typical concern with dysfunctions and pathology. She presents two cases of couples she had seen in therapy who illustrate the heights that people can reach when they relinquish conventional sexual rules and roles. Both couples, one initially heterosexual and "vanilla" while the other identified from the outset as "leather dykes," chose instead to be fully alive and engaged with each other in SM play. Kleinplatz lists ten lessons taught by these two courageous couples. Ordinary couples and ordinary sex therapists have much to gain by going beyond "us and them" perspectives and by regarding those we have marginalized as on the cutting edge of sexual potential.

We would like to thank Irving B. Weiner, PhD, William T. Hoyt, PhD, Dalit Weinberg, BA, Carol Motuz, MA, Dino Zuccarini, BA, Alvin R. Mahrer, PhD, Ronald E. Fox, PhD, and John P. De Cecco, PhD, for their generous help during the review and editorial phases of this project.

Sadomasochism and the Social Sciences: A Review of the Sociological and Social Psychological Literature

Thomas S. Weinberg, PhD

Buffalo State College

SUMMARY. Recent literature about sadomasochism in Sociology and Social Psychology is reviewed. Studies include survey research and questionnaire studies, content analyses, ethnographic research, and critical essays. The current state of our knowledge of sadomasochism, including its defining characteristics, sadomasochistic identities, and sadomasochistic subcultures is briefly summarized. *[Article copies available for a fee from The Haworth Document Delivery Service: 1-800-HAWORTH. E-mail address: <docdelivery@haworthpress.com> Website: <http://www.HaworthPress.com> © 2006 by The Haworth Press, Inc. All rights reserved.]*

KEYWORDS. Sadism, masochism, sadomasochism, dominance, submission, leathersex

---

Thomas S. Weinberg, PhD, is Professor of Sociology at Buffalo State College. He wishes to thank Dr. Charles Moser and Dr. Peggy J. Kleinplatz for their critical reading of this manuscript and helpful suggestions.

[Haworth co-indexing entry note]: "Sadomasochism and the Social Sciences: A Review of the Sociological and Social Psychological Literature." Weinberg, Thomas S. Co-published simultaneously in *Journal of Homosexuality* (Harrington Park Press, an imprint of The Haworth Press, Inc.) Vol. 50, No. 2/3, 2006, pp. 17-40; and: *Sadomasochism: Powerful Pleasures* (ed: Peggy J. Kleinplatz, and Charles Moser) Harrington Park Press, an imprint of The Haworth Press, Inc., 2006, pp. 17-40. Single or multiple copies of this article are available for a fee from The Haworth Document Delivery Service [1-800-HAWORTH, 9:00 a.m. - 5:00 p.m. (EST). E-mail address: docdelivery@haworthpress.com].

doi:10.1300/J082v50n02_02

17

Early psychoanalytical approaches to the topic of sadomasochism, such as those of Freud (1938, 1953, 1959, 1961), Krafft-Ebing (1965), and Stekel (1965), viewed sadomasochism as evidence of an underlying psychopathology. Krafft-Ebing, for example, saw masochism as "a peculiar perversion of the psychical sexual life in which the individual affected, in sexual feeling and thought, is controlled by the idea of being completely and unconditionally subject to the will of a person of the opposite sex; of being treated by this person as by a master, humiliated and abused" (Krafft-Ebing, 1965, p. 86). Krafft-Ebing derived the term masochism from the name of the writer Leopold Ritter von Sacher Masoch (1836-1905), whose novels, such as *Venus in Furs (Venus im Pelz)*, reflected his personal erotic preoccupation with pain, humiliation, and submission (Cleugh, 1952). The word sadism can be traced to French literature and is linked with the name of Comte Donatien-Alphonse-Francois, marquis de Sade (1740-1814), whose life and erotic writings were filled with incidents and images of sexual cruelty. Freud believed that "Sadism would . . . correspond to an aggressive component of the sexual instinct which has become independent and exaggerated and has been brought to the foreground by displacement" (Freud, 1938. p. 569). He also considered masochism to be a perversion and believed it to be "nothing but a continuation of sadism directed at one's own person in which the latter at first takes the place of the sexual object" (Freud, 1938, p. 570). He pointed out that masochism is not easily separable from sadism. In fact, he noted that "the most striking peculiarity of this perversion lies in the fact that its active and passive forms are regularly encountered together in the same person" (Freud, 1938, p. 570).

The perspective taken by the early psychoanalysts is understandable. The literary works with which they were familiar, such as those by de Sade and Sacher Masoch, described extreme obsessions and behaviors. The only sadists and masochists with whom they had contact were patients, many of whom had come for help with other problems (Stekel, 1965). The psychoanalysts' theories about these behaviors were therefore derived from a very limited and narrow experience. Moreover, Freud and Krafft-Ebing, the most prominent psychoanalysts of their time, had lived most of their lives during the Victorian era, a time of very conservative attitudes toward sexuality. Their perspective, however, is still prevalent. Ross (1997), for example, sees sadomasochists as having been abused as children, experiencing "irrational guilt," being filled with "unconscious rage and the desire for revenge," and having a "'fragile sense of identity,' which in turn leads to indistinct personal boundaries between themselves and others. These are reflected in the frequently fluid roles played by sexual sadists and sexual masochists" (Ross, 1997, pp. 90-91, as cited in Westheimer & Lopater, 2002, p. 650). His observations, however, are based on his clinical research and experience, rather than on a large sample of sadomasochists who have not sought help.

Since the publication of anthropologist Paul Gebhard's seminal article, "Fetishism and Sadomasochism" (1969), there has been a growing body of literature on sadomasochism from the viewpoint of the social sciences, especially that of sociology and social psychology, which I have previously reviewed (Weinberg, 1987, 1994). Recognizing that psychoanalytical interpretations do not accurately address the situations of many contemporary sadomasochists, modern writers have begun to broaden the perspective taken by clinicians. Sadism and masochism are treated as sociological phenomena, dependent upon meanings which are culturally produced, learned and reinforced by participation in sadomasochistic subcultures. Unlike earlier writers, whose source of information was largely confined to case studies of patients in therapy, recent researchers utilize a variety of methods of data collection. These methods include survey research and questionnaire studies (Alison, Santtila, Sandnabba, & Nordling, 2001; Breslow, 1987; Breslow et al., 1985, 1986; Donnelly & Fraser, 1998; Levitt, Moser, & Jamison 1994; Moser & Levitt 1987; Sandnabba, Santtila, & Nordling, 1999; Santilla, Sandnabba, Alison, & Nordling, 2002; Spengler, 1977); content analyses of SM publications (Houlberg, 1991), letters and stories appearing in sexually oriented magazines (Baumeister, 1988b; Naerssen et al., 1987), analyses of graffiti (Innala & Ernulf, 1992), and materials collected from the Internet (Ernulf & Innala, 1995); ethnographies (Brodsky, 1993; Lieshout, 1996; Moser, 1998; Myers, 1992; Weinberg, Williams, & Moser, 1984), theoretical essays (Baumeister, 1988a, 1997; Baumeister & Tice, 2001), critical examinations of the assumptions implicit in psychiatric categories used by clinicians (Moser & Kleinplatz, n.d.) and court decisions involving sadomasochism (Green, 2001; Hoople, 1996; Thompson, 1995; Williams, 1995), and reviews of the state of knowledge on the topic (Breslow, 1989; Moser, 1988; Weinberg, 1987, 1994). There is also a growing number of articles appearing in popular magazines that frequently cite the work of these researchers (Apostolides, 1999; Levitt, 1992). This more recent literature focuses on the social organization of sadomasochism, sadomasochistic interactions, socialization to sadomasochism, characteristics of sadomasochists, the functions of sadomasochistic subcultures and organizations for their members, norms and values, and sadomasochistic preferences and practices. Importantly, many of these studies have been done outside of the United States, and thus provide important cross-cultural comparative data.

In this paper I will first survey some of the recent literature on SM and related behavior that has been published since my last review. Then I will update my assessment of what it is that we now know about sado-masochism.

SURVEY RESEARCH AND QUESTIONNAIRE STUDIES

Anonymous questionnaire studies can provide valuable insights when entree into deviant subcultures is made difficult because of the need for secrecy. While sadomasochistic clubs and behavior have become more visible, this is a relatively recent phenomenon, and the possibility of stigmatization and negative consequences is still very much a concern of SMers, especially among those in the heterosexual community. Researchers are therefore often dependent on the cooperation of contact magazines and other sadomasochistically oriented publications for access to samples or the good will of SM clubs and organizations. This generally requires extensive interaction with club officers and the building of rapport and establishment of trust. Not only do questionnaire studies have the disadvantage of low return rates typical of most surveys, but, importantly, they remove the researcher one step further from the subculture itself, causing reliance on accounts of interaction rather than on first hand observations. Nevertheless, much can be learned from questionnaire studies.

Since my last literature review (Weinberg, 1994), there have been a few additional studies with large samples, which confirm the findings of earlier studies. One of the most ambitious of these is the research carried out in Finland by N. Kenneth Sandnabba, Pekka Santtila, Niklas Nordling, and Laurence Alison (Sandnabba et al., 1999; Alison et al., 2001; Santilla et al., 2002). Participants in this study were 164 men and 22 women, who were members of two sexually oriented clubs. One of these, MSC-Finland, is an association with mainly gay male members interested in sadomasochism and leathersex (n = 91). Sadomasochism, the eroticization of dominance and submission, is differentiated from leathersex, which is the eroticization of a macho, masculine image, symbolized by wearing leather clothing and costumes derivative of the cowboy, motorcycle rebel, etc. According to Lieshout (1995), "For many gay men leather is not only a style-item, but also and especially a sexual fetish" (p. 23). While there is an overlap between the two scenes, they are not the same (Lieshout, 1995).

The other organization, Kinky Club (n = 95), had predominantly heterosexuals of both sexes who have an interest in several kinds of exotic sexual activities. A 237-item questionnaire was distributed to all members of both clubs. In the first report of their study (Sandnabba, et al., 1999) women were eliminated from the analysis, so that only the self-identified male sadomasochists were examined. Comparisons were made with the general Finnish population from data obtained from the Statistical Yearbook of Finland, and heterosexuals and homosexual subgroups within the sample were also compared. Additionally, a comparison was made between those with dominant and submissive orientations. Sandnabba and his colleagues report that their sample of sadomasochists had statistically significant higher levels of education and income than did the general Finnish population, and they were more likely to work in white-collar occupations. Sixty-one percent of the subjects had prominent positions at work, and 60% were involved in community service, findings that tend to support the idea that most sadomasochists function well socially.

Sandnabba et al. found that their subjects first became aware of their sadomasochistic interests between the ages of 18 and 20, and they both had their first SM experiences and began to regularly participate in this behavior between the ages of 21 and 25. Awareness of SM interests in this sample occurred somewhat later than in the Breslow et al. (1985) study, where half of the males recognized their sadomasochistic interests by the age of 14. Recognition was slightly earlier than in the sample described by Moser and Levitt (1987), in which "coming out" was at age 26. However, the age of the first SM experience of men is consistent with findings of Moser and Levitt (1987), whose subjects first participated in SM at the age of 23. Exclusively heterosexual subjects both became aware of their SM interests and had their first sadomasochistic experiences at a younger age than did exclusively gay men. The majority of men had enjoyed their first SM experience.

Sandnabba and his colleagues found that over 88% of their sample had engaged in nonsadomasochistic sex, and that fewer than 5% no longer did so. However, slightly over one-fourth of the sample agreed that only SM sex could satisfy them. Regarding frequency of SM activity, slightly more than one-third of the sample had practiced SM sex two to five times within the previous 12 months, with the next highest percentage, about 20%, having engaged in this behavior from 11 to 20 times in

that period. Gays and bisexuals reported more SM sessions than did heterosexuals, a finding consistent with that of Spengler (1977). The sample reported more frequent masturbation than that found in the general
Finnish population. Sandnabba et al. explain this as probably the result
of having fewer permanent sexual relationships. "Although the participants seemed to have difficulties in finding partners," they write,
"they still had a positive and ego-syntonic view of their sexual behavior" (p. 278). The researchers conclude that, "Although the results do
not suggest significant impairment of social and psychological functioning among sadomasochistic males, a full understanding of these
characteristics requires in-depth analysis from a more individual perspective delineating, for example, the developmental background of
sadomasochistic individuals" (p. 282).

In the two other papers based on the same research (Alison et al.,
2001; Santilla et al., 2002), the writers used sophisticated statistical procedures to examine the relationships among sadomasochistic behaviors.
In the first of these papers (Alison et al., 2001), the authors examined
the types of behaviors engaged in during a sadomasochistic encounter
and the empirical relationships among them. They arranged SM behaviors into types or themes: hypermasculinity, administration of
pain, humiliation, and physical restriction. They then were able to develop a correlational map, showing which behaviors fit into which of
these types or themes and how closely they were related to one another. For example, cockbinding, fistfucking, dildo use and catheters
fit into the hypermasculinity region of their map, while flagellation,
faceslapping, and verbal humiliation fit into the humiliation region.
They could also tell which behaviors within a given theme region were
more closely related to others in contiguous regions. They note that,
"This . . . suggests that sadomasochism can be conceptualized as a set of
interrelated behaviors where individuals give different emphases to particular themes rather than it being a label of convenience for a number of
independent phenomena" (p. 7). When they compared male and female
subjects, the researchers found that women engaged in significantly
more humiliation behaviors, while men engaged in hypermasculinity
behaviors. This finding, however, may be a function of the composition
of the male sample, rather than reflecting male-female differences.
Ninety-five of the 162 men studied came from the predominantly gay
organization, and this may have skewed the results. What the authors
see as male/female differences may really be gay male/heterosexual female differences. As Alison et al. note, many of the behaviors located
within the hypermasculinity region, such as fistfucking (i.e., anal fist-

ing), enemas, and catheters are commonly associated with the gay male leathersex subculture. Terms such as "fisting" or "vaginal fisting" are more common in the heterosexual or lesbian communities such as in California (C. Moser & P. Kleinplatz, personal communication, February 17, 2003). Alison et al.'s comparison of gay and heterosexual male SMers appears to support my caveat; they found that male heterosexuals engaged more in behaviors of the humiliation region, while gays engaged in those of the hypermasculinity region.

Relating their findings to the literature, the authors conclude that "the administration and receiving of pain may take on rather different meanings depending upon the context within which it is received and, of course, depending upon the intensity of the sensation delivered/experienced" (p. 10). Further, "results suggest that for the gay male group, the administration and reception of pain was a more intense and real perception and that the symbolic representation of pain was more important for the women and the heterosexual men" (p. 10).

The third report of the research group (Santilla et al., 2002), examined how the individual behaviors contained within the four themes they identified in the second paper represent different scales of intensity. Using the concept of "scripts," they looked not only at behaviors within a given scenario, but also at how they progress over several encounters. Focusing on individual behavior, the researchers attempted to find out if there is an underlying ordered structure for SM behaviors. That is, they attempted to develop a cumulative scale, in which some behaviors would normally proceed others with a higher intensity. The authors conclude that SM behaviors are not randomly combined with one another but represent a structured pattern, and that some of these "partially cumulative structures . . . can be likened to sexual scripts for ordinary heterosexual sexual behavior" (p. 193).

Eugene E. Levitt and his colleagues (1994) studied a sample of 34 women, gathered as part of an earlier larger research project (Moser, 1979). The sample was obtained through meetings of the Society of Janus and The Eulenspiegel Society. A special attempt was made to compare their study results with that of Breslow et al. (1985). In the Levitt et al. study the mean age of recognizing one's SM interests or "coming out" was 22.7 years, compared to 21.6 years in the Breslow et al. survey, a non-significant difference. While Levitt and his colleagues found differences from Breslow et al. in reported frequency of participation in sadomasochistic scenes, with their own sample reporting a higher activity level, the difference is explained in terms of educational level and marital status. Examining preference for SM activities, the authors found similarities between the two samples, with women preferring bondage, spanking, oral sex, and master-slave scenarios. Despite differences in sample selection, in some of the questions asked, in ways in which variables were combined, and in techniques for eliminating prostitutes from their studies, Levitt et al. draw some conclusions about women in the sadomasochistic subculture. They note that women in the SM scene tend to be better educated and more likely to be single than those in the general population, that they become aware of their interests as young adults, that a "plurality consider themselves submissive in the S/M role but a substantial minority enjoy, or are at least able to play, either dominant or submissive. Those who express a clear preference for the dominant role are a smaller minority" (p. 472). Most importantly, however, the authors state that "Four out of five are satisfied with their S/M orientation" (p. 472).

Denise Donnelly and James Fraser (1998) studied a sample of 320 undergraduate students from a large university in the Southeast to test three competing hypotheses. These are the male arousal hypothesis (because of socialization emphasizing sexual aggression and experimentation, males will be more aroused by both sadism and masochism than women), the female arousal hypothesis (because of socialization to passivity, women will be more aroused by masochistic activities than males), and the convergence hypothesis (male and female attitudes and behavior have converged, and this is shown in similarities in responses to sadomasochistic stimuli). The 220-item questionnaire was administered in a range of sociology classes. Seventy-two percent of the subjects were female and 28% were male. It is important to note here that this sample was not self-identified as sadomasochistic, since the researchers were only studying responses to SM stimuli in a general population. Among a variety of questions asked were those about the frequency of being aroused by fantasizing about certain sadomasochistic behaviors and participating in those behaviors. The authors found that the men in the study were significantly more likely to become aroused by both fantasizing about and participating in SM behavior. This holds true for being dominant during sex but not for being dominated. Males, however, were significantly more likely to become aroused by fantasizing about and participating in bondage and discipline and more likely to be aroused by fantasizing about being restrained and by being spanked, which appears to contradict the first finding. The researchers conclude that the male arousal hypothesis is supported, but not the others. The findings of this study are of limited utility, however, in understanding SM as a social phenomenon for a number of reasons. First, the subjects were not self-identified as sado-masochists, nor were they, as far as we know, regular participants in SM scenes or subcultures. Secondly, as the authors acknowledge, the sample was a convenience one, limited in age and gender and not randomly selected, so the findings are not, therefore, generalizable beyond the sample itself. Third, it is difficult to ascertain how much of the difference between men and women is attributable to the men's responding to general sexual imagery rather than to specifically sadomasochistic imagery. Fourth, mislabeling of their tables (Table II should be captioned, "Male-Female Differences in Arousal Over Being Dominated," and Table III should be labeled, "Male-Female Differences in Arousal Over Fantasizing and Participating in Watching Bondage and Discipline") makes this report confusing to read.

CONTENT ANALYSES

Content or secondary analyses of a variety of sources including magazine content, letters, graffiti, and material gathered from the Internet, although another step further removed from direct observations of the SM scene, provide an alternative way of gathering useful data. However, there are at least two problems with content or secondary analyses. First, the researcher's data are limited to materials that have already been produced, usually for reasons unrelated to his or her hypotheses. Second, because this method relies heavily on the researcher's insights to develop ways of categorizing information, there is a danger that the organization of data and the conclusions drawn from the analysis may reflect the coder's perspectives more than they do the perceptions of sadomasochists. This technique is probably best used as a supplement to other methods of data gathering.

Kurt Ernulf and Sune Innala (1995) analyzed 514 messages appearing in an international computerized discussion group on sexual bondage, which was part of the Internet/USENET news system. They were interested in finding out "what experiences in sexual bondage are sexually stimulating, what experiences lead to sexual satisfaction, and how experiences differ between individuals" (Ernulf & Innala, 1995, p. 639). They pointed out that previous studies of sexual bondage used either clinical samples, which have a pathological bias, or interviews with members of sadomasochistic organizations, who may try to give a favorable impression about their interests. By using content analysis, the authors hoped to avoid these problems.

They found that eighty percent of the posted messages whose origin they could determine were from the United States, probably, they speculated, because of greater access to the Internet. Other messages came from Australia, Canada, Finland, Germany, Japan, The Netherlands, Norway, Sweden, and the United Kingdom. Almost three-fourths of the messages were written by males, and of those who stated their sexual orientation, 81% said they were heterosexual, 18% said they were homosexual, and 1% claimed to be bisexual.

Categorizing messages in terms of the writers' experiences during bondage, Ernulf and Innala found that 60 of them (12%) mentioned bondage as play, 19 (4%) saw the experience as an exchange of power, and 15 (3%) claimed that bondage intensified sexual pleasure. Thirteen messages (2.5%) reported tactile stimulation and bodily sensations from being bound, and 12 others (2.3%) said that bondage enhanced their visual enjoyment of their partner. Other motivations for bondage included partners' sexual pleasure and control of the sexual stimulation and prolonged orgasm, both cited in 11 messages (2%), and fulfillment of sexual fantasy scenarios, sexual experimentation, trust and care, not knowing what will happen, objectifying of partner, and a lifestyle, all fewer than 10 mentions each.

Ernulf and Innala distinguished among sadomasochism, bondage and discipline, and dominance and submission, as did many of the writers of the messages they analyzed. However, in one-third of the messages analyzed, sadomasochism was mentioned either as part of bondage or as occurring with it. The authors noted that there was no consensus among the subjects about whether bondage is part of sadomasochism.

In all subcultures, there are norms that serve to define members' expectations and to control their interaction. For the bondage subculture, these involve the intertwined issues of safety and trust. Ernulf and Innala found 36 messages with safety as a theme. They note that "Subjects reported that there are workshops about safety at community meetings, and strict safety standards exist among members. A member who breaks the rules of safety will often be expelled from the community" (p. 650). This response is similar to that noted by Lee (1979).

Some of the messages discussed the desirable characteristics of a good "top," or what Ernulf and Innala term the "dominant-initiator." Implicit in these discussions are the issues of trust and safety. The good top is one who knows the bottom's limits and is watchful for signs that they are being reached or pushed. The top is sensitive to the bottom's needs and wishes the interaction to be experienced as pleasurable by the bottom.

The writers found some differences between male heterosexual and homosexual participants. Heterosexuals were much more likely to prefer the dominant-initiator role than were gays. This finding is at odds with that of Sandnabba et al. (1999), who describe the proportion of sadistic gay male participants in their study as "quite high" (Sandnabba et al., p. 280).

ETHNOGRAPHIC RESEARCH

Ethnographic research involves intimate contact with members of the SM subculture. By immersing him- or herself in the SM world, the researcher is able to observe actual behavior and to interact with sadomasochists, providing fertile ground for theory development. There are, however, a number of difficulties in doing ethnographic research. The greatest challenge for researchers is gaining entree into the SM world, and finding a role within it, which explains the paucity of ethnographic data. In general, the gay leathersex scene in most middle-sized cities is much more accessible than the heterosexual sadomasochistic subculture. Gay SM bars are well known in the gay community and, with the exception of some private clubs, they are not difficult to enter. With the possible exception of the largest metropolitan areas, heterosexual sadomasochistic groups are almost invisible. Even in the larger cities, SM groups are not easy to find or to study without a member who will vouch for the researcher. Compared to surveys, ethnographic research takes a tremendous amount of time and has inherent difficulties in the analysis and presentation of data. It relies heavily on the perceptiveness, attention to detail, and creativity of the researcher. One important problem is that the role taken in the setting may restrict one's ability to observe some types of interaction, particularly those not accessible in common areas of the setting. Participant observation necessarily requires the ability to interact and question participants about both private behavior and their perceptions of what is going on.

Maurice van Lieshout (1995), who studied homosexual encounters in a Dutch highway rest area and an adjoining wood (the Mollebos), did not have the kinds of difficulties noted above, since he was first a participant in the behavior he studied. He writes, "From my fourth or fifth visit, my role became a mixed one: for some time during the evening and night I was an observing participant, for some time a participating observer. Approximately 80 percent of the time I spent there focused on my role as participant *observer*" (Lieshout, 1995, p. 25, emphasis in original). A gay man who had had experience in leather bars and cruising areas, Lieshout says that he felt, "at ease almost immediately" (p. 25). He was able to get respondents to talk to him, because they perceived him as a sympathetic co-participant.

The Mollebos, which was closed after his study, served as an additional venue for the activities of SMers and leathermen (Lieshout makes a distinction between leathersex and SM. Not all leathermen are interested in sadomasochism, and not all SMers are involved in the leather scene) on Monday evenings. After describing the setting, which had specific areas or zones designated for activities such as getting a first impression of other participants, making social contacts, cruising, and engaging in orgies, Lieshout shows how leathermen use spatial strategies in the Mollebos similar to those used in leather bars. His discussion of courting practices makes it clear that there are implicit rules that are followed during interactions ("In cruising situations 'No' always means 'No.' A negative response is mostly given in a non-verbal way and has not to be taken personally," p. 33), an observation also made by Brodsky (1993) in his ethnography of the Mineshaft, a bar and sex club that existed in New York City in the 1980s. When the rules of the game are broken, for example, by a dominant initiating rough play too soon, the encounter is immediately broken off. Role interests (top or bottom) are often indicated through attire and the placement of key rings and other symbols, and encounters appear to follow role expectations of other settings. Similar to Brodsky's observation that the Mineshaft served a "variety of integrative social and cultural functions for gay men at the communal level" (Brodsky, 1993, p. 234), Lieshout notes that "For many patrons the Mollebos also supplies a social function: they see acquaintances, sometimes friends with whom they can exchange news and information (not only about the leather scene)" (Lieshout, 1995, p. 28).

Charles Moser's paper, "S/M (sadomasochistic) interactions in semi-public settings" (1998) provides a retrospective analysis of his observations of sadomasochistic parties, which he attended during the course of 25 years of research in the SM community. While the parties he observed varied widely in size, style, exclusivity, and setting, they had some common characteristics. They all provided a setting for SMers to meet, interact, and "display their personal style of S/M behavior in a semi-public setting" (Moser, 1998, p. 19). Another commonality is that all parties are structured by rules. "The rules of behavior at a party," he writes, "are quite serious and explicitly stated" (p. 20). Although he notes that "The rules related to an etiquette that is actually quite varied throughout the S/M community," Moser points out that "the issues are constant" (p. 21). These issues pertain to acceptable forms of interaction, prohibited sexual behavior, and confidentiality. Some rules, like those prohibiting inebriation, are universal. Like most non-SM parties, a starting time is specified, but unlike them, a door closing time is usually also maintained.

Probably the most important reason for parties is that they serve an integration and socialization function for participants. SMers get to know others like themselves, learn the rules of interaction and specific SM techniques, and most importantly, are able to normalize their interests and feelings. As Moser writes, "Clearly individuals are attracted by an atmosphere that encourages them to be themselves and validates their behavior. An acceptance of S/M identity and role is clearly part of the reason that individuals attend" (p. 25). These are, of course, common functions of all subcultures, particularly those in which behavior occurs that is deemed deviant by the larger society.

An interesting observation made by Moser is that although most parties do not prohibit sexual activity, coitus or genitally focused orgasmic behavior is unusual. This appears to be the case, even though voyeurism is encouraged, and many participants are exhibitionists. When he asked about this, several partygoers told Moser that this activity was too personal for public exhibition. This is different from the observations made by Brodsky (1993), although similar to those of Lieshout, who noted that, compared to regular gay sex in public places, SM and leathersex are "less penis-oriented" and that "the sexual act is not by definition aimed on orgasm" (Lieshout, 1995, p. 28).

CRITICAL ESSAYS

Some recent critical papers have attacked the psychoanalytical perspective. There are two ways in which this has been done. First, the scientific validity of the psychiatric classification of the Paraphilias, found in the Diagnostic and Statistical Manual of the American Psychiatric Association (DSM-IV-TR) has been challenged (Moser & Kleinplatz, 2005). Second, other writers have critiqued legal decisions concerning sadomasochism (Green, 2001; Hoople, 1996; Thompson, 1995; Williams, 1995), whose underlying assumptions reflect a psychoanalytical view of this behavior.

A Challenge to DSM Nosology

Charles Moser and Peggy J. Kleinplatz (2005) have questioned the categorization of the paraphilias as mental disorders by the *DSM-IV-TR*. By so doing, they attack the underlying psychoanalytic assumptions of the Paraphilia section. They begin by using a social constructionist approach to point out that conceptions of mental disorders are made within a sociocultural context, thus making scientific definitions of healthy sexual behavior difficult to find. Noting that "The equating of unusual sexual interests with psychiatric diagnoses has been used to justify the oppression of sexual minorities and to serve a political agenda," they assert that a "review of this area is not only a scientific issue, but also a human rights issue" (Moser & Kleinplatz, 2003, p. 93). In their analysis, Moser and Kleinplatz make a number of important points. First, they deny that the paraphilias are mental disorders, noting that research has not provided data supporting this classification. In fact, they say, "The non-clinical studies of individuals with unusual sexual interests demonstrate that these individuals are indistinguishable from those with 'normophilic' (i.e., conventional) sexual interests" (p. 96) and that even "clinical studies do not identify a discernible group who have anything more in common than their shared sexual interest" (p. 96). Second, Moser and Kleinplatz point out inconsistencies and contradictions within the *DSM* classification. Third, they give specific instances in which statements appearing as fact in the section are not supported by research, including assertions about the sex ratio among masochists, the extent of injuries stemming from this behavior, and the prevalence of certain sexual practices. They note that although the *DSM* editors claim to have carefully reviewed the appropriate literature, the Paraphilia section is not consistent with the current state of knowledge. The writers assert that, "The *DSM* criteria for diagnosis of unusual sexual interests as pathological rests on a series of unproven and more importantly, untested assumptions. *The implicit belief system, which infuses this classification, remains unscrutinized*" (p. 96, emphasis added). They conclude by stating, "Although it is a radical solution, we favor removal of the entire category from the *DSM* as the most appropriate remedy for the problems outlined" (p. 96).

Critiques of Legal Decisions

A number of writers have been concerned with the implications of the decisions rendered in R. v. Brown, popularly known as the "Spanner" case. This was a nationally publicized court case in the United Kingdom, in which sixteen men were arrested in 1987 and convicted for consensual sadomasochistic activities that violated The Offences Against the Person Act, originally passed in 1861 (Green, 2001; Hoople, 1996; Kershaw, 1992; Thompson, 1995; Williams, 1995). "The Act states, 'whoever shall unlawfully and maliciously wound or inflict any grievous bodily harm on any other person, either with or without any weapon or instrument, shall be liable to imprisonment'" (Green, 2001, p. 544). While the victims made no complaints to police, during the course of unrelated investigations, officers found videotapes of these activities, which had been duplicated and distributed to participants. Although all activities were consensual, this was deemed irrelevant to the charges against the men, and ". . . 11 men received sentences of up to four-and-a-half years for assault; 26 others were cautioned for the offence, thought to be unique, of aiding and abetting assaults on themselves" (Kershaw, 1992, p. 6). The Court of Appeal, Criminal Division, the House of Lords, the European Commission of Human Rights, and the European Court of Human Rights upheld convictions (Green, 2001).

Green's analysis of the case examines whether the behaviors prosecuted in the Spanner case should be protected either under the right to privacy or by the right to consent to bodily injury extended, for example, to professional boxers. He reviews two post-Spanner cases. In one, a man who had used nipple clamps and nipple piercing during bondage with a female partner was acquitted when she testified that she had consented. In another case, a man was first convicted for branding his initials on his wife's buttocks with a hot knife. His conviction was overturned on appeal, "with the Court noting that the wife not only consented to the act, but she instigated it, and that there was no aggressive intent on his part" (Green, 2001, p. 544). Green cites these cases to question the Spanner decision. Unlike these two cases, the issue of consent in the Spanner case was deemed irrelevant, and the question is why? Although the trial judge discounted the sexual orientation of the participants as affecting the case, and the European Court felt that the decision was based on the extreme behaviors (e.g., using hot wax, needles, fishhooks, and sandpaper on the genitals) and not on any anti-homosexual bias, one is still left with doubts about whether the homosexuality of the defendants had a bearing on the outcome. In the court case itself, the issue of privacy was not brought up by the defense. The defendants argued, however, that they were entitled to the right of sexual expression. The European Court did not accept this. Their response is not unlike statements made by Krafft-Ebing (1965), reflecting a psychoanalytical bias: "There was no evidence to support the men's assertion . . . that the SM activities were essential to their happiness but the argument would be accepted if sadomasochism were only concerned with sex (and not violence) as the men contended" (Green, 2001, p. 547). For Green, the law should be consistent; either activities like boxing and SM should both be banned, or they should both be permitted.

Hoople's (1996) take on the Spanner case is different from Green's. Analyzing the case from an SM perspective, the case, he says, is about the issue of representation. Who should have the authority to represent SM? "I would argue, " he writes, "that SM practitioners were never really represented in *R. v. Brown*. Rather, SM practitioners were represented *as* a stereotype, as a gross caricature of a Sadeian libertine, or, perhaps more to the point, as 'normal' society's diabolical 'other,' as the social's Mr. Hyde, so to speak" (Hoople, 1996, p. 186, emphasis in original). The problem, as he sees it, is that "how SM practitioners 'see' and represent themselves and their practice often conflicts with how others 'see' them, and thus there is a struggle over how to represent SM, a struggle with potentially dire consequences for practitioners" (p. 190). He notes that even the defense used stereotypes about SM. Portraying SMers as only being sexually aroused by inflicting and receiving pain, as the defense did, is inaccurate. He points out that these acts do not always cause sexual arousal in SMers. Hoople says that bottoms willingly grant control to their tops, and that "control can only be exercised up to the limits imposed by the willing consent of one's partner, and if these limits are intentionally transgressed, an SM relation becomes a relation of oppression and thus abusive (and therefore legitimately subject to prosecution)" (p. 213).

WHAT WE KNOW ABOUT SADOMASOCHISM

In the 37 years since Gebhard's (1969) essay, there has been an accumulation of knowledge about SM. Some early assumptions, for example that women were rare in that subculture, have been discarded with more empirical research (Alison et al., 2001; Breslow et al., 1985; Levitt et. al., 1994; Moser & Levitt, 1987). While there are some disagreements about some of the features of SM, there is a great deal of consensus among researchers. What follows is a summary of what we know about SM.

Characteristics of Sadomasochism

Sociologists and social psychologists have identified a number of defining characteristics of sadomasochism. It is about dominance and submission and not necessarily about pain. Acts of dominance and submission outside the sexual arena are simply not perceived by participants as fitting the criteria of sadomasochism. Outside the sadomasochistic scene, dominants are not cruel, nor are submissives necessarily passive. It is only within the sexual context that such behavior is perceived as appropriate. While it is true that pain is important to some sadomasochists, and it is certainly possible that pain can be eroticized, definitions of sadomasochism that focus exclusively on pain miss the essence of SM, the ritualization of dominance and submission. SMers often consider their behavior to be a power exchange (Ernulf & Innala, 1995; Hoople, 1996; Moser, 1988). This is a common theme among sadomasochists. In fact, a number of organizations use the term in their names, including the Arizona Power Exchange (APEX), People Exchanging Power (PEP) headquartered in New Mexico, and the Memphis Power Exchange in Tennessee.

SM is recreational or play-like behavior (Magill, 1982; Moser, 1998), which is set aside from other aspects of life. SMers do not see it as "real" in any sense but acknowledge it as a means of temporarily escaping from the everyday world. Sadomasochistic behavior thus involves fantasy in varying degrees (Brodsky, 1993; Sandnabba et al., 1999). Fantasy is critical to sadomasochistic interactions. Frequently, sadomasochistic scenarios are scripted; individuals play designated roles during their interaction. This serves to confine the behavior only to that episode, keeping it from spilling over to other aspects of life. Using fantasy, sadomasochistic scenes are framed by social definitions that give the behavior a specific contextual meaning (Lee, 1979; Weinberg, 1978). It is this fantasy frame that allows people to engage in behaviors or roles that are usually not permitted in everyday life, as, for example, when a man dressed as a maid allows himself to be dominated by a woman. Common fantasies include the severe boss and the naughty secretary, queen, mistress or master and slave (Sandnabba et al., 1999), employer and servant or maid, teacher and pupil, owner and horse or dog, and parent and child (Juliette, 1995; Sandnabba et al., 1999). Thus, the framing of interaction enables the participants to enjoy themselves without feeling guilt (Weinberg, 1978).

Sadomasochistic scenes are both consensual and collaboratively produced (Baumeister, 1988b; Hoople, 1996; Weinberg, 1978; Weinberg & Falk, 1980). What may appear to the uninitiated observer to be spontaneous behavior is often carefully planned. In this way, the kinds of uncertainties one faces in everyday life do not exist. All parties to the interaction must agree to participate. Forced participation is not acceptable within the subculture; it is only the *illusion* that individuals are coerced that is approved by sadomasochists. Participants must agree on what will take place during the scene and carefully discuss limits to the interaction, insuring that both derive pleasure from their participation. Moser points out, however, that when SMers know each other well, this discussion may not always take place (Moser, 1998). Often safe words (Moser, 1998), such as "yellow" (for slow down) or "red" (for stop), are used to indicate to one's partner that one is nearing one's discomfort limit. Participants have a very good idea of what will transpire. Sometimes, however, the dominant partner will test the submissive's limits, going just a bit beyond the agreed upon boundaries. Naerssen et al. (1987) found that limits were determined during the interaction, but that only two of a few hundred reported interactions were defined by the participants as having been too hard. Pushing the limits adds a feeling of authenticity to the scene, making the submissive believe that what is happening is "real." Upon receiving any indication that the interaction is becoming too intense, the dominant will back down. This is usually done very subtly, so that the mood is not broken and interaction can continue on a lower level of intensity (Weinberg, 1978). When SMers know each other well, pushing the limits or going beyond the agreed upon limits (Weinberg et al., 1984) may not be seen as a violation. Skilled dominants carefully observe the submissive's response and immediately decelerate the intensity of the interaction (Ernulf & Innala, 1995; Weinberg, 1994). Interaction with others less well known is problematic, bringing up issues of trust and safety. Before consenting to participate in a scene with someone who is not an intimate, SMers may learn something about the reputation of the potential partner from others who know him or her (Lee, 1979). Limits are discussed as well as specific fantasies or scenarios (Moser, 1998). In these relatively small subcultures, an individual's reputation for skill and trustworthiness serves as a mechanism of social control. Those SMers who are perceived as not being safe have difficulty in obtaining partners (Brodsky, 1993; Kamel, 1980; Lee, 1979). Both Kamel (1980) and Lee (1979) point out that risk is reduced through agreement on norms and values within the subculture.

Sadomasochistic behavior is highly symbolic; a variety of devices, such as clothing (sadomasochists often wear costumes of black leather, vinyl or rubber) (Brodsky, 1993; Moser, 1998), the use of language, the utilization of restraints, and so forth, serve to indicate a participant's role, either dominant or submissive, in the interaction. There are, for example, slave harnesses and other restraints indicating to potential partners the individual's preferred role in the interaction. Among male homosexuals in the "leathersex" subculture, dominance or submission is signaled by wearing key chains or colored handkerchiefs. Usually, wearing keys on the left indicates that the individual is a top, and the right side signals that he is a bottom. The preference for a specific act is symbolized by the color of the handkerchiefs; color codes are generally agreed upon within the subculture.

Sadomasochistic Identity

Kamel (1980; Kamel & Weinberg, 1983), who was particularly interested in how people become sadomasochists, demonstrated that it was part of an interactive process or "career," during which the individual becomes aware of role expectations and is socialized into the community. The first sadomasochistic experience often, but not always, precedes "coming out," which refers to the process of coming to terms with a sadomasochist self-identity and entrance into the subculture (Moser & Levitt, 1987). There may be gender differences in this process, although the literature on coming out is unclear. Some people, who have not previously recognized any SM interests, become involved in sadomasochism through a variety of relationships. Breslow et al. (1985) found that another person had introduced over 60% of the women they studied to SM. While Breslow et al. (1985) found that men reported first discovering an interest in SM on the average five years earlier than females (14.99 years vs. 21.58 years), Moser and Levitt (1987) found that women and men came out and participated in sadomasochistic behavior at about the same age. Coming out in the Moser and Levitt sample occurred at 22.9 years for males (Moser & Levitt, 1987) and 22.7 years for females (Levitt et al., 1994). What we are still missing in the literature is information on coming out as a sadomasochist *as a process*. With the notable exception of Kamel's (1980, 1983) work on becoming a leatherman, qualitative information on the process of identity formation is lacking. Are there, for example, progressive stages in the SM career for heterosexuals similar to those Kamel found for gay SMers?

Sadomasochistic Subcultures

It is inaccurate to speak generically of the sadomasochistic subculture. There are many different sadomasochistic worlds organized around sexual orientation, gender, and preferred activities. For example, there are heterosexual (Breslow et al., 1985; Levitt et al., 1994; Moser, 1979, 1984, 1988; 1998; Scott, 1983; Weinberg, 1978), gay male "leathersex" (Brodsky, 1993; Innala & Ernulf, 1992; Kamel, 1980, 1983; Lee, 1979; Lieshout, 1996; Naerseen, et al., 1987), and lesbian (Califia, 1979; Hopkins, 1994; Lewis & Adler, 1994) subcultures. There are more specialized subcultures devoted to bondage and discipline (B & D), which is used to describe the combination of restraint and control with punishment or humiliation (Ernulf & Innala, 1995) and body modifications like genital piercing, branding, burning, and cutting (Myers, 1992). Some SM practitioners make distinctions between sadomasochism, dominance and submission, and bondage and discipline (Ernulf & Innala, 1995). Often, however, there are blendings and overlaps among these subcultures, and a variety of practitioners may interact in parties or clubs (Moser, 1998).

Sadomasochists enter their subcultures in a variety of ways. In addition to being introduced to these practices by another person, they meet others by placing and responding to advertisements in specialized publications, through chatrooms on the Internet, by joining formally organized SM clubs such as the Eulenspiegel Society or the Society of Janus, or by attending SM bars in which sadomasochists can find one another and engage in sadomasochistic scenes. During the mid-1980s, these bars were closed down because of the AIDS epidemic, either by departments of public health or voluntarily (Brodsky, 1993). These institutions reopened in the 1990s, at least in the larger cities. Additionally, sadomasochists hold private parties, sometimes with more than 500 participants (Moser, 1998).

Sadomasochistic organizations have existed for a long time. In the eighteenth and nineteenth century, private clubs, whose activities included birching and caning, could be found in London (Falk & Weinberg, 1983). The oldest modern organization for sadomasochists, the Eulenspiegel Society, was founded in New York City in 1971. The Society of Janus, the second oldest BDSM (Bondage and Discipline, Dominance and Submission, and Sadomasochism) society was founded in San Francisco in 1974. Other organizations can be found scattered around the U.S. These societies function as support groups and agents of socialization into SM. They provide information about sadomasochistic practices and develop and maintain justifications, ideologies, and neutralizations, which allow members to engage in these activities while avoiding a deviant self-identity. Some organizations, like the Eulenspiegel Society, publish magazines or newsletters and maintain Websites on the Internet. Their literature includes sophisticated statements of purpose, asserting the normalcy of sadomasochistic behavior and the rights of individuals to practice it, and they provide their members with a variety of services and opportunities to interact.

Sadomasochistic nightclubs and bars allow SMers to meet others in the scene. Often in out-of-the-way spots such as warehouse districts, in the largest cities, these places are difficult to find for the uninitiated. Unremarkable in appearance, these nightclubs or bars often have no signs and an unobtrusive entrance. An entrance fee is usually charged, often with males paying more than females. Discounts are generally given for members of local SM organizations. Inducements to attend include special theme nights and programs for their habitues. These include slave and master/mistress auctions, demonstrations, and the like. Signals used to control the interaction are often nonverbal and very subtle (Weinberg, 1995). Gay leather bars are less hidden than the heterosexual SM nightclubs, and their locations are usually well known within the larger gay community (Brodsky, 1993; Lieshout, 1995). In both kinds of clubs, various devices for restraining submissives and acting out fantasies are available. These establishments usually have several rooms in which interaction takes place in full view of observers. In fact, being observed by others during a scene is a frequent fantasy, so that voyeurs may be incorporated into the scene without their realizing it as participants in the submissive's humiliation.

In conclusion, social science research in sadomasochism over the past three decades indicates that this is a complex social phenomenon, not easily nor accurately summed up by psychoanalytical perspectives. Contrary to the psychoanalytical view that SM is an individual psychopathology, sociological and social psychological studies see SM practitioners as emotionally and psychologically well balanced, generally comfortable with their sexual orientation, and socially well adjusted.

REFERENCES

Alison, L., Santtila, P., Sandnabba, N. K., & Nordling, N. (2001). Sadomasochistically oriented behavior: Diversity in practice and meaning. *Archives of Sexual Behavior, 30,* 1-12.

Apostolides, M. (1999). The pleasure of the pain, why some people need S&M. *Psychology Today, 32*(5), 60-65.

Baumeister, R. F. (1988a). Masochism as escape from self. *Journal of Sex Research* *25*, 28-59.

Baumeister, R. F. (1988b). Gender differences in masochistic scripts. *Journal of Sex Research 25*, 478-499.

Baumeister, R. F., & Butler, J. L. (1997). Sexual masochism: Deviance without pathology. In D. R. Laws & W. O'Donohue (Eds.), *Sexual deviance. Theory, assessment, and treatment. (*pp. 225-239). New York: The Guilford Press.

Baumeister, R. F., & Tice, D. M. (2001). *The social dimension of sex.* Boston: Allyn and Bacon.

Breslow, N. (1987). Locus of Control, Desirability of Control, and Sadomasochists. *Psychological Reports 61*, 995-1001.

Breslow, N. (1989). Sources of Confusion in the Study and Treatment of Sadomasochism. *Journal of Social Behavior and Personality 4*, 263-274.

Breslow, N., Evans, L., & Langley, J. (1985). On the prevalence and roles of females in the sadomasochistic subculture: Report on an empirical study. *Archives of Sexual Behavior, 14*, 303-317.

Breslow, N., Evans, L., & Langley, J. (1986). Comparisons among heterosexual, bisexual, and homosexual male sadomasochists. *Journal of Homosexuality 13(1)*, 83-107.

Brodsky, J. I. (1993). The Mineshaft: A retrospective ethnography. *Journal of Homosexuality 24(3/4)*, 233-251.

Califia, P. (1979) A secret side of lesbian sexuality. *The Advocate* (December 17), 19-23.

Cleugh, J. (1952). *The Marquis and the Chevalier.* Boston: Little, Brown.

Donnelly, D., & Fraser, J. (1998). Gender differences in sado-masochistic arousal among college students. *Sex Roles: A Journal of Research, 39*, 391-407.

Ernulf, K. E., & Innala, S. M. (1995). Sexual bondage: A review and unobtrusive investigation. *Archives of Sexual Behavior 24*, 631-654.

Falk, G., & Weinberg, T. S. (1983). Sadomasochism and popular Western culture. In T. Weinberg & G. W. L. Kamel (Eds.) *S and M: Studies in sadomasochism* (pp. 137-144). Buffalo, NY: Prometheus Books.

Freud, S. (1938). The basic writings of Sigmund Freud. A. A. Brill (Trans.). New York: Modern Library.

Freud, S. (1953). Three Essays on Sexuality. In J. Strachey (Ed. & Trans.) in *The standard edition of the complete psychological works of Sigmund Freud. Vol. 7* (pp. 135-230) London: Hogarth Press. (Translated from the German edition; original work published 1905).

Freud, S. (1959). The economic problem in masochism. In E. Jones (Ed.) & J. Riviere (Trans.). *Sigmund Freud, collected papers. vol. 2.* (pp. 255-276). New York: Basic Books. [Translated from the German edition; original work published in 1924).

Freud, S. (1961). *Beyond the pleasure principle.* J. Strachey (Ed. & Trans.). New York: Liveright. (Translated from the German edition; original work published 1920).

Gebhard, P. (1969). Fetishism and Sadomasochism. In J.H. Masserman (Ed.). *Dynamics of deviant sexuality.* (pp. 71-80). New York: Grune & Stratton.

Green, R. (2001). (Serious) sadomasochism: A protected right of privacy? *Archives of Sexual Behavior, 30*, 543-550.

Hoople, T. (1996). Conflicting visions: SM, feminism, and the law. A problem of representation. *Canadian Journal of Law and Society 11(1)*, 177-220.

Hopkins, P. D. (1994). Rethinking sadomasochism: Feminism, interpretation, and simulation. *Hypatia 9*, 116-141.

Houlberg, R. (1991). The magazine of a sadomasochistic club: The tie that binds. *Journal of Homosexuality 21(1/2)*, 167-183.

Innala, S. M., & Ernulf, K. E. (1992). Understanding male homosexual attraction: An analysis of restroom graffiti. *Journal of Social Behavior and Personality 7*, 503-510.

Juliette. (1995). Autobiography of a dominatrix. In T. S. Weinberg (Ed.). *S & M: Studies in dominance & submission.* (pp. 61-70) Amherst, N Y: Prometheus Books.

Kamel, G. W. L. (1980). Leathersex: Meaningful aspects of gay sadomasochism. *Deviant Behavior: An Interdisciplinary Journal 1*, 171-191.

Kamel, G. W. L. (1983). The leather career: On becoming a sadomasochist. In T. Weinberg and G.W.L. Kamel (Eds.). *S and M: Studies in sadomasochism.* (pp. 73-79) Buffalo, NY: Prometheus Books.

Kamel, G. W. L., & Weinberg, T.S. (1983). Diversity in sadomasochism: Four S&M careers. In T. Weinberg and G.W.L. Kamel (Eds.). *S and M: Studies in sadomasochism.* (pp. 113-128). Buffalo, NY: Prometheus Books.

Kershaw, A. (1992). Love hurts. *The Guardian Weekend*, 6-10, 12 (November 28).

Krafft-Ebing, R. von. 1965. *Psychopathia sexualis.* F.S. Klaff (Trans.) New York: Stein & Day. (Translated from the German edition; original work published 1886).

Lee, J. A. (1979). The social organization of sexual risk. *Alternative Lifestyles 2*, 69-100.

Levitt, E. E., Moser, C., & Jamison, K. V. (1994). The prevalence and some attributes of females in the sadomasochistic subculture: A second report. *Archives of Sexual Behavior 23*, 465-473.

Levitt, S. (1992). The scary lure of sado-masochism. *Cosmopolitan (November)*, 212-215.

Lewis, R., & Adler, K. (1994). Come to me baby or what's wrong with lesbian SM. *Women's Studies International Forum 17*, 433-441.

Lieshout, M. van. (1996). Leather nights in the woods: Homosexual encounters in a Dutch highway rest area. *Journal of Homosexuality 29*, 19-39.

Magill, M. S. (1982). Ritual and symbolism of dominance and submission: The case of heterosexual sadomasochism. Unpublished manuscript. Department of Anthropology, State University of New York at Buffalo, Buffalo, NY.

Moser, C. (1979). "An Exploratory-descriptive Study of a Self-defined S/M (sadomasochistic) Sample. Ph.D. dissertation, Institute for Advanced Study of Human Sexuality. San Francisco, CA.

Moser, C. (1984). Dominant women-submissive men: An exploration in erotic dominance and submission. [book review]. *The Journal of Sex Research 20*, 417-419.

Moser, C.(1988). Sadomasochism. *Journal of Social Work and Human Sexuality 7(1)*, 43-56.

Moser, C. (1998). S/M (sadomasochistic) interactions in semi-public settings. *Journal of Homosexuality 36*, 19-29.

Moser, C., & Levitt, E. E. (1987). An exploratory-descriptive study of a sadomaso-chistically oriented sample. *Journal of Sex Research 23*, 322-337.

Moser, C., & Kleinplatz, P. J. (2005). DSM-IV-TR and the paraphilias: An argument for removal. *Journal of Psychology & Human Sexuality, 17(3/4)*, 91-109.

Myers, J. (1992). Nonmainstream body modification: Genital piercing, branding, burning, and cutting. *Journal of Contemporary Ethnography 21*, 267-306.

Naerssen, A. X. van, van Dijk, M., Hoogveen, G., Visser, D., & van Zessen, G. (1987). Gay SM in pornography and reality. *Journal of Homosexuality 12(2/3)*, 111-119.

Ross, J. M. (1997). *The sadomasochism of everyday life*. New York: Simon & Schuster.

Sandnabba, N. K., Santtila, P. & Nordling, N. (1999). Sexual behavior and social adap-tation among sadomasochistically-oriented males. *Journal of Sex Research 36*, 273-282.

Santtila, P, Sandnabba, N. K., Alison, L., & Nordling, N. (2002). Investigating the un-derlying structure in sadomasochistically oriented behavior. *Archives of Sexual Be-havior, 31*, 185-196.

Scott, G. G. (1983). *Dominant women-submissive men: An exploration in erotic domi-nance and submission*. New York: Praeger Publishers.

Spengler, A. (1977). Manifest sadomasochism of males: Results of an empirical study. *Archives of Sexual Behavior 6*, 441-456.

Spengler, A. (1979). *Sadomasochisten und ihre Subkulturen*. Frankfurt, West Ger-many: Campus Verlag.

Stekel, W. (1965). *Sadism and masochism, the psychology of hatred and cruelty. vol. 2*. New York: Grove Press. (Original work published in 1929).

Thompson, B. (1995). *Sadomasochism: Painful perversion or pleasurable play?* New York: Cassell.

Weinberg, M. S., Williams, C. J., & Moser, C. (1984). The social constituents of sado-masochism. *Social Problems 31*, 379-389.

Weinberg, T. S. (1978). Sadism and masochism: Sociological perspectives. *The Bulle-tin of the American Academy of Psychiatry and the Law 6*, 284-295.

Weinberg, T. S. (1987). Sadomasochism in the United States: A review of recent socio-logical literature. *The Journal of Sex Research 23*, 50-69.

Weinberg, T. S. (1994). Research in sadomasochism: A review of sociological and so-cial psychological literature. *Annual Review of Sex Research 5*, 257-279.

Weinberg, T. S. (1995). Sociological and social psychological issues in the study of sadomasochism. In T. S. Weinberg (Ed.) *S & M: Studies in dominance & submis-sion* (pp. 289-303) Amherst, NY: Prometheus Books.

Weinberg, T. S., & Falk, G. (1980). The social organization of sadism and masochism. *Deviant Behavior: An Interdisciplinary Journal 1*, 379-393.

Westheimer, R. K., & Lopater, S. (2002). *Human sexuality: A psychosocial perspec-tive*. New York: Lippincott, Williams & Wilkins.

Williams, C. J. (1995). SM in the sceptred isle. *Journal of Sex Research 32*, 170-172.

Differences and Similarities Between Gay and Straight Individuals Involved in the Sadomasochistic Subculture

Niklas Nordling, MPsych

Åbo Akademi University

N. Kenneth Sandnabba, PhD

Åbo Akademi University

Pekka Santtila, PhD

Åbo Akademi University

Laurence Alison, PhD

University of Liverpool

Niklas Nordling is a PhD student at the Department of Psychology at the Åbo Akademi University and an authorised psychologist. He is currently preparing his PhD thesis on sadomasochism. Dr. N. Kenneth Sandnabba is Professor of Applied Psychology at the Department of Psychology at the Åbo Akademi University and an authorised psychotherapist and clinical sexologist. His research interests include sexual behavior, aggressive behavior, and gender issues. Dr. Pekka Santtila is a Docent in Forensic Psychology at the Department of Psychology at the Åbo Akademi University. His research interests include sexual behavior and forensic psychology. Dr. Laurence Alison is affiliated with the Centre for Critical Incident Research, School of Psychology, University of Liverpool. His research interests include sexual behavior, forensic psychology and offender profiling. This study was financially supported by grants from the Rector of Åbo Akademi University and the SETA Foundation.

[Haworth co-indexing entry note]: "Differences and Similarities Between Gay and Straight Individuals Involved in the Sadomasochistic Subculture." Nordling et al. Co-published simultaneously in *Journal of Homosexuality* (Harrington Park Press, an imprint of The Haworth Press, Inc.) Vol. 50, No. 2/3, 2006, pp. 41-57; and: *Sadomasochism: Powerful Pleasures* (ed: Peggy J. Kleinplatz, and Charles Moser) Harrington Park Press, an imprint of The Haworth Press, Inc., 2006, pp. 41-57. Single or multiple copies of this article are available for a fee from The Haworth Document Delivery Service [1-800-HAWORTH, 9:00 a.m. - 5:00 p.m. (EST). E-mail address: docdelivery@haworthpress.com].

doi:10.1300/J082v50n02_03

41

SUMMARY. Results from some new analyses as well as a selective review of the results of six empirical studies on a self-identified sample of sadomasochistically-oriented individuals (22 women and 162 men) with an emphasis on differences between gay and straight participants are presented. The gay male respondents seemed to be better educated, to hold white-collar occupations and to be more sadistically oriented. The gay male respondents became aware of their sadomasochistic preferences and had their first experiences at an older age. They showed a preference for leather outfits, anal intercourse, rimming, dildos, wrestling, special equipment and uniform scenes, and the straight male respondents for verbal humiliation, mask and blindfold, gags, rubber outfits, cane whipping, vaginal intercourse, cross dressing, and straitjackets, and different role plays except for uniform scenes. Four separate sexual themes were identified: hypermasculinity; administration and receiving of pain; physical restriction and psychological humiliation. Gay male participants showed a preference for hypermasculinity and straight men respondents for humiliation. The number of lesbian respondents was too low to draw any definite conclusions. Differences between gay and straight male sadomasochists in the present sample were found. Clearly, sadomasochism cannot be thought of as a unitary phenomenon: People who identify themselves as sadomasochists mean different things by these identifications. *[Article copies available for a fee from The Haworth Document Delivery Service: 1-800-HAWORTH. E-mail address: <docdelivery@ haworthpress.com> Website: <http://www.HaworthPress.com> © 2006 by The Haworth Press, Inc. All rights reserved.]*

KEYWORDS. Homosexuality, sadomasochism, masculinity, gender stereotypes

The relationship between sadomasochistic preferences and sexual orientation has not been thoroughly explored although it has been suggested that sexual orientation issues are usually clarified prior to engagement in sadomasochistic sex (Falk & Weinberg, T. S., 1983; Moser & Levitt, 1987). (Throughout the paper the expressions 'sadistically oriented' and 'masochistically oriented' refer to the individuals preferring the sadistic or masochistic role respectively in a consensual sexual encounter with sadomasochistic elements.) The aim of the present paper is to present some new data on the relationship between sadomasochistic interests and sexual orientation issues as well as to review some of the earlier literature on the matter.

According to Moser (1988), there is no commonly accepted definition of what constitutes sadomasochistic sexual behavior. A non-clinical definition of consensual sadomasochistic sex by Townsend (1983) identifies six characteristic features in a sadomasochistic scene: a relation of dominance and submission, infliction of pain that is experienced as pleasurable by both partners, using fantasy or role-playing by one or both partners, deliberate humiliation of the other partner, fetishistic elements (clothes, devices, scenery), and one or more ritualistic activities, e.g., bondage, whipping. Other definitions have been offered by, for example, Weinberg, M. S., Williams and Moser (1984) and by Kamel (1983). There has been little attention to differences in behaviors engaged in as a function of sexual orientation. However, Weinberg, M. S. et al. (1984), Lee (1979) and Kamel (1983) refer to a subset of behaviors commonly associated with the gay male 'leather' scene that, to observers, appears to be sadomasochistic in origin although the participants not necessarily consider themselves as sadomasochists. These behaviors include enemas, catheters, anal fisting and scatological practices and are sometimes described by the subjects as displays of 'masculinity and toughness' (Weinberg, M. S. et al., 1984, p. 387). One of the studies reviewed in the present paper explored whether a preference for such "hypermasculinity" (Alison, Santtila, Sandnabba, & Nordling, 2001) behaviors over other possible behaviors would be related to a homosexual orientation in male sadomasochists.

Weinberg, T. S. (1978) emphasizes the importance of sadomasochistic clubs in developing attitudes supportive of sadomasochism. These attitudes enable individuals who are integrated in the subculture to justify their sexual desires more easily. This does not imply that individuals who do not participate in the sadomasochistic subculture would necessarily have problems in accepting their sadomasochistic interests; it may just be more difficult for them to find likeminded partners. Previous studies (Spengler, 1977; Kamel, 1983) have shown gay men to be more integrated in the sadomasochistic subculture. However, during the last two decades sadomasochism has become more visible and it may be that such differences no longer exist. To the extent that gay male sadomasochistic subculture still offers more role-models and possibilities of engaging in sexual behavior than the straight sadomasochistic subculture (Kamel, 1983), it would be expected that gay male sadomasochists would be more satisfied with their sex lives than straight male sadomasochists.

There is a lack of research into the childhood experiences of practitioners of sadomasochism. For example, attachment theorists (e.g., Shaver, Hazan, & Bradshaw, 1988) have shown that attachment style affects the expression of sexuality in a number of areas including trust, desire for reciprocation, and fear of closeness. They also suggest that for every feature of adult love-relationships, there is either a documented or a plausible infant parallel. Although there is no single and accepted explanation of variations in either sexual orientation or sadomasochistic preferences, it cannot be excluded *a priori* that no associations exist between early family dynamics and sexual behaviour in the group of sadomasochistically oriented individuals.

Likewise, the question of whether childhood abuse experiences lead to sadomasochistic behavior has been largely ignored. Due to the complexity of sadomasochistic sexual behavior and the significance of social influences on it, it is unlikely that any simple associations between childhood abuse experiences and later sadomasochistic sexual behavior could be found. Nevertheless, it is important to ascertain empirically what the role of sexual abuse–if any–is for the development of sadomasochistic sexual interests.

The present article reports the results from some new analyses as well as a selective review of the results of six empirical studies (Alison et al., 2001; Nordling, Sandnabba, & Santtila, 2000; Sandnabba, Santtila, Nordling, Beetz, & Alison, 2002; Sandnabba, Santtila, & Nordling, 1999; Santtila, Sandnabba, & Nordling, 2000; Santtila, Sandnabba, Alison, & Nordling, 2002) on a self-identified sample of Finnish sadomasochistically oriented individuals with a special emphasis on differences between gay and straight participants. Throughout the present article, earlier reported findings are cited in the text. Results from new analyses are reported with full statistical details whereas those reported earlier have no statistical details or at most the significance level reached.

In total, 186 respondents (two questionnaires had not been adequately filled in and were discarded leaving 22 women and 162 men) who were members of two sadomasochistically oriented organisations provided information for the studies. Ninety-five respondents were recruited from Kinky Club, an association for mainly straight persons with a variety of sexual preferences. Ninety-one respondents were recruited from the MSC-Finland association for mainly gay male members. Most of the members are only loosely connected with the clubs with their main connection to the organizations being reading the newsletter and occasionally going to parties organised by the club. The organizations are not clubs in a stricter, more organized sense of the word. They are more like loose associations of likeminded people from all over Finland. At the time of research, these were the only organizations in Finland specifically for persons interested in sadomasochistic sexuality and in targeting both of them our aim was to acquire about equal numbers of both gay and straight respondents. Details on the questionnaire and the procedure can be found in the previously published reports listed above. It should be noted, however, that as both above mentioned organizations had members with differing sexual preferences it was emphasized that only individuals who defined themselves as sadomasochists would complete the instrument. It should be noted that there is always the possibility of differences between sadomasochistically oriented individuals who are involved in organizations and those who are not which limits the generalizability of the findings.

The questionnaire that was used had been specifically created for the research. It contained 237 questions on 18 pages. The length of the questionnaire precluded the inclusion of additional significant areas of inquiry such as the relationship between HIV/AIDS and SM-sex. The questionnaires were mailed to all the members of the two clubs with the approval and cooperation of the boards for the two organizations. Full confidentiality was guaranteed and the individuals who volunteered sent their addressed and stamped return envelopes to the researchers. As both organizations had members with differing sexual preferences it was emphasized that only individuals who defined themselves as sadomasochists would complete the instrument. The response rate was 35%, which, considering the nature of the study and the fact that the clubs also had members other than sadomasochists, was deemed to be acceptable.

As a consequence of the small number of female respondents (and an even smaller number of lesbian respondents), we were not able to carry out as thorough analyses regarding them as regarding the male respondents.

DIFFERENCES BETWEEN GAY AND STRAIGHT RESPONDENTS IN DEMOGRAPHIC FEATURES

The respondents were highly educated with over a third having a university degree when the corresponding figure for the general population was 5.5% (Sandnabba et al., 1999). In spite of some differences in age distribution (approximately 10% of the respondents were over 50 years old) the difference is robust. In terms of sexual orientation there was some indication that the gay male respondents would have been better educated (43% had university exams) compared to straight men (29% had university exams), although this difference failed to reach statistically significant levels ($p < .06$). The gay male respondents also had a higher income level than the population in general. In terms of age, no differences were found as a function of sexual orientation. However, there were differences between the gay male and the straight male respondents in the rate of their placement in different occupational areas ($p < .001$). Comparison of the responses showed that the gay male respondents primarily held white-collar occupations (e.g., administration and education) while the straight respondents held more blue-collar positions (e.g., industry and service). To the extent that educational attainment is viewed as a measure of social and psychological well-being, it seems that the gay male respondents had succeeded well in this respect (Sandnabba et al., 1999).

SEXUAL ORIENTATION
AND SADOMASOCHISTIC PREFERENCE

Table 1 shows the sexual orientation categories of male and female respondents separately. More female respondents reported a hetero- or bisexual orientation (72.7%) compared to male respondents (45.0%), $\chi2 (4) = 16.74$, $p < .002$. This effect is likely to be an artifact based on the selection procedure: The MSC Finland association was mainly open for gay male individuals while the Kinky Club attracted mainly straight males and females leading possibly to an underrepresentation of lesbian sadomasochists. Also, there were relatively equal numbers of gay and straight respondents in the sample. This could be explainable by both of

TABLE 1. Sexual orientation of the male and female respondents.

	Male respondents n = 164	Female respondents n = 22
Exclusively heterosexual	28.4	18.2
Predominantly heterosexual	12.3	40.9
Bisexual	4.3	13.6
Predominantly homosexual	17.3	9.1
Exclusively homosexual	37.7	18.2

the organizations being situated in the metropolitan area of Finland with a relatively high concentration of gay individuals whereas heterosexually oriented sadomasochists are probably more evenly distributed throughout the country leading to a sampling bias favoring gay respondents. It would seem likely that the actual distribution of sadomasochistically oriented persons with different sexual orientations would be close to the distribution of sexual orientation in the general population.

Correlations between sexual orientation (rated on a five-point scale with anchors exlusively homosexual and exclusively heterosexual with the middle point being bisexual) and sadomasochistic preference (also rated on a five-point scale with anchors exclusively sadistic and exclusively masochistic with the middle point being equally sadistic and masochistic) were computed separately for male and female respondents using Spearman's ρ. Both male and female respondents with a more heterosexual orientation were more likely to have a more masochistic preference while the more gay respondents were more likely to be sadistically oriented. This association was stronger in female ($\rho = -.66$, $p < .001$) when compared to male ($\rho = -.16$, $p < .042$) respondents.

The gay male respondents became aware of their sadomasochistic preferences at an older age than the exclusively heterosexual males. Further, the gay males had their first experience at an older age than the exclusively heterosexual males. In a similar manner, there was a tendency for the gay males to differ from the other groups in terms of the onset of regular sadomasochistic activity (Sandnabba et al., 1999).

It was also found that 88.4% of the respondents had practiced consensual heterosexual or homosexual sexual activity without sadomasochistic elements, before engaging in sadomasochism. The percentage of the respondents who no longer practiced such sex was 4.9%; the mean age at which these respondents stopped having such sex was 25 years. On the other hand, 27.2% of the male respondents endorsed a statement suggesting that only sadomasochistic sex could satisfy them. The straight males showed a nonsignificant tendency to endorse this statement more often than the gay males (Sandnabba et al., 1999).

These results suggest that the development of sadomasochistic sexual behavior starts after experience with more sexual behavior without sadomasochistic elements and the establishment of a sexual orientation. Specifically, the exclusively gay male respondents became aware and started practising their sadomasochistic interests later which accords well with findings showing that gay male individuals establish their sexual orientation later than straight males (Coleman, 1982; Kontula & Haavio-Mannila, 1993). This is also consistent with Kamel's idea of sadomasochism as a reaction to dissatisfaction with the ordinary gay male scene (Kamel, 1983).

When exploring the changes in sadomasochistic preference it was found that 48.9% of the gay men and 50.0% of the lesbian respondents had not changed their sadomasochistic role preference. Changes toward sadistic behavior were not significantly more prevalent than changes toward masochistic behavior. This contradicts Baumeister's (1988) hypothesis of such a change towards a more sadistic position.

DIFFERENCES BETWEEN GAY AND STRAIGHT RESPONDENTS IN SEXUAL BEHAVIOR

Table 2 presents significant differences between the frequencies with which the gay male and straight male respondents had participated in different sexual behaviors and role plays. Clear differences in the frequencies of sexual and sadomasochistic behaviors and role plays between the straight and gay male respondents were found, e.g., the gay male respondents were more fond of leather outfits, anal intercourse, rimming, dildos, wrestling, special equipment and uniform scenes, while the straight respondents more often enjoyed verbal humiliation, mask and blindfold, gags, rubber outfits, cane whipping, vaginal intercourse, cross dressing, and straitjackets. Different role plays, except for uniform scenes, were involved more often in the sexual repertoires of the straight male respondents.

Also, sadomasochistic activity did not seem to be associated with extensive substance abuse during or before sadomasochistic sex. However, the use of poppers and alcohol by the gay male respondents was an exception to this pattern and could perhaps be understood as a distinctive pattern of the gay male subculture (Sandnabba et al., 1999).

Only male respondents had engaged in sexual behavior with animals (Sandnabba et al., 2002). There were no differences between gay male and straight male participants in the likelihood of engaging in such behavior; five respondents from each group (as well as two bisexual respondents) reported having done so.

Table 3 shows the frequencies with which lesbian and straight female respondents had engaged in different sexual behavior and role plays. No significance tests were carried out due to the low numbers of participants. Most frequently reported behaviors among the lesbian respondents were the use of leather outfits, flagellations, use of dildos, bondage, oral sex as well as blindfolds, whereas in contrast to the

TABLE 2. Various sexual and sadomasochistic behaviors and role-plays during the last twelve months with significant differences between the exclusively and predominantly straight and the exclusively and predominantly gay male participants.

Behavior	Gay Men % n = 90	Straight Men % n = 67	χ^2
Leather outfits	96.60	79.70	11.24***
Anal intercourse	95.30	71.00	16.92***
Rimming	86.50	70.50	5.81**
Dildos	78.40	61.30	5.21*
Flagellation	77.30	90.60	4.66*
Cock binding	75.00	61.30	3.22+
Verbal humiliation	65.90	81.00	4.14*
Wrestling	63.20	23.30	22.68***
Mask, blindfold	57.50	77.80	6.72**
Rubber outfits	47.70	65.60	4.62*
Special equipment, e.g, slings, crosses, cages	46.50	30.60	3.78*
Gag	44.80	67.70	7.66**
Cane whipping	44.30	63.40	5.17*
Electric shocks	11.50	21.30	2.63+
Straitjacket	10.30	27.40	7.33**
Cross dressing	9.20	52.40	34.31***
Role plays			
Uniform scenes	55.3	22.8	14.76***
Master/Madame-Slave	36.5	83.9	33.77***
Teacher-Student	20	44.6	9.80**
Hospital scenes	7.1	32.7	15.23***

Note. Percentages have been calculated on the basis of only those participants who have answered a particular question.
+$p < .10$. *$p < .05$. **$p < .01$. ***$p < .001$.

straight female participants, the lesbian respondents did not participate in scenes including rubber outfits, weights, hypoxyphilia, mummifying and straitjackets. Straitjackets and rubber outfits were especially preferred by the straight male participants.

A question on the frequency at which the male respondents had practiced sadomasochistic sex during the preceding 12 months showed that the highest relative frequency (34.1%) was in the 2-5 sessions bracket. The gay male respondents had more sessions than the straight respon-

TABLE 3. Various sexual and sadomasochistic behaviors and role-plays during the last twelve months with significant differences between the exclusively and predominantly straight female and the exclusively and predominantly lesbian participants (n = 22).

Behavior	Lesbian respondents % N = 6	Straight female respondents % N = 13
Oral sex	100	100
Flagellation	100	92
Dildos	100	92
Bondage	100	92
Leather outfits	100	85
Mask, blindfold	100	77
Handcuffs	80	92
Biting	80	77
Spanking	80	77
Ice	80	39
Face-slapping	80	62
Chains	60	85
Anal intercourse	60	83
Verbal humiliation	60	77
Clothespins, clamps	60	62
Caning	60	46
Rimming	60	31
Hot wax	60	23
Knives, razor blades	60	15
Cross dressing	50	46
Gag	40	67
Wrestling	40	62
Special equipment	40	31
Skin branding	40	23
Water sports (urolangia)	40	15
Fist-fucking	20	39
Piercing	20	39
Odors	20	25
Electric shocks	20	-
Rubber outfits	-	58
Weights	-	31
Hypoxyphilia	-	31
Enema	-	23

Behavior	Lesbian respondents % N = 6	Straight female respondents % N = 13
Mummifying	-	15
Scat (coprophilia)	-	15
Straitjacket	-	8
Role plays		
Rape scenes	100	67
Master/Madame-Slave	80	69
Uniform scenes	60	27
Teacher-Student	40	36
Hospital scenes	40	18
Execution scenes	20	9

dents. The modal number of sadomasochistic sessions that the male respondents had had during the last twelve months is rather low. However, it should be remembered that only a minority of the respondents could only be satisfied by sadomasochistic sex and only about 5% do not engage in other sexual activity besides sadomasochism (Sandnabba et al., 1999).

COMBINATIONS OF BEHAVIORS TYPICALLY ENGAGED IN BY GAY MALE RESPONDENTS

Sadomasochism can be seen as a label of convenience for a set of related sexual activities of particular subcultures. Facets include physical restriction and bondage (Baumeister, 1988) and humiliation (Moser & Levitt, 1987; Baumeister, 1988; Weinberg, 1987) among others. Weinberg, M. S. et al. (1984), Lee (1979) and Kamel (1983) refer to a subset of behaviors commonly associated with the gay male 'leather' scene that, to observers, appears to be sadomasochistic in origin although the participants not necessarily consider themselves as sadomasochists. These behaviors include enemas, catheters, anal fisting and scatological practices and are sometimes described by the subjects as displays of 'masculinity and toughness' (Weinberg et al., p. 387). Using a multidimensional scaling analysis it was possible to identify four separate sexual themes which in the Alison et al. (2001) article were labeled: hypermasculinity; administration and receiving of pain; physical restriction and psychological humiliation. These are, of course, labels of convenience and other possibilities might exist. There were significant differences between the gay and straight male respondents in terms of their involvement in the hypermasculinity (involving rimming, watersports, cockbinding, fistfucking, scatologia and the use of dildos, enemas and catheters) and humiliation (involving faceslapping, flagellation, the use of a gag, the use of knives and razors and verbal humiliation) regions. As expected, the gay male subjects were more likely to engage in a larger number of the behaviours of the hypermasculinity region ($p < .01$) compared to the straight male subjects whereas the latter were more likely to engage in a larger number of humiliation behaviors ($p < .01$). The facets appear to take on different functions for the gay men and straight men on the other hand (Alison et al., 2001). There were no significant differences between sadistically and masochistically oriented individuals in this regard.

However, in the above analysis, there was no attempt at establishing the order of these behaviors. That is, there was no discussion or examination of the intensity of the behaviors or the structure of the behaviours in the context of sets of actions. Therefore, it was not possible to discern whether particular behaviors are always preceded by others thereby creating cumulative structures of various SM-scenarios. In the Santtila et al. (2002) study the intention was, in other words, to examine the relationship that individual actions may have in the context of learned and developing sequences of behaviors in much the same way that studies of conventional heterosexual activity have examined the progression of kissing to intercourse. It could, for example, be hypothesised that people who use straitjackets in their SM-scenarios would previously have engaged in bondage. An attempt was thus made to explore the responses further in order to identify any such cumulative structures.

For example, the results from the eight hypermasculinity behaviors which were preferred by the gay male respondents indicated a cumulative scale where those respondents engaged in *watersports* had also engaged in *rimming*. *Cockbinding*, was, however, a qualitatively different aspect of hypermasculinity. Further, those respondents engaged in *fistfucking* most certainly also had experienced *scat* and respondents with experience of *scat* in turn had also experienced *enemas*. The presence of these behaviours combined with either the *rimming/watersports* dimension or the *cockbinding* dimension identified SM-practitioners with the most experience. Use of *dildos* together with *catheters* had no clear relationship with either dimension. This may have something to do with their being pieces of technical equipment (Santtila et al., 2002).

EARLY EXPERIENCES AND CHILDHOOD SEXUAL ABUSE

The question of how different patterns of family interaction are related to sexual orientation in a group of sadomasochistically oriented individuals was also explored.

Correlations between sexual orientation and the respondents' general description of their relationships to their fathers and mothers as distant or close were computed using Spearman's ρ separately for male and female respondents. Sexual orientation was not related to the closeness of the father. However, male respondents identifying themselves as exclusively or predominantly homosexual tended to describe their relationships to their mothers as closer than more heterosexual respondents did ($\rho = -.16, p < .037$). In contrast, female respondents with a more homosexual orientation described their relationships to their mothers as more distant than did the more heterosexual respondents ($\rho = .45, p < .035$).

Sexual orientation was not related to the respondents' descriptions of their fathers or mothers on the dimension of dominance-submissiveness. Likewise, the classifications of the respondents as either securely, avoidantly or ambivalently attached to their mothers and fathers were not associated with their sexual orientation. Both these analyses were conducted separately for male and female respondents (Santtila et al., 2000). The distribution of different attachment styles in the present sample was almost identical to distributions obtained in previous studies with general adult samples using similar methods of measurement (Shaver, Hazan, & Bradshaw, 1988) indicating the comparability of this sample with non-sadomasochistic individuals. This again suggests that conclusions drawn from clinical case reports based on people who have sought psychological help cannot be generalized to the majority of men practicing SM-sex.

The occurrence, type, and frequency of childhood sexual abuse as well as the identity of the perpetrator were also explored. The prevalence of reported sexual abuse (for one person the abuse was only verbal, i.e., speech of erotic content inappropriate for the age of the child, in nature–for the others it included physical touching defined as touching of erogenous zones of the body) was higher in the present study as compared to the findings of a study of sexual abuse (defined as physical touching of the erogenous zones) of children in Finland (Nordling et al., 2000). In the present sample 7.9% of the males reported sexual abuse compared to 1-3% in the general population (Sariola & Uutela, 1994). The corresponding figures for females were 22.7% and 6-8%. For one participant the sexual abuse was solely verbal in nature whereas for the remaining 17 participants it also included physical sexual contact. Sexual abuse had occurred for a significantly larger portion of the female respondents. Sexual abuse experiences were equally distributed across the different sexual orientation categories also when male and female respondents were considered separately.

CONCLUDING THOUGHTS

The main conclusion that emerges from the present comparison of gay and straight individuals engaged in sadomasochistic behavior is that differences do exist and this has consequences for our understanding of sadomasochism. Clearly, it cannot be thought of as a unitary phenomenon: People who identify as sadomasochists probably mean different things by these identifications. This would also mean that a particular behavior may be understood by somebody as sadomasochistic whereas somebody else would not consider it in this way. For example, some researchers suggest that fist-fucking is not sadomasochistic (Naving, 1981).

One of the most striking differences between the gay male and straight male sadomasochists is the fact that more gay male sadomasochists are sadistically oriented and that they have a preference for masculinization of their sexual behavior. The gay male sadomasochistic subculture exaggerates the male aspects of sexual behavior while the straight men seem to play down these aspects and adopt more submissive roles with emphasis on pain and humiliation. However, it is important to remember that these differences were group differences reaching statistical significance: Many gay men preferred primarily the behaviors in the humiliation theme and many straight men engaged in behaviors in the hypermasculinity region.

When drawing conclusions regarding the differences between gay and straight sadomasochists found in the present study, it should be remembered that it cannot be totally determined if these are just differences between gay and straight individuals in general or if the sadomasochism plays a specific part. Indeed, a single behavior can seldom be classified unambiguously as sadomasochistic or not without knowing the context of the behavior and the interpretation the individuals engaging in the behavior give to it. Certainly, non-sadomasochistic gay men also can be interested and engage in behaviors here classified into the hypermasculinity theme of sadomasochistic behavior. The same criticism applies to differences between gay and straight sadomasochistic subcultures as well as to family interaction.

This finding is interesting as a major aspect of the stereotypes linked to gay and lesbian individuals has been that they do not fit the accepted stereotypes for their own gender (Lips, 2001, p. 27). Also, the stereotype of gay men has as a central aspect the notion of femininity (Deaux & Lewis, 1984). However, the gay male participants in our sample accentuate their masculinity, acting in direct opposition of the stereotype. This does not mean that the gay males in the sample are necessarily more masculine than other gay men–accentuating masculinity can be interpreted as a reaction to still prevailing stereotypes. Also, previous research has indicated that a lot of gay men have anti-effeminacy prejudice (Taywaditep, 2001). In light of these findings, the hypermasculinity of gay men within the sadomasochistic subculture could be understood as a reaction against these stereotypes and a coping strategy to handle the conflict between internalized aspects of such a stereotype and anti-effeminacy attitudes held at the same time. At the same time, some gay men adopt an exaggerated feminine pose probably in an attempt to handle the same conflict by internalizing the stereotype completely and denying any anti-effeminacy attitudes. The number of lesbian respondents was too low to draw any definite conclusions. Likewise, the straight men who have sadomasochistic sexual interests may be escaping from the pressures of their narrow gender role demanding that they be strong, masculine, active, dominant, and successful. The masochistic role in a sadomasochistic sexual encounter is to some extent the exact opposite of such a role and it is therefore interesting that many of the straight men in our sample were, in fact, masochistically oriented. Further, it can be speculated that the small numbers of women engaging in sadomasochistic sex could be related to the female gender role being broader in these respects.

The lack of unity in the phenomenon of sadomasochism makes it easy to understand that no one description–let alone explanation–can suffice for it. Our results suggest that a person's sadomasochistic interest may be influenced by a number of factors. Individual sadomasochistic behavioral repertoire is also most certainly influenced by social and cultural features which may be one of the reasons why gay and straight respondents show different repertoires. It can be speculated that sadomasochism can be both a creative part of an individual's sexual life (as suggested by Foucault, 1999) or have a protective function as a neosexual creation in order to prevent severe psychological disturbances from appearing (as suggested by McDougall, 2000).

REFERENCES

Alison, L., Santtila, P., Sandnabba, N. K. & Nordling, N. (2001). Sadomasochistically-oriented behaviour: Diversity in practice and meaning. *Archives of Sexual Behavior, 30,* 1-12.

Baumeister, R. F. (1988). Masochism as escape from self. *Journal of Sex Research, 25,* 28-59.

Deaux, K., & Lewis, L. L. (1984). Structure of gender stereotypes: Interrelationships among components and gender label. *Journal of Personality and Social Psychology, 46,* 991-1004.

Falk, G. & Weinberg, T. S. (1983). Sadomasochism and popular western culture. In T. S. Weinberg & G. W. Kamel (Eds.) *S and M Studies in Sadomasochism,* pp. 137-146 (NY, Prometheus Books).

Foucault, M. (1999). Sexualitet, makt och identitetens politik. *Lambda Nordica, 2,* 122-137.

Kamel, G. W. (1983). Leathersex: Meaningful aspects of gay sadomasochism. In T. Weinberg & G. W. Kamel (Eds.) *S and M Studies in Sadomasochism,* pp. 162-174 (New York, Prometheus Books).

Kontula, O. & Haavio-Mannila, E. (1993). *Suomalainen Seksi.* (Juva, WSOY).

Lee, J.A. (1979). The social organization of sexual risk. *Alternative Lifestyles, 2,* 69-100.

Lips, H. M. (2001). *Sex and Gender: An Introduction.* Mayfield: London.

McDougall, J. (2000). Sexuality and the neosexual. *Modern Psychoanalysis, 25,* 155-166.

Moser, C. (1988). Sadomasochism. In D. M. Dailey (Ed) *The Sexually Unusual,* 43-56 (New York, Harrington Park Press).

Moser, C. & Levitt, E. E. (1987). An exploratory-descriptive study of a sadomaso-chistically oriented sample. *The Journal of Sex Research, 23,* 322-337.

Navin, H. (1981). Medical and surgical risks in handballing: Implications of an inadequate socialization process. *Journal of Homosexuality, 6,* 67-76.

Nordling, N., Sandnabba, N. K. & Santtila, P. (2000). The prevalence and effects of self-reported childhood sexual abuse among sadomasochistically oriented males and females. *Journal of Child Sexual Abuse, 9,* 53-63.

Sandnabba, N. K., Santtila, P. & Nordling, N. (1999). Sexual behavior and social adaptation among sadomasochistically oriented males. *Journal of Sex Research, 36,* 273-282.

Sandnabba, N. K., Santtila, P., Nordling, N., Beetz, A. M., & Alison, L. (2002). Characteristics of a sample of sadomasochistically-oriented males with recent experience of sexual contact with animals. *Deviant Behaviour: An Interdisciplinary Journal, 23,* 511-529.

Santtila, P., Sandnabba, N. K. & Nordling, N. (2000). Retrospective perceptions of family interaction in childhood as correlates of current sexual adaptation among sadomasochistic males. *Journal of Psychology and Human Sexuality, 12,* 69-87.

Santtila, P., Sandnabba, N. K., Alison, L. & Nordling, N. (2002). Investigating the underlying structure in sadomasochistically-oriented behaviour: Evidence for sexual scripts. *Archives of Sexual Behavior, 31,* 185-196.

Sariola, H., & Uutela, A. (1994). The prevalence of child sexual abuse in Finland. *Child Abuse & Neglect, 18,* 827-835.

Shaver, P., Hazan, C. & Bradshaw, D. (1988). Love as attachment: The integration of three behavioral systems. In R. J. Steinberg & M. L. Barnes (Eds.) *The Psychology of Love,* pp. 68-99 (New York, Vail-Ballou Press).

Spengler, A. (1977). Manifest sadomasochism of males: Results of an empirical study. *Archives of Sexual Behavior, 6,* 441-456.

Taywaditep, K. J. (2001). *Marginalization among the marginalized: Gay men's negative attitudes toward effeminacy.* An unpublished doctoral dissertation. University of Chicago.

Townsend, L. (1983). *The Leatherman's Handbook* (New York: Modernismo Publications).

Weinberg, M. S., Williams, C. J. & Moser, C. (1984). The social constituents of sadomasochism. *Social Problems, 31,* 379-389.

Weinberg, T.S. (1987). Sadomasochism in the United States: A review of recent sociological literature. *Journal of Sex Research, 23,* 50-69.

Sexual Spanking, the Self, and the Construction of Deviance

Rebecca F. Plante, PhD

Ithaca College

SUMMARY. Using interview and observation data from a group of consensual, heterosexual adults interested in sexual spanking, I describe members' sexual stories and stigma neutralization techniques. Sexual stories are situated within broader cultural contexts that help individuals construct meaning and identities. I describe group members' stories about their initial interest in sexualized spankings. Focusing on a specific event at one party, I show how these stories help to create scene-specific stigma neutralization techniques. Participants strive to differentiate themselves from sadomasochistic activities and to create normative behavioral expectations within their scenes. I conclude that all of this can ultimately be viewed as part of the complex sexual adaptations that people make. *[Article copies available for a fee from The Haworth Document Delivery Service: 1-800-HAWORTH. E-mail address: <docdelivery@haworthpress.com> Website: <http://www.HaworthPress.com> © 2006 by The Haworth Press, Inc. All rights reserved.]*

KEYWORDS. Sexual stories, sexual spanking, stigma neutralization, sexual scripts

Rebecca F. Plante is affiliated with the Department of Sociology, Ithaca College.

[Haworth co-indexing entry note]: "Sexual Spanking, the Self, and the Construction of Deviance." Plante, Rebecca F. Co-published simultaneously in *Journal of Homosexuality* (Harrington Park Press, an imprint of The Haworth Press, Inc.) Vol. 50, No. 2/3, 2006, pp. 59-79; and: *Sadomasochism: Powerful Pleasures* (ed: Peggy J. Kleinplatz, and Charles Moser) Harrington Park Press, an imprint of The Haworth Press, Inc., 2006, pp. 59-79. Single or multiple copies of this article are available for a fee from The Haworth Document Delivery Service [1-800-HAWORTH, 9:00 a.m. - 5:00 p.m. (EST). E-mail address: docdelivery@haworthpress.com].

Available online at http://www.haworthpress.com/web/JH
doi:10.1300/J082v50n02_04

I know I have long promised you an account of the reason of my penchant for the rod, which, in my estimation, is one of the most voluptuous and delicious institutions of private life, especially to a supposed highly respectable old maid like your esteemed friend. (Anonymous, 1968, p. 6)

Thus begins the story of Miss Coote, the central character in this "tale of voluptuousness," reportedly first published in *The Pearl*, an underground magazine originally distributed in England from 1879 to 1880. And what is the reason she gives for her penchant for the birch flagellation rod? Early childhood socialization, of course.

The history of spanking, a traditional type of corporal punishment, or its umbrella term, flagellation, is an old and venerable one. The *Kama Sutra*, the ancient Hindu version of the modern sex manual, includes a section on "love blows," giving detailed instructions on how to administer the most arousing slaps and punches (Danielou, 1995). Historically, sex workers used flagellation as one way to excite their clients. Caning was often used in British schools to discipline wayward pupils, and was only finally outlawed in 2000 (Farrell, 2003). And of course, parents in many Western cultures have historically employed some sort of spanking as actual (or threatened) punishment.

The specific activity described in this article is simply called erotic spanking. The focus is on spanking in a sexualized context, as a form of sexual discipline, not as corporal punishment. Erotic spanking is generally regarded as a form of bondage/domination and sadomasochism; spankings may be done over clothing, undergarments, or on the bare buttocks. The purpose of erotic spanking is for the emotional and sexual gratification of either or both parties. This kind of spanking is exactly the kind pop music star Madonna sang about: "Treat me like I'm a bad girl, even when I'm being good to you, I don't want you to thank me, you can just spank me. Mmm" (Madonna & Leonard, 1990). This is spanking as an erotic punishment, as part of fantasy scenes of misbehavior, but not as part of a wider array of sadomasochistic activities.

The research highlights the activities of a group of heterosexual men who like to spank consensual heterosexual women. Several questions frame this research. How do "sexual minorities" understand and make sense of their socially stigmatized sexual interests? How do they mitigate the effects of stereotypical and negative sexual scripting? And what is the larger social context for a type of sexual conduct that might appear, at first glance and for the average audience, to be the province of only a few individuals?

After reviewing the literature on sadomasochism, spanking, and stigma, observation and interview data are analyzed. This article is an attempt to describe several aspects of erotic, sexual(ized) spanking. Social context provides a lens through which participants situate their sexual interests. Participants know about broader cultural narratives and constructions of "normal," and are aware that their interests are often stigmatized and defined as deviant. In this vein, they work to redefine deviance via several strategies and techniques for neutralizing stigma. They collect and share pop cultural references to sexualized spanking and suggest that most people are interested in spanking but simply do not know it. The participants in this research also differentiate themselves from sadomasochistic practitioners, defining themselves as solely interested in "the bottom," or the buttocks, and in fantasies and scenes specifically involving the erotic tableau of a man spanking a woman.

This article focuses on a party attended by the group of heterosexual men and women referred to above, that is, primarily men who wished to spank women and women who wished to be spanked by men. There appeared to be a few "switches," men who wanted to be spanked, but only one woman who wanted to spank men. Other permutations of spanking do exist–women who wish to be spanked by other women, men who wish to be spanked by women, and men who wish to be spanked by other men. However, research participants were committed to spanking done by men for women, and no one indicated anything other than heterosexual sexual orientation.

SADOMASOCHISM

Spanking could be seen as one small element within broader bondage, domination, and sadomasochistic activities. This encompasses a very wide range of practices, including but not limited to flagellation, humiliation, restraints, torture, and blindfolding (Moser & Levitt, 1987). As a set of sexual practices and interests, sadomasochism (SM) is ecumenical, with gay, lesbian, bisexual, heterosexual, pansexual, and transgendered practitioners. The fluidity of identities, roles, and fantasies opens SM to a diverse range of people, although interest groups do form within other communities (e.g., gay leathermen, heterosexual infantilism). McClintock defines SM as "The sexual organization of social risk, for one of S/M's characteristics is the eroticizing of scenes, symbols, contexts, and contradictions which society does not typically recognize as erotic: domestic work, infancy, boots, water, money, uniforms, and so on" (1993, p. 108).

There is still a relatively small body of social scientific research on the broader practice of sadomasochism. Pioneering research delineated the first efforts to describe SM in sociological and destigmatizing contexts (Spengler, 1977; Weinberg, 1978; Moser, 1979; Kamel, 1980; Weinberg, Williams, & Moser, 1984). Previous inquiries had been concerned with the deviance and pathology of SM, seeking to describe it as aberrant (e.g., Krafft-Ebing, 1893/1933). In transcending the pejorative qualities of psychoanalytic and medical reports of SM practices, researchers in the last twenty years have tended to adopt broad, neutral or positive definitions. Compiling first-person narratives and commentaries, Thompson offers a very broad definition of "radical sex" (1994): It is "about the exploration of eros" and the liberation of erotic potential from Puritan ethics (1994).

Social science research has attempted to describe some demographic characteristics of SM aficionados, such as age of first noted interest in SM activities, disclosure to partners, appeal of specific practices, gender and sexual orientation differences, and participation in organized clubs or groups (Breslow, Evans, & Langley, 1985; Moser & Levitt, 1987; Houlberg, 1991; Thompson, 1994; McKenna & Bargh, 1998; Sandnabba, Santtila, & Nordling, 1999; Alison, Santtila, Sandnabba, & Nordling, 2001; Santtila, Sandnabba, Alison, & Nordling, 2002). These accounts are limited due to the difficulty of conducting ethnographic and in-depth interview studies.

Moser (1998) did describe what SM parties are like, using a retrospective analysis of 25 years of observations. He wrote, "S/M parties are similar to other parties, in that they are a place for socializing, refreshments are usually available, and they are an enjoyable way to spend time" (p. 19). The main difference between SM or scene parties and "other parties" is that SM parties include much less alcohol and other drugs, the clothing is mostly scene and role-specific, and participants are in a non-stigmatized space. This report clarifies that there are patterns, rules, and order underlying participation in the scene.

Recently, Taylor and Ussher (2001) studied SM practitioners via interviews, searching for a way to understand their lived experiences and meaning-making process. Fourteen men and ten women participated in open-ended interviews designed to provide a window into the ways in which they understood and interpreted their sexualities. The researchers identified an array of discursive strategies, including SM as fun, as learned behavior, and as intra-psychic. One respondent suggested, "I must have an SM personality" (p. 307).

The color or flavor of the broad array of SM activities has largely been offered by practitioners themselves. An early attempt to document what Thompson (1994) calls "radical sex" came in the form of an editorial plea from the editors of "Bizarre Life," a privately produced booklet of clothing "fetishes":

> We already have wide-ranging material (especially on the subjects of tight-lacing and high-heels), from earlier days (although more is always welcome), and now we are concerned in building up a library of authentic 'case-histories' of practices today. We are convinced that a great deal of original and exciting material is to be had from practicing fetishists whose experience and inventiveness could help us build up a really complete picture of the wonderful fetishist world. (Anonymous, 1964, p. 40)

In the subsequent questionnaire, the editors asked, "What combination of fetishes do you have? Allied to what other non-fetishist sexual variations?" Brame, Brame, and Jacobs (1993) presented a very broad range of activities, contextualized by expert commentaries but focusing on participants' narratives. In *The Kiss of the Whip*, Prezwalski includes his own and other gay men's accounts of "coming out" to SM and leather (1994). Califia helps novices navigate the terrain of SM sexualities in *Sensuous Magic*, a how-to guide for opposite and same sex couples (1993). But none of these focus only on spanking.

An obscure book about buttocks and fetishes did describe heterosexual spanking:

> One ritual, virtually as old as man himself, is the time-honored swat across the buttocks of a beloved female. While spanking, the logical punishment for an errant wife, has not attained the popularity it deserves, this form of flagellation is far from obsolete. There are many case histories . . . that testify to the frequency of spanking, both as chastisement and as an aid to sexual satisfaction. (Dione, 1966, unnumbered)

But there appears to be only one academic article about spanking, a theoretical analysis of the discourses that give rise to the sexualization of this activity (Butt & Hearn, 1998). They ask how someone could eventually come to see spanking as sexual, given that many people experience it first as nonsexual corporal punishment. Butt and Hearn conclude by suggesting that there are larger social contexts within which "sexualized corporal punishment" needs to be placed.

"SELF STORIES":
THE CONTEXT OF SEXUALIZED SPANKING

In some sense, the need for research on SM and spanking is related to the usual questions posed about these adaptations to standard, stereotypical sexual scripts. Those questions can be reduced to, "Why does someone have this deviant sexual interest?" Really the question should be, "Why does anyone have the sexual interests he/she has, whether those interests are 'mainstream' or outside the mainstream?"

To begin to answer the latter question, it is useful to consider the sociological and cultural scripting of sexuality. Gagnon and Simon (1973) first advanced the idea of sexual scripts, the sociological blueprints that shape our sexual interests. Scripts specify the who, what, where, when, why and how of sexualities and sexual practices. Scripts can be cultural, subcultural, interpersonal, or intrapsychic. Intrapsychic scripts include the stories we tell ourselves, our memories, our internal rehearsals; we develop intrapsychic, or mental, scripts based on cues from culture, subculture, and interactions. Interpersonal scripts develop primarily from interactions we have with others. Subcultural scripts would include discourses, ideologies, and expectations at the local or small-group level, e.g., according to ethnic or religious group. Cultural scripts include discourses, ideologies, and expectations at the national level.

Standard cultural scripts do not include such things as sexualized spanking. Rather, the standard script eroticizes the basics of (hetero)sexual activity: kissing, breast fondling, genital stimulation, and penile-vaginal intercourse (Laumann, Gagnon, Michael, & Michaels, 1994). How then would someone adapt this basic cultural script? How would an individual with a larger cultural context for sexuality expand the script to include sexualized spanking? And how does one adapt the script to include an attribute that is potentially stigmatizing?

Stigma is defined as an attribute that is discrediting to an individual's self (Goffman, 1963). Those interested in spanking can be said to have a discreditable stigma, or one that can be hidden. Goffman wrote, "Even where an individual has quite abnormal feelings and beliefs, he is likely to have quite normal concerns and employ quite normal strategies in attempting to conceal these abnormalities from others" (p. 131). Awareness of a stigmatizing condition requires impression management, to determine to whom the attribute will be revealed, with the goal of maintaining control over the discreditable attribute. The two "coping mechanisms" most applicable to this research are acceptance of the attribute, and overt rejection of the dominant norms that compel the discrediting in the first place. Some of this norm rejection can be seen when a spanking aficionado implies that everyone is actually interested in spanking (we just may not know it yet).

Brekhus described another form of rejection of dominant norms. He suggests, "Minority subcultures . . . develop oppositional constructions that parody the 'sexual mainstream'" (1996, p. 513). One strategy is to label those who do not engage in radical sex as "vanilla." The implication is that those with 'mainstream' sexual interests are conformist, bland, uninteresting, and unadventurous, representing the lowest common denominator of sexualities (Taylor & Ussher, 2001). Turning the mainstream into a negatively-labeled population enables the sexual radical to reject standard cultural scripting, thus normalizing the self. This is a fairly straightforward form of stigma management.

One strategy for rendering the sexual self is to construct a story describing its attributes, tracing its history, and locating it within the nexus of cultural sexual scripting. Plummer studied the "sexual stories" in circulation at century's end, arguing that there are patterned discourses, constructed in social contexts, and given individual meaning within these contexts (1995). In fact, Plummer's initial foray into sexual stories began with people who thought of themselves as sexually different. He said, "Most of these stories have been taken as signs of a truth: they have been presented to us as 'fact' and presumed to tell us something about our sexual natures" (1995, p. 5). The stories that spanking aficionados construct are patterned and do describe the nature of the interest, its genesis, and the normalization techniques the individual employs. But it is worth noting that nearly all sexual stories–Plummer also details rape survivor narratives–address how the actor fits him or herself into broader social contexts.

In describing postmodern sexualities, Simon noted the tendency to essentialize sexualities of all forms, locating them within genes or innate tendencies (1996). The culturally-motivated interest in essentializing is linked to the social construction of acceptable and unacceptable sexual practices. Simon said, "Once the normal is constructed, its explanation organizes our understanding of all other variations by moving us to conceive of all other outcomes as violations or variations of the logic of the normal" (p. 14). So spanking is viewed within this context as a violation of the normal, thus requiring an explanation of how and why the interest develops.

In a longitudinal study of bisexuality, another seeming violation of "normal," Weinberg, Williams and Pryor (2001) reported that by midlife, study participants had made larger commitments to other social roles and felt they had mostly lost the support of bisexual communities. The authors attributed this to the finding that self-constructions of sexuality changed. "As the bisexuals aged, rather than focusing on the nature of their current sexual lives as the important dimension, more of them turned to their history of sexual feelings–their having sustained a dual attraction over such a long time" (Weinberg et al., 2001, p. 202). This illustrates the concept that behavior alone does not and cannot determine the sexual self. Part of modern sexual storytelling then is an attempt to describe how salient 'normal' identities, such as work or professional roles, compete with sexual identities for meaning and priority.

So for those interested in sexual spanking, the construction of the self relies on cultural contexts and recognition of the reality of stigma. There are "vanilla" cultural scripts providing the foundation for identity development, wherein aficionados see that their interests deviate from the narrowly-rendered norms. To address these stigmatizing interests, individuals must develop coping strategies and design culturally and subculturally meaningful "sexual stories." The spanking aficionados' stories that follow address the management of external stigma and provide a script for stigmatizable behavior within the group.

METHODS

Participants and Fieldwork

This research describes fieldwork with participants in a loosely-organized group of consensual adults interested in sexual spanking. All participants were informed of the nature of the research and gave oral consent to be included. All identities and identifying characteristics are masked and names are pseudonyms. Because of the sensitivity of the topic, participants are described as generally as possible. Since this research included observation, it is appropriate to explicitly situate the author in the fieldwork. Access to the group occurred via a key informant, Jim, a longtime member of the "scene." After meeting at a professional conference, we had had many general, nonsexual conversations before he mentioned that he had always been interested in spanking; he wanted to see whether he could trust me. Jim was also curious to see if I would express any interest in being spanked. About 13 months later he confirmed that he had been hoping that I was an avid "bottom," because men outnumber women (particularly young ones) in the scene. The fieldwork was thus not devoid of the conflicts and ambiguities that often accompany qualitative research (Sanders, 1997). Regardless, Jim was aware that my interests were solely research-related. Unlike one researcher's foray into gay lives in Japan, I never led him on or misrepresented myself to gain access (McLelland, 2002). All research was confined to observation only.

Jim provided access to a complex and dynamic community of spanking aficionados. The fieldwork included spanking parties, discreetly held in small-town hotels on floors far from hotel traffic, formal interviews and casual conversations, and observations of private scenes between two people. Supplemental research included reading spanking stories, spanking newsletters and magazines. Participants' toy boxes were examined, replete with paddles, straps, hairbrushes, and whips. The research ultimately expanded to include other aspects of the larger world of sadomasochism. This led to observations in sex clubs, scanning of Web sites, interviews with those who incorporate SM into their sexual activities, and visits to commercial ventures, such as Boston's "Fetish Fair." Analysis of the local context of spanking is enhanced by an understanding of the larger context of sexual radicals. The fieldwork took place in Boston, New Hampshire, metro New York, New Jersey, and Atlanta, beginning in 1993 and ending in 2000.

Similarly to SM practitioners, men outnumbered women at this party almost three to one (Brame, Brame & Jacobs, 1993). Most of the approximately 50 attendees were from the East Coast, were between the ages of 30 and 70, and were white-collar professionals. All but one of the attendees were Caucasian. Not all attendees participated in formal and informal interviews; however, about 25 did.

Spanking Stories and Strategies of Neutralization

The narratives offered by the participants to explain or situate their interests in spanking are strikingly similar to narratives offered by others who adapt standard cultural sexual scripts. Men who like to spank said that they had had this interest for as long as they could remember, similarly to gay men who are asked to explain the origin of their same-sex interests. Women who like to be spanked said that it took them many years to realize that they were interested, perhaps similarly to some lesbians who reported many heterosexually active years before realizing a same-sex orientation (e.g., Whisman, 1996). The men tended to essentialize their interests while the women tended to locate them in interpersonal scripting, describing partners who assisted the development of the interest. Both men and women, but particularly men, explained their interests by asserting that everyone has hidden desires about spanking.

Nonetheless, research on SM has documented gender gaps. Breslow et al. (1985) surveyed 130 men and 52 women, self-identified SM practitioners. They found that 90% of the men and 60% of the women had acknowledged SM interests by their early twenties. But by age 14, more than 50% of men had identified an SM interest. In Damon's study of 342 male SM participants, the overwhelming majority of the sample (93%) reported having childhood/adolescent SM related fantasies (2002). As an impression management strategy to neutralize stigma, essentializing culturally-defined deviance is not uncommon, as in, "I was born this way, this is hard-wiring, I have no choice, so don't discriminate against me."

Some did offer stories of having been spanked as children, and having made a connection at those early moments between sexual arousal and the punishment being received. This neutralization strategy seems designed to imply that the individual has not consciously orchestrated or chosen this sexual interest. Taylor and Ussher commented, "Such discourse usually involved some awareness of SM as having a neuro-physiological component in which pain and arousal become inseparably paired" (2001, p. 307). Others were never spanked as children but asserted a long-standing interest in spanking nonetheless. Christina told me her "coming-out" story, as she called it. Ever since she could remember, she thought about spanking (as a five-year-old, for example) and wanted to be spanked. She thought she was weird and thought it best to keep it to herself for most of her life. Preston recalled vividly the first time he developed an interest in spanking: He was 12 years old and saw an ad depicting "a beautiful woman's bottom." He looked at it and thought, "That's ripe for a spanking."

But the narratives differed slightly from person to person and encompassed broader aspects of the interest. Jim had been married for over 30 years. He could not precisely pinpoint the development of his interest in spanking, and although he had started a related business, in his private life there was a disjuncture. His wife knew that he enjoyed spanking but refused to participate and did not attend parties. Jim, Christina, and other participants described spanking relationships that did not include intercourse or other stereotypically sexual activities. These relationships were forged with trust–female participants noted that trust was essential for a good scene–and comfort. The focus was on playing out fantasy scenes and men providing erotic/sexual discipline. However, Christina and Belinda had confessed their interests to the men whom they later married. These husbands were able to adapt their sexual scripts to include spanking and discipline along with more "vanilla" sexual practices. Including spanking in these relationships enabled these and other women participants to feel much less alone, "less freakish," as Christina said.

Outside the context of relationships, it was difficult for participants to fully accept and understand themselves. Initially, Michael thought that he was the only person in the world who was into this "bizarre perversion." Once he had "been in the scene" for 4 or 5 years and discovered publications on spanking, he felt that he was not alone. He initially felt that his affinity for spanking was "bizarre," a perspective that seemed to be borne out in the midwestern state where he lived. Officials there had threatened to outlaw spanking publications, asserting that they represented violence against women. Michael noted that it was especially important that he eventually found publications by "real" spanking aficionados, because the original items he found "were done by people just looking to make a buck." They were less realistic and arousing than the later publications he found.

Several participants combed more general publications for mentions of spanking. Jim was extremely knowledgeable about popular culture references to spanking, even nonsexualized but seemingly sexually-charged references. He situated his interest by arguing that everyone needs to try sexualized spanking, and that there is nothing "deviant" about his interests. About spanking aficionados, he did say, "We wonder about ourselves and our 'perversion' endlessly."

Newer participants were especially prone to these musings. Andrew said, "You know, I can't believe that I'm here. I look around and wonder what the hell I'm doing here. I mean, I'm not like these other people. This isn't all I do or anything." He was trying to neutralize any stigma to himself by comparing himself to the other party-goers. He implied that the others had a single-minded focus on spanking–but he was "normal," his interest in spanking was just a small piece of his identity. He had also told me that he found me "stereotypically attractive." He was trying to neutralize the perceived stigma of spanking partially because he wanted me to find him attractive as well.

Another stigma neutralization followed this path, an attempt to broaden spanking parties beyond the ostensible reason for gathering. Several male party-goers noted that the parties they had attended seemed "especially sterile." Michael said, "Especially among the men, there's this tendency to talk about sports, politics–anything but spanking." In dancing around and/or avoiding the subject that had drawn the group together, participants could diminish its seeming importance and, like Andrew, present the impression that they have interests and identities beyond spanking.

Another stigma neutralization strategy was common among spanking aficionados. Many men took care to mention that those interested in spanking were "different" from those who were interested in SM more generally. There is a spectrum of activities included in SM, including play with whips, bondage devices, clothing (e.g., latex, leather), and role playing. Much of the scene-specific lingo has been reluctantly borrowed from SM, according to participants. Spanking and other forms of flagellation are sometimes included in SM activities, thus the apparent need for participants to differentiate themselves from SM practitioners. But participants generally defined SM as "truly kinky" and "where the real weirdos go." In this strategy, one group denigrates another "fringe" group in order to mitigate the stigmatizing effects: "We are more normal than they are; they are the true deviants."

The Party and Subcultural Rules

At the party that is the focus of this article, something occurred that constituted a defining moment in the attempt to differentiate (and normalize) spanking versus SM. As noted above, the party included about 50 people, perhaps 15 women and 35 men, almost all Caucasian and middle to upper-middle class. Some had traveled from the West Coast and the Midwest to this East Coast event. It was a social event where people of like minds could meet; some planned rendezvous with people they had only corresponded with previously. Some planned scenes with people who were essentially regular spanking dates. Rendezvous and planned scenes tended to be focused on spanking and fantasies only. Penile-vaginal and oral intercourse were limited to marital and dating partners, according to most participants. One married couple described their spanking scenes as separate from but also integral to intercourse.

Party organizers had leeway in terms of how much planning to do. Men tended to simply arrange the time, place, and some basic snacks, while women tended to make more elaborate preparations, including decorating and organizing public spankings and demonstrations. Occasionally, partygoers would provide their own public demonstrations, playing out a scene in the main gathering space while attendees watched avidly.

The organizer of this particular party had planned a "Bid-A-Swat" auction. The women at the party would bid on men with the number of swats they wanted to receive. The men were expected to display forearms, biceps, and handspans. The female auction host demonstrated her handspan for comparison, so that bidding women could assess the spanking potential of the men. Finally, each man was told to say, in his sternest possible voice, "Young lady, get over my knee now!" The most stereotypically attractive men, the men with the largest handspans, and two men who were known to be "good spankers" were bid on the most.

A group of six women monopolized the bidding. Many of the women made comments about one particular woman, Annalisa, because of her bidding behavior. She had won a cute young man with a high bid of 600 swats, after already having won a large-handed man with a bid of 400 swats. When two other women grouped their bid to get a total of 500 swats from Michael (known as a "good spanker," someone with just the right touch, sternness, and trustworthiness), they asked Annalisa if she was splitting her 600-swat bid with anyone.

"No," she responded emphatically, and seemed offended at the suggestion that she would share her swats with anyone. Behind Annalisa's back, the other women were moved to judge her behavior. One said, "There's no way she can do all that! She's going to need a pillow on the plane back!" The other women who had been bidding whispered to each other, "Wow, she's crazy," and looked at her disdainfully.

These women attributed her apparent desire to receive over 1000 swats from several men as simply a function of masochism–vaguely defined as, "a person who specifically enjoys receiving pain" (Wiseman, 1996, p. 372). The women at the party did not link spanking with masochism, pain, or SM. Belinda told me, "It's more about knowing that someone cares enough to discipline me, to keep me in line when I act like a brat." In other words, the women's desire to be spanked was seen as an emotionally-laden activity within a caring context, not as a desire for pain or humiliation. One man captured the group's shared distinction between SM and spanking:

> It's tough for male first-timers to get to spank anyone, because there is a shortage of women and they like to go with men they know they can trust. It's also difficult to know a woman's limits

the first few times you spank, because there she is crying out "No, no, stop," and your natural inclination is to heed her cries.

This hints at a presumed difference between sadism and spanking, with participants believing that men who spank do so for the emotional fulfillment of women–not to hurt them. This narrative is supported in numerous spanking short stories and fantasies, and in Belinda's words about someone caring enough to "provide discipline." Other male and female participants described their interests in similar terms, though men more readily acknowledged a sexual element. Male participants did admit that there was an erotic charge in having "a squirming, bare-bottomed woman over your knee," as Cooper explained. Thus the apparently unspoken "Goldilocks" rule was revealed: There is a just-right amount of spanking to administer or receive, a just-right amount of discipline to desire, and a just-right amount of eroticism. Bidding for too many swats was constructed in this context as beyond the pale–no longer just about having been a "brat," but more about pain and masochism.

Other apparently unspoken rules were revealed when one woman dared to offer to spank men. Since this party was billed and constructed as a gathering of women who liked to be spanked and men who liked to do the spanking, most of the women were offended by this act of switching. Only four men ended up bidding on the woman's services; she looked uncomfortable throughout the mini-auction. She refused to say, "Young man, get over my knee, now!" Finally, she offered to let all the men come to her room, so she could line them up and spank them all.

Some of the party-goers were in awe of this woman's offer, but most seemed disdainful of the fact that she was switching, knowing that she would spank men and also be spanked herself. "She doesn't even know what she is," one woman said. The woman who switched did have her limits, however. Melanie asked if she would spank women too and the very cold response was "No." While she was clearly seen as deviant in this particular setting, she remained resolutely heterosexual, in accordance with broader cultural scripts about sexual orientation.

However, in line with the subcultural scripting in this particular community, all of the behavior described above was transgressive. A woman wanting too many swats, from more than one man, all of whom were strangers to her–this was outside the unspoken rules. A woman offering to spank men at an event that had been constructed with specific roles and rules–only men spank women–was also deviant for this community. Before the party, a male participant had said, "Women who want to spank are borderline with being tops in the SM scene. Most [heterosexual] men in the spanking scene would be loathe to admit an interest in being spanked, as opposed to men in the SM scene." The most bitter judgment was reserved for transgressive women and not levied on the men who offered their bottoms or their multiple swats, most likely because women's participation in the constructed and overt order of things was crucial. With women outnumbered almost three to one, men were eager to become accepted in the scene, trusted by the women, and thus desired as spanking partners. Women were the gatekeepers for men being able to participate in "what they came for," according to Brett. The men had come to spank willing women, not to be spanked.

DISCUSSION

The Cultural Context of Sexualized Spanking

The participants in this field study delighted in publicizing and analyzing public and pop cultural references to spanking, as a way to inscribe the "normality" of their interests. Particularly pleasing were anecdotes that participants thought hinted at the sexualized component of the activity, even if one needed to split hairs to find the sexual symbolism. For example, several participants recounted the spanking activities in the household of all-American singer and entertainer Pat Boone. One said, "There was far too much spanking going on in that house for it to lack any sexual charge for him." Many knew that page 37 of Cherry Boone O'Neill's autobiographical account of anorexia nervosa (1982) contains the following:

> I knew disobedience would result in swift, sure punishment. For the most part I was compliant, so spankings were relatively infrequent. I was strangely thankful for the uncommon spanking I did receive because it created a kind of penitential release for me—a victory over the nagging, inner torment of guilt. There would be a time of praying, crying, and hugging after the punishment and this seemed to give me a new lease on life.

This was precisely the kind of anecdote my informants enjoyed most, because they interpreted it to mean that Cherry actually enjoyed this form of punishment. However, it is a stretch to interpret this passage as having sexual symbolism. Chances are that the average reader would not have seen this as an example of erotic, sexual(ized) punishment. Rather, the average reader would probably see this as a child reflecting on a parent's corporal punishment.

More contemporary cultural references to more sexualized spanking were recounted by participants. Did you know that a London politician raved about the joy of spanking children on a popular morning television program (Wheen, 1996)? Or that the British Chancellor of the Exchequer rented his basement to a dominatrix who said, "I'll test your limits with caning. There are two ways of hitting–where you leave a mark and where you don't" (Barber, 1991). Or that a Maryland lawyer spanked secretaries and clients, making one teenaged employee write, "If I continue to make stupid, no-brainer mistakes . . . I will have to be turned over Mr. Goldsborough's knee" (Roberts, Grove, Hendrickson, & Harden, 1992). A dean at Louisiana State University spanked a professor, chanting "You're a bad girl," while another dean apparently watched and laughed (Ruark, 1999).

Madonna's casual and favorable treatment of spanking in a song also delighted participants (Madonna & Leonard, 1990), and around that time, sparked a wave of celebrity references to spanking. The *Arsenio Hall Show*, an early 1990s late-night talk show hosted by a comedian/actor, twice had guests who extolled the virtues of a good spanking. Actor Robert Pastorelli of *Murphy Brown*, a popular early 1990s sitcom depicting a stubborn, clever female television journalist, commented that actor Candice Bergen (who played Murphy Brown) could use a good spanking. When Hall asked him if all assertive women ought to be spanked, and if Pastorelli did this sort of thing often, Pastorelli said that he had never spanked a woman who didn't deserve it. Singer Johnny Gill commented that singer Bobby Brown (both formerly of the 1980s pop band New Edition) would have to get a spanking if he did not stop challenging Gill to public singing competitions. Participants also pointed out that FM radio talk show host and "shock jock" Howard Stern mentioned spanking quite a bit in his autobiography, *Private Parts*, and that actors Ryan O'Neal and Farrah Fawcett had made veiled references to her being spanked during their long-term relationship. Stern had also tried to get NBC to broadcast him spanking a woman on host Jay Leno's late-night television variety show, but censors refused.

Popular references to spanking seemed to spring up everywhere. In New York, an SM restaurant opened in 1997, offering patrons spankings from the "Special Fare" menu; dinner and wine, without any corporal extras, ran about $50 for one (Marin, 1998 p. 85).

It's Planet Kinkywood, outfitted with all the requisite tools of this potentially very rough trade. Patrons can opt to dine in a confining little jail called the Prisoner's Cell. A scaffold with manacles is available for those whose idea of a tasty appetizer is flagellation with a cat-o'-nine-tails. The menu also includes Verbal Abuse and Spanking, at just $20 a pop. (Warning: the chicken receives similarly nasty treatment in the kitchen.)

Commentators noted that SM-related themes had become trendy. "Does naughty fashion need a spanking?" asked Guy Trebay in a report on the spring designer collections, which were influenced by leather and fetishwear (2000, p. 12). A 2003 episode of MTV's *The Real World* featured some of the cast of the Las Vegas season spanking each other in a public skit in a nightclub.

What is the significance of these widely available references to an activity that may have clear sexual meanings to some but only punitive meanings to others, and both to still others? For spanking aficionados, these references are like unpolished gems, indicative of the larger social context of their particular sexual interests. They believe that the more casual and nonsexual anecdotes show an overwhelming cultural fascination with corporal punishment in all forms, and offer these anecdotes as proof that they are neither alone nor deviant in their interests. The efforts within the spanking community to delineate themselves from and disavow SM practices are offered as proof, again, that they are not deviant or, at the least, not as deviant as others.

Would spanking folk ever agree with this quote about the wider array of SM activities: "Though sadomasochism is most often regarded as an exotic and unusual pleasure, it is in truth part of all of us, though maybe showing itself only in timorous and unrecognized ways" (Hughes, 1993, p. 31). Is this indeed true? How do spanking aficionados understand and explain themselves?

CONCLUSIONS

The context for sexual spanking is also borne out in the multiple publications, Internet interest groups, videos, and toys focused on this sexual practice. It appears as if one intention of these items is to draw a distinction between SM and spanking. My fieldwork included observation in a workshop for novices by "Governess Margaret." She described three different types of or reasons for spanking: punishment, erotic, and maintenance. In discussing spanking positions, approaches (e.g., scolding phrases versus erotic words), and implements, the Governess suggested that some of these are more [spanking] purist versus being more SM in perspective.

A translated book of French spanking stories and line drawings includes the following, somewhat incongruous text:

> I struck without restraint, certain she could bear even more. Besides, I was so aroused that I could never have harmed her. Only cold-blooded sadists hurt their victims. Such practices have nothing to do with the gentle and playful art of spanking. . . . (Manara & Enard, 1993, unnumbered)

In *The Female Disciplinary Manual*, the author wishes to clarify that there are distinctions between SM and spanking; the two have nothing to do with each other (Snow, 1997). An obscure book, *Buttocks!: A Study of Fetishisms*, asserts a very close kinship only between bare bottoms and "flagellation": "Buttock fetishism and flagellation are closely related, and in many cases inseparable. The sight of the naked buttocks is very important in stimulating the flagellant" (Dione, 1966, unnumbered). The implication is that there is no intervening variable, and that the "flagellant" has a sexual focus that can manifest itself in spanking.

The differences between and among spanking, flagellation, and SM are obscured by casual use of all three terms. Even in the introduction to his encyclopedic text *Thy Rod and Staff*, Anthony (1995) uses the three terms without clearly defining them or acknowledging any differences in the practices implied by each term. Later he asks, "Has human knowledge . . . been very greatly advanced by . . . slide-rule gradations of perversity and its drearily impoverished terminology?" (Anthony 1995, p. 76).

The Eulenspiegel Society, an outpost for the exploration of the wide world of SM, has recognized that there may be some particular properties of spanking. A monthly spanking group meets in the Society's meeting space in New York, so experts and novices can find like minds. Using Eulenspiegel's example, spanking devotees can construct narratives that distance themselves from broader SM communities and practices, thereby normalizing the self. In New York and other urban areas, it is physically possible for this distance to be achieved, but in smaller communities, spanking aficionados face difficulties. Participants described joining SM groups in spite of "lifestyle differences," contrasted in this way: "I am not interested in a full SM lifestyle, just in erotic spankings and discipline with members of the opposite sex." Repeatedly, an invisible line is drawn between and among these practices and practitioners.

So what does this brief foray into one sexual subculture suggest about sexual scripts, neutralization of stigma, impression management, and the development of the sexual self? First, we might conclude that social norms are pervasive, even in a sexually radical subculture. This subculture's participants compared themselves to each other, made microlevel distinctions about the just-right, or Goldilocks, amount of spanking, and offered justifications for their interests. There were within-group judgments, redefinitions, and stigma neutralization techniques. This echoes the discourses that surround us in the cultural scripting of "normal" and "deviant" (e.g., Simon, 1996).

As for the development of both adaptive sexual scripts and the sexual self, it is harder to make conclusive statements based on these minimal data. It is safe to say that sexualities are enormously complex. The sexual self is clearly fluid, variable, and is simultaneously individually and culturally contextualized. Sexual scripts are basic blueprints, yes, but clearly they can be adapted and revised for the user. Sexual spanking should be viewed as one of the many sexual adaptations individuals make, based on interactions and changes to intrapsychic and interpersonal scripts. An expanded view of sexualities, seen as the potent interaction between cultures and individuals instead of as a series of "rights and wrongs," can only benefit all who seek to find sexual paths of comfort, pleasure, and pain.

It is inadequate to ask about the justifications and self stories of those who participate in sexualized spanking. We need to ask larger questions. Why does anyone do what they do sexually? Why be so concerned about "normal" or "abnormal" sexuality involving consenting adults? Ultimately, there is far more work to be done in this and other subcultures, and, as importantly, in the wide open 'mainstream' of sexualities.

REFERENCES

Alison, L., Santtila, P., Sandnabba, N.K., & Nordling, N. (2001). Sadomasochistically oriented behavior: Diversity in practice and meaning. Archives of Sexual Behavior 30, 1-12.

An editorial plea. (1964). Bizarre Life 2, 40-42.

Anonymous. (1878-1880/1968). The pearl. New York: Grove Press.

Anthony, E. (1995). Thy rod and staff. London: Abacus.

Barber, L. (1991, April 21). Lynn Barber's base thoughts. The Independent, p. 21.

Brame, G. G., Brame, W. D., & Jacobs, J. (1993). Different loving: An exploration of the world of sexual dominance and submission. New York: Villard Books.

Brekhus, W. (1996). Social marking and the mental coloring of identity: Sexual identity construction and maintenance in the United States. Sociological Forum, 11, 497-522.

Breslow, N., Evans, L., & Langley, J. (1985). On the prevalence and roles of females in the sadomasochistic subculture: Report on an empirical study. Archives of Sexual Behavior, 14, 303-317.

Butt T. & Hearn, J. (1998). The sexualization of corporal punishment: The construction of sexual meaning. Sexualities, 1, 203-227.

Califia, P. (1993). Sensuous magic: A guide for adventurous couples. New York: Masquerade Books.

Damon, W. D. (2002). Patterns of power: A test of two approaches to understanding sadomasochistic sexual behavior in heterosexual men. Unpublished manuscript. University of Illinois, Chicago.

Danielou, A. (1995). The complete Kama Sutra: The first unabridged modern translation of the classic Indian text. Rochester, VT: Inner Traditions International.

Dione, B. (1966). Buttocks!: A study of fetishisms. New York: Debon Distributors.

Farrell, C. (2003). Frequently asked questions. Retrieved July 27, 2003, from http://www.corpun.com.

Gagnon, J. H. & Simon, W. (1973). Sexual conduct: The social sources of human sexuality. Chicago: Aldine Publishing Company.

Goffman, E. (1963). Stigma: Notes on the management of spoiled identity. New York: Touchstone/Simon & Schuster.

Houlberg, R. (1991). The magazine of a sadomasochistic club: The tie that binds. Journal of Homosexuality, 21, 167-183.

Hughes, G. 1993. The dominant species. In T. Woodward (Ed.), The best of skin two (pp. 31-40). New York: Masquerade Books.

Kamel, G. W. L. (1980). Leathersex: Meaningful aspects of gay sadomasochism. Deviant Behavior: An Interdisciplinary Journal, 1, 171-191.

Krafft-Ebing, R. von. (1933, originally published 1893). Psychopathia sexualis. Brooklyn, NY: Physicians and Surgeons Book Company.

Laumann, E. O., Gagnon, J. H., Michael, R. T., & Michaels, S. (1994). The social organization of sexuality: Sexual practices in the United States. Chicago: University of Chicago Press.

McKenna, K. Y. A. & Bargh, J. A. (1998). Coming out in the age of the Internet: Identity "demarginalization" through virtual group participation. Journal of Personality and Social Psychology, 75, 681-694.

Madonna, & Leonard, P. (1990). Hanky panky. On I'm breathless: Dick Tracy, music from and inspired by the film [CD]. Los Angeles: Warner Brothers.

Manara M. & Enard, J. (1993). Art of spanking. New York: NBM/Erotica Press

Marin, R. (1998, January 5). Lick me, flog me, buy me! Newsweek, p. 85.

McClintock, A. (1993). Maid to order: Commercial fetishism and gender power. Social Text, 37(Winter), 87-116.

McLelland, M. (2002). Virtual ethnography: Using the internet to study gay culture in Japan. Sexualities, 5, 387-406.

Moser, C. (1979). An exploratory-descriptive study of a self-defined s/m (sadomasochistic) sample. Unpublished doctoral dissertation. Institute for Advanced Study of Human Sexuality.

Moser, C. (1998). S/M (sadomasochistic) interactions in semi-public settings. Journal of Homosexuality, 36, 19-29.

Moser, C. & Levitt, E. E. (1987). An exploratory-descriptive study of a sadomasochistically oriented sample. The Journal of Sex Research, 23, 322-337.

O'Neill, C. B. (1982). Starving for attention. New York: Continuum.

Plummer, K. (1995). Telling sexual stories: Power, change, and social worlds. London: Routledge.

Prezwalski, J. (1994). The kiss of the whip: Explorations in sm. San Francisco CA: Leyland Publications.

Roberts, R., Grove, L., Hendrickson, P., & Harden, B. (1992, December 31). Whatever happened to . . .? The Washington Post, p. C1.

Ruark, J. (1999, January 29). LSU professor charges that dean spanked her. Chronicle of Higher Education, p. A16.

Sandnabba, N. K., Santtila, P., & Nordling, N. (1999). Sexual behavior and social adaptation among sadomasochistically-oriented males. The Journal of Sex Research, 36, 273-282.

Sanders, C. (1997). Earn as you learn: Connections between doing qualitative work and living daily life. Qualitative Sociology, 20: 457-464.

Santtila, P., Sandnabba, N. K., Alison, L. A. & Nordling, N. (2002). Investigating the underlying structure in sadomasochistically oriented behavior. Archives of Sexual Behavior, 31, 185-196.

Simon, W. (1996). Postmodern sexualities. London: Routledge.

Snow, R. (1997).The female disciplinary manual: A complete encyclopaedia of the correction of the fair sex. England: LPC.

Spengler, A. (1977). Manifest sadomasochism of males: Results of an empirical study. Archives of Sexual Behavior, 6, 441-456.

Taylor, G. W. & Ussher, J. M. (2001). Making sense of s&m: A discourse analytic account. Sexualities, 4, 293-314.

Thompson, B. (1994). Sadomasochism: Painful perversion or pleasurable play? London: Cassell.

Trebay, G. (2000, October 31). A detour into naughty for last season's nice girls. The New York Times, p. 12.

Vatsyayana. (1994). The complete kama sutra. Rochester, VT: Park Street Press.

Weinberg, M. S., Williams, C. J., & Moser, C. (1984). The social constituents of sadomasochism. Social Problems, 31, 379-389.

Weinberg, M.S., Williams, C. J. & Pryor, D. W. (2001.) Bisexuals at midlife: Commitment, salience, and identity. Journal of Contemporary Ethnography, 30, 180-208.

Weinberg, T. S. (1978). Sadism and masochism: Sociological perspectives. The Bulletin of the American Academy of Psychiatry and the Law, 6, 284-295.

Wheen, F. (1996, October 31). Swish of the big stick. The Guardian, p.T2.

Wiseman, J. (1996). SM101: A realistic introduction. San Francisco: Greenery Press.

Whisman, V. (1996). Queer by choice: Lesbians, gay men, and the politics of identity. New York: Routledge.

24/7 SM Slavery

Peter L. Dancer, PhD

Institute for Advanced Study of Human Sexuality

Peggy J. Kleinplatz, PhD

University of Ottawa

Charles Moser, PhD, MD

Institute for Advanced Study of Human Sexuality

SUMMARY. This study describes the nature of 24/7 SM slavery as practiced within the SM (sadomasochistic) commmunity. These SM participants, who attempt to live full-time in owner-slave roles, represent a small proportion of those with SM interests. SM slaves have not been studied systematically to determine if and how they differ from other SM practitioners. An online questionnaire was used to obtain responses from individuals who self-identified as slaves. A total of 146 respondents participated, 53% female and 47% male, ranging in age from 18 to 72. We explored the depth of their relationships, how well they ap-

Peter L. Dancer is affiliated with the Institute for Advanced Study of Human Sexuality, San Francisco, CA. Peggy J. Kleinplatz is affiliated with the Faculty of Medicine and School of Psychology, University of Ottawa, Ottawa, ON, Canada. Charles Moser is Professor and Chair of the Department of Sexual Medicine, Institute for Advanced Study of Human Sexuality, San Francisco, CA. Correspondence may be addressed: Peter L. Dancer, PhD, 2 Pappert Place, Rochester, NY 14620.

[Haworth co-indexing entry note]: "24/7 SM Slavery." Dancer, Peter L., Peggy J. Kleinplatz, and Charles Moser. Co-published simultaneously in *Journal of Homosexuality* (Harrington Park Press, an imprint of The Haworth Press, Inc.) Vol. 50, No. 2/3, 2006, pp. 81-101; and: *Sadomasochism: Powerful Pleasures* (ed: Peggy J. Kleinplatz, and Charles Moser) Harrington Park Press, an imprint of The Haworth Press, Inc., 2006, pp. 81-101. Single or multiple copies of this article are available for a fee from The Haworth Document Delivery Service [1-800-HAWORTH, 9:00 a.m. - 5:00 p.m. (EST). E-mail address: docdelivery@haworthpress.com].

doi:10.1300/J082v50n02_05

proximated "slavery," and how their relationships were structured to maintain distinct roles. Data showed that in long-term SM slave relationships, a power differential exists which extends beyond time-limited SM or sexual interactions. Owners and slaves often use common, daily life experiences or situations, such as the completion of household chores, money management, and morning or evening routines, to distinguish and maintain their respective roles. In addition, contrary to the perception of total submission, results revealed that slaves exercise free will when it is in their best interests to do so. These relationships were long-lasting and satisfying to the respondents. *[Article copies available for a fee from The Haworth Document Delivery Service: 1-800-HAWORTH. E-mail address: <docdelivery@haworthpress.com> Website: <http://www. HaworthPress.com>*

KEYWORDS. BDSM, sexual slavery, sexual lifestyles, alternative lifestyles, relationship contracts

The present study describes the nature of self-defined 24/7 (24 hours a day, 7 days a week) sadomasochistic (SM) slavery relationships. Do such relationships exist or are they an elaborate fantasy? Are the relationships viable? If so, how are they sustained? What kinds of interactions and structures characterize SM slavery? In this study, the phenomenon of SM slavery will be examined from the slave's perspective. The key characteristics of SM slave relationships will be explored. The term "slave" is used throughout this article to describe the self-definition of these individuals. We will examine the differences between traditional slavery and these relationships in detail.

SM is a colloquial term used to describe an interest in giving or receiving intense stimulation, bondage, or the purposeful enacting of dominant and submissive roles, usually for sexual gratification. There are numerous schema for categorizing SM behavior, interactions or relationships. One schema is by differentiating between SM interactions that are part-time or time-limited versus those that are full-time and long-term. Time-limited SM encounters are circumscribed by rules and roles that are established only for the duration of that encounter. Such "scenes" (SM interactions) are often built around a theme which defines the participants' roles and the parameters of behavior. These scenes can occur within the context of established relationships, which are self-defined as sexually conventional, and on occasion incorporate an SM scene. For example, a couple may decide to role-play a school mistress and naughty school boy; these roles provide the framework within which the encounter transpires. Once the scene or the encounter has ended, the rules and the roles are abandoned and no longer apply. The ordinary, egalitarian status of the participants is resumed.

SM, which is limited to some or even all sexual interactions within a relationship, is sometimes referred to as, Erotic Power Exchange (EPE) and does not extend into other areas of the relationship. Others choose or find that their SM interests color other aspects of their relationship, aside from sex. Some relationships specifically choose to incorporate their SM interests as a basis for the entire relationship, in all domains. Some of these relationships strive for "total power exchange" (TPE), also called "total power transfer" (TPT), in which the submissive partner consciously yields all control to the dominant partner. SM slavery relationships are a subset of these TPE relationships; in this type of relationship the submissive person "chooses" to be seen as a slave and identifies as such. Other TPE relationships are created around other roles (e.g, parent-child, often called daddy-boy or boi regardless of the sex of the individuals).

Individuals interested in any activity display different levels of interests. This spectrum includes mere acknowledgment of an interest or participation in an occasional event to incorporating the interest into their identities. SM is no different. Accepting an identity of "slave" does not imply that the person is actually a slave. Continued participation in the relationship and identification as a slave is voluntary; forced slavery is clearly illegal and unenforceable.

In long-term SM relationships, the adopted rules and roles are expected to be in place indefinitely. They extend beyond discrete "scenes." There may be SM or sexual encounters where the roles are more explicit, but once that scene is over, the power exchange is still in place. Rules and roles are expected to remain in force whether or not the partners are engaging in what viewers might recognize as overtly sexual or SM interactions. Full-time, SM slave relationships, the topic of this study, are prime examples of this second SM subgroup.

All SM relationships have several common attributes: The relationships are consensual, both partners agree to the general power differential framework of the relationship. The partners overtly state their limits, that is, what will or will not be allowed. These limits can be "hard," not to be broached, or "soft," some exploration is possible. Some individuals feel that the process of setting limits gives the submissive partner too much control, which is contrary to the premise of these relationships. TPE relationships are often described as consensual non-consent. Although these relationships are reportedly without limit, the process of deciding to enter into the relationship is such, that the submissive partner rarely finds the dominant's desires incompatible with his or her own.

A key element of SM "slavery" is the desire of the slave to allow the other partner (the owner) to control all aspects of his or her life. Mundane behaviors such as being able to go out alone, when and what to eat, where to sit, and what to wear (usually associated with everyday life rather than with sexual interaction), become tinged with SM undertones by virtue of the continuing dynamic among the participants.

These relationships are poorly understood by SM participants themselves or sexological researchers. It is unclear why someone would willingly and totally submit to another person or what appeal such relationships hold. It might be assumed that slave relationships share little in common with those of a more egalitarian nature. This belief bears investigation.

Much of the existing literature related to sadomasochism tends to be focused on time-limited or scene-specific SM interactions (Kamel, 1983; Kamel & Weinberg, 1983; Sandnabba, Santilla, & Nordling, 1999; Scoville, 1985). Research to date has failed to provide specific or detailed information about SM slavery as a distinct subgroup of SM relationships. SM slavery is referred to in indirect and inferential ways only. At best, such literature has taken scene-specific dynamics and made general inferences to Owner/slave roles and lifetime relationships. Whether or not existing findings can be extrapolated accurately to SM slavery is not yet known. This is the first study of which we are aware that has focused primarily on this type of long-term relationship.

Many authors discuss the key characteristics of scene-specific SM interactions and cite the importance of consensuality (Ernulf & Innala, 1995; Kamel, 1983; Kamel & Weinberg, 1983). The consensual nature ensures that neither party involved is subjected to activities or behaviors to which they have not agreed beforehand. In this way, ". . . either party has the ability to withdraw their consent at any point during an SM encounter" (Truscott, 1991). This is an important consideration in this study. Slavery entails a full-time relationship in which the slave has given up all rights to participate in decision-making within the relationship. How does this fit with the emphasis on consent? How do the participants create an environment in which both the appearance of a total power exchange and the slave's active consent to participate co-exist?

Some commentators have suggested that long-term SM relationships are not viable nor likely to last (Baumeister, 1989, 1997). There is no reason to assume, however, that deep and caring feelings are counterproductive to the establishment and maintenance of long-term 24/7 SM slave relationships, as is suggested by others (Brame & Brame, 1993; Gosselin, Wilson, & Barrett, 1987; Moser, 1988).

METHOD

Participants

The sample was recruited via the Internet and participation was voluntary. Respondents were required to be 18 years of age or older and to self-identify as "24/7 slaves." A total of 153 individuals responded; 7 questionnaires which did not meet the inclusion criteria or failed to complete basic demographic data were not included in the final analyses. This left a total of 146 respondents, 66 males and 80 females. City or country of origin was not collected. Respondents ranged in age from 18 to 72, the mean age was 38 (SD = 10.1). The duration of respondents' slavery relationship ranged from 3 weeks to 22 years; the mean duration was 41.2 months (SD = 49.3) and the median was 24 months.

Respondents were primarily white, accounting for 94% of all respondents. There was one African-American, one Hispanic, and one Asian respondent. Six people (4%) indicated that they belonged to groups other than those noted, including "American Indian" and Métis (a Canadian people who trace their ancestry to the French and to Native Canadians). As indicated earlier, 53% of respondents were women, 46% were men, and 1 was a male-to-female transsexual. There were no female-to-male transsexual respondents in this study.

Although respondents self-identified as heterosexual (41%), bisexual (26%) or homosexual (33%), it is not clear whether this self-identification reflected "intrinsic" interest or actual behavior. There were two male respondents who self-identified as heterosexual, yet their questionnaires indicated that their owners were male and that their sexual contact was exclusively with men. Of the 66 male respondents, 51 were involved with another male and 15 with a female. Of the 80 female respondents, 74 were involved with a male and 6 were involved with another female.

Apparatus

A survey instrument was developed for this study (available from the first author, P.D.). The final survey contained 49 questions covering a wide range of topics including basic demographic information, household tasks, rules and rituals, sexual behaviors, and questions related to satisfaction with the slave experience.

Given the focus on 24/7 slavery as opposed to scene-specific SM interactions, questions regarding everyday activities issues were deemed important. It is with the purpose of capturing the dynamic within such relationships that specific situations were selected for inquiry. For example, questions included: Are you bound or tethered in any way while you sleep? Do you have any bank accounts in your name only? The aspects these questions attempt to explore are not typically relevant within time-limited SM scenes. These questions do, however, hold the potential for elucidating information regarding an unequal distribution of power.

The study received necessary approvals by the Institute for Advanced Study of Human Sexuality. Prior to implementation, the survey was reviewed by leaders of the SM community to ensure that the questions were unambiguous, non-offensive, and that the questionnaire was adequate in detail and comprehensiveness.

Procedure

The survey was posted on the Internet at a commercial site (FormSite. com), specifically catering to survey research; this site allows anonymous survey submission. Requests to participate and general information about the project were posted on one SM Web site, distributed to several SM community leaders so that they could solicit participants, and sent to a variety of SM organizations and online SM groups to solicit their members. The survey was available on the Internet for a period of three months in 2001.

RESULTS

Everyday Life

We assumed that slaves would be expected to do the usual household chores. The data revealed that slaves are most often responsible for menial day-to-day tasks, but were not exclusively responsible for these (see Table 1). Some tasks seemed to be divided along stereotypical gender roles. For example, 30% of the female versus 82% of the male slaves took out the garbage. Conversely, male owners were more likely to drive the car than female owners and female owners were more likely to do laundry than male owners. There was little difference in tasks that are generally considered to be gender neutral (e.g., shopping, paying bills).

Rituals, Rules and Discipline

The establishment of rituals was another method of reinforcing the slave's role. The use of rituals was reported by 86% of the respondents. Receiving discipline (e.g., punishment) was cited by 67% of the sample as the most meaningful of these rituals. Discipline can be physical (e.g., spanking), psychological (e.g., standing in the corner), or both. Other rituals involved the particulars of going to bed, greeting one's owner, and getting up in the morning. Many respondents indicated that they were bound or tethered for sleep, and there was often a ritual associated with the tethering. Collars are also a common symbol of SM slavery and were often used to signify formal ownership. Rituals concerning the collar (e.g., putting it on, taking it off, asking permission to wear it) were also quite common.

The data revealed that the vast majority (99%) of all respondents had rules (see Table 2). These rules involved limitations or obligations

TABLE 1. Division of Common Household Chores by Number of Respondents[1] and Percentage (%)

Chore	Individual Responsible		
	Slave	Owner	Shared/Other
Taking out garbage	77 (53)	21 (14)	47 (32)
Doing housework	103 (71)	1 (1)	41 (28)
Cooking	92 (63)	14 (10)	38 (26)
Cleaning up after meals	110 (75)	3 (2)	31 (21)
Doing laundry	98 (67)	7 (5)	39 (27)
Balancing bank accounts	49 (34)	60 (41)	35 (24)

[1] N = 146

TABLE 2. Number[1] and (%) of Respondents with Formal Rules Surrounding Daily Activities

Rules

Have any rules	144 (99)
Touching one's body	95 (66)
Dressing rules	91 (63)
Speaking to owner	75 (52)
Sitting rules	71 (49)
Being bound when sleeping	64 (45)[2]
Bathroom use	64 (44)
Speaking to others	59 (41)
Eating rules	59 (41)
Eye contact with owner	41 (28)
E-mail use	36 (25)
Contact with friends	33 (23)
Telephone use	32 (22)
Contact with family	21 (15)

[1] N = 146, unless otherwise specified
[2] N = 143

applicable to the slave that are in place at all times and in all situations. Among respondents, 85% reported that they participate regularly in established rituals (see Table 3). Approximately two-thirds of the respondents (67%) cited receiving discipline as a ritual, but it is unclear if the other respondents were not subject to discipline or if it was just not ritualized. Other key ritual areas included going to bed, greeting one's owner, and getting up in the morning. Rituals described by respondents ranged from extremely simple to very complex. An example of a simple ritual is, "Kneeling beside the bed, handing M [Master] my collar, letting Him padlock it around my neck, then asking permission to sleep beside Him."

"Out of Role"

Owners and slaves often portrayed or carried out the elements of their relationship differently depending on their settings and surroundings.

TABLE 3. Number[1] and (%) of Respondents with Formal Rituals Surrounding Daily Activities

Rituals	
Have any rituals	123 (85)[2]
Receiving discipline	98 (67)
Arising in the a.m.	70 (49)
Going to sleep	76 (53)
Entering the owner's presence	57 (40)
Eating	45 (31)

[1] N = 146, unless otherwise specified
[2] N = 143

These changes are referred to as "forms" or "conduct modes." For example, one respondent stated that regardless of circumstances, "i am never out of role but that doesn't mean that everyone around me knows i'm a slave. i serve my owner at work but no one there has any idea of my slavery." The roles are in place but no one need know but the owner and slave.

The demands of working, activities of daily living, and social prejudice against SM practitioners often require the owner-slave couple to be surreptitious about their relationship. In many instances, slaves would say that they were always "in role," but there are times when the slavery was less formal. Although slaves may be required to address their owners as Mistress or a similar honorific at home, Kathy is the usual form of address among work acquaintances or family. A simple neck chain worn at work may replace the more obvious collar required at home. This more relaxed or less formal aspect of the relationship was most commonly reported when visiting family, when at work, and when sick. More than 75% of the male owners, all of the female owners of males and 4/6 female owners of females allowed their slaves out of role under some condition (see Table 4).

Respondents' comments provided additional insight into the question of role. One reported being allowed out of role "when out in the world with Him [owner]." Another is allowed out of role only in part, stating, "Within parameters at work, i still have duties i must perform even at work." Other respondents referred to differences in how they embrace their slave persona based on where they are or who is present.

TABLE 4. Number[1] and (%) of Respondents Who Indicated Situations When They Could Be Out of Role or Refuse an Order

Out of role	
When sick	47 (32)
When with family	76 (52)
When at work	69 (47)
Refuse order	
Risk of bodily harm	63 (43)
Risk to job	47 (32)
Risk of arrest	58 (40)

[1] N = 146

Limits and Safewords

Approximately half of all respondents (51%) reported being able to refuse orders at some time (Table 4). Comments received from respondents flesh out these results. For example, one wrote:

> . . . If my Owner tells me to do something, he trusts that i'll do it, and i do. In turn, i trust him not to ask things of me that are truly beyond me, or things that will damage me physically or emotionally. While there are no situations where i have the "right" to refuse an order, he is aware that i will nevertheless refuse any order that compromises my principles, consequences be damned.

Another wrote, "The concept of limits and safewords do not exist in the M/s [Master/slave] relationship with which i am involved." A third respondent wrote, ". . . i trust my Master and He knows my needs and limits therefore this is no issue for me." A last respondent wrote what appears to be a contradiction. He first stated, ". . . i would submit to Her in all things, even when those things were hard on me or even at times hurt me, but that i would mold myself to Her will." Later, he wrote, "Do i have rights and limits, some limits . . . rights, no. Mistress will listen to me, if things bother me, but ultimately She will do what She desires to do, and it is my job to either figure it out and realize how to make it work or leave . . ." This slave initially said that he would submit to his mistress completely, yet later stated that if he could not find a way to make the relationship work, he would leave. This is a telling contradiction.

As mentioned earlier, the concept of limits and safewords (i.e., a word or gesture that indicates one participant needs to stop the scene) are part of most SM relationships, although some slaves would state that limits or safewords are antithetical to the concept of slavery. None of the respondents reported use of a safeword, but that does not mean that they were unable to communicate the need to stop a scene. It only implies that a designated safeword was not used.

We also enquired about the how malleable the slave's limits were. We found that almost three-quarters (74%) had engaged in behavior that had seemed inconceivable at the start of the relationship. "Pushing limits" is common within SM relationships. The sense of surrender and belief that the "slavery" is real, is confirmed when slaves participate in behavior that previously seemed beyond them. Given the data on relationships that ended because the dominant partner had gone too far, this maneuver can prove to be risky. Nevertheless, such behavior appears to be common.

Sexual and SM Activities

We found that sexual and SM activities were varied and extensive. Except for physical impossibilities (e.g., female-female couples did not engage in penile-vaginal sex), the repertoire of the slaves was extensive and all relationship types engaged in all possible combinations and communications of sexual and SM interactions. Common SM activities included bondage (80% of participants), spanking and whipping (83% of participants), and 73% of paticipants were the recipients of "tit torture." "Cock and Ball Torture" (CBT) was common for male slaves, with 81% reporting participation. In contrast, only 58% of the female slaves reported "cunt torture."

All the relationships were sexual. It was not uncommon for a slave to take a role sometimes characterized superficially as "dominant"during in sex. For example, 21% of male slaves of female owners took part in penile-anal sex, 43% engaged in penile-vaginal contact and 36% were orally stimulated by their owner. Masturbation (self-stimulation) with orgasm was reported by 54% of the sample and without orgasm by 51%. We assume that masturbation without orgasm implied that orgasm was forbidden as part of the relationship at least part of the time.

The gay leather scene, which is related to SM but not synonymous, is known for its interest in "fisting" (placing one's hand in his partner's rectum). Surprisingly only 38% of the male-male relationships indicated this occurred; the female-male relationships reported only slightly lower rates, with 29%. In contrast 83% of the female-female relationships and 23% of the male-female relationships included vaginal "fisting."

Ability to Leave

Historically, a distinguishing characteristic of traditional slavery has been the inability to leave. Almost half the respondents (70/146) had had a previous owner. We inquired into the reasons and circumstances in which these prior relationships ended. These relationships ended for a variety of reasons, including the owner's death, the slave's dissatisfaction, the owner's dissatisfaction, or mutual agreement. The respondents indicated that they initiated their release in 69% of the instances, while termination was initiated by the owners in 24%. In the remaining 7% of cases, termination was mutual or no data were reported.

Of the 48 slaves who initiated their own release, 8 (17%) left because their limits were not respected, 5 (10%) left because the relationship was stale, 13 (27%) left because they felt unsafe in the relationship, 5 (10%) left because of risk for bodily harm or death, 9 (19%) left because the relationship was no longer fulfilling, and we lacked data to classify the remaining 8 (17%) respondents.

One way of reinforcing the role, creating a sense of dependence, and limiting the ability of the slave to flee, would be to limit the slave's access to money. This was not a common method for these couples. Over 60% of the respondents had their own bank accounts, almost 40% had joint bank accounts with their owners, and 15% had a joint bank account with someone other than their owners. Only three respondents had no access to a bank account in their own names.

Satisfaction

A large majority of respondents (88%) indicated that they were satisfied or completely satisfied with their current relationships. Additionally, almost 71% of the sample indicated the relationship was more satisfying or significantly more satisfying now than when it began. Nonetheless, when asked if they would seek other owners if their current relationships ended, 50% of the respondents indicated that they would not.

DISCUSSION

This section will explore the major characteristics of 24/7 SM slavery, focusing on four distinguishing themes or features: (1) The relationship reinforces the slave mind-set. (2) The participants must often tionship reinforce aspects of the relationship surreptitiously. (3) The relationship is structured to safeguard the slave. (4) The relationship contract parallels conventional relationship arrangements.

The Relationship Is Designed to Create and Reinforce the Slave Mind-Set at All Times

The most prominent feature of these relationships is their pervasiveness and all-encompassing nature. In order to make 24/7 SM slavery "real," non-scene-specific aspects of daily life must be structured by an unequal power differential. Getting up in the morning is an unremarkable part of most people's day. Within an SM slave relationship, however, it is often an opportunity, carried out faithfully every day, through which the boundaries of the relationship are reaffirmed.

Creating such a power differential within non-SM and nonsexual activities and tasks replaces or augments the ropes and chains of the time-limited scene. The bondage of SM slavery *is* the responsibility for menial tasks; it *is* the more subtle public form even as much as it is the collar and the shackles which bind to the slave every night. Owner and slave who try to maintain the slave relationship based exclusively on the interactions within a discrete SM scene risk running into difficulties when they leave the dungeon and pay bills, do chores, or decide in which restaurant to eat. The power exchange that is so clearly demarcated in the scene can lose its power outside of such a structured environment unless it is formally considered and applied to other daily situations.

Although the data demonstrated that slaves are most likely to be responsible for menial day-to-day tasks, a finding which was not unanticipated, we did not find that the slave was overwhelmingly responsible for these tasks. Slavery typically entails servitude. Cleaning up after meals is not generally regarded as a sexual act, but it can be constructed as part of the owner-slave relationship. This differs from scene-specific SM, where the activity is typically focused on overtly sexual and/or overtly SM interactions between the participants. Responsibility for household tasks, though characterized by a power differential in SM slavery, is not generally factored into time-limited scenes. Unique to

24/7 SM *relationships*, however, the power exchange does not end when the SM or sexual scene has ended. Rather, it is one example of how the power exchange helps to maintain and support the relationship outside of these scenes.

Just over 50% of all respondents are bound or tethered while they sleep. Although bondage is a common aspect of SM scenes, the slave while "nothing is going on" serves as a symbolic restraining tion and heightens awareness of the power differential. This may be portant for the owner and slave in their attempts to realize as fully as possible their respective roles. Bondage during the night may appear on the surface to be an extension of an SM encounter and could be part of a time-limited scene. The SM slave relationship can use these obviously ritualistic demonstrations to reinforce the overt power differences desired by both partners. Similarly, rules existed in the relationships of 94% of the respondents. These included involvement in such areas of life as where to sit and what to eat. The application of restrictions beyond a time-limited scene further confirms the 24/7 nature of this type of SM relationship.

Established rituals existed in 86% of respondents' relationships. Rituals are a part of everyone's life, whether SM focused or not. The types of ritual described in this study relate primarily to non-scene-specific activities (e.g., getting up in the morning, going to bed at night, or greeting one's owner) and are intended to heighten the awareness of the structure and pervasive nature of these relationships.

The Participants Must Often Engage in Their Relationship Surreptitiously

The second element involves the need to modify the overt representation of one's slavery when in public as another means by which the slavery can be maintained 24/7, outside of the traditionally viewed scene or sexual encounter. Within the confines and structure of one's home, the owner and slave roles can be embraced with relative ease. Most people, however, will have to interact with and join the outside world at some point. This is similar to the issues that homosexual-identified individuals report when having to be "in the closet." By altering form (as defined below) both owner and slave can still feel the boundaries and structure of the established slave relationship. Failure to do so can result in role and boundary confusion.

Respondents do not cease being slaves when they are apart from their owners or outside of the slavery household. Rather, they alter their behavior in order to fit in with the world around them. The behavioral expectations change even while their status as slaves remains intact. This change in expectation is often referred to as "form" within the SM community (e.g., private form, public form, or friendly form). In "private form," the slave is bound by the strict rules of the relationship and these would be in effect when alone together in the owner's space as well as in the presence of others who are aware of the arrangement. "Friendly form" may be in effect in such places as leather bars where the dress, demeanor and appearance of the owner and slave would be understood for what they are and viewed sympathetically by casual onlookers. Some rules might not apply so as not to bring undue attention to the couple (e.g., nudity), but other rules would be enforced. "Public form" rules would apply to situations in which the owner-slave relationship would not be understood or accepted by those present. Behavior or speech that might reveal the relationship status would be avoided, but other rules which would not be obvious to onlookers would still be in force. Thus, owner and slave weave their relationship and their power imbalance throughout the course of the day in many different ways and in a variety of settings.

More than 75% of all respondents indicated that their owners allowed them (i.e., slaves) to be out of role at certain times or in certain situations. The concept of whether slavery constitutes a role which one can move into and out of is avidly debated by participants. Comments ranged from "I'm often out of role, life's demands require it for us on a regular basis," to "OUT OF ROLE? This is NO roleplaying here . . . this is 24/7."

The Relationship Is Structured to Safeguard the Slave

Paradoxically, the third key element found in owner-slave relationships was the presence of a "safety net" maintained for slaves and in case the relationship ended. Although superficial appearances reflect a person without rights (i.e., powerless and bound to the whims of another), this appears to be part of the structure, framework, or agreement between owner and slave. The participants in SM slavery go to great lengths to experience their desired relationships but their basic human and civil rights remain and cannot be relinquished legally.

The comments on the survey indicated that limits within the relationship were respected. This allows the slave and owner to state that they do not have any limits or do not need "safewords" within the established framework of their slavery. The lack of "safewords" or "consensual

non-consent" relationships, however, is part of the ambiance of the relationship. The predetermined parameters define and clarify where the
"edge" is so that all participants can play freely within these boundaries.
Within the space created by the participants, there may not, in fact, be
any need for safewords given the deep level of trust and respect established prior to entering into the owner-slave relationship. These limits
are not immutable and 73% indicated that they had participated in activities that they had not thought initially they ever would engage in, as the
relationship progressed. Conversely, some slaves had left previous
relationships because their limits were not respected.

This complexity is illustrated in the management of finances within
the SM slave relationship. Many respondents indicated that they turned
over any money earned to their owners. The owner often provided the
slave with an allowance, thereby monitoring the slave's expenditures,
even though most slaves had access to a bank account. The fact that
60% of respondents reported having bank accounts in their own names
suggests that these slaves maintain some level of independence in spite
of their slavery. This may also suggest the means to support themselves
in the event that the slave relationship should end.

While the results clearly indicated that this type of relationship extends throughout the day and the life of those involved, it also provided
insight into how it differs from surface appearances or traditional understanding of slavery and servitude. Many responses reflected an assumption that owners would not recklessly push slaves to do physically or
emotionally dangerous things, or that slaves could refuse such orders
even while stating that they do not have the right to do so. This suggests
that slaves could exercise their "denied" rights, if and when necessary.

Furthermore, the data indicated that of the 70 respondents who had
prior owner-slave relationships, 48 respondents initiated their own re-
leases from their prior relationships. Thus, notwithstanding the appearance of utter dependence on the owner, the slave is apparently able to
exit the relationship if necessary. Approximately 19% (13/70) of those
with a previous 24/7 relationship left that relationship because their limits were not respected, they felt unsafe, or both.

The Relationship Contract Parallels Conventional Relationship Arrangements

The fourth key characteristic of SM slavery is the extent to which
such relationships mirror more conventional relationships. In all long-
term, live-in relationships, the housework must be done, meals must be

prepared, finances must be organized, etc. All homes have routines and parameters for acceptable behavior. Faithfulness to explicit and implicit contracts governing the participants' conduct and the extent to which the individuals involved maintain their commitments affects the quality and duration of the relationship. In marriage, these may be formalized in the marital vows. In SM slavery, these may be articulated in the owner-slave contract. Once the nature of these relationships has been negotiated, the participants are better able to "let down their guards" and to embrace what they have created within the framework set forth together. Thus, at least at the outset, these relationships are predicated on mutual consent.

We did not inquire about romantic feelings of the slave (or owner), but we assume that there is a romantic aspect of these relationships. Most of these relationships have the appearance of romantic couples, as manifested by being allowed out of role when non-scene individuals are present; the slave was not introduced as a servant. The slave is taken to family events and treated as a partner rather than a slave at these times. A traditional slave would have been left at home or eaten with the other servants.

Most slaves are not traded permanently and the process of finding a partner is not simple. The prospective slave chooses very carefully. There are numerous Internet services that attempt to help prospective owners and slaves to connect with each other. Nevertheless, there are numerous e-mail postings decrying the lack of prospective dominant partners who meet the slaves' requirements, thus suggesting that these "matchmaking" services are not overwhelmingly successful. These relationships, like most committed relationships, are meant to be permanent. Despite that intention, most relationships end. One would expect that slaves' movements and access to money would be tightly controlled. We did not ask about how tightly their movements were controlled. Most do have access to money and many initiate termination of their relationships. Again, this pattern is more reminiscent of traditional marriage than of traditional slavery.

Overwhelmingly, the respondents indicated that they were satisfied with their relationships and more satisfied than when the relationship began. Those unhappy with their relationships would have been unlikely to participate in the present study or "slaves" may not have felt it was their "place" to complain. Nevertheless, the level of satisfaction is noteworthy. The participants seemed to like these relationships. There was no indication that anyone was coerced into staying, when the relationship was no longer fulfilling.

These were clearly SM couples and the sexual and SM activities within these relationships resembled those in other SM interactions. We did not ascertain how rigorously the "rules" were enforced, how fairly the discipline was meted out, or how the participants responded to the discipline.

There was no indication that the respondents were "battered" in the traditional sense (i.e., suffered significant injury or participated against their will). Nevertheless, it is possible that some spousal abusers could use such arrangements to legitimize or otherwise find support for their abusive inclinations or intentions. Perusal of the relationship advertisements suggests the "slaves" are keenly aware of this danger and perpetrators of domestic violence are shunned in this community. Superficially similar behaviors can be governed by different motivations and goals. These relationships appear to be more similar to traditional marriages than to spousal abuse situations. Nevertheless, the line between marital abuse and traditional marriage is not always clear in the general population. Within the SM community, it also can be difficult to classify. The clarity of the power dynamics entering the relationship may prevent some of the degeneration into abuse that occurs in more ambiguously defined (i.e., conventional) power dynamics.

There is also a subgroup of these relationships that models the power dynamics on religion and traditional marriage (e.g., www. submissivewife. org, groups.yahoo.com/group/dmstcdspln, www.themarriagebed.com/dd. shtml). In summary, this may be a very interesting area for further research.

The desire for ritual within relationships is understandable. People often create rituals in their lives and it is not surprising that rituals would surround any important area of life. Why this is so is beyond the scope of this paper. We often create rituals surrounding going to bed, arising in the morning, eating, etc. When individuals adopt roles or behavior patterns as part of their identities, it follows that rituals would be created to confirm their identities. Various symbols are also adopted to signify one's identity/identities.

LIMITATIONS AND DIRECTIONS FOR FUTURE RESEARCH

The present study is exploratory and employs a non-random, self-selected sample. It is unlikely that individuals not interested in SM relationships would have found the study. The number of participants who found the study in the relatively short time that the survey was posted on the Internet suggests that these relationships are more common than previously thought. Also, finding male and female owners and slaves suggests that all relationship combinations exist. We did not explore one owner-multiple slaves relationships nor multiple owners-single slave relationships, but are aware that they exist.

These relationships are satisfying to the slaves, but there is evidence that they can disintegrate. Either slaves or owners can initiate the separation process. Further research on the separation process and what happens to the participants after separation is needed. It is not clear how many of the individuals who indicate that they would or would not seek another owner actually follow through with the spirit of that statement.

Additional research is called for by these results. Future studies should explore the various ways in which forms are structured and used to ensure the continuity of slavery in a variety of settings. Also, several respondents indicated that their slavery is simply who they are, whether they are in a slave relationship at the time or not. Further research should examine whether or not for some participants slavery or submission is akin to a distinct orientation and the extent to which such a belief affects the need for more firmly identified boundaries and parameters.

CONCLUSIONS

Clearly, SM owner-slave couples exist and the relationships can flourish. The relationships focus on the power differential between the partners, but are between partners rather than stereotypical owners and slaves. The sexual aspects of the relationships are similar to other SM relationships, though the intensity and frequency of these behaviors was not quantified in the present study.

There is no reason to believe that these "slaves" need saving or freeing. There is no indication that they are more likely to be abused than in other relationships. It would appear that some of the shock from disclosing participation in this type of relationship relates to the terms used to describe the relationship, rather than the actual behavior within the relationship.

Another key characteristic of SM slavery is the extent to which such relationships mirror more conventional relationships. Once the nature of these relationships has been negotiated, the participants embrace the roles created within the accepted framework. Thus, at least at the outset, these relationships are predicated on mutual consent.

   This study has provided concrete evidence of the presence of 24/7 SM slavery as a unique and definable subset of SM interactions and relationships. Specific measurable characteristics of overall slavery have been identified. Each of the defining characteristics together flesh out the framework without which 24/7 SM slavery would not be possible. This study has revealed that SM slavery constitutes a distinct and fulfilling lifestyle. In addition, 24/7 SM slavery has been shown to provide for very specific and clearly defined needs for those who participate in it.

REFERENCES

Baumeister, R. F. (1989). *Masochism and the self.* Hillsdale, NJ: Laurence Erlbaum Associates.

Baumeister, R. F. (1997). The enigmatic appeal of sexual masochism: Why people desire pain, bondage, and humiliation in sex. *Journal of Social and Clinical Psychology, 16* (2), 133-150.

Brame, G. G., & Brame, W. D. (1993). *Different loving.* New York: Villard Books.

Dancer, P.L. (2001). *24/7 SM Slavery: A descriptive study from the slave's perspective.* Unpublished doctoral dissertation. The Institute for Advanced Study of Human Sexuality, San Francisco.

Deutsch, H. (1995). The significance of masochism in the mental life of women. In M. Hanley (Ed.), *Essential papers on masochism* (pp. 411-422). New York: New York University Press.

Donnelly, D. (1998). Gender differences in sado-masochistic arousal among college students. *Sex Roles, 39* (5-6), 391-407.

Eisenbud, R. J. (1967). Masochism revisited. *The Psychoanalytic Review, 54* (4), 561-582.

Ernulf, K. E., & Innala, S. M. (1995). Sexual Bondage: A review and unobtrusive investigation. *Archives of Sexual Behavior, 24* (6), 341-356.

Gero, G. (1962). Sadism, masochism, and aggression: Their role in symptom formation. *The Psychoanalytic Quarterly, 31,* 31-42.

Gosselin, C. C., Wilson, G. D., & Barrett, P. T. (1987). The sadomasochistic contract. In G. D. Wilson (Ed.), *Variant sexuality: Research and theory* (pp. 229-257). Baltimore: John Hopkins University Press.

Kamel, G. W. L. (1983). Toward a sexology of sadomasochism. In T. Weinberg, & G. W. L. Kamel (Eds.), *S and M: Studies in sadomasochism* (pp. 197-203). Buffalo, NY: Prometheus Press.

Kamel, G. W. L., & Weinberg, T. (1983). Diversity in sadomasochism: Four S&M careers. In T. Weinberg, & G. W. L. Kamel (Eds.), *S and M: Studies in sadomasochism* (pp. 113-128). Buffalo, NY: Prometheus Press.

Lee, J. A. (1983). The social organization of sexual risk. In T Weinberg, & G. W. L. Kamel (Eds.), *S and M: Studies in sadomasochism* (pp. 149-161). Buffalo, NY: Prometheus Press.

Money, J. (1986). *Lovemaps*. New York: Irvington Publishers, Inc.

Moser, C (1988). Sadomasochism. *Journal of Social Work and Human Sexuality, 7* (1), 43-56.

Novick, K. K., & Novick, J. (1995). The essence of masochism. In M. Hanley (Ed.), *Essential Papers on Masochism* (pp. 237-273). New York: New York University Press.

Panken, S. (1967). On masochism: A re-evaluation. *The Psychoanalytic Review, 54* (3), 527-541.

Rosen, I. (1964). *The pathology and treatment of sexual deviation: A methodological approach*. London: Oxford University Press.

Sandnabba, N. K., Santilla, P., & Nordling, N. (1999). Sexual behavior and social adaptation among sadomasochistically-oriented males. *The Journal of Sex Research, 36* (3), 273-282.

Schad-Somers, S. P. (1982). *Sadomasochism: Etiology and treatment*. New York: Human Sciences Press, Inc.

Scoville, J. W. (1985). *Sexual domination today: Sado-masochism and domination-submission*. New York: Irvington Press.

Truscott, C. (1991). S&M: Some questions and a few answers. In M. Thompson (Ed.)., *Leatherfolk: Radical sex, people, politics, and practice* (pp. 15-36). Boston: Alyson Publications, Inc.

Weinberg, T. (1983). Sadism and masochism: Sociological perspectives. In T. Weinberg, & G. W. L. Kamel (Eds.), *S and M: Studies in sadomasochism* (pp. 99-112). Buffalo, NY: Prometheus Press.

Mainstreaming Kink:
The Politics of BDSM Representation
in U.S. Popular Media

Margot D. Weiss, PhD

Sweet Briar College

SUMMARY. This article explores nonpractitioners' understandings of and responses to the increasingly mainstream representation of BDSM in U.S. media, focusing on the film *Secretary* (Shainberg, 2002). Survey, focus group, and interview data indicate that popular images of SM promote the acceptance and understanding of sexual minorities through two mechanisms: *acceptance via normalization,* and *understanding via pathologizing.* Rather than challenging the privileged status of normative sexuality, these mechanisms reinforce boundaries between protected/privileged and policed/pathological sexualities. Instead of celebrating increased representation, this article argues that political energy

---

Margot D. Weiss is Visiting Assistant Professor of Anthropology, Sweet Briar College. The author thanks Anne Allison, Naomi Greyser, and Kimberly Wright for their careful reading and helpful comments and suggestions, and the participants in the focus group, survey, and interviews. This research is part of a doctoral dissertation on BDSM practitioners, entitled *Techniques of pleasure, scenes of play: SM in the San Francisco Bay Area.* Correspondence may be addressed: 108 Gray Hall, Sweet Briar College, Sweet Briar, VA 24595 (mweiss@sbc.edu).

[Haworth co-indexing entry note]: "Mainstreaming Kink: The Politics of BDSM Representation in U.S. Popular Media." Weiss, Margot D. Co-published simultaneously in *Journal of Homosexuality* (Harrington Park Press, an imprint of The Haworth Press, Inc.) Vol. 50, No. 2/3, 2006, pp. 103-132; and: *Sadomasochism: Powerful Pleasures* (ed: Peggy J. Kleinplatz, and Charles Moser) Harrington Park Press, an imprint of The Haworth Press, Inc., 2006, pp. 103-132. Single or multiple copies of this article are available for a fee from The Haworth Document Delivery Service [1-800-HAWORTH, 9:00 a.m. - 5:00 p.m. (EST). E-mail address: docdelivery@haworthpress.com].

doi:10.1300/J082v50n02_06

might be directed toward the desire that the popularity of BDSM representations signifies: the desire to encounter authentic, undisciplined, and non-commodified representations that would transgress the sexual norms of American postmodern consumer culture. *[Article copies available for a fee from The Haworth Document Delivery Service: 1-800-HAWORTH. E-mail address: <docdelivery@haworthpress.com> Website: <http://www.HaworthPress.com> © 2006 by The Haworth Press, Inc. All rights reserved.]*

KEYWORDS. BDSM, SM, sexuality, media, popular culture, consumption, politics of representation, postmodern American culture, late-capitalism

This article explores representations of BDSM in U.S. mainstream and popular media, focusing on the film *Secretary* (Shainberg, 2002). This text uses both *BDSM* and *SM* to denote depictions, perceptions, and interpretations of sexual bondage, domination/submission, pain/sensation play, power exchange, leathersex, role-playing, and some fetish. Although nonpractitioners tend to use *S&M* almost exclusively, this analysis draws on understandings of BDSM derived from the community of practitioners, and research on those communities (e.g., Califia, 1994; Thompson, 1991; Weinberg, William, and Moser, 1984; and Weinberg, 1995). In these communities, *BDSM* and *SM* are more common; the use of both terms recognizes the relatively recent coinage of *BDSM*, while maintaining historical continuity with the use of *SM* as the inclusive term.

Mainstream media representation of alternative sexualities, including BDSM, has increased dramatically in the last 20 years. First noted in 1983 (Falk & Weinberg), this trend shows no signs of abating today. As evidence of SM's mainstreaming, this paper first catalogues examples of BDSM representations appearing in ads, television, film, music, and newspapers from 1985-2003. SM has saturated popular culture, and in this saturation, SM has come to mean something more mainstream and less risqué, more conventional and less exotic. Popular depictions of SM have shifted from images of the shocking, dangerous other to representations both pathological *and* normal. Against the backdrop of the increasingly kinky mainstream, this article queries the political effect of these representations. Arguing against the understanding that there is a causal relationship between increased media representation and political progress, this paper documents the political perils of such visibility.

Drawing on survey, focus group, and interview data, the analysis focuses on the reception of representations of BDSM by a "mainstream" audience, defined broadly here as those who do not identify as practicing BDSM. For these media consumers, increased exposure to representations of SM has not resulted in progressive or politically useful feelings of acceptance or understanding. This article defines *acceptance* as: expressing tolerance of BDSM; admitting SM into mainstream social groupings; and/or categorizing BDSM as proper, normal, or approved. It defines *understanding* as: grasping the reasonableness of BDSM; having a thorough acquaintance of, and familiarity with, SM; and/or showing a sympathetic or tolerant attitude toward BDSM and its practitioners.

Instead of promoting politically progressive forms of acceptance or understanding, these representations offer *acceptance via normalization*, and *understanding via pathologizing*. In the former mechanism, SM is acceptable only when it falls under the rubric of normative American sexuality. In the latter mechanism, SM is understandable only when it is the symptom of a deviant type of person with a sick, damaged core. Both mechanisms offer a form of acceptance or understanding, but these forms do not further the cause of sexual freedom. They allow the mainstream audience to flirt with danger and excitement, but ultimately reinforce boundaries between protected and privileged normal sexuality, and policed and pathological not normal sexuality. These mechanisms solidify the ideological dichotomies that animate American understandings of sexuality, where normal is heterosexual, monogamous, romantic, private, married, and suburban, while abnormal is nonheterosexual, nonmonogamous, unromantic, public, unmarried, and urban (e.g., Rubin, 1984/1993). When viewers accept or understand BDSM in these ways, they utilize a mode of *distanced consumption*, where representations of SM offer a tantalizing glimpse of something other (sexy, exotic, kinky) that is safely viewed and evaluated from a detached, privileged, and normative position.

Rather than celebrating increased representation, this article argues that desire and disappointment are more promising sites for political intervention. The mainstream public expresses disappointment and boredom when confronted with representations of BDSM that have been predigested by the ideological schemas of normal/abnormal, healthy/pathological, or privileged/policed. These feelings are an emotional response to contemporary U.S. consumer culture, a culture that is increasingly media-saturated and spectacle-driven (e.g., Gómez-Peña, 2001; Jameson, 1991). Viewer-citizens of this postmodern culture privilege sexuality–especially alternative, nonnormative sexualities–as a site of authenticity and transgression. They are disappointed when these representations fail to challenge boundaries and transgress norms, when instead popular culture presents a disciplined, commodified version of BDSM, already bound by these ideological dichotomies. The continued popularity of mainstream media representations of SM signifies the growing desire of the public to experience something authentic, unalienated, undisciplined, and noncommodified. This article reads this disappointment and desire as a nascent political protest. This protest is especially important as the state continues to police and marginalize alternative sexualities, and the U.S. cultural landscape becomes more sensationalistic and media-driven.

METHOD

This study employed several methods: (a) a survey of media representations, newspaper, and magazine documentation of the "mainstreaming of S&M"; (b) a focus group and Internet survey conducted in 2001; and (c) interviews with 12 nonpractitioners conducted in 2002 and 2003. The survey of popular culture references compiled over the course of this research (2000-2003) included references in ads, newspaper, and popular magazine articles, on TV and film, and other media (including music). Representations were located through searching on Websites and newspaper and other databases, and by referrals from friends, colleagues, BDSM practitioners taking part in the larger research project, SM media watch organizations, and several Internet mailing lists.

The informal focus group was conducted in a graduate seminar on popular culture in the Department of Cultural Anthropology at Duke University on April 17, 2001. The fourteen students in class agreed to watch and respond to two ads: the 2001 "Organized Neighbors" Ikea furniture ad, and the "Oh La La" Dannon yogurt ad from the La Crème series (2001-2003). The Ikea ad depicted a heterosexual couple discussing their neighbors' newly organized living room. The woman said, "I wish we could be that organized," to which the man replied, "People like that never have fun. They're uptight." As they watched, a man ran through the living room of the neighbors' apartment, pursued by a woman, in a dominatrix outfit, who cracked a whip on the sofa. The first woman turned to the man and deadpanned, "They don't seem that uptight." The Dannon ad portrayed a woman in a French maid outfit, sitting on a man's lap and sexily feeding him yogurt. Suddenly, two teenage girls opened the door, surprising the couple. One girl said to her friend, "My parents are so weird," to which the woman (suddenly mother) replied, "You're home early." Twelve of the participants in the focus group were female, two were male; ten were graduate students, and four were undergraduates. The discussion was digitally taped (with verbal permission), and transcribed. From an initial prompt asking whether these ads were "about BDSM," participants discussed what made a depiction about SM, what other audiences might think about these ads, and other related topics.

The 28 people who responded to the anonymous Internet survey distributed in the spring of 2001 ranged in age from 17-58 (averaging 29 years), specifically indicated that they were not "into BDSM," and lived in the U.S. Among these respondents, 16 were male and 12 were female. Participants were recruited via e-mail using snowball sampling from my initial social and academic networks. The survey asked respondents to view the two above ads (using the Internet ad database AdCritic.com) and answer several questions, including "When you hear the words *S&M, sadomasochism, SM* etc., what do you think of?" and "Do you think [this ad] is 'about SM'? . . . Why, or why not?" Respondents had an unlimited textbox in which to record answers. In what follows, survey and focus group participants are not named; they are identified as "focus group participant" or "survey respondent" in the text.

The majority of this analysis draws on in-depth, semi-structured interviews conducted in 2002 and 2003 with 12 individuals from the San Francisco Bay Area, Chicago, and New York who had (a) seen the film *Secretary*; and (b) identified as not being into BDSM. These participants ranged in age from 20-37 (averaging 28 years), and were recruited using snowball sampling of informal social and research networks. Of these interviewees, five were men and seven were women, eleven were White and one was Asian American. All participants were given an opportunity to choose a verbal, anonymous consent process (where all potentially identifying information was dissociated from the interview itself), or a written, nonanonymous consent process. These interviews ranged from 45 to 120 minutes, were recorded on digital media (with permission), and transcribed. Working from a set of common prompts, the interviews were tailored to the idiosyncratic responses of participants. In every interview, respondents were asked general questions about SM (e.g., what images come to mind when you think about SM, what would you posit as the key definition of BDSM, how would you describe key differences between SM and non-SM sex) and questions about the film *Secretary* (e.g., why did you watch the film, did you learn anything about SM from the film, do you feel the film was an "accurate" portrayal of BDSM). The interview participants are identified in this text by a first name they have chosen and brief demographic information (age, occupation, and location).

REPRESENTATIONS OF BDSM IN MAINSTREAM MEDIA, 1985-2003

In the last 20 years, SM images, iconography, and style have become increasingly prevalent in mainstream U.S. popular culture, in various media forms such as print ads, billboards, television sit-coms, news programs, movies, and commercials. As Weinberg and Magill (1995) began to document, the diffusion of SM iconography into mainstream mass media has meant that such representations are no longer confined to haute fashion or the occasional reference; SM has saturated popular culture. From the relative invisibility of SM 20 years ago, today these images appear in a wide variety of media, are used to sell a wide range of products, function in multiple ways, and encode a variety of contradictory personalities. There has not been a clear shift in the tenor of these representations (e.g., from negative to positive); rather, these depictions are at once mocking and sincere, normalizing and pathologizing. This flood of increasingly spectacular images marks the entry of BDSM into the postmodern and media-driven mainstream consumer landscape.

Print, billboard, and television ads that depict SM have been produced by a wide array of clothing and shoe companies, alcohol companies, and even a breath mint company (Altoids). For example, a 1997 Bass Ale beer print campaign featured a male "slave" drooling over a woman's blue patent-leather boot. Network television aired a series of Axe deodorant spray commercials from 2002-2003; one ending included a paunchy leatherman eyeing an aromatically irresistible nerd in an elevator. These two examples indicate that marketers have tapped into the allure and exoticism of SM sexuality to sell an ever-widening array of products; SM not only appears in high fashion, but also in beer ads. Although clothes that made "frank allusion to bondage, fetishes, and sadomasochism" date from the 1980s, media commentators have now noted "the diffuse way fetish wear turned up on the runways, in collections from designers of all stripes" (Trebay, 2000, p. B-12; see

Bienvenu, 1998, and Steele, 1999, for historical analyses of the development of fetish fashion). As Menkes argued, "There's nothing to be shocked at anymore. It's as if a designer said, 'This is the day dress, this is the cotton chiffon, this is the S/M.' It's just another tool" (cited in Trebay, 2000, p. B-12). No longer confined to runways, these images of BDSM have shifted from exotic to mundane, from "celebs at award shows to your neighbor on bingo night" (Shanahan, 2003, p. 38). The accessibility of SM as "tool," or spotting fetish wear on "your neighbor," indicate the ways that BDSM has penetrated the mainstream, and has become more everyday in this penetration.

This shift means that representations of SM are no longer confined to shocking, exotic, and exciting depictions. While these representations persist, when SM appears on television, in films, and in popular music today it is also depicted as something everyday, mundane, and conventional. On television, viewers are offered not only sexy and scandalized depictions on late night cable television shows, docudramas, or primetime crime dramas, but also friendly and upbeat depictions on primetime situation comedies, soap operas, and home and garden shows. For example, on a 2001 episode of *Will & Grace* (Herschlag & Burrows, 2001), Grace, an interior designer, had a client who needed a dungeon converted into a nursery. The punch line: The jolly jumper and changing table can stay. Even The Learning Channel's dowdy home design show *Trading Spaces* included Frank, the country-kitsch designer, crafting a "bondage rocking chair" for a bachelor's bedroom (Cramsey, 2002). Cinematic depiction has also broadened to include lighter and more permissive representations (e.g., the goofy SM-themed caper *Exit to Eden* [Marshall, 1994]), although dark and criminal representations remain popular (e.g., the SM-leads-to-murder in *The General's Daughter* [Neufeld & West, 1999]). Yet films like *Sick: The Life & Death of Bob Flanagan, Supermasochist* (Dick, 1997), *Quills* (Kaufman, 2000), and *Secretary* demonstrate that SM is no longer limited to the underworld; like the television examples cited above, SM is not just scary, dangerous, and exciting, but also funny, romantic, and safe enough to appear on The Learning Channel. Similarly, lyrics celebrating SM dynamics are in the repertoire of alternative bands like Nine Inch Nails ("Head Like a Hole" [1989, track 1]) and Puddle of Mudd ("Control" [2001, track 1]), but also in the work of the very pop Janet Jackson ("Rope Burn" [1997, track 19]) and Britney Spears ("I'm a Slave 4 U" [2001, track 1]). These more ordinary representations of SM in mainstream media were less common 20 years ago.

The mainstreaming of BDSM means that SM appears in more popular, mainstream locations (primetime, Hollywood movies, ads for beer) and also that the meaning of SM has shifted from exotic other to something both pathological and normal. Coverage of SM in the news follows this trend as well; mainstream newspapers and magazines no longer confine discussion of BDSM to scandalized and sensationalistic crime stories, but also produce balanced stories on the consensual, adult BDSM community. For example, the Ohio paper *Columbus Alive!* ran a front-page story on a friendly "S&M dungeon where everybody knows your name" (Mozzocco, 2002).

These depictions of SM reveal the complex popular attitudes about SM; SM is simultaneously exciting and other, and conventional and everyday. For example, when newspapers revealed that Sarah Kozer, the second-to-last contestant on FOX's reality dating game show *Joe Millionaire*, had participated in several fetish (foot worship and bondage) videos, she was unrepentant and seemingly unperturbed ("I'm not embarrassed at all," Kozer informed *Access Hollywood* [cited in Haberman, 2003, ¶ 6]). Yet the message boards at the *Millionaire* Website revealed that the show's fans were decidedly less blasé about it; she was described with words like tramp, freak, liar, sleazy, bondage slut, and Sarah-the-slut (from http://forums.prospero.com/foxjoem/messages; this site is no longer online). In late December 2002, several newspapers breathlessly revealed that Jack McGeorge, one of the UN arms inspectors deployed to Iraq, was also a founder of Black Rose (an SM organization in the DC area). Although he never denied or tried to hide his SM activities and activism, McGeorge was nevertheless the butt of jokes on late night talk shows, in cartoons featuring him in a leather harness, and in news articles with such clever pun-titles as "A taste of the whip for Saddam" (Lauerman, 2002) or "The UN's foray into Saddamasochism" (Steyn, 2002). Both of these stories were initially offered as shocking exposés, yet when Kozer was not embarrassed, and Hans Blix (the head of the team of UN weapons inspectors) seemed unconcerned and refused to accept McGeorge's proffered resignation, the media attention dissipated.

Mainstream representations of BDSM are sometimes jokey sight-gags (e.g., *Friends* [Kurland & Bonerz, 1997]), sometimes deviant underworld explorations (e.g., *8mm* [Schumacher, 1999]), sometimes all about fetish fashion (e.g., *The Matrix* [Wachowski & Wachowski, 1999]), and sometimes earnest explorations (e.g., Marech, 2001). They are certainly not all positive depictions. Yet what must be highlighted here is that as BDSM has begun to saturate popular culture, appearing more often and in more contexts, it has also come to signify something more mainstream and more conventional, something less exceptional, extreme, or unusual. As Rosie O'Donnell's character said in *Exit to Eden*, "It's just another alternative lifestyle." Or, as Marin (1997-1988) argued, "S&M . . . has been mainstreamed from deviant perversion to just another wacky lifestyle choice . . . S&M has become so common-place, so banal, that it can safely be used to sell beer" (p. 85).

Twenty years ago, SM was (at least in fantasy) something dark and mys-terious, unspoken and invisible; today, representations of BDSM are ev-erywhere. A commonsense tenet of American liberal politics is that mainstream, positive, and realistic representation is the first step toward the greater social acceptance, understanding, and tolerance of a minority group. Thus, many would argue that all of this mass representation–which now at least sometimes includes more positive, accepting, or sympathetic representations of BDSM–is politically effective. As one participant in the focus group said, "The Ikea ad shows that even normal people do this . . . [it] takes away the . . . perversity attached to SM, so even the most normal of the normal, even people who go shopping at Ikea [do SM]." This tenet must be examined: How does the mainstream public understand and re-spond to these representations? Do these increasingly mainstream images result in a greater understanding or acceptance of BDSM, and if so, is this acceptance or understanding necessarily politically progressive?

An analysis of critical and interview responses to the film *Secretary* indicates that increasingly mainstream depictions yield both acceptance and understanding of BDSM. Like the representations above, *Secretary* depicts SM as exotic, sexy, and other *and* conventional, mainstream, and normal. However, the form of acceptance that these mainstream representations promote is predicated on conformity to normative American sexuality (acceptance through normalization). Similarly, the form of understanding that these mainstream representations promote is reliant on the classification as an abnormal, damaged type (understanding through pathologizing). Both mechanisms reinforce boundaries between normal, protected, and privileged sexuality, and abnormal, policed, and pathological sexuality. Together, these dual mechanisms diminish any positive political outcome of the mainstreaming of BDSM.

RECUPERATION BY ROMANCE: ACCEPTANCE THROUGH NORMALIZATION

Lion's Gate released *Secretary* in the fall of 2002. An adaptation of a Mary Gaitskill short story of the same name, the film told the story of a young woman saved by sadomasochism. In brief, the plot involved a young, naïve girl (Lee Holloway), just released from a mental institution (for self-cutting), who got her first job as the secretary of a repressed, tightly wound lawyer (Mr. Grey). The two developed a relationship involving power exchange, sexual discipline, and control. When their dynamics became too emotionally intense, Mr. Grey fired Lee, ending the relationship. With the crushing reality of a marriage with vanilla boyfriend Peter looming, Lee returned to Mr. Grey's office and demonstrated her determination and love for him. In the end, this was enough; she won him back, they married, and lived happily ever after in the suburbs.

Although it was an independent release, *Secretary* was one of the more popular small films of the year. It garnered praise and the Grand Jury Prize for Originality at its debut at Sundance Film Festival, and was subsequently nominated for several other awards (Maggie Gyllenhaal, the actress who played Lee, was nominated for best actor awards from five award-giving bodies, including the Golden Globes and the Independent Spirit Awards. The latter also nominated the film for Best Feature; screenwriter Erin Cressida Wilson won Best First Screenplay). It played in art and independent theaters in major U.S. cities for 21 weeks; grossed $4,046,737 in its U.S. theatrical release (Box Office, n.d.); and generated much press, both critical and popular. When *Secretary* was released, several SM activists expressed guarded hope; perhaps this was a first step toward mainstream acceptance, understanding, and tolerance of BDSM.

In American liberal political paradigms, the mainstream representation of sexual minorities is a sign of progress. The time line is as follows: first representation and visibility, next acceptance or tolerance of the minority, then an empathetic form of understanding, and finally sexual freedom. There are assumed causal links between increased visibility, acceptance, understanding, and such political gains as the ability to assert rights and privileges, and the freedom from unjust persecution. This paradigm presupposes that with acceptance and understanding, sexual minorities will gain legitimacy in the mainstream of American politics.

While it is true that *Secretary*'s mainstream audience professed acceptance of BDSM sexuality and relationships after seeing the film, this acceptance was predicated on normalization. Presenting a very conventional love story with some kinky bits of the other, the film allowed viewers to accept SM only as long as it remained squarely normal. Critics described the movie with terms like tender, sweet, poignant, sweet-natured, charming, kindhearted, touching, gentle, warm-hearted, and life-affirming, sometimes with the word *oddly* preceding these adjectives (e.g., Edelstein, 2002b; Zacharek, 2002). Described as "the world's first S&M date movie" (Burr, 2002, p. C-1) and a "feel good movie about sadomasochism" (Ansen, 2002, p. 70), *Secretary* was so oddly sweet because it was a tried and true romantic comedy, "a *Pretty Woman* for the bondage set" (Edelstein, 2002b, ¶ 1). Reviewers described *Secretary* as an oddball, screwball, or quirky romance (e.g., Weiskind, 2002), a Cinderella story with a kink, whose main message (as in all romantic comedies) was that there is someone perfect for everyone. As in all fairy tale endings, "Both suspect there is no one else they're ever likely to meet who will understand them quite so completely" (Ebert, 2002, p. 31). Or, as Suzy, a 32-year-old graduate student living in Oakland, noted, "There's a lid for every pot." Following the conventions of the genre (they meet, they struggle, they overcome, they love forever and ever), *Secretary* turned out to be less hardcore perversion and more a "gently bent old-fashioned romance about two people who are so ideally suited for each other that they seemed doomed to never get it together" (Dargis, 2002, p. 17). Indeed, a turning point in the film was a cliché found in many romantic comedies: Lee fled her impending wedding–in her wedding dress–to be with her one true love.

Interviewees agreed; Inna, a 30-year-old lawyer in San Francisco, said, in the end "He gives in and realizes he's found his perfect mate. It's a love story. It *is* a love story! It is!" Ty, a 22-year-old college student in Chicago, described it as "a dark love story," a version of female need and male remoteness (or inability to be intimate) gussied up with bondage, spanking, and some more serious D/s (dominance and submission). Jenny, a 29-year-old computer contractor in the Bay Area, thought "the end when they're having their wedding and she's strapped to the tree" was a funny twist on her own fantasies of marriage and happily ever after: "It's so antithetical to any wedding bell images that I've ever had in my mind, and yet they're obviously enjoying themselves thoroughly; it's just funny." These interviewees enjoyed the "twist" on the classic *Secretary* portrayed. The story worked the same way the mainstream images documented above worked; it flirted with danger without actually being dangerous (whether this is the same reason SM is appealing to practitioners is a topic for another paper). It was what Nye termed the "riskless risk" (cited in Hannigan, 1998, p. 71) of clean, commodified experience, prepackaged for the slightly adventurous consumer.

In this way, *Secretary* offered a glimpse of something sexy and exciting that, in the end, was not alienating, was just a traditional–if odd–love story. The film promised what hooks (1992) called "a bit of the other" as a sort of exotic/erotic prop for the self. Like representations of the native other, the dark other, or the dangerous other, the sexual other is tied to a long practice of distanced consumption. This mode of viewership enables the privileged use of the other in a way that gives the normative audience familiarity, knowledge, and even intimacy of the other, all the while shoring up a basic power differential that maintains the one's power, and the other's essential alterity (see also Allison, 2001, for a discussion of the orientalist "distant intimacy" involved in fan reactions to A. Golden's [1999] novel *Memoirs of a Geisha*). These representations reinforce boundaries between normal and not normal by allowing the viewer to consume a bit of the kinky other while buttressing the privilege, authority, and essential normalcy of the self.

The reinforcement of normative American sexuality at the end of the film clearly reveals this dynamic. The romantic story line in *Secretary* limits the potential transgressiveness of Lee and Mr. Grey's relationship–and SM sexuality by extension–by folding it back into a mainstream, domesticated version of romance. As Rubin (1984/1993) argued, privilege is bestowed on sexuality that is heterosexual, marital, monogamous, reproductive, noncommercial, coupled, vanilla, without "manufactured objects," relational, homo-generational, and at home (pp. 13-14); sexuality that falls within these boundaries is considered good, normal, and natural. "Bad, abnormal, unnatural, damned sexuality" (Rubin, pp. 13-14) describes sexuality that is homosexual, unmarried, promiscuous, nonprocreative, commercial, alone or in groups, casual, cross-generational, in public, or with objects; these sexualities are stigmatized, pathologized, policed, and oppressed. Ideologically, SM sexuality is on the bad side of this dichotomy, classified, conceptually, as abnormal. In the popular, public imagination, BDSM sexuality is nongenital, nonprocreative, nonmonogamous, often commercial, public, and not relationally-oriented.

When asked about their own understandings of SM relationships, many interviewees imagined SM sex between two people who did not know one another, or nonmonogamous couples, or between a professional dominatrix and a client, or in a public setting like a club, or, as Dan, a 22-year-old college student in Chicago half-joked, "on a gross group scale or a cult scale in an abandoned warehouse." In contrast, Lee's relationship with Mr. Grey was between married partners, in the context of a traditional, monogamous relationship. Shannon, a 37-year-old designer and Web producer living in San Francisco, argued, "It's two people that know and care about each other"; it is "a complete package." She thought the ending showed that they "were able to have a full, well-rounded relationship, not just this relationship of SM. . . . They were able to be a couple . . . They could have this aspect of their relationship, but they were able to make the bed . . . They're sharing the everyday things too."

Interviewees characterized typical SM sex as hard, rough, painful, cold, distant, exposed, or not tender, and thus expressed surprise at the domestic depiction at the end of the film. The film's resolution, which featured a soft and "tender" bathing and lovemaking scene, and final snapshots of domestic bliss (Lee and Mr. Grey making their bed together, Lee straightening Mr. Grey's tie, and Lee sitting in a rocking chair on the porch of their suburban home as Mr. Grey drives off to work), defanged the representations of SM in the film. Many interviewees had never imaged that SM could, as Jenny said, extend "to picking out china patterns and making the bed." Ty said,

> They turn out to be real lovers in the end. . . . I never really thought that SM people have, of course they didn't have a normal relationship, but it seemed like they were pretty happy and they were living in a regular place and stuff like that. . . . I always thought that the partners wouldn't live together, as a married happy couple, and have interactions like a normal husband and wife.

Had the film depicted SM sexuality as the happy ending; it would have challenged the hierarchy of American sexuality. As it was, the film's happy ending redeemed BDSM by refolding it back into normative constructions of sexuality, thus making the representational argument that SM/nonnormative sexuality is acceptable as long as it turns out, after all, to be not-SM/normative sexuality. The images presented at the end of the film recuperate SM back into the tightly bounded, enforced, and policed norm of American sex and intimacy. The film allowed viewers to accept SM sexuality, but only insofar as it could be normalized.

The acceptance via normalization mechanism in *Secretary* allows the viewer to identify with the love story and accept the characters as long as the characters are recognizably mainstream. Adam, a 23-year-old interviewee working as a biologist in Chicago, explained,

> My problem with [the ending] is that their interaction was more conventional . . . he takes her up to this room and lays her down,

and then she sort of becomes this housewife, like on the porch waving goodbye, and so then it almost becomes like you are saying . . . that being OK means you have to be conventional [instead of saying that] SM is OK, and that it can be practiced in a healthy way.

In this way, the traditionalist ending of the film constrains any challenge to normative American sexuality that the representation of SM might present. The bits of the other the film delivered upfront (e.g., the spanking, masturbation, and D/s scenes) were overwhelmed in the end by the normative romantic resolution (Lee and Mr. Grey firmly enmeshed in a monogamous, heterosexual, married, suburban, professional husband/housewife setting). The dynamic here granted the normative viewer access to BDSM through a normalizing gaze. Like the SM in *Will & Grace* or beer ads, this mode of representation co-opts or appropriates SM to put a funny, cool, or hip twist on something essentially normative. These images do not challenge normative sexuality and relationships; rather they flirt with exoticism and excitement while reinforcing the borders between normal and not normal sexuality. Rather than being a clearly positive first step, this form of acceptance is quite politically dangerous. The dynamic of acceptance via normalization means that BDSM is acceptable to the mainstream only when it turns out to be not SM at all.

THE MASOCHIST:
UNDERSTANDING THROUGH PATHOLOGIZING

Similarly, while many responded to mainstreamed images of BDSM with a form of understanding, here understanding was predicated on viewing SM as a kind of sickness. This second dynamic in *Secretary*, understanding via pathologizing, allowed the normative viewer to understand SM only insofar as it is understood as a damaged, pathological identity. The audience maintained a first person identification with Lee, yet this identification was double-edged; she was "'kinky' and strange, as well as sympathetic" (Fuchs, 2002, ¶ 8). Lee is accessible and understandable; as Gyllenhaal said, "Almost everyone seems to say, 'I understand her'" (cited in Wloszczyna, 2002, p. 14D). However, the cost of this understanding is pathologizing; the characters might be "lovable basket cases" (Edelstein, 2002a), but they are lovable and sympathetic because they are ill. As Ty noted, "You get inside the secretary's head, and you see what her home life, her family life is, and you see the cause and effect, what might have driven her to, caused her to become that way." As one critic wrote, Gyllenhaal's performance "makes it possible for us to understand the person beneath the pathologies" (Weiskind, 2002, p. 27). It should be noted that in some contexts, consensual SM is still officially considered pathological: The movie received its R rating in part for what the Motion Picture Association of America (the organization responsible for film ratings) called "depiction of behavioral disorders" (see also Moser & Kleinplatz, 2005, for an argument advocating the removal of paraphilias–including sexual sadism and masochism–from the current *Diagnostic and Statistical Manual of Mental Disorders [DSM-IV-TR]*).

Secretary presented Lee as, above all, a masochist. Her masochism is "inside [her] makeup"; "deep inside . . . part of [her] being," as Chris, a 36-year-old software marketer and manager living in San Francisco, remarked. Inna thought that the film "really opened my eyes" because it showed that sexual masochism was "a natural extension" of "the whole cutting yourself thing"; or, as Shannon said, "Instead of abusing herself, she's letting someone else abuse her." Closer to older, sexological definitions of masochism than to contemporary understandings of the dynamics of D/s and SM, viewers understand Lee as a person whose sickness (masochism) becomes the driving identity in her life (she is a masochist). This mode of sex-based categorization is reminiscent of (the last) turn of the century sexological classifications, where the spectrum of sexual practices, behaviors, and desires were rigidified into stable psychosexual (and pathological) types. As Foucault (1978/1990) documented, this careful cataloging of pleasure and sex resulted in new species of deviants, named and "entomologized" on the basis of their sexuality (pp. 42-46). The effuse desires, detached pleasures, and other ambiguities of sexuality became instead more formal and inflexible means of classifying persons. Sexuality thus became the most real, natural, and essential categorization of a person, the truth of the subject. These classificatory systems are based on the categories of normal and abnormal, healthy and sick, that remain entrenched in American sexual ideology. In *Secretary*, fixing SM desires and relationships to a deviant type of person (here a masochist) allows the viewer to understand Lee as person who is defined by a pathological sexuality.

As Adam said, "After I saw the movie, I realized that there are people that consider themselves sadists, and people that consider themselves masochists." For him, viewing SM as a type of person (a masochist or a sadist) rather than as a practice allowed him to move beyond understanding SM as wrong, but at the same time, it further differentiated normal people from *those* people. Shannon asked, "Do people who are self-abusers become submissive? Do they get into this lifestyle?" Suzy worried about this depiction; she thought the film's argument was that "If it were OK for people to be like this, she wouldn't have had to do all the things she did. . . . She doesn't have to cut herself now that she's found him." But this portrayal is hard for Suzy to identify with, because she has "definitely had some hot experiences with it [spanking] and that doesn't mean I'm a masochist."

This comment alludes to a differentiation between sexuality as a practice, a behavior, a style, or a fun thing to do in the city, and sexuality as the truth of the subject. As long as sexuality serves as the basis of authentic subjectivity, it leads directly into the classification of subjects as either normal (heterosexual, married, etc.) or pathological (homosexual, kinky, etc.). Thus, these respondents differentiated SM as a preference or recreational activity from SM as a lifestyle, identity, a natural disposition, or sexual orientation, like being gay. Chris remarked, "The thing that left the biggest impact . . . is that it seems more like a mental disorder, or a mental trait, or personality, almost something that is innate. It's almost like homosexuality, innate; you don't have a choice." Several interviewees felt that there might be several "levels" of BDSM involvement; Adam said, "For some it is just a preference, and maybe for others, maybe they were abused when they were younger" and thus develop more stable SM identities. Shannon said, "I think that it's hard to understand if it becomes like a whole lifestyle," something people are "obsessed with"; "I get why people would do it occasionally, but . . . if it's all the time, to the point where it becomes a need, it seems like there must be underlying reasons why people participate." In *Secretary*, as Steve, a 30-year-old software developer living in Marin County, remarked, "It wasn't just something they did for fun; they needed it to fulfill an emotional void. They needed it to function."

This mode of representation allows the hip consumption of SM while always keeping the normative viewer safely removed from the perverts. As Jenny said, the movie "sort of posited both of them as damaged people. I felt like they were saying this behavior . . . would only work for those who have severe emotional scars, as a way to differentiate what they're doing from the audience." Eleanor, a 29-year-old teacher living in Oakland, felt that "If I were in the SM community. . . . I would feel like 'this doesn't represent me'" because "They made the characters so weird. They were both kind of insane."

Presenting SM as a (pathological) identity rather than a practice works to shore up boundaries between normal and abnormal. Offering understanding through pathologizing, this representation reinforces boundaries between the person who might take a slightly kinky trip to Good Vibrations (a San Francisco sex store) and the full-on pervert with a sick core. It allows the normative viewer access and understanding to BDSM through a pathologizing, stigmatizing gaze. Like the moralizing crime drama or scandalized exposé discussed above, this mode of representation reinforces the essential abnormality of BDSM. The dynamic of understanding via pathologizing means that the mainstream understands SM through diagnosis as a damaged type.

THE DOUBLE GAZE:
AGAINST VISIBILITY

As images of SM become more mainstream, it is tempting to regard more mainstream representations of BDSM as signs of, or potential moments for, political progress. Yet the analysis of media consumption offered here suggests that there is no easy correlation between the increased visibility, understanding, and acceptance of sexual minorities, and activist goals. By offering modes of acceptance and understanding that reinforce the division of sexuality into normal/abnormal, privileged/policed, and healthy/pathological, these mainstream representations of SM disrupt the assumption of causation between visibility and political progress. As Champagne (1995) argued, "The desire of cultural minorities to achieve increased visibility must be considered alongside modern disciplinary society's demands for a normalization linked to increased forms of surveillance" (p. 71). This comment draws on Foucault's (1977/1995) understanding of discipline; for Foucault, disciplinary power "imposes on those whom it subjects a principle of compulsory visibility. In discipline, it is the subjects who have to be seen. Their visibility assures the hold of the power that is exercised over them" (p. 187). The authoritative gaze of power here offers subjectivity only insofar as sexual minorities conform to the categories a disciplinary society offers. The increased visibility of BDSM in mainstream media renders it increasingly vulnerable to this dynamic of normalizing and pathologizing.

The quest to categorize populations on the basis of sexuality (what Foucault termed "bio-power" [Foucault, 1978/1990]) continues to be an essential form of power in contemporary late-capitalism (see also

Lowe, 1995, and Singer, 1993). This mode of categorization is a form of social control; by offering acceptance or understanding only insofar as BDSM sexuality conforms to the ideological categories of normal/not-SM or not normal/pathological SM, these representations do not challenge the systems of privilege and power currently governing sexuality in the U.S. They are not a moment of political progress, but rather suggest the entrenched machinations of power and control over sexual minorities.

Mainstream representations of SM reinforce boundaries between normal and not normal sexuality by granting the viewer access to something kinky and other in a way that does not challenge the normative positionality of the self. These depictions display sexual minorities as a sort of freak show for a mainstream audience. Like the paradoxical "normalization through freak show" that Gamson (1998, p.19) documents on TV talk shows, the dynamic of visibility offered to sexual minorities in mainstream media is limited to a spectacular, exciting display (a push at normative boundaries) followed immediately by the reabsorption into convention (a rearticulation of those boundaries). Opportunities for understanding or accepting these minorities are restricted to majority terms. Whether the other is granted normativity (Lee and Mr. Grey's romance), or the other is consigned to pathology (Lee as Masochist), when the other enters the mainstream viewing landscape s/he is pinned by a disciplining gaze.

This distanced consumption provides a safe location for the viewer, especially as SM remains policed, feared, and deviant. It could be that this position of safe, if titillated, distance is especially attractive right now as the U.S. swings further into an anti-sex regime (continuing the "moral panic" chronicled by Rubin, 1984/1993). In the context of attacks on sex education, hatred of sexual minorities, and AIDS, sex that does not leave the hands dirty may be quite compelling. As Califia argued, "The machine of pop culture steals from minorities. It comes to us for titillation and rips off our symbolism. At the MTV level, s/m looks more acceptable. The reality, for actual perverts, is it's not" (cited in Trebay, 1997, p. 32). Or, as Buchanan noted, "Candle wax and ice may be okay for Janet Jackson, but that doesn't mean you'll ever see branding at the mall" (cited in Trebay, 1997, p. 32).

A branding kiosk might conceivably appear at the local mall, but if this ever happened, branding would cease to mark the dividing line between in-here normal and out-there abnormal. These comments about appropriation refer to the ways that current mainstream representation does not break down the boundaries around which American sexuality revolves. Instead, these representations provide new entry points for strengthening boundaries and disciplining minorities. As bits of SM move into the mainstream, other bits of SM stand as the new outside; if spanking is now OK, then branding or cutting is not. Here spanking becomes normalized, accepted because it's not *really* SM, and branding becomes pathological, understood as not normal and other. Like the punks Hebdige (1979) documented, mainstream representations co-opt subcultural style and practice through commodification and ideological incorporation (like labeling and typing), so that in the end what was clearly "resistant" (or outside) becomes "incorporated" (or inside) (pp. 92-99).

The dynamics of normalizing and pathologizing mean that when BDSM enters the mainstream, it is either normalized out of existence (e.g., BDSM in sit-coms or in the song or dress of Britney Spears), or exiled to pathological other (e.g., BDSM in crime dramas or *8mm*). It is either labeled, coded, and entomologized as pathological, or rendered accessible, visible, and comfortably normal (i.e., not really SM). Both dynamics enforce boundaries between normal and not normal, and the systems of privilege and power that work through these distinctions. When BDSM becomes mainstream (incorporated), it is a disciplined SM, an SM that has been appropriated by systems of control and is granted existence only in relation to those dominant categories and rules.

DISAPPOINTINGLY NORMAL: SEXUALITY AND DISCIPLINE IN U.S. CONSUMER CULTURE

If increased representation does not equate with a form of acceptance or understanding that is politically useful, what, if anything, can be said for such representations? Why are they so popular? What do these images stand in for, and how do the consumers of such imagery respond to this incorporated, disciplined BDSM? Reactions to these images suggest that BDSM remains popular because it continues to stand for something that can disturb these dominant categories, even as it is absorbed. When mainstream representations of SM result in the rearticulation of borders and boundaries, viewers express disappointment that, in the end, SM does not stand outside the "machine of pop culture," that instead the machine disciplines, regulates, and controls this sexuality as it incorporates it. The popularity of SM images in mainstream media encodes a desire for realness, for transgression, and for authenticity.

Viewer-citizens expect BDSM sexuality to be something dangerous, outside the law, taboo, and other. Yet, due in part to the accelerations of the media-driven late-capitalist U.S., mainstream media representations of BDSM are doomed to disappoint. Viewers do not want BDSM to be something acceptable (and normal) or something understandable (and pathological); they want BDSM to be somehow outside these systems of power and privilege, discipline and control.

Some voice this disappointment as sanitation, making the argument that once these representations are displayed in mainstream contexts, they cease to be exciting. Here respondents are protesting the ways that the mainstreaming of BDSM means that it appears everywhere, but once it does, it is perceived as too safe, too commercial, and too clean. The fact that one can buy leather floggers on eBay and at Drugstore.com (in the bondage section of "sex toys & games") ruins the illusion that SM exists outside mainstream, consumer capitalism, somewhere truly other, truly outside. Similarly, when *Vogue* editor Kate Betts (1997/ 1998) called fetish fashion "last year's trend" because "You can buy leather pants at the Gap" (cited in Marin, p. 85), she is recognizing that the mainstreaming of fetish fashion, and BDSM by extension, has brought SM out of the fashion underground and into the local mall. This link to banal consumerism incorporates BDSM into a popular consumer landscape at once too accessible, too mundane, and too available to be satisfyingly exotic or other. As one Internet survey respondent wrote in his definition of SM, "I used to walk by the display windows in San Francisco and think, it doesn't look so terrifying, but not so awfully sexy either. More like a trip to the dentist's office."

In spite of this disappointment, BDSM imagery remains popular, even as critics and respondents dismiss SM as just another trend, just another marketing campaign, and just one of many mix-and-match styles of postmodern American consumer culture. Its continued popularity indicates that there is something else people are looking for when they look at BDSM. One survey respondent wrote, "I grow quickly bored of the images and the supposed 'extreme' nature of it all. I'm much more curious about the really sick and twisted side, less commonly seen and not in any Ikea ads."

In the popular imagination, the "really sick and twisted side" of SM cannot be tainted by capitalism or appear in America's suburban living rooms. It exists *outside* these banal locations, somewhere unreachable, unviewable, and unseen. It is something undisciplined and transgressive; to respondents, BDSM symbolizes something risky, dangerous, mysterious, extraordinary, glamorous, urban, underground, scary, off-limits, and cool. Yet as soon as SM appears in a beer ad, or in a Hollywood movie, it is immediately too suburban, uncool, demystified, safe, and banal. When one focus group participant argued that the French maid Dannon ad could not be about SM because "That form of role-playing is lame, that's like the most stock American form of exoticized sexuality," she is arguing that SM ceases to be SM when it becomes lame, stock, and banal. When sexuality is on display, it risks becoming ordinary.

This complex situation is a result of contemporary American postmodernity, often described as a hyperreal, surface-orientated, hyper-visual, inauthentic, and depthless cultural terrain (e.g., Baudrillard, 1986/1988; Jameson, 1991). The late-capitalist cultural landscape is increasingly a frenzied spectacle of visual surfaces. Performance artist Gómez-Peña (2001) called this the "culture of the mainstream bizarre," a *cultura in extremis* characterized by a flood of extreme images of sex, sports, violence, and reality crime shows. This field of "sharp edges and strong emotions" is pitched to viewer-citizens who flip from lifestyle reality show to open-heart surgery on TV (p. 13). BDSM representation in mainstream media parallels this frenzied spectacle. As mainstream representation becomes increasingly extreme, it is no longer unusual to see SM play on primetime television, or Britney Spears in leather. Yet at the same time, even as the mainstream becomes more "bizarre," sexuality continues to represent something that exists outside or beyond this visual field.

Many popular writers covering the fashion and advertising industries have suggested that the mainstreaming of SM is inexorably linked to consumer capitalism: It is the latest (sexy) identity that can be harnessed to sell anything. This is a pop version of Lowe's (1995) argument, where he asserted that late-capitalism is now increasingly involved in formerly independent practices like sexuality. BDSM can be used to generate consumption in general by linking sexuality (a new, nonreproductive, exchange-based sexuality) with nebulous "product characteristics" (Lowe, 1995, pp. 133-134). Thus, marketers associate the myriad meanings of SM in the popular imagination with various products: The outsider status of fetish fashion lends a punch to the Altoids breath mint, the risqué-ness of D/s dynamics enlivens the staid Bass Ale, or the coolness of SM play resignifies being uptight/organized in the Ikea ad. This dynamic indicates that SM continues to represent, at least in fantasy, something dangerously outside, even as the representations themselves become more mainstream.

In the contemporary U.S., sexuality symbolizes something real, something unalienated, undisciplined, and nonconsumptive. It is a privileged location for these expectations; sexuality is a placeholder for various forms of boundary transgression, including boundaries between selves, and between normative and deviant expressions and desires. As Singer (1993) argued, sexuality in late-capitalism is imagined as "a mechanism for resistance, transgression, opposition to the sphere of demand"; it is an "emblem . . . of freedom" from an "alienating social system" (pp. 36-37). Even though late-capitalism works in part through the regulation, production, and incitement of sexuality and sexual identities, and even as sexuality has become increasingly bound to consumptive practices, still somehow sexuality is imagined as outside of these forces, a privileged locus of authenticity, and an antidote to modern capitalist alienation.

Although this configuration describes all sexualities under late-capitalism, alternative sexualities shoulder the dual expectations of remaining somehow outside while still delivering a satisfying punch. And while this expectation for boundary challenging applies to all visible, nonheterosexual sexualities, at this particular historical moment, BDSM sexuality is a privileged site for these cultural contestations. It is only in the last 20 years that SM sexuality has become visible to the mainstream, and in this mainstreaming, subject to the perils of this visibility (although it should be noted that much of the theoretical work on the perils of visibility was first developed in relation to the mainstreaming of gay, and to a lesser extent lesbian, sexuality). BDSM sexuality is supposed to be real, raw, and dirty, something that goes beyond the cleanly commodified, spectacular landscape, something that disrupts clear boundaries between privileged, normal sexuality and stigmatized, not normal sexuality. In part, this is because BDSM is positioned outside the norm of American sexuality. In part, this is because SM is a persistently vilified form of sexuality, bearing the full weight of legal, psychiatric, and social damnation. But always, SM's meanings are bound to the expectation that it will, as Abby, a 20-year-old college student in New York said, "[break] the boundaries of what is normal." It is sexuality that is supposed to be, in the words of Adam, "hard enough to leave marks," supposed to break down boundaries between self and other, normal and not normal.

Thus even interviewees who enjoyed the love story in *Secretary* expressed disappointment that these images of the other were too mainstream, too conventional, too mundane, or too consumerist. Ty thought that if real SM is "violent, dark, and more depressing," the representation in *Secretary*, "tone[s] it down a little bit" and "cast[s] a nice humorous light" on BDSM. Suzy thought *Secretary* made it "a little bit safe," while Jenny thought the film was a little "too Hollywood." Abby said that, in *Secretary*, "SM was portrayed as like not as harsh [but as] something that could bring two people together, and you know, make them fall in love with each other. It was just like more subtle SM, softer." Suzy described it this way: "It's a starter kit; it's bringing something that has a very diverse set of practices to the mainstream in a way that it can be swallowed more easily, for people who don't know that it's there." These interviewees are pointing to a basic disappointment: Nothing *truly* shocking and out-there can appear in the in-here consumer culture. Once mainstreamed, these images of BDSM are a little too safe, a little too nice, and a little too easy to swallow.

Even the *TV Guide* review (hardly a cutting edge publication) complains about such neutering: "Mr. Grey's interest flags, Lee tries everything in the book to get him back, and this once-seriously edgy film assumes the guise of a silly madcap comedy, spiced up [with] an air of naughty chic" (Fox, n.d., ¶ 1). These complaints about the effect of mainstreaming point to complex desires for sex to be transgressive, nonnormative, undisciplined, and resistant to commercialization and marketing. Like all desires under capitalism, SM sexuality (in a popular representational form) promises satisfaction in the form of something brand new, dangerously other, or unimaginable, but leaves the viewer unsatisfied, always wanting more. Eleanor said she had hoped the film would be "a little exciting, titillating, you know, to go see kinky sex," but then remarked, "You kind of expected more kinky stuff." Steve said, "I was disappointed that there wasn't more hardcore SM." Laura, a 20-year-old college student in Chicago, said, "So the moral of the story is she gets the guy, and now she is a housewife, so that was unnerving. . . . It would be cooler if she became a career woman, but they still were nasty and SM-y all the time." Abby thought the film's ending was "totally bogus. The making the bed together, and her sitting there, and her being all happy. . . . I just thought it was a lame ending." Interviewees thought the SM in *Secretary* was too domestic, nice, and happy; as one reviewer wrote, "By the final scene, the film has rendered safely trite everything it once deemed subversive" (Sutton, 2002, ¶ 6). Promising a walk on the wild side–a come-on evidenced by the film's poster featuring a bent-over Gyllenhaal with the tag-line "Assume the Position"–*Secretary* instead delivered something too neatly contained. Shepherd (2002), a *Portland Mercury* reviewer, wrote:

> The ending sucks a bunch of ass–this huge, demanding movie, with its riveting, hot loads of tension, turns into just another goddamn fluff flick, and Lee and Mr. Grey degenerate into a yuppie couple worthy of a Snuggle dryer sheets commercial. . . . The filmmakers copped out. (¶ 5)

When mainstream images of BDSM appear, in the end, too safe, they provoke disappointment masquerading as boredom. *Secretary* reviewers wrote that it was "a real bore" (Rodriguez, 2002, ¶ 1), "crushingly mundane" (LaSalle, 2002, p. D-5), and "deeply conventional" (Rainier, 2002, ¶ 5). "It's just rather boring . . . considering its plot revolves around sadomasochism" (Brunt, 2002, ¶ 4). *The San Francisco Chronicle*'s review of the movie began:

> The movie, radiant with self-satisfaction, seems to have been intended as a provocation and as a daring exploration of sexuality. But it gets tripped up on two points: It provokes nothing but yawns, and the sex it explores is stuff everybody knows about and says, 'so what?' (LaSalle, 2002, p. D-5)

The main issue here seems to be that it "should have been a lot riskier, given its subject matter" (Rainer, 2002, ¶ 5), that it was, "pretty tame, more sweet than salacious" (Dargis, 2002, p. 17), and that it was not "even titillating" (Oppenheimer, 2002, ¶ 6). This is the mechanism of boredom qua disappointment: When BDSM appears so closely bound to mainstream, consumer capitalism, it disappoints those hoping for edgy titillation. As the U.S. popular cultural landscape becomes increasingly beholden to sex-as-spectacle, sex-as-consumption, these mainstream representations will always fail. SM promises a taste of something real and authentic, something deep and satisfying, and when these representations dissatisfy (as, of course, they must), viewers experience boredom.

The lame, domestic, too safe version of kink presented in *Secretary* is disappointing because viewers want to see something dangerous, something transgressive, and something outside the machinations of normativity. It is disappointing, even boring, when these representations fail, when instead of something real, authentic, undisciplined, and nonconsumptive, viewers are stuck with a story about two lovers, mass marketed imagery, entomologized perverts, or other mainstreamed versions of fully-commodified, controlled, and disciplined selves. Yet the desire to see something really other can also be read as transgressive; after all, this desire is also a desire to experience something that would blur, uproot, or unfix the boundaries between normal and not normal. Even as increased representation provides avenues for increased stigmatization, the desire to see something else carries political potential.

IN CONCLUSION:
THE POTENTIAL OF DESIRE

There is no question that mainstream representations of BDSM have increased dramatically, spreading further and further into popular culture. Instead of challenging systems of sexual privilege and power, mainstream representations of SM (both normalizing and pathologizing) reinforce the normativity of the distanced viewing subject. SM promises a fantasy of kinkiness that can titillate the viewer-citizen out of the banal and lifeless existence of socially compliant bodies, while at the same time it serves as a limit against which a normal, vanilla, procreative, heterosexual, and suburban sexuality is defined.

Yet as long as American culture remains ideologically bound to a vision of sexuality that privileges heterosexual, monogamous marriage, that simultaneously disavows and persecutes sexual minorities, and that rigorously attempts to strengthen boundaries between normal and not normal, it is imperative to find ways to contest this vision. As activists, researchers, and advocates, we cannot pin political hope on valorizing positive representations of SM; this argument denies the dangers of surveillance, disciplining, normalizing, and pathologizing documented in this article. Instead, we might return to the emotional aftermath of this distanced consumption, to that feeling of letdown when the other appears so neatly displayed within a clean, commercial field.

As SM becomes more mainstream, the desire for something real, raw, and hard grows. This desire is elusive; it reveals itself when viewers are left feeling hollow and empty, disappointed that they were not sufficiently shocked or turned on (or, ideally, both). This disappointment points to the fantasy the mainstream public continues to treasure: There is something *else*, something more, something that is really real, that is really authentic. Abby struggled with this feeling that BDSM is always something that cannot be represented in mass media like *Secretary*:

A: I feel like it just nicked the surface of it. Because there wasn't any–it didn't really deal with SM that much. Like, I feel like the producers and directors went as far as they could in our society, but they didn't go fully into it.

MW: What was missing?

A: Um. I don't know, maybe just more explicit? Like I feel like this was one of those . . . like they just sort of had a kinky relationship, it wasn't like full-blown SM, it was just like, I just think they did a lot of role playing, like he was the dominating one and she was like the one who liked to get humiliated and liked to be his little slave and stuff, which you know, definitely is a part of SM, but I don't know. I don't know.

MW: Is it because it's about power and not pain, bondage, black leather?

A: No. The power thing, I mean that's what SM is all about. I mean it really did show [that] I don't know because you don't need the toys and the bondage and you don't need to be wearing black leather to really be SM. I don't know. I feel like the movie was kind of safe.

In this way, SM can never *really* be mainstreamed, because there will always seem to be a bit that remains out there, just out of reach. In the context of critical reception of Madonna's *Sex* (1992), Champagne (1993) described, "the continued difficulty of recuperating the impure and filthy heterogeneity of male homosexuality for an elevated, capitalist consumption" because even for Madonna, there is something a little "gross" about being gay (p. 138). It is this heterogeneity, this dirtiness, and this taint that remains even as SM becomes more clearly positioned within the mainstream. This taint marks the ways SM continues to signify contradictory desires for authenticity, for realness, for the meaningful transgression of social norms and docile, mapped-out bodies. Mainstream representations of SM embody always-excessive desires, and these desires protect its disruptive potential even as SM moves into the circle of the mainstream. Late-capitalism works by inciting and capitalizing on these desires, yet it can never control the emotional effect of this excess.

The respondents and reviewers chronicled in this text are reaching for the out-there, the uncontained, and it is in this reaching that political potential lies. Using the language of disappointment, they are protesting the failure of transgression, decrying the ways sexual strangeness is disciplined out of existence. I find their disappointment hopeful; it suggests that, even as the state dedicates itself to policing and marginalizing alternative sexualities, even as the popular landscape becomes more sensationalistic and media-driven, even as sexuality becomes increasingly bound to consumption, there is nascent protest against these constraints. The mainstream public documented here continues to look to BDSM as an inspiration for norm violation, a location that promises an attack on borders, boundaries, and closed-down options. They want something harder or realer, something that could jolt the viewer out of a complacent, easy, defined, consumptive world. They want something truly outside, disobedient, and undisciplined; something that can break the rules and transgress the bounds; something hard enough to leave marks. Although it is unclear whether mainstream media representations can ever satisfy these desires, the desire itself retains potential.

REFERENCES

Allison, A. (2001). Memoirs of the Orient. *Journal of Japanese Studies, 27*, 381-398.

Ansen, D. (2002, October 7). Hostile work environment [Review of the motion picture *Secretary*; electronic version]. *Newsweek*, 70.

Baudrillard, J. (1988). *America* (C. Turner, Trans.). New York: Verso. (Original work published 1986)

Bienvenu, R. V., II. (1998). The development of sadomasochism as a cultural style in the twentieth-century United States (Doctoral dissertation, Indiana University, 1998). Retrieved May 10, 2003, from http://www.americanfetish.net/NFHome.html

Box office data for Secretary. (n.d.). Retrieved May 10, 2003, from http://www.the-numbers.com/movies/2002/SCTRY.html

Brunt, C. (2002, September 20). Quirky 'Secretary' doesn't entertain [Review of the motion picture *Secretary*]. *The Daily Cougar, 68*. Retrieved May 10, 2003, from http://www.stp.uh.edu/vol68/19/arts/arts1.html

Burr, T. (2002, September 27). S&M gets tender, amusing twist in 'Secretary' [Review of the motion picture *Secretary*; electronic version]. *The Boston Globe*, p. C-1.

Califia, P. (1994). *Public sex: The culture of radical sex*. Pittsburgh, PA: Cleis Press.

Champagne, J. (1993). Stabat Madonna. In L. Frank & P. Smith (Eds.), *Madonnarama: Essays on sex and popular culture* (pp. 111-138). Pittsburgh, PA: Cleis Press.

Champagne, J. (1995). *The ethics of marginality: A new approach to gay studies*. Minneapolis: University of Minnesota Press.

Cramsey, D. (Producer). (2002). Maine: Joseph Drive [Television series episode]. In D. Cramsey (Producer), *Trading spaces*. Maine: The Learning Channel.

Dargis, M. (2002, September 20). In buoyant 'Secretary,' romance for consenting adults [Review of the motion picture *Secretary*; electronic version]. *Los Angeles Times*, p. 17.

Dick, K. (Director/Producer). (1997). *Sick: The life and death of Bob Flanagan, supermasochist* [Motion picture]. United States: Kirby Dick Productions.

Ebert, R. (2002, September 27). 'Secretary' handles delicate matter skillfully [Review of the motion picture *Secretary*; electronic version]. *Chicago Sun-Times*, p. 31.

Edelstein, D. (Reviewer). (2002a). New film 'Secretary' [Audio review of the motion picture *Secretary*]. *Fresh Air with Terry Gross*, National Public Radio, airdate September 20, 2002.

Edelstein, D. (2002b, September 20). Spanking good time [Review of the motion picture *Secretary*]. *Slate Magazine*. Retrieved May 10, 2003, from http://slate.msn.com/id/2071275.

Falk, G., & Weinberg, T. S. (1983). Sadomasochism and popular Western culture. In T. S. Weinberg & G. Levi Kamel (Eds.), *S&M: Studies in sadomasochism* (pp. 137-144). Amherst, NY: Prometheus Books.

Foucault, M. (1990). *The history of sexuality. Volume one: An introduction* (R. Hurley, Trans.). New York: Vintage Books. (Original work published 1978)

Foucault, M. (1995). *Discipline and punish: The birth of the prison* (A. Sheridan, Trans.). New York: Vintage Books. (Original work published 1977)

Fox, K. (n.d.) Under my thumb [Review of the motion picture *Secretary*]. *TV Guide Online*. Retrieved May 10, 2003, from http://www.tvguide.com/movies/database/ShowMovie.asp?MI=44007

Fuchs, C. (2002, September 26). Giving in [Review of the motion picture *Secretary*]. *PopMatters*. Retrieved May 10, 2003, from http://popmatters.com/film/reviews/s/secretary.shtml

Gamson, J. (1998). *Freaks talk back: Tabloid talk shows and sexual nonconformity.* Chicago: University of Chicago Press.

Gómez-Peña, G. (2001). Somewhere between corporate multiculturalism and the mainstream bizarre. *TDR, 45,* 7-30.

Haberman, L. (2003, January 31). Joe's "dirty soled" girl comes clean. *E! Online News*. Retrieved May 10, 2003, from http://www.eonline.com/News/Items/0,1,11217,00.html

Hannigan, J. (1998). *Fantasy city: Pleasure and profit in the postmodern metropolis.* New York: Routledge.

Hebdige, D. (1979). *Subculture: The meaning of style.* London: Routledge.

Herschlag, A. (Writer), & Burrows, J. (Director). (2001). Cheaters [Television series episode]. In J. Burrows (Producer). *Will & Grace.* Studio City, CA: NBC.

hooks, b. (1992). *Black looks: Race and representation.* Boston: South End Press.

Jackson, J. (1997). Rope burn. On *The velvet rope* [CD]. New York: Virgin Records.

Jameson, F. (1991). *Postmodernism, or, the cultural logic of late capitalism.* Durham, NC: Duke University Press.

Kaufman, P. (Director/Producer). (2002). *Quills* [Motion picture]. United States: Fox Searchlight.

Kurland, S. (Writer), & Bonerz, P. (Director). (1997). The one with the 'cuffs [Television series episode]. In M. Kauffman & D. Crane (Creators/Producers), *Friends.* Burbank, CA: NBC.

LaSalle, M. (2002, September 27). Also opening today [Review of the motion picture *Secretary*; electronic version]. *The San Francisco Chronicle*, p. D-5.

Lauerman, K. (2002, December 4). A taste of the whip for Saddam. *Salon.* Retrieved May 10, 2003, from http://www.salon.com/news/feature/2002/12/03/un_sm/index_np.html

Lowe, D. M. (1995). *The body in late-capitalist USA*. Durham, NC: Duke University Press.

Marech, R. (2001, October 19). Greenery Press specializes in off-color topics. *San Francisco Chronicle*, p. EB-3.

Marin, R. (1997-1998, December 29-January 5). Lick me, flog me, buy me! The mainstreaming of S&M has turned us into a jaded culture of kink. *Newsweek, 131*, 85.

Marshall, G. (Director). (1994). *Exit to Eden* [Motion picture]. United States: Savoy Pictures.

Moser, C., & Kleinplatz, P. (2005). *DSM-IV-TR and the paraphilias: An argument for removal. Journal of Psychology & Human Sexuality, 17(3/4)*, 91-109.

Mozzocco, J. C. (2002, October 10). The ties that bind. *Columbus Alive!* Retrieved May 10, 2003, from http://www.columbusalive.com/2002/20021010/

Neufeld, M. (Producer), & West, S. (Director). (1999). *The general's daughter* [Motion picture]. United States: Paramount Pictures.

Nine Inch Nails. (1989). Head like a hole. On *Pretty hate machine* [CD]. New York: TVT Records.

Oppenheimer, J. (2002, September 19). Type caste [Review of the motion picture *Secretary*]. *New Times Los Angeles*. Retrieved May 10, 2003, from LexisNexis database.

Puddle of Mudd. (2001). Control. On *Come clean* [CD]. North Hollywood, CA: Geffen Records.

Rainer, P. (2002, September 23). Girls gone wild [Review of the motion picture *Secretary*]. *New York Magazine, 35*, 60-61. Retrieved May 10, 2003, from http://www.newyorkmetro.com/nymetro/movies/reviews/n_7702/

Rodriguez, R. (2002, September 27). Secretary [Review of the motion picture *Secretary*]. *The Miami Herald*. Retrieved May 10, 2003, from LexisNexis database.

Rubin, G. (1993). Thinking sex: Notes for a radical theory of the politics of sexuality. In H. Abelove, M. A. Barale, & D. Halperin (Eds.), *The gay and lesbian studies reader* (pp. 3-44). New York: Routledge. (Original work published 1984)

Schumacher, J. (Director/Producer). (1999). *8mm* [Motion picture]. United States: Columbia Tri-Star.

Shainberg, S. (Director/Writer/Producer). (2002). *Secretary* [Motion picture]. United States: Lion's Gate Films.

Shanahan, L. (2003, February 3). Designated shopper [electronic version]. *Brandweek, 44(5)*, 38.

Shepherd, J. (2002, October 9-15). A spanking a day [Review of the motion picture *Secretary*]. *The Portland Mercury, 3*. Retrieved May 10, 2003, from http://www.portlandmercury.com/2002-10-09/film2.html

Singer, L. (1993). *Erotic welfare: Sexual theory and politics in the age of epidemic*. New York: Routledge.

Spears, B. (2001). I'm a slave 4 U. On *Britney* [CD]. New York: Jive Records.

Steele, V. (1996). *Fetish: Fashion, sex, and power*. Oxford, England: Oxford University Press.

Steyn, M. (2002, December 2). The UN's foray into Saddamasochism [electronic version]. *National Post*, p. A14.

Sutton, T. (2002, October 2). Then & then [Review of the motion picture *Secretary*]. *Citypages, 23*. Retrieved May 10, 2003, from http://www.citypages.com/ databank/ 23/1139/article10747.asp

Thompson, M. (Ed.). (1991). *Leatherfolk: Radical sex, people, politics, and practice.* Boston: Alyson Press.

Trebay, G. (1997, November 11). No pain, no gain: The mainstreaming of kink. *The Village Voice*, p. 32.

Trebay, G. (2000, October 31). A detour into naughty for last season's nice girls. *The New York Times*, p. B-12.

Wachowski, A., & Wachowski, L. (Directors/Writers). (1999). *The matrix* [Motion picture]. United States: Warner Brothers.

Weinberg, M., Williams, C., & Moser, C. (1984). The social constituents of sadomasochism. *Social Problems, 31*, 379-389.

Weinberg, T. S., (Ed.). (1995). *S&M: Studies in sadomasochism* (Rev. ed.). Amherst, NY: Prometheus Books.

Weinberg, T. S., & Magill, M. S. (1995). Sadomasochistic themes in mainstream culture. In T. S. Weinberg (Ed.), *S&M: Studies in sadomasochism* (Rev. ed., pp. 223-230). Amherst, NY: Prometheus Books.

Weiskind, R. (2002, October 11). Bossed around: 'Secretary' is an odd, dark comedy about sexual dominance [Review of the motion picture *Secretary*; electronic version]. *Pittsburgh Post-Gazette*, p. 27.

Wloszczyna, S. (2002, September 27). For Gyllenhaal, no pain means no gain [Review of the motion picture *Secretary*; electronic version]. *USA TODAY*, p. 14D.

Zacharek, S. (2002, September 19). Secretary [Review of the motion picture *Secretary*]. *Salon.com*. Retrieved May 10, 2003, from http://archive.salon.com/ent/ movies/review/2002/09/20/secretary/

Understanding Sadomasochism:
An Empirical Examination
of Four Perspectives

Patricia A. Cross, PhD

Carleton University

Kim Matheson, PhD

Carleton University

SUMMARY. Three studies assessed current understandings of sado-masochism (SM). In Study 1 questionnaires testing four academic views of SM were administered to individuals who self-defined as involved in SM. The psychoanalytic, psychopathology/medical model, radical feminist and escape-from-self perspectives were not supported. Study 2 examined "virtual" sadomasochism as a source of information about sadomasochists in the real life world. Cluster analyses indicated that real-life and virtual sadomasochists share unique sexual proclivities. Study 3 examined an alternative view that identifies power as the commodity of importance in SM play. Content analysis of online SM encounters indicated that both "top" and "bottom" role-players used

Patricia A. Cross and Kim Matheson are affiliated with Carleton University, Ottawa, Ontario, Canada. Correspondence may be addressed: Patricia A. Cross, 44 Merriman Street #1, Rochester, NY USA 14607 (E-mail: patriciacross@hotmail.com).

[Haworth co-indexing entry note]: "Understanding Sadomasochism: An Empirical Examination of Four Perspectives." Cross, Patricia A., and Kim Matheson. Co-published simultaneously in *Journal of Homosexuality* (Harrington Park Press, an imprint of The Haworth Press, Inc.) Vol. 50, No. 2/3, 2006, pp. 133-166; and: *Sadomasochism: Powerful Pleasures* (ed: Peggy J. Kleinplatz, and Charles Moser) Harrington Park Press, an imprint of The Haworth Press, Inc., 2006, pp. 133-166. Single or multiple copies of this article are available for a fee from The Haworth Document Delivery Service [1-800-HAWORTH, 9:00 a.m. - 5:00 p.m. (EST). E-mail address: docdelivery@haworthpress.com].

several specific techniques to create a power differential. These studies suggest that, contrary to many academic theories, power, and not the giving and receiving of pain, is at the core of SM. *[Article copies available for a fee from The Haworth Document Delivery Service: 1-800-HAWORTH. E-mail address: <docdelivery@haworthpress.com> Website: <http://www.HaworthPress.com> © 2006 by The Haworth Press, Inc. All rights reserved.]*

KEYWORDS. Sadomasochism, escape-from-self, role-play, power, SM

Sadomasochism (SM) presents us with an apparent paradox: How is it that the pursuit of sensual pleasure can become intimately connected with physical and psychological pain? Is this, as current perspectives contend, the domain of the mentally ill, the misogynistic, the neurotic? The usefulness of current academic theories to understand SM, which focus on pain as central to the phenomenon, has been called into question by SM participants themselves, who offer a different perspective on what their activities mean and why they engage in them. The purpose of this research was to assess the major academic perspectives, and explore an alternate conceptualization provided by those who practise SM.

CURRENT UNDERSTANDINGS OF SM

Current scholarly viewpoints on SM can be broken down into two general orientations: those perspectives that regard SM as evidence of individual pathology–that is, disease, maladjustment, or congenital defects (the medical and psychoanalytic models belong here), and those seeking to explain SM by reference to cultural and social context (the gender inequities and escape from self-awareness viewpoints belong here). A third perspective, emerging not from academia but from the world of SM participants themselves, defines SM as highly ritualized, mutually enjoyable role-play, in which pain is emblematic of power or powerlessness, rather than being sought for its own sake.

Medical/Psychoanalytic Perceptions of SM

Despite their differences, psychoanalytic and medical theorists agree that SM is symptomatic of sickness or maladjustment. For example,

Freud (1906/1953) explained masochism as a maladaptive transmuta-
tion of the death instinct, and saw sadism as evidence for a weak superego and ego, resulting in the id being permitted to find expression in
sexual violence. Krafft-Ebing (1886/1965), the father of scientific medical inquiry into SM, suggested that sadomasochism is a congenital disorder, rather like hermaphroditism. These conceptualizations are clear
in their message that sadomasochism is associated with inferior health,
inferior adaptation, or inferior maturation.

Specifically, the psychoanalytic perspective argues that those who
actively seek pain in a sexual context do so because of feelings of shame
and guilt that must be satisfied (Charme, 1983; Freud, 1924/1961;
Price, 1983). The association in SM of punishment and immobilization
with sexual activity creates an illusion of non-consent, placating the superego's strictures against actively seeking sexual pleasure. The pain
desired by the masochist provides the punishment demanded by the superego as payment for sexual pleasure. As for the sadists, their need to
act out sadistic fantasies is seen as a reflection of a weak or nonexistent
superego or an ineffectual ego, permitting the id too much free reign
(Freud, 1900/1954). Thrill-seeking, impulsive behaviors are therefore
typical of these id-driven individuals.

The *DSM-IV-TR* (American Psychiatric Association [APA], 2000)
lists Sexual Sadism and Sexual Masochism as sexual disorders. Their
inclusion as paraphilias is a clear indication that bondage, pain, and humiliation in the context of sexual pleasure is regarded by mainstream
psychiatry and clinical psychology as indicative of illness or mental disorder. The diagnostic criteria require, at a minimum, simply having
SM-related fantasies that cause some concern. It is not uncommon in
the psychiatric literature to see sadomasochism linked with such antisocial behaviors as rape and murder (e.g., Ehm & Patrick, 1995; Gratzer &
Bradford, 1995). Thus sadists may be seen as psychopathic would-be
rapists or killers, and masochists as suffering from a severe mental disorder resulting in a desire for self-harm.

Social/Context-Based Perceptions

The radical feminist view. While not all feminists share this perspective, some from the radical feminist camp regard SM as fundamentally
misogynistic (Bar-On, 1982; Butler, 1982). Adherents of this view argue that SM borrows its script from the patriarchal framework of Western culture, in which women are frequently subject to violence and
injustice at the hands of men. Thus endorsement of sadomasochistic

sexuality is seen as necessarily anti-feminist and misogynistic, even in situations in which a man is submitting to a woman. They argue that the enjoyment of the degradation and torture associated with sadomasochistic sex, regardless of who is submitting to whom, inevitably indicates an over-arching acceptance of patriarchal dogma, from whence, they argue, all notions of domination and submission ultimately derive.

Escape-from-self. A perspective that has emerged out of Baumeister's (1988, 1989) social psychological interpretation of the concept of selfhood argues that masochism provides a temporary and powerful escape from higher-level self-awareness. Baumeister (1988) describes several aspects of selfhood which make masochism seem, at first, like paradoxical behavior. Since the self develops in order to facilitate the organism's quest for happiness and avoidance of suffering, it is oriented towards controlling the environment, and towards perceiving itself as having control. The self also strives to maintain a positive evaluation, both in others' eyes and in its own. Masochism seems to challenge these functions. Whereas the self seeks to avoid suffering, masochists seek it out. Whereas the self strives for control, masochists apparently relinquish it. Whereas the self seeks to maintain and increase esteem, masochists seek humiliation. Thus masochism represents a systematic attempt to temporarily eradicate the main features of the self. Why would some people wish to do this?

Baumeister (1988) asserts that selfhood can become burdensome at times. Sometimes people enjoy self-awareness, but sometimes they may wish to escape and avoid it (e.g., after experiencing an interpersonal rejection [Gibbons & Wicklund, 1976]). Desire to escape from self- awareness has been linked to the use of several commonly available drugs such as alcohol and tobacco (e.g., Hull, 1981; Hull & Young, 1983; Wicklund, 1975). It is also plausible that escape from self-awareness is an underlying goal in other recreational activities, such as spectator sports, watching movies, and reading novels (Baumeister, 1988).

A successful self in particular may become emotionally draining (Jones & Bergals, 1978); thus it makes sense that successful people in particular might occasionally seek to escape from self-awareness. High levels of esteem and responsibility produce the most complex and elaborate selves, which may be the most burdensome selves. As a result, Baumeister says, such individuals may seek the strongest modes of escape, one of which may be sexual masochism.

Baumeister (1988, 1989) also asserts that since masochists are far more plentiful than sadists, a great number of so-called "sadists" are in fact masochists who have had to learn to be flexible until such time as they get their turn at playing the submissive role. It is not the case, though, that preference for the sadistic role does not exist. There are people who genuinely prefer this role, though they are not as common as those who prefer the masochistic role.

Baumeister (1988, 1989) speculates that those few who do prefer the sadistic role may be doing so not out of a need to escape the self, but out of a need to bolster the self-concept. The sadistic role provides for an enhanced high-level self-awareness, in that the individual actively controls the scene and actively takes measures to avoid injury to the masochist. Thus there is no opportunity to slip into a lower level of self-awareness for the sadist. What is possible, though, is an awareness of self that is enhanced by the dynamics of the scene. Feelings of potency, of power, and of control are experienced by the sadist because within the scene he or she embodies these characteristics and is treated as though he/she was in fact such a formidable individual. In this way, the role might appeal to those for whom such elements are lacking in their everyday self-concepts. Thus, according to this perspective, sadists may require a nurturing of a precarious sense of self, and a reinforcement of notions of personal power and authority.

SM-centered perspective. Some who participate in SM activities argue that SM is best understood as an eroticized, consensual exchange of power (Califia, 1983). They say that, contrary to popular belief, SM is not about the infliction of pain per se (Califia, 1983). Rather, pain is one of many techniques that help delineate power and status, and it is the experience of a power differential that is sought.

OVERVIEW OF THE PRESENT INVESTIGATION

Study 1

Our first study was aimed at assessing the current academic perspectives, specifically the psychoanalytic, psychopathological, radical feminist, and escape from self views. We obtained our sample of self-defined SM participants through postings on sadomasochism-related Internet news groups (e.g., alt.personals.spanking, alt.sex.bondage). Interested individuals contacted us via e-mail. This technique can be especially useful when seeking members of unusual or reticent groups, as is the case with sadomasochists. In this way, we were able to simultaneously reach a large number of potential research participants from numerous countries, and ended up with a relatively large sample size for studies in this area. Specifically, our sample of N = 93 sadomasochists, while not large by normal standards, was substantially bigger than the sample sizes of numerous studies in this area, many of which are case studies involving only a few individuals (e.g., Awad, 2000; Bader, 1993; Fakhry, 1997; Gagnier & Robertiello, 1993; Lerner, 2001; Panter, 1999; Sandnabba et al., 2002; Seelig & Person, 1991; Taylor & Ussher, 2001; Weille, 2002). Those studies with comparable sample sizes to ours tended to involve only sadomasochists who were members of SM clubs (e.g., Alison et al., 2001; Houlberg, 1991; Spengler, 1977), while ours did not have that limitation. We also obtained a sample of non-sadomasochists for comparison purposes by soliciting their participation on non-SM-related online bulletin boards (e.g., soc.singles, alt.romance.adult). All our participants completed a battery of psychometric measures, sent either in electronic or hard-copy format, that had been selected to put the academic theories to the test.

Studies 2 and 3

As a follow-up, we then sought to examine the alternative perspective put forth by SM practitioners that sadomasochism is primarily about power, and not pain. To do this, we wanted to observe SM activities in progress so as to analyze the importance of power and the means by which it is exercised, implemented and controlled. However, obtaining access to SM interactions in progress proved to be difficult. To get around this, we took advantage of the fact that SM activities take place not only in private clubs and individuals' bedrooms, but also in Internet SM chat rooms. A number of such online venues for the exploration of SM were available; their existence seemed ideal for the observation of sadomasochistic interchanges. These online "dungeons," as they are sometimes called, provide an opportunity for individuals to explore sadomasochistic activities in a relatively nonthreatening "virtual" environment. They differ from online bulletin boards or news groups, in that while these provide a forum for the exchange of ideas and the discussion of issues surrounding SM, the dungeons provide a venue for its practise, albeit virtual.

Clearly, online SM and real-life SM have some important differences. The fact that the online experience is text-based while real-life SM is not suggests that the "virtual" version may not be as intense or as visceral as the real thing. Further, since online participants can terminate the session at any time by simply logging out, it is not clear that submission and powerlessness, or domination and powerfulness, are experienced to the same degree or in the same way as with real-life encounters. However, if one construes the virtual SM encounter as an interactive sadomasochistic fantasy, then there is every reason to expect that the contents of these scenes can reveal much about what sadomasochists want and enjoy. As well, it makes sense that these virtual scenes can allow us a glimpse into how these goals are negotiated and communicated to one's partner. Such negotiations also have to take place in real-life SM, as two individuals work together to create a mutually satisfying encounter. Therefore, we were optimistic that an analysis of virtual SM activities would prove to be a valuable source of information about real-life SM.

To justify this hunch, we sought to establish that the sexual tastes of real-life and virtual sadomasochists are in fact similar. Study 2, then, was a comparison of the sexual proclivities of virtual and real-life sadomasochists with those of non-sadomasochists, including people who enjoy other types of online role-playing, in an effort to determine if virtual sadomasochists are sufficiently comparable with real-life sadomasochists to justify their use for research purposes.

It was only once this similarity was established that Study 3, the observation of several real-time, online SM encounters, was then conducted. These encounters were analyzed for clues as to the importance of power in SM scenes, and the means by which it is manipulated.

STUDY 1

Method

Participants and procedure. The SM group (N = 93) was solicited through postings on sex-related Internet news groups. In the sample, 27 self-identified as sadists (21 males, 6 females), 34 as masochists (26 males, 8 females), and 32 as switches (i.e., willing to adopt either role) (22 males, 10 females). We obtained a non-SM comparison group (N = 61, consisting of 46 males and 15 females) from postings on non-sex-related Internet news groups. The average age of participants did not differ by group (M = 35.03, SD = 11.72). All participants responded via e-mail and were sent the package of questionnaires, along with an informed consent form, either through regular mail or as attachments via e-mail. The informed consent form included information about the purpose of the research, the task requirements, including a warning concerning the frank sexual content of some questionnaires, the researchers' commitment to safeguarding participants' anonymity and confidentiality, and participants' right to withdraw at any time. Participants were not paid for their participation. Participation time averaged approximately two hours. All participants were sent a debriefing letter via e-mail or via regular mail after we received their completed packages, which included the researchers' reasons for using a sample solicited via the Internet, a description of the theories being evaluated, and contact information.

Sexual behaviors. Numerous measures were selected or created by the authors to test the validity of current academic views on SM. The Sexual Behaviours Inventory (SBI) (available from the authors) was constructed to assess participants' sexual activities and proclivities, sexual guilt, and judgments as to the morality of various sexual behaviors. These were variables that were important to our assessment of the Escape-from-Self and Psychoanalytic theories. We also piloted an early version of the inventory with a small sample of sadomasochists (N = 10) solicited online, who were asked whether any items ought to be added, removed, or altered. Based on their input, some minor changes were made, resulting in the 79 items that currently make up the instrument.

With this questionnaire, participants were asked to rate the extent to which they engaged in, wanted to engage in, and the morality of a variety of sexual behaviors, ranging from "deep kissing" to "being heavily whipped." Using this information, measures of SM and mainstream sexual behaviors and proclivities were obtained. By counting the number of activities that the participant indicated engaging in or wanting to engage in, but which he/she also considered morally wrong, a "sexual guilt" scale could be constructed. Factor analysis indicated nine factors, providing information on experiences, desires, and disapproval of submissive acts, dominant acts, and non-SM sexual acts. These measures were found to have good internal reliability with the current sample, from $r = .76$ to $r = .93$.

A number of other established inventories and questionnaires were selected to assess the various theories. All measures not constructed by the authors had been shown in previous research to be valid tools. These measures, comprising our battery of questionnaires, are presented here as they pertained to each theory under scrutiny.

Psychopathology view. The Psychopathology perspective suggests that the desire for self-harm reflects significant mental disorder in masochists. To test this concept, we included several measures of psychopathology in our battery: The Stress subscale of the Differential Personality Questionnaire (DPQ) (Tellegen, 1976); the Neuroticism subscale of the Eysenck Personality Inventory (EPI) (Eysenck, 1964); the Symptom Checklist-90 (Revised) (SCL-90-R) (Derogatis, 1983) which yields measures of somatic complaints, interpersonal sensitivity, anxiety, hostility, and psychoticism; the Dissociative Experiences Scale (Carlson & Putnam, 1993); and the Rosenberg Self-Esteem Scale (RSES) (Rosenberg, 1965).

This view also argues that sadism is associated with Antisocial Personality Disorder. To test this, we included the Social Personality Inventory (SPI) (Hill & Wong, 1995), which measures psychopathy. We also included the Social Potency and Authoritarianism subscales of the DPQ (Tellegen, 1976), which provide measures of social dominance, and interpersonal aggressiveness, traits related to psychopathy.

These measures were found to have good internal reliability with our sample, ranging from $\alpha = .75$ to $\alpha = .91$.

Psychoanalytic view. Given that this perspective views masochism as reflecting sexual guilt, we sought to measure this construct with the Sexual Guilt scale from the SBI, reasoning that if the psychoanalysts are correct, then masochists would score higher on it than others. This measure was found to have high internal reliability with our sample, $\alpha = .95$. Further, given that the psychoanalytic view sees sadism as reflecting an id-driven personality, we sought to assess this with several measures, including our psychopathy tool (SPI). Psychopathy is understood by psychoanalysts as being the result of an unconstrained id (Dorr & Woodhall, 1986; Kegan, 1986; Newcomb & McGee, 1991). Thus according to this view the presence of psychopathic behaviors is consistent with the id-driven tendencies of the sexual sadist. This tool was also used as part of our assessment of the psychopathology hypothesis, as its results can be interpreted as either reflecting psychopathy, or, in the case of the psychoanalytic perspective, reflecting id-driven behaviors. We also included a measure of thrill-seeking with the Danger-Seeking subscale of the DPQ, reasoning that id-driven individuals, being more likely to engage in impulsive reckless acts, ought to score higher on this measure than others. This subscale demonstrated good internal reliability with our sample, $\alpha = .78$.

Radical feminist view. Given that some radical feminists see SM as inherently misogynistic and indicative of a wholesale acceptance of patriarchal values, we sought to test this by obtaining measures of feminist attitudes versus endorsement of traditional gender roles. We combined the Feminist Attitudes Scale (Matheson, 1996) and the Spanos Attitudes Towards Women Scale (Spanos & Dubreuil, 1991) to yield a single measure reflecting feminist attitudes. We reasoned that if the radical feminists were correct, then those who engage in SM would be less likely to endorse feminist beliefs than non-sadomasochists. Both of these questionnaires demonstrated high internal reliability with our sample (α = .90 for both).

Escape-from-self view. This theory sees masochism as a means of escaping a burdensome sense of self. To test this, we included several measures of escapism, reasoning that such individuals would likely seek more than one method for escaping their burdensome self-identity. These measures included the Danger-Seeking subscale of the DPQ (also relevant to the psychoanalytic perspective, above). We reasoned that if masochistic activity is sought because of its ability to reduce awareness to the here-and-now, as Baumeister (1988, 1989) suggests, then so should activities from this subscale, like skydiving, being near a volcano when it erupts, etc. We also included the Role-Play Inventory (RPI) (Fletcher & Averill, 1984), which provides a measure of role-playing proclivity. Role-playing is an activity that provides for a temporary release from normal identity, and so should be attractive to masochists, if Baumeister is correct. For the same reason we included the following scales: the Day-Dream Scale from the Imaginal Processes Inventory (IPI) (Singer & Antrobus, 1970), which provides a measure of fantasy proclivity, indicative of a capacity to "escape" into fantasies, a much-valued skill for those seeking to escape the burden of selfhood; the Inventory of Childhood Memories and Imaginings (ICMI) (Wilson & Barber, 1987) as an alternate convergent measure of the propensity to get lost in fantasy; self-report information regarding the use of recreational drugs (the Drug-Use Inventory, available from the authors), as this represented another obvious means by which one might seek escape from the burden of one's self-identity.

This theory also argues that masochists have especially burdensome selves, due to stressful interpersonal and professional roles, and the fact that they feel responsible for outcomes in their lives. Consequently, they typically have a need to be in control, an urge which they periodically must escape from via activities such as sexual masochism. Several measures were included to assess this idea: The Desirability of Control Inventory (DCI) measures enjoyment of situations in which the respondent is in control (e.g., "I enjoy being able to influence the actions of others"). We also included the Locus of Control Scale (LOC) (Rotter, 1957), reasoning that if Baumeister were correct, then masochists would be more likely to have internal loci of control, reflecting the belief that they are responsible for outcomes in their lives.

The escape-from-self perspective on sadism argues that most sadists are in fact masochists waiting to take their turns at submission. To test this, we used the Submissive Proclivities Factor from the SBI to assess whether our sample of sadists in fact indicated a desire to engage in submissive activities.

This view also asserts that those few sadists who genuinely enjoy the sadistic role seek out the experience of power and authority that sadomasochism provides for them because they do not have such experiences in real life. Thus one would expect that sadists would be more likely to hold lower-status jobs or to be unemployed. Therefore we included an item in our demographics questionnaire asking about their level of employment.

Results

Demographic findings. In addition to standard questions about age, sex, and marital status, the demographics questionnaire also sought information about sexual orientation, current employment status, and sexual history, including the number of sex partners one has had. With these results we were able to construct a tentative sexual profile of our participants.

Sexual profile. Participants were categorized as being seriously involved (i.e., married, living together, seriously dating, or engaged) or uninvolved (i.e., single and not seriously dating, or divorced/separated/widowed and not seriously dating). A chi-square analysis on relationship status was significant, χ^2 (3) = 7.75, $p < .05$. In our sample, 70.4% of the sadists (n = 19) and 76.5% of the masochists (n = 26) reported being involved, in comparison to the Internet comparison group in which 50.0% (n = 30) reported being involved. However, since many of our comparison group participants were solicited from dating news groups and bulletin boards, it is not clear that this finding reflects genuine differences between sadomasochists and non-sadomasochists generally.

Sexual orientation was evaluated in terms of whether participants self-defined as exclusively heterosexual or bisexual/homosexual. (We were unable to use a more sensitive categorization because we would have had too many cells with expected values of less than 5.) A chi-square analysis was significant, χ^2 (3) = 16.29, $p < .001$, in that SM participants were overall more likely than non-SM respondents to report bisexual/homosexual orientations. Specifically, 37.0% of the sadists and 47.1% of the masochists, and 67.6% of the switches and only 18.1% of the control group indicated a non-strictly heterosexual orientation.

It was left up to the participants to define for themselves what constitutes a sexual partner. The sadists, for example, reported numbers from 1 to 1000 sexual partners ($M = 79.3$, $SD = 200.8$). Thus the mean score did not adequately describe this widely distributed set of responses. Overall sadomasochists reported having had more sexual partners than did the non-SM group. Specifically, sadists (44.0%, n = 11), masochists (38.2%, n = 13) and switches (37.5%, n = 12) all reported more than 15 sexual partners in their lives, in comparison to the group (21.3%, n = 13).

In sum, the sadomasochists in our sample were relatively more likely to be in ongoing relationships than our comparison group, relatively more likely to report bisexual or homosexual proclivities, and tended to report more partners in their sexual histories than the comparison group. Taken together, a tentative picture emerges of our s/m sample as individuals whose sexual experiences and tastes in sexual partners may be broader than those of our sample of non-sadomasochists.

Assessing the psychoanalytic hypothesis. To examine the hypothesis that masochists suffer from sexual guilt, a one-way between-subjects ANOVA on the sexual guilt measure from the SBI was conducted. It was not significant.

To test the psychoanalytic idea that a weak superego or an ineffectual ego is behind sadistic urges and acts (Freud 1900/1954), responses of sadists on the two measures of psychopathy (intrapersonal and interpersonal) obtained from the SPI were examined. Also pertinent were sadists' responses on the Danger-Seeking subscale of the DPQ, measuring impulsive, id-driven behaviors. A one-way between-subjects MANOVA on these three measures was not significant.

In sum, we could not find support for the psychoanalytic contentions that masochists are guilt-ridden when it comes to sex or that sadists are id-driven or exhibited psychopathy.

Assessing the psychopathology hypothesis. A number of measures of mental health were chosen to assess mental disorder among masochists. In the interests of reducing the number of variables, the SCL-90-R subscales, the Neuroticism EPI subscale, and the Stress DPQ subscale were subjected to principal components analysis. A principal components extraction yielded a one-component solution with an eigenvalue >1. Component loading for each variable was high, ranging from .71 to .89. This was dubbed the "Mental Instability Component," and was interpreted as representing psychological problems. Internal reliability was good for this component, $\alpha = .88$. This component, along with the DES and the RSES, assessed whether masochists were more psychologically disturbed or distressed than the others. A one-way between-subjects MANOVA conducted on the Mental Instability component, the RSES, and the DES was not significant. Therefore masochists were not found to be more prone to psychological distress or mental instability than the other groups.

To test if sadists suffer from antisocial personality disorder, a one-way between-subjects MANOVA was conducted on the standardized scores from the Hostility and Authoritarianism measures from the DPQ and the two psychopathy indices from the SPI. This test was significant, Pillais $= .04$, F (9, 447) $= 2.04$, $p < .05$. Follow-up univariate F-tests revealed that only the Authoritarianism variable was significant, F (3, 149) $= 3.76$, $p < .05$, $\eta^2 = .07$. Importantly, post-hoc analyses (Tukey's HSD) showed that the Internet comparison group ($M = 0.11$, $SD = 0.98$) scored higher than switches ($M = -0.55$, $SD = 0.84$) on this measure, while no other comparisons were significant (masochists, $M = -.14$, $SD = 1.02$; sadists, $M = -.36$, $SD = .92$). In other words, the SM participants scored equivalent to or lower than the non-SM comparison group on Authoritarianism, a finding that is contrary to the expectations of the psychopathology hypothesis.

In sum, we could not find support for the psychopathology/medical-model contention that sadists are antisocial or psychopathic and that masochists suffer from some sort of mental disorder.

Assessing the radical feminist hypothesis. According to radical feminists, if one's sexual life involves scripts reflecting domination and submission, then this indicates a large-scale acceptance of patriarchal values. If this view is accurate, then SM practitioners should be less likely to endorse feminist values and more likely to endorse traditional notions of female gender roles. Differences between SM practitioners and non-SM comparison groups were sought on an index derived from the two measures of feminist beliefs: the Feminist Attitudes Scale (Matheson, 1996) and the Spanos Attitudes Towards Women Scale (Spanos & Dubreuil, 1991). A one-way between-subjects ANOVA conducted on this composite score was not significant.

The raw scores were examined to determine how anti- or pro-feminist the subsamples were: The Matheson Feminist Attitudes Questionnaire has a minimum possible raw score of 15, and a maximum of 105. The lower the raw score, the more pro-feminist the person's attitudes. The sadists in the present study obtained a mean raw score of $M = 38.12$,

SD = 19.52. The masochists scored M = 35.82, SD = 13.52. The switches scored M = 35.25, SD = 12.82. The non-SM comparison group scored M = 40.44, SD = 15.92. Thus all four groups indicated generally pro-feminist attitudes. Similarly, a low score on the Spanos Attitudes Towards Women Scale reflects non-endorsement of traditional gender roles. All four groups' scores indicated beliefs consistent with feminist tenets of equality for the sexes and breaking free of traditional gender roles.

Interestingly, though, a difference did emerge when the standardized responses for males were compared to those of females collapsed across groups by means of a one-way between-subjects ANOVA, F (1, 151) = 12.43, p < .001, η^2 = .08. Males scored higher than females on endorsement of traditional gender role beliefs (M = .01, SD = .87) relative to females (M = $-$.53, SD = .59). However, examination of raw scores on both original inventories indicates that the males' scores, while higher on average than the females', both were still well within the range of relatively pro-feminist views.

Thus, while some potentially interesting differences emerged as a function of sex, no evidence was found suggesting that sadomasochists espoused anti-feminist beliefs or traditional gender roles to a greater extent than the non-sadomasochists sampled. We were unable to find support for the radical feminist contention that SM reflects anti-feminist beliefs.

Assessing the escape-from-self hypothesis. A number of measures relating to escapism were included in the battery. Of these measures, two were pertinent to other hypotheses as well (the DES and the Danger-Seeking subscale of the DPQ) and were therefore left as individual measures. In the interests of reducing the number of variables, the remaining questionnaires (RPI, Day-dreaming Scale from the IPI, ICMI) were factor-analyzed, using principal components extraction, yielding one factor with eigenvalues > 1. Loadings for the three indices ranged from .70 to .84. This factor was dubbed "Imaginal Propensities," with a reliability of α = .75. A one-way between-subjects MANOVA on the Drug-Use index, the Imaginal Propensities factor, the LOC and the DCI was not significant.

To address the prediction that genuine sadists seek out power because of a lack of power in their everyday lives, participants were asked to indicate whether they were employed, and if so, what kind of job they held. A chi-square analysis on reported job categories was not possible, as too many cells had expected values of less than five. Responses were therefore collapsed into two categories: employed for pay and not employed for pay. A chi-square analysis on these categories was significant, $\chi^2 (3) = 7.80$, $p < .05$. Importantly, and contrary to the expectations of this perspective, the sadists did not differ from the non-sadomasochists in their levels of employment. The significant findings were due to the masochists and switches reporting somewhat higher levels of employment as compared to the sadists and the non-SM comparison group (masochists: 86.7% employed; switches: 71.0% employed; sadists: 58.3% employed; non-sadomasochists: 59.3% employed).

Thus we found no support for the idea that masochists were more inclined to engage in escapist behaviors such as drug-taking, day-dreaming, or fantasizing than any of the other groups. Nor were they more likely to have internal loci of control. They were, however, more likely than sadists and non-sadomasochists to be employed, which is not inconsistent with the theory that masochists have a more burdensome sense of self.

To address Baumeister's (1988, 1989) idea that many sadists are in fact masochists who have learned to be patient and flexible as they wait their turn to take the submissive role, the Submissive Sexual Proclivities factor from the SBI was utilized. A one-way between-subjects ANOVA conducted on this measure was significant, $F (3, 150) = 52.27$, $p < .001$, partial $\eta^2 = .51$. Post-hoc analyses (Tukey's HSD) revealed that the masochists ($M = 1.08$, $SD = 0.95$) and switches ($M = 1.06$, $SD = 0.77$) both scored higher than the Internet comparison group ($M = -0.52$, $SD = 0.49$) and the sadists ($M = -0.12$, $SD = 0.82$). These findings suggest strongly that contrary to the prediction of Baumeister's theory, submissive acts and desires are preferred by masochists and switches relative to sadists, who do not in fact differ on this index from non-sadomasochists.

In sum, while we did find that masochists are more likely to be employed than sadists and non-sadomasochists, we failed to find any other compelling support for the escape-from-self perspective on SM.

Discussion

None of the prevailing academic perspectives on SM explored in the present investigation was supported by the data. We ended up with predominantly null findings. Support for the null hypotheses is generally regarded as inconclusive, and given the possibility of sample biases, inappropriate operationalizations of key constructs, and insufficient power in the present study, these results should be viewed with caution. That being said, these findings should at the very least result in questions concerning the validity of the theoretical perspectives we examined. Sample biases in participants recruited from socially covert groups are always a risk, and no doubt biases did exist in the present study. However, the use of an Internet sample may have in fact minimized some of the biases that are evident in other samples of SM practitioners, in that the sample was not restricted to those who participated in the club scene (and hence are potentially more public about their sexual proclivities), or to those who were familiar to one another (as in the use of snowball techniques). The highly anonymous nature of the Internet recruitment and participation perhaps opened up the possibility that this sample was broader (and larger) than that found in many other studies on SM.

Finally, although differences among the groups were not found in the theoretical constructs of interest, we did find some interesting, albeit predictable, differences in participants' sexual histories and activities. The sample of sadomasochists reported being more sexually active, with a wider range of sexual activities in their repertoire, and a broader range of partners. Perhaps, then, those who engage in SM tend to be people who engage in a variety of sexual activities. One might speculate that sadomasochists could be understood as sexual gourmets with diverse and sophisticated tastes. These findings suggest that sadomasochism may simply be a form of sex play, providing those individuals with a sufficiently adventurous attitude towards sex with the experience of intense and intimate encounters. Further, rather than pain, bondage, and humiliation being at the core of the SM experience, Califia (1980) suggests that these behaviors are better understood as tools to assist in the mutual creation of differential status. That is, power may be the core phenomenon; the exchange of power in an erotic context may become, for some, a vehicle for the experience of sexual pleasure. While genuine rape, torture, and humiliation are crimes against humanity, the consensual simulation of such acts may represent an opportunity to play with the icons of power and authority for purposes of exploring and developing erotic fantasies.

If this is so, it should be informative to focus on the exchange of power in sadomasochistic scenes, examining the means by which the power exchange occurs, the methods by which it is maintained throughout a scene, and how such an exchange would provide a framework for erotic pleasure.

One way to do this is to observe SM encounters in progress, with an eye to uncovering the power dynamics within the scene and the techniques used for their instigation and maintenance. While examination of real-life SM scenes would be ideal, the difficulties inherent in obtaining access to such encounters are often prohibitive. However, SM activities take place not only in private clubs and individuals' bedrooms, but also in Internet SM chat rooms. The existence of these online SM venues may provide an excellent forum to allow for the observation of sadomasochistic interchanges. Studies 2 and 3 were undertaken with this goal in mind.

STUDY 2

The ready availability and accessibility of Internet SM "clubs" seems ideally suited to participant-observer research. The text-based nature of the encounters makes it easier to collect and analyze scripts of the encounters than would be the case with real-life interactions, which require visual and auditory interpretation on the part of the observer. Making use of online SM for purposes of exploring SM more generally assumes that virtual sadomasochists are like real-life sadomasochists in terms of their sexual proclivities. However, "virtual" SM may differ in important ways from real-life SM. The present study therefore sought to compare the sexual proclivities of virtual sadomasochists with real-life sadomasochists. Comparison samples of non-sadomasochists, including a group of non-sadomasochistic fantasy role-players, were also collected. Given that sexual proclivities were the only variables that distinguished SM practitioners in Study 1, we reasoned that if the virtual SM group was found to have sexual proclivities similar to those of real-life sadomasochists, then we can be more confident that the study of SM in the virtual realm can inform current understandings of SM more generally.

Method

The data from 10 individuals obtained for Study 1 was examined. These individuals' responses had not been included in the Study 1 sample because they had reported engaging in SM exclusively via the Internet. Of the 10 participants, 3 reported taking the dominant role, 4 preferred the submissive role, and 3 self-identified as switches. They were compared to a sample of ten real-life sadomasochists randomly selected from the Study 1 group who were matched for role preference.

None of the real-life SM participants indicated engaging in SM in these online environments. Also included was a randomly selected sample of ten individuals from the non-SM Internet comparison group from Study 1. And finally, a sample of 10 individuals who engaged in online fantasy role-play games such as "Dungeons and Dragons" was obtained. The goal was to determine whether the virtual SM group had more in common, in terms of sexual proclivities, with the real-life sadomasochists, the role-players, or the non-SM Internet group, or whether, alternatively, they were unique unto themselves. These alternatives were based on the assumption that virtual sadomasochists would either be from the same population as real-life sadomasochists in terms of sexual proclivities, or, alternatively, that they would have been attracted to virtual SM venues for other reasons. These other reasons include the possibility that virtual SM has more in common with fantasy role-play games like "Dungeons and Dragons" than it does with real-life SM. Another possibility is that "normal" people might simply be indulging their curiosity in these online venues, in which case they would have more in common with non-sadomasochists. The fantasy role-players were solicited by posting a request for volunteers on several online news groups devoted to discussions of fantasy role-play games. This online fantasy group filled out the same Sexual Behaviors Inventory (SBI) that was included in the Study 1 battery. Thus data on sexual proclivities were obtained for all participants.

Results

Agglomerative hierarchical cluster analyses were used to compare participants in all four groups. The measures used to form the basis of this analysis were derived from the SBI, and included scores on masochistic sexual proclivities, sadistic sexual proclivities, and non-SM sexual proclivities. A matrix of difference scores for each pair of subjects was computed. Cluster analyses were then conducted on this matrix, using three different linkage methods (complete linkage, average linkage, and single linkage), each yielding a dendogram for interpretation.

The cluster analyses yielded five to eight distinct clusters, depending on which linkage method was used. We looked primarily at the complete linkage analysis, since it typically yields the most straightforward dendograms with the most highly similar clusterings. Eight clusters were obtained with this technique.

The overall pattern was of two major clusterings, one containing all the non-sadomasochists, and the other containing the virtual and real-life sadomasochists, which in turn separated out into smaller clusters. Thus at the broadest level of differentiation, non-sadomasochists were clearly distinct from sadomasochists. Second, within the SM cluster, real-life sadists and switches tended to group with virtual sadists and switches. Another cluster was formed comprising real-life and virtual masochists. Thus this secondary clustering distinguished between sadistic versus masochistic propensities, but not between the real-life and virtual forums. This same basic pattern was found irrespective of the linkage method used (see Figure 1).

As a reliability check, the analysis was reconducted, using a second random sample of ten individuals from the real-life SM group, and a second random sample of ten individuals from the Internet comparison group. A similar pattern was again detected, grouping the virtual and real-life sadomasochists together, and apart from the non-sadomasochistic cases. Therefore, it appears that the virtual SM group was similar to real-life sadomasochists and dissimilar to non-sadomasochists, including fantasy role-players, on the self-report indices of sadomasochistic sexual proclivities. These findings provided some justification for making use of a virtual SM participant pool as a source of data relevant to SM in the real world.

STUDY 3

Study 3 was conducted to assess the importance and role of power in SM interactions. Interpersonal power has been defined as the ability to get another person or persons to do or to believe something they would not necessarily have done or believed of their own volition (Johnson, 1976). Intimately tied to this notion is the concept of status (Berger, Rosenholtz & Zelditch, 1980; Turkle, 1995). According to Expectation Status Theory (Berger et al., 1980), higher status is an indicator of power expressed as a greater ability to alter directly other people's behaviors and/or beliefs.

One's status affects the strategies one employs when attempting to influence others (Berger et al., 1980; Falbo & Peplau, 1980). Specifically, persons of higher status utilize direct tactics (e.g., direct statements or commands to indicate one's preference) while those with lower status utilize indirect tactics (e.g., suggestions or nonverbal cues such as facial expressions) (Falbo & Peplau, 1980). Status differences

FIGURE 1. Dendogram using complete linkage, showing the pattern of cluster-ing of real-life and virtual sadomasochists in terms of sexual proclivities.

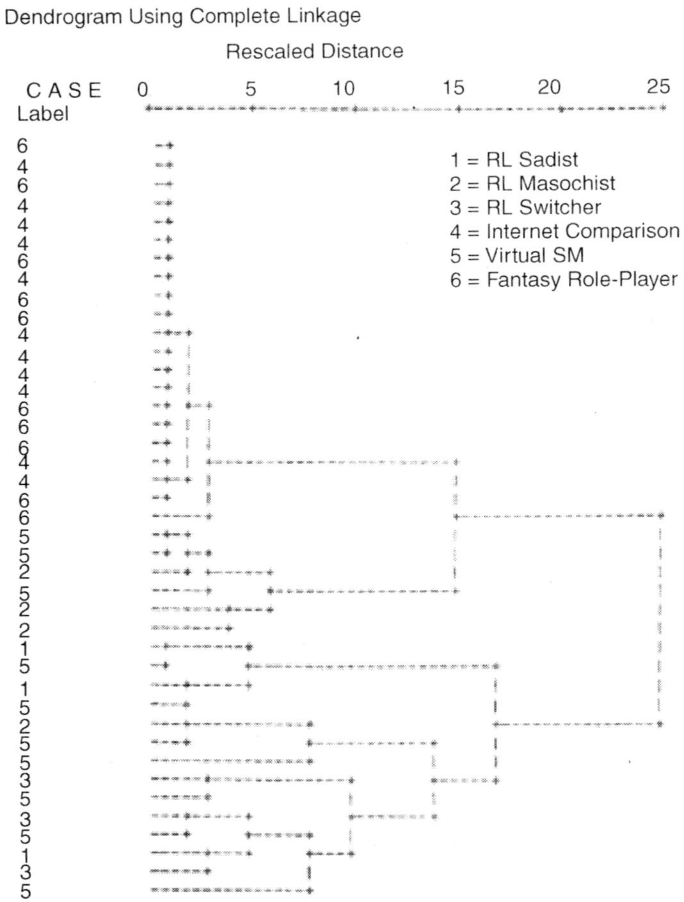

Dendrogram Using Complete Linkage

Rescaled Distance

1 = RL Sadist
2 = RL Masochist
3 = RL Switcher
4 = Internet Comparison
5 = Virtual SM
6 = Fantasy Role-Player

are revealed in instances in which one individual obeys the orders of an-other (Falbo & Peplau, 1980). As well, indicators of one individual be-ing "owned" by another, such as statements like, "I am yours," or "you are my possession" indicate a clear status differential. Further, indica-tors of status are derived not simply from actual behavior or influence, but also involve socially constructed symbols that identify directions of power and influence. For example, one indicator of status might be the manner in which an individual is addressed (Falbo & Peplau, 1980). If one individual refers to another as "master," or "mistress," this indicates a conferring of higher status upon the person being addressed. If an individual is addressed as "pet," or "slave," or "slut," this indicates his or her lower status. This also extends to parental forms of address, such as "child" or "little one." Even expressions of concern and caring can indicate power and status (Falbo & Peplau, 1980), to the extent that such expressions can imply a responsibility on the part of one individual for the welfare of the other, suggesting an almost parental relationship.

Another indicator of power and powerlessness specific to the context of virtual SM may involve the participants' online anonymity. In the world of Internet chat rooms, anonymity permits for feelings of safety and comfort. The sharing of such real-life information as name, location, or age may serve to reduce or eliminate the individual's sense of comfort and safety, something a higher-status individual would be less likely to feel compelled to do.

If a power exchange is the core phenomenon with SM, then pain may be understood as one of many possible tools useful for helping to establish and maintain the requisite power differential. Pain is thus seen not as definitive of the SM experience in itself, but as one of several techniques for clearly differentiating the powerful from the powerless.

Method

Several online SM-themed chat rooms served as the venue for soliciting the participation of SM couples. After identifying myself (P.C.) as a researcher, and providing information regarding my credentials, contact information, participants' confidentiality, and the right of the participants to withdraw at any time, I accompanied consenting couples to one of the many private "rooms" available at each site to observe their encounter. Afterwards, participants were individually interviewed online to collect such information as gender, age, familiarity with online and real-life SM, and familiarity with the partner. Participants were also asked to describe how the dynamic of dominance and submission had been established and maintained in their encounters. By way of a debriefing, I discussed the purposes of the study with participants, provided them again with contact names, e-mails, and telephone numbers, and reiterated that the data would be confidential and anonymous.

Eight interactions (N = 16 individuals) were collected for analysis. Of these, six were reportedly heterosexual dyads, and two were female same-sex dyads. Of the heterosexual pairs, five took the form of female masochist/male sadist and one took the form of male masochist/female sadist. Ages ranged from 21 to 47 years, with no differences as a function of role (M = 28.8 years, SD = 7.3). Three of the eight dyads consisted of partners who had been together before, while for the remaining five the observed scenes were their first together.

Transcripts of the sessions were captured for content analysis with the aid of a computer program called "Quick Link" (Sperling & O'Leary, 1989). This program has a "capture text" function, which permits the verbatim recording of text-based communications.

The categories described below and derived from power and status theories as well as examination of the transcripts were coded by two independent judges. Inter-rater reliabilities were good, ranging from phi = .67 to 1.00, and all disagreements were resolved by discussion. The unit of analysis was defined as a discrete utterance from either partner.

Establishment of a power exchange. The items in this category were coded to reflect the ways in which the power exchange was established and maintained. Theories of interpersonal power suggest that strategies for communication differ as a function of one's power level (e.g., Berger, Rosenholtz & Zelditch, 1980; Falbo & Peplau, 1980; Johnson, 1976). Therefore we expected to find differences in our sample as a function of role. Three distinct techniques for establishing and maintaining a status differential were identified and coded for. The first was whether the individual utilized direct modes of communication, such as clear statements, commands, or requests, versus indirect modes of communication, including nonverbal strategies like moans or pouting and the use of hints to guide the scene's progress. It may seem peculiar on the face of it to refer to nonverbal strategies as elements of an online encounter, given that the entire experience is textual. In fact, though, such elements are integral to the interchange. For example, if one individual wishes to show approval of the partner's actions, instead of simply stating approval directly, one has the option of having his or her online persona moan passionately, tremble in anticipation, smile, or engage in any other "action" that can be dreamed up.

Second, the provision of real-life personal information, such as a description of physiological arousal, physical appearance, real name, or geographical location, was noted. This may be interpreted as a means by which one partner asserts control over the other, by denying the partner the comfort and security of complete anonymity.

Third, expressions of caring and concern for one's partner were coded for (e.g., using terms of endearment such as "my love"). Such expressions can be strategically used to indicate status (e.g., if one person concerns him- or herself with the other's well-being, this implies responsibility for that person, and therefore superior status).

Mutuality in creating a power exchange. A number of items were noted which indicate that the power exchange was mutually constructed, as opposed to being imposed by one partner upon the other. First, masochists' and sadists' relative use of status indicators was examined so as to determine whether both masochists and sadists were actively maintaining differential status within the dyad through the use of mode of address (e.g., the masochist calling the sadist "Sir" or "Ma'am"; the sadist calling the masochist "slave" or "pet"). As well, other status indicators, like obedience to commands and indicators of ownership, were looked at in terms of the relative frequency with which they were invoked by masochists versus sadists.

We also examined instances of individuals stepping outside of the role so as to indicate pleasure or displeasure, suggest directions for the scene, or inquire into their partners' enjoyment. Instances of masochists' and sadists' deviation from their roles for these purposes were compared so as to determine whether sadists or masochists were relatively more likely to direct the scene in this way.

Results

Mode of communication. To assess whether the sadist and masochist roles differed in their use of direct modes of communication, a dependent groups t-test was conducted. Sadists ($M = 10.01\%$ of utterances, $SD = 3.04$) were far more likely than masochists ($M = 1.50\%$ of utterances, $SD = 2.54$) to utilize direct modes of communication, such as expressing approval or disapproval directly, or telling the partner to do something directly, $t(7) = 5.80, p < .001, \eta^2 = .83$. Conversely, masochists ($M = 9.71\%$ of utterances, $SD = 6.32$) were more likely than sadists ($M = 5.74\%$ of utterances, $SD = 3.60$) to utilize indirect forms of communication, such as hinting and body language, $t(7) = -2.10, p < .05, \eta^2 = .38$.

Masochists ($M = 2.32\%$ of utterances, $SD = 2.45$) were more likely than sadists ($M = 0.18\%$ of utterances, $SD = 0.34$) to provide real-life information during the course of the scene, $t(7) = -2.36, p < .05, \eta^2 = .51$, thereby indicating a willingness to compromise their own anonymity.

A dependent groups t-test conducted on indicators of caring and tenderness displayed to the partner was significant. Sadists ($M = 5.27\%$ of utterances, $SD = 3.17$) were far more likely than masochists ($M = 0.69\%$

of utterances, $SD = 0.96$) to use expressions of caring towards their partners, $t(7) = 4.59$, $p < .01$, $\eta^2 = .75$.

Mutuality in creating a power exchange. A dependent groups t-test looking at the percentage of utterances containing indicators of status differential was not significant. Both the sadists and the masochists were equally likely to make use of indicators of status. On average, masochists made use of indicators of status differential in $M = 20.2\%$ of utterances per scene, $SD = 8.70$. This did not differ significantly from sadists, who made use of such indicators in $M = 19.1\%$ of utterances per scene, $SD = 8.80$. That is, the power differential was set up and maintained by both partners working to construct this situation actively.

A dependent groups t-test looking at the percent of utterances containing instances of stepping outside of the role and the scene in order to comment on preferences, the progress of the scene, or to inquire as to the partner's enjoyment, was not significant. Thus both sadists and masochists were equally likely to break out of role so as to elucidate preferences and check on their partners' enjoyment of the scene. On average sadists did this in $M = 2.0\%$ of utterances, $SD = 1.62$, while masochists did this in $M = 1.4\%$ of utterances, $SD = 2.40$.

Participants' own reports. Those individuals who participated in the post-scene interview (n = 13) were asked to explain the aspects of the scene that, in their opinions, established and sustained the sadist's power over the masochist. Two strategies by which the power exchange was instigated and maintained emerged from these interviews. The primary strategy involved expressing specific actions which designate power (described by n = 6 out of the thirteen people interviewed). For example, some identified the sadist's use of high-power behaviors, such as the administration of discipline, to signal greater status, e.g., "... when she didn't call me 'Sir' I made sure she knew that was not going to be tolerated again." Others mentioned the use of low-power behaviors on the part of the masochist to indicate relative status, e.g., "... I treat her with respect and I obey her," and "well, I was chained to the wall! So I was totally helpless for most of it. "

The second, though by no means unrelated, method for establishing a power differential that was described by a number of participants was through understanding and acting in accordance with the implicit or explicit rules of conduct within an SM scene (reported by $n = 5$ individuals). In some instances the rules of conduct were signaled by the specifics of the scene. "I guess when she wanted me to call her 'Mommy,' that's when I clued in to the kind of scene she was into." In two instances the rules were tacit, establishing an implicit paradigm within which virtual sadomasochism exists. "It's like there are rules of behaviour you have to follow. There are things I do as a sub and there are things he does as a Dom," and "The power thing is set up before it even starts." Five people also mentioned that the rules of conduct were established explicitly through dialogue prior to engaging in a scene. "We talk before we do a scene, especially if it's for the first time. We get to know each other, feel out our likes and dislikes."

Three individuals indicated that preferences for behavior could be signaled through the use of informative pseudonyms, e.g., "My name is a Domme name. Like her name is submissive . . . so I knew I was going to be the top."

Four participants' comments indicated an understanding of this power exchange as essentially illusory, e.g., "The only power he's got is what I let him have. . . .We shop for what they have to offer. If we don't like it, then we don't play" and "To say I have the power and the control is misleading. We are out to please each other." Thus it seems clear that many of the participants considered the power exchange to be mutually constructed, maintained by tacit and explicit rules and conventions, and, ultimately, illusory.

Discussion

Both sadists and masochists made use of various techniques to create and sustain relative power and powerlessness. Sadists were more likely to use direct forms of communication, consistent with their higher status roles, whereas masochists were more likely to use indirect forms of communication, as would be expected, given their less-powerful status. Such role-specific preferences served to maintain the illusion of a power and status differential in the dyad. Sadists were more likely to express tenderness and caring toward their partners, suggesting an almost parental role, also indicative of greater power. Masochists, on the other hand, were more than 10 times more likely than sadists to reveal real-life information about themselves, reflecting their lower status and thus their greater vulnerability relative to their partners. Further, both sadists and masochists used these various indicators of status frequently and to an equivalent extent; both partners therefore shared the responsibility for creating and maintaining the power differential. What is more, the care with which both sadists and masochists maintained roles and behaviors that delineated a clear status differential suggests that this power differential was in fact of paramount importance to the SM experience. The use of status-specific roles and the careful orchestration of events indicate that more was sought than the simple enactment of an exchange of pain. Roles were selected, behaviors were enacted, and language was utilized such that one partner was accorded higher status and ostensibly had control, while the other was rendered of lower status and ostensibly did not have control.

This conceptualization of what is happening in a sadomasochistic encounter is quite different from views that seek to explain these behaviors as a function of a desire to give and/or receive pain. Although pain (both physical and psychological) is common to SM scenarios, some practitioners have argued that pain is not sought for its own sake, but rather is utilized for the creation of a particular power dynamic (Califia, 1983); our observations are consistent with this idea. Still others argue that some SM participants may not experience intense sensations in SM contexts as painful and note that only particular types of "pain" are sought (Kleinplatz & Moser, 2003).

One must bear in mind the potential limitations to generalizability of these findings to real-life SM participants. Although Study 2 established a general similarity between virtual and real-life sadomasochists concerning their sexual proclivities, clearly virtual SM does not involve the use of real pain, whereas real-life SM may do so. It may be that although virtual SM appears to focus on the manipulation of power, real-life SM serves different goals. Nonetheless, the fact that real-life sadomasochists themselves tend to describe their encounters in terms of a power exchange suggests that these virtual scenarios may not be so very different from the real-life versions after all. Further, if in fact on-line SM encounters represent sadomasochistic fantasies, then the virtual events that transpire can reasonably be expected to reflect the aspects of SM that people find most desirable. One logical consequence of this is that if pain is what is sought, then it will be "written into" the script. Indeed, if this is so, one might expect encounters that get right to the point, and involve one person simply and directly inflicting virtual pain upon another. This was not, however, what we found. Instead we witnessed complex scenarios of submission and domination that seemed to use pain, if it was present at all, as more of a tool than a goal. What is needed at this point is a replication of these findings with a real-life SM sample. Such a sample would yield a clearer picture of the importance of pain, particularly whether it is used for its symbolic power, for the physical sensations, or both.

GENERAL DISCUSSION

The findings from Study 1 suggested that current scholarly understandings of SM may be inadequate. By administering carefully selected psychometric tools, and comparing the responses of sadomasochists to those of non-sadomasochists, we sought evidence for several theories currently being used to explain SM. We found no support for the view that sadomasochism is an illness—our measures of mental illness did not differentiate sadomasochists from non-sadomasochists. Likewise we could not find evidence for the psychoanalytic view that SM reflects sexual guilt on the part of masochists or an id-driven personality on the part of sadists—our measure of sexual guilt did not differentiate masochists from others, and our measures of id-driven behavior did not differentiate sadists from others. We also could not find evidence that sadomasochists are anti-feminist—our measure of feminist attitudes did not differentiate sadomasochists from non-sadomasochists. Finally, we failed to find compelling support for Baumeister's (1988, 1989) contention that masochists are seeking escape from their stressful high-powered everyday lives, while sadists are either would-be masochists or are seeking power to make up for everyday powerlessness. While we did find that masochists were more likely to report being employed than sadists and non-sadomasochists, we did not find that sadists reported wanting to engage in masochistic activities, or that sadists inhabit low-powered social strata to a greater extent than others. Thus we began to speculate that the phenomenon of SM may not best be explained via any of these perspectives.

Study 2, in establishing the similarity of sexual proclivities among virtual and real-life sadomasochists, opened the door to making use of online SM sites as a viable source of information about this elusive population. Implications for future research are exciting; the Internet provides researchers with a ready and almost instantaneous subject pool, which may facilitate research into sexuality and other aspects of personality and human behavior. Further research is needed, however, before we can comfortably make the conceptual leap from Internet-based activities to activities in the real world.

Study 3 provided a glimpse into the dynamics of SM encounters as they transpired online. The manipulation of indicators of power so as to create and maintain an illusion of a power differential in the dyad was clearly demonstrated. Both sadists and masochists worked at sustaining this illusion throughout their encounters by various means, including altering their mode of address and their conduct towards one another.

Many participants reported afterwards that they were well aware of tacit and explicit rules of conduct specific to their current roles, indicating the existence of an SM "schema" for appropriate behavior. Thus it appears that the roles of masochist and sadist carry with them mutually understood standards of behavior that are to be obeyed if the dynamic of a power differential is to be sustained.

However, these three studies have important limitations that restrict our confidence in generalizing the results to the SM population at large. For one thing, Study 1 solicited its participants from the Internet, which may have resulted in a non-representative sample. Although we were able to obtain participants from several countries and of both sexes, it is not clear whether they differ in some systematic ways from a sample collected by more conventional means. Future research should attempt to replicate these findings using alternative measures, and with a sample of sadomasochists obtained in some manner other than via the Internet. It is possible that the specific forms of psychopathology hypothesized in the existing theories, not found in this study, would become apparent using an alternate set of psychometric instruments.

Another limitation to this research derives from the fact that the validity of our examination of virtual SM in Study 3 rests on the assumption that virtual sadomasochists are sufficiently similar to real-life sadomasochists to be used as convenient "stand-ins." Although Study 2 found some evidence for these two populations sharing sexual proclivities in common, more data needs to be collected to establish this for a certainty. It is possible, despite our findings in Study 2, that virtual SM is really a very different activity than real-life SM, and is engaged in for different reasons and by different people. It may be, for example, that many of those who engage in SM online would never actually try it in real life. Future research, then, should involve an examination of real-life SM scenes to see whether power and status are managed in similar ways, and to assess the viability of the idea that pain in this context is a means of establishing power, and not a goal unto itself.

Subsequent to completion of this research, we were faced with the question of whether or not SM represented sexual behavior for those in our sample. This reflects the larger issue of whether or not SM is about sex, or whether, instead, it can be about the gratification of some other need or needs. Clearly, there are those who use SM as a form of "foreplay," or as a context within which to place arousal, intercourse, or orgasm. For example, an examination of the transcripts in Study 3 contains numerous sexual elements, including instances of arousal, intercourse, and orgasm. Our research made the assumption that SM was sexual, springing initially, as it did, from a desire to question the diagnostic entities of sexual sadism and sexual masochism. In retrospect, however, we cannot be sure that all participants shared this implicit definition. Therefore, in collecting information about the number of sex partners and frequency of sexual activity, it may have been the case that some of our SM respondents were not referring to SM partners and SM activity in their answers, but were instead discussing a different set of behaviors conceptually separate from their sadomasochistic experiences. This may further limit the interpretability of our findings. Future research should work to clarify these issues. For example, it would be essential to obtain insight into participants' own assumptions as to whether SM is sexual for them or not. If in fact SM turns out to serve a nonsexual purpose for many sadomasochists, then it would become important to assess what other needs these activities may be addressing. Certainly, the results of our research are consistent with the idea that SM is predominantly sexual behavior. In addition to our transcripts containing abundant instances of arousal, intercourse, and orgasm, none of our participants asked for clarification when answering questions about their sexuality, interspersed, as they were, with questions about their SM activities. For example, when answering questions about sex drive, number of partners, and the like, no one asked us, "Do you mean my SM activities or my sexual activities?" One would think, if these were two distinct domains of behavior, that someone would have pointed out to us that we were at risk of confusing the two with the wording of our questions. The fact that this did not happen is perhaps some indication that the assumptions we had made about SM as being sexual were assumptions that our respondents shared. Nevertheless, future research should directly examine sadomasochists' views on this matter.

Sadomasochism is, like any interpersonal social behavior, a complex phenomenon. Sadomasochists in this research reported having had more sex partners and a greater likelihood of having explored non-heterosexual experiences. They were also more likely to be sexually active relative to non-sadomasochists. One might wonder, on the basis of these findings, whether sadomasochists are simply individuals for whom sex and sexuality play a relatively important role. One might wonder whether SM ought to be understood best as a game explored by the sexually sophisticated and adventurous, involving the manipulation of power for erotic purposes. Further research is needed to determine whether these preliminary impressions are in fact accurate. In particular, research with samples collected from sources other than the Internet, and observations of SM activity in real-life situations would be helpful in overcoming the limitations of the current research.

REFERENCES

Adams, M., Palmer, A, O'Brien, J, & Crook, W. (2000). Health of the nation outcomes for psychiatry: Are they valid? *Journal of Mental Health-UK, 9*(2), 193-198.

American Psychiatric Association (2000). *Diagnostic and statistical manual of mental disorders, fourth edition, text revision.* Washington, D.C.: American Psychiatric Association.

Alison, L., Santtila, P., & Sandnabba, K.N. (2001). Sadomasochistically oriented behavior: Diversity in practice and meaning. *Archives of Sexual Behavior, 30*(1), 1-12.

Awad, G.A. (2000). The development and consequences of an aggressive symbiotic fantasy. *Psychoanalytic Study of the Child, 55*, 180-201.

Bader, M.J. (1993). Adaptive sadomasochism and psychological growth. *Psychoanalytic Dialogues, 3* (2), 279-300.

Bagley, C., Bolitho, F., & Bertrand, L. (1997). Norms and construct validity of the Rosenberg Self-Esteem Scale in Canadian high school populations: Implications for counseling. *Canadian Journal of Counselling, 31* (1), 82-92.

Bagley, C. & Mallick, K. (2001). Normative data and mental health construct validity for the Rosenberg Self-Esteem Scale in British adolescents. *International Journal of Adolescence and Youth, 9* (2-3), 117-126.

Bar-On, B.A. (1982). Feminism and sadomasochism: Self-critical notes. In *Against sadomasochism: A radical feminist analysis.* San Francisco: Frog In The Well.

Baumeister, R.F. (1988). Masochism as escape from self. *Journal of Sex Research, 25*, 28-59.

Baumeister, R.F. (1989). *Masochism and the self.* Hilldale, N.J.: Lawrence Erlbaum & Associates Inc.

Berger, J., Rosenholtz, S., & Zelditch, M. (1980). Status organizing processes. *Annual Review of Sociology, 6*, 479-508.

Burger, J.M. & Cooper, H.M. (1979). The desirability of control. *Motivation and Emotion, 3*, 381-393.

Butler, J. (1982). Lesbian s & m: The politics of dis-illusion. In *Against sadomasochism: A radical feminist analysis.* San Francisco: Frog In The Well.

Califia, P. (1983). A secret side of lesbian sexuality. In T. Weinberg & G. Kamel (Eds.), *S and M: Studies in sadomasochism* (pp. 129-136). Buffalo, N.Y: Prometheus.

Carlson, E.B. & Putnam, F.W. (1993). An update on the dissociative experiences scale. *Dissociation Progress in the Dissociative Disorders, 6* (1), 16-27.

Carlson, E.B., Putnam, F.W., Ross, C.A., & Torem, M. (1993). Validity of the Dissociative Experiences Scale in screening for multiple personality disorder: A multicenter study. *American Journal of Psychiatry, 150* (7), 1030-1036.

Charme, S.L. (1983). Religion and the theory of masochism. *Journal of Religion and Health, 22* (3), 221-233.

Crowne, D.P., & Marlowe, D. (1960). A new scale of social desirability independent of psychopathology. *Journal of Consulting Psychology, 24,* 349-354.

Cundiff, G. & Gold, S. (1979). Daydreaming: A measurable concept. *Perceptual and Motor Skills, 49* (2), 347-353.

Derogatis, L. R. (1983). *SCL-90-R Administration, Scoring, Procedures Manual II for the Revised Version* (2nd ed). Towson, MD: Clinical Psychometric Research.

Derogatis, L. R. (2000). The SCL-90-R and Brief Symptom Inventory (BSI) in primary care. In Maruish, M. (Ed.), *Handbook of psychological assessment in primary care settings* (pp. 297-334). Mahwah, NJ: Lawrence Erlbaum.

Dorr, D. & Woodhall, P.K. (1986). Ego dysfunction in psychopathic psychiatric inpatients. In *Unmasking the Psychopath*, W.H. Reid, Ed. New York: W.W. Norton.

Ehm, S. & Patrick, K (1995). Sexual sadists who murder: A leading sex-psychiatrist speaks out. *Notes from the Underground, 8 (2),* 1.

Eysenck, H.J., & Eysenck, S.B.G. (1964). *Eysenck Personality Inventory.* Sevenoaks: Hodder and Stoughton.

Fakhry-Davids, M. (1997). Sadomasochism as a defence. *Psychoanalytic Psychotherapy in South Africa, 5* (2), 51-64.

Falbo, T., & Peplau, L. A. (1980). Power strategies in intimate relationships. *Journal of Personality and Social Psychology, 38,* 618-628.

Ferrando, P. (2001). The measurement of neuroticism using MMQ, MPI, EPI and EPQ items: A psychometric analysis based on item response theory. *Personality and Individual Differences, 30* (4), 641-656.

Fletcher, K.E. & Averill, J.R.(1984). A scale for the measurement of role-playing ability. *Journal of Research in Personality, 18,* 131-149.

Freud, S. (1900/1954). *The interpretation of dreams.* London: Allen & Unwin.

Freud, S. (1906/1953). My views on the part played by sexuality in the etiology of the neuroses. *Standard Edition, VII.* London: Hogarth.

Freud, S. (1924/1961). The economic problem of masochism. In J. Strachey (Ed. And Trans.), *The standard edition of the complete psychological works of Sigmund Freud, 19,* 159-170.

Freud, S. (1938). Sadism and masochism. In A.A. Brill (Ed. and Trans.), *Basic writings of Sigmund Freud.* New York: Modern Library.

Gagnier, T.T., & Roberiello, R.C. (1993). Sadomasochism as a defense against merging: Six case studies. *Journal of Contemporary Psychotherapy, 23* (3), 183-192.

Gibbons, F.X., & Wicklund, R.A. (1976). Selective exposure to self. *Journal of Research in Personality, 10,* 98-106.

Gold, S., Teague, R., & Jarvinen, P. (1981). Counting daydreams. *Journal of mental imagery, 5* (1), 129-132.

Goodman, S.H., & Waters, L.K. (1987). Convergent validity of five locus of control scales. *Educational and Psychological Measurement, 47* (3), 743-747.

Gratzer, M.D. & Bradford, J.M.W. (1995). Offender and offense characteristics of sexual sadists: A comparative study. *Journal of Forensic Sciences, JFSCA, 40 (3),* 450-455.

Harper, H., Oei, T., Mendalgio, S., & Evans, L. (1990). Dimensionality, validity, and utility of the I-E scale with anxiety disorders. *Journal of Anxiety Disorders, 4* (2), 89-98.

Hill, J.K. (2000). Development of a psychopathy self-report measure (Social Personality Inventory). *Dissertation Abstracts International, 60* (7-B), 3615.

Houlberg, R. (1991). The magazine of a sadomasochism club: The tie that binds. *Journal of Homosexuality, 21* (1-2), 167-183.

Huba, G., Aneshensel, C., & Singer, J. (1981). Development of scales for three second-order factors of inner experience (Imaginal Processes Inventory). *Multivariate Behavioral Research,* 16 (2), 181-206.

Hull, J.G. (1981). A self-awareness model of the causes and effects of alcohol consumption. *Journal of Abnormal Psychology, 90,* 586-600.

Hull, J.G., & Young, R.D. (1983). Self-consciousness, self-esteem, and success-failure as determinants of alcohol consumption in male social drinkers. *Journal of Personality and Social Psychology, 44,* 1097-1109.

Jacobs, K.W. (1977). Intercorrelations of the Sensation-Seeking Scale, Eysenck Personality Inventory, and Rotter's Internal-External Control Scale. *Southern Journal of Educational Research, 11* (1), 9-16.

Johnson, P. (1976). Women and power: Toward a theory of effectiveness. *Journal of Social Issues, 32,* 99-110.

Jones, E.E., & Bergals, S.C. (1978). Control of attributions about the self through self-handicapping strategies: The appeal of alcohol and the role of underachievement. *Personality and Social Psychology Bulletin, 4,* 200-206.

Kegan, R.G. (1986). The child behind the mask: Sociopathy as developmental delay. In *Unmasking the Psychopath,* W.H. Reid, Ed. New York: W.W. Norton.

Kleinplatz, P. J., & Moser, C. (2003) *Is Sadomasochism Psycopathology?* Paper presented at the Annual Meeting of the American Association of Sex Educators, Counselors and Therapists, Las Vegas, U.S.A., June 5, 2003.

Krafft-Ebing, R. Von (1886/1965). *Psychopathia sexualis* (F.S. Klaf, trans.). New York: Bell.

Larstone, R., Jang, K., Livesley, W., Vernon, P., & Wolf, H. (2002). The relationship between Eysenck's P-E-N model of personality, the five-factor model of personality, and traits delineating personality dysfunction. *Personality and Individual Differences, 33* (1), 25-37.

Lerner, H.D. (2001). A two-systems approach to the treatment of a disturbed adolescent. *Psychoanalytic Social Work, 8* (3-4), 123-142.

Matheson, K. (1994). The Matheson Feminist Attitudes Scale. Unpublished scale. Carleton University, Ottawa, Canada.

Newcomb, M.D. & McGee, L. (1991). Influence of sensation seeking on general deviance and specific problem behaviours from adolescence to young adulthood. *Journal of Personality and Social Psychology, 61* (4), 614-628.

Panter, A. (1999). An exploratory study of female sadomasochists' sexuality: Behavior, fantasy, and meaning. *Dissertation Abstracts International, Section B: The Sciences and Engineering, 60* (4-B), 1867.

Price, R.M. (1983). Masochism and piety. *Journal of Religion and Health, 22* (2), 161-166.

Rhue, J.W., & Lynn, S.J. (1987). Fantasy proneness: Developmental antecedents. *Journal of Personality, 55* (1), 121-137.

Robins, R., Hendin, H., & Trzesniewski, K. (2001). Measuring global self-esteem: Construct validation of a single-item measure and the Rosenberg Self-Esteem Scale. *Personality and Social Psychology Bulletin, 27* (2), 151-161.

Rosenberg, M. (1965). *Society and the adolescent self-image.* Princeton, NJ: Princeton University Press.

Rotter, J. (1966). Generalized expectancies for internal versus external control of reinforcement. *Psychological Monographs: General and Applied, 80,* (1), 87-123.

Samois (1987). *Coming to power.* Boston, MA: Alyson.

Sandnabba, K.N., Santtila, P., Nordling, N, Beetz, A.M., & Alison, L. (2002). Characteristics of a sample of sadomasochistically-oriented males with recent experience of sexual contact with animals. *Deviant Behavior, 23* (6), 511-529.

Seelig, B.J., & Person, E.S. (1991). A sadomasochistic transference: its relation to distortions in the rapprochement subphase. *Journal of the American Psychoanalytic Association, 39* (4), 939-965.

Singer, J.L., & Antrobus, J.S. (1970). A factor-analytical study of daydreaming and the conceptually related cognitive and personality variables. *Perceptual and Motor Skills, Monograph Supplement 3-V17.*

Siuta, J. (1990). Fantasy-proneness: Towards cross-cultural comparisons. *British Journal of Experimental and Clinical Hypnosis, 7* (2), 93-101.

Spanos, N.P. & Dubreuil, S. (1991). Sexual Beliefs Scale. Unpublished manuscript. Carleton University, Ottawa, Canada.

Spengler, A. (1977). Manifest sadomasochism of males: Results of an empirical study. *Archives of Sexual Behavior, 6* (6), 441-456.

Sperling, A. & O'Leary, R. (1989). *Quick link communications program, version 1.2.0.* Property of Smith Microsoftware Incorporated, New York.

Taylor, G.W. & Ussher, J.M. (2001). Making sense of S&M: A discourse analytic account. *Sexualities, 4* (3), 293-314.

Tellegen, A. (1976). *Differential personality questionnaire.* Minneapolis: University of Minnesota.

Thompson, M. (1991). *Leatherfolk: Radical sex, people, politics, and practice.* Boston, MA: Alyson.

Turkle, S. (1995). *Life on the screen: Identity in the age of the Internet.* New York: Simon & Schuster.

Warren, S.C. (1997). The disavowal of desire: A relational view of sadomasochism. *Psychoanalysis and Psychotherapy, 14* (1), 107-123.

Weille, K. (2002). The psychodynamics of consensual sadomasochistic and dominant-submissive sexual games. *Studies in Gender and Sexuality, 3* (2), 131-160.

Weinberg, T., & Kamel, G. (1983). *S and M: Studies in sadomasochism.* Buffalo, N.Y: Prometheus.

Weiss, P.A. (2002). *Self-esteem: A study of methods of measurements. Disseration Abstracts International, Section B: The Sciences and Engineering, 62* (9-B), 4242.

Wicklund, R.A. (1975). Discrepancy reduction or attempted distraction? A reply to Liebling, Seiler & Shaver. *Journal of Experimental Social Psychology, 11,* 78-81.

Wilson, S.C. & Barber, T.X. (1987). The creative imagination scale as a measure of hypnotic responsiveness: Applications to experimental and clinical hypnosis. *American Journal of Clinical Hypnosis, 20*, 235-249.

Zerega, W.D., Tseng, M.S., & Greever, K.B. (1976). Stability and concurrent validity of the Rotter Internal-External Locus of Control Scale. *Educational and Psychological Measurement, 36* (2), 473-475.

The Spanner Trials and the Changing Law on Sadomasochism in the UK

Chris White, PhD

University of Bolton

SUMMARY. In the United Kingdom in 1989 a group of gay men who had been engaging in consensual SM activities were put on trial and found guilty of assault. The dominants/tops were charged with assault, and the men who participated in the activities as "bottoms" or submissives were convicted of aiding and abetting assaults upon themselves. This article discusses these Spanner trials–as they came to be called–and the issues of consent and privacy on which they were argued. UK and potentially European law are being subjected to pressure for redefinition as a result of the Spanner case, as SM practitioners are beginning to experience the implications and fallout from the prosecutions. While there have been proposals to reform the laws about what has been

---

Chris White is Senior Lecturer in English, University of Bolton, UK; editor of *Nineteenth-Century Writings on Homosexuality* (Routledge 1999); and co-editor of *What Lesbians Do in Books* (Women's Press 1991).

Author note: With grateful thanks to the Spanner Trust and all the SMers who have contributed their knowledge and ideas to this essay. I have not documented, for reasons of space, the long-standing, courageous and vigorous campaigning work of the organization which began as Countdown to Spanner, and which has become the Spanner Trust. For a full account of their ongoing work, visit their Website which is cited in the references.

[Haworth co-indexing entry note]: "The Spanner Trials and the Changing Law on Sadomasochism in the UK." White, Chris. Co-published simultaneously in *Journal of Homosexuality* (Harrington Park Press, an imprint of The Haworth Press, Inc.) Vol. 50, No. 2/3, 2006, pp. 167-187; and: *Sadomasochism: Powerful Pleasures* (ed: Peggy J. Kleinplatz, and Charles Moser) Harrington Park Press, an imprint of The Haworth Press, Inc., 2006, pp. 167-187. Single or multiple copies of this article are available for a fee from The Haworth Document Delivery Service [1-800-HAWORTH, 9:00 a.m. - 5:00 p.m. (EST). E-mail address: docdelivery@haworthpress.com].

deemed self-destructive and socially dangerous behavior, little has changed to date. The story of the prosecutions and appeals, and the pressures for a new legislative approach to decriminalize consensual SM, will be situated in the context of public interest claims to control the private actions of individuals in the interest of public health. Differences in interpretation that occur when gay men are involved as compared to heterosexual couples will also be discussed. *[Article copies available for a fee from The Haworth Document Delivery Service: 1-800-HAWORTH. E-mail address: <docdelivery@haworthpress.com> Website: <http://www.HaworthPress. com>*

KEYWORDS. Sadomasochism, law, British, Spanner, trial

In December 1990, sixteen men involved in sadomasochistic activities were charged and convicted of assault, having been denied a defense that the activity was consensual. This case, which came to be known as the Spanner case, set in motion a chain of events and created public pressure that may ultimately clarify the laws related to sadomasochism in both the United Kingdom and in Europe. This is the story of how this has come about; a story that bears telling in detail, and one that connects not only with the future legality of consensual SM in the UK and Europe, but also with political understandings of privacy and the public good. The first part of this article documents the sequence of events, beginning with the prosecution of a group of gay men as a result of Operation Spanner. The second part of the article examines the conceptual framework underpinning the contentious public debate that arose in the Spanner trial around consent in SM, and when the state can intervene in a "private" activity.

THE FACTS IN THE CASE

Throughout the late 1970s and 1980s, a group of gay men photographed and videotaped their play parties (gatherings to practice SM), documenting the SM activities that took place at a number of private properties in the UK Midlands. The Greater Manchester police came into possession of one of those videotapes which showed a number of identifiable men engaging in activities including beatings, genital abrasions and lacerations. Having viewed the tape the police searched the home of the owner and his associates as part of "Operation Spanner" (an investigation headed by the Obscene Publications Squad into paedophile rings and child pornography), claiming they were engaging in a murder enquiry because the videotape had convinced them that gay men were being killed during perverted, violent sex. One of the Spannermen, Roland Jaggard, has written:

> What did they see on that first video tape? Well we cannot be certain which of the many homemade tapes they saw first. However during the investigation they confiscated numerous tapes . . . [which] depicted among other things: Beatings of buttocks, legs, cocks and balls with leather straps, canes, nettles etc. Hot wax being dripped onto genitals, torsos, legs etc. Play piercings of tits, scrotums, cock knobs, shafts, and foreskins. Genital application of heat (hair driers) and cold (ice cubes). Genital bondage and manipulation etc, ball weights, safe electrical play (just adaptation for electrical sexual play, of the muscle toning gear used by health clubs). Scrotal stretching and pinning out with needles etc. Nipple and cock branding. (Jaggard, [n.d.])

In the ensuing enquiry, between two and three hundred individuals were interviewed. None of the men in the videos had been murdered, or suffered injuries that required medical attention, a fact never contested at any point in the legal process. As a result of the interviews, in late 1989, 16 men were charged with assault, aiding and abetting assault and keeping a disorderly house, while a further 26 were cautioned. (In cautioning, the individuals admit to the crime but it does not count as a conviction; however, if there are future incidents, the charges can be resurrected.) The men who participated in the activities as submissives were accused of abetting assaults upon themselves. Specific charges included grievous and/or actual bodily harm on oneself and/or others, aiding and abetting grievous bodily harm on oneself; conspiracy to commit assault, publishing indecent material, conspiracy to distribute indecent material, and keeping a disorderly house. Penalties included jail terms ranging from 12 months to four and one half years, probation, conditional discharge, suspended sentences and/or fines. Jaggard expands upon the nature of the charges against him:

> Actual Bodily Harm (ABH) for cock waxing & play piercing; unlawful wounding for cock caning, play piercing & abetting the Master while he cut his slave's cock with a scalpel; aiding & abetting assault occasioning ABH for doing the scalpel video; unlaw-

ful wounding for sticking things down my mate's urethra & play piercing his foreskin; ABH for beating a guy's bum with a leather strap. Also the Master was charged [among other things] with ABH for sandpapering my testicles. (Jaggard, [n.d.])

In December 1990 the Spanner case came to trial at the Old Bailey in London, the Central Criminal Court in the UK (one of 90 sites of the Crown Court, a court capable of dealing with serious offences). This venue was chosen because the seriousness of the offences and the geographical spread of the defendants across England and Wales. Judge Rant, who presided over the trial, decided that the activities in question fell outside the exceptions to the law of assault and ruled that a defense of consent was ineligible. As a consequence of Rant's decision, 16 of the men pleaded guilty on legal advice to a number of offences and were sent to jail or fined.

In 1980, the Attorney General, Lord Lane, had declared that activities deemed to be "in the public interest" would be immune from legal sanction. He listed a number of such activities, including boxing, rugby and mountaineering, concluding his list with 'etc.' A ruling made by the Court of Appeal following a reference by the Attorney General in 1980 allowed for a defense of consent in such activities that caused physical injuries (Attorney-General's Reference, 1980). A number of the defendants appealed their convictions and sentences on the basis that the 'etc.' included sadomasochistic activities. The appeals were heard at the Court of Appeal in January 1992. The Appeal Court (and subsequent courts) responded by asserting that it was not "in the public interest" to allow people to engage in such activities. The convictions were upheld but the sentences reduced on the grounds that the defendants might have been unaware that their activities were illegal. The Appeal Court noted, however, that the grounds for appeal allowed would not apply to similar cases in the future. The Spannermen were warned by the presiding judge, Lord Lane, that if they were arrested on repeat offences they "could expect no mercy from the courts and any sentences would be substantial" (CAR: 498 E).

The case was next taken to the House of Lords, the highest court of appeal in England and Wales, where the convictions were upheld by a majority of three to two, with the two dissenting Lords noting that the case was about sexuality and not violence, and therefore the charges of violence were inappropriate. Having exhausted all legal avenues in the UK, three of the men, Roland Jaggard, Tony Brown, and Colin Laskey, took their case before the European Court of Human Rights (ECHR). In

March 1993 they registered a case with the ECHR at Strasbourg, alleging that the UK Government was principally in breach of Article 8 of the European Convention on Human Rights (1950), which establishes a right to privacy, normally taken to include private expression of sexuality. In December 1995 the European Commissioners reviewing the case decided that the case should go to the ECHR, with the recognition that the case was about "mutual sexual gratification" and not about violence. They offered the opinion that the UK government was within its rights to intervene. In October 1996 the ECHR heard the Spanner Appeal in a three-hour hearing, and on February 19, 1997, unanimously upheld the UK judges' verdict, ruling that governments have a right to intervene in the private sexual activities of their citizens for the sake of public health.

SEX AND VIOLENCE

The understandings of SM in general, and homosexual sadomasochism in particular, evinced through these legal considerations and judgments, reveal an implicit, interlocking set of assumptions about pleasure, the body and gender identity that affected the case. Also acting in the situation is a notion of the social good that is potentially antithetical to private, deviant indulgence.

At an early stage in the Spanner case, there was a collapsing of gay SM into activities that attract straightforward condemnation. By their own account, the police believed, on first viewing the video tapes, that they were watching a snuff movie and were thus compelled to act swiftly and decisively in response to the apparent murder of gay men. This claim by the police gains credence only if considered in light of the video footage used as evidence. Of 16 hours of video tape available to the police, the jury were shown an edited tape, three hours in length, that highlighted acts most readily readable as barbaric, cruel and violent, removing all context, negotiation and evidence of pleasure. An indication of the effect of the editing process is the depiction, amongst the acts perpetrated, of one individual who apparently had his penis nailed to the floor. In fact, the nail was inserted into a pre-existing penile piercing before being knocked into the wood, but this information was removed from the original footage. And the myth of the penis nailing persisted:

> When the context, tone and meaning of an act are removed, sensuality, pleasure and intimacy are removed also, making the consensual appear to be violent abuse. Outside of a consensual

sadomasochistic encounter, the acts committed would be regarded as criminal assaults, but, through the editing process, a wholly inaccurate impression of the Spannermen's activities was created, the horrific nature of which caused a white-faced Judge Rant to ask for an adjournment after watching one video, later saying, "I am not likely to forget that one. No one would." (Young, 1990)

Despite the fact that none of the participants required medical treatment following the private parties, the original investigators persisted in raising the spectre of the snuff movie in the press:

Det Supt Michael Hames, head of Scotland Yard's Obscene Publications Squad, said after the trial that sadistic pornography was becoming more bizarre, more violent and more widespread. He issued a warning that it would eventually lead to a death being filmed. (Young, 1990)

The House of Lords, in considering the appeal, also saw SM as violence, even while acknowledging the sexual dimension:

The Lords make very clear their understanding of SM as violence, not as sex. Charges under the [Offences Against the] Person Act of 1861 are concerned with violence. The violence of sadists and the degradation of their victims have sexual motivations but sex is no excuse for violence. (R v Brown, 1993, 2 WLR 556)

Lord Templeton represented the Lords' overriding preoccupation with the violence of SM:

In my opinion sado-masochism is not only concerned with sex. Sado-masochism is also concerned with violence. The evidence discloses that the practices of the appellants were unpredictably dangerous and degrading to body and mind and were developed with increasing barbarity. . . . (Lord Templeman, R v Brown [1993] 2 All ER 75)

Asserting that "the [manacled] victim had no control over the harm which the sadist, also stimulated by drink and drugs, might inflict" (Lord Templeman, R v Brown [1993] 2 All ER 75) they describe a version of SM that no practitioner of erotic domination and submission would recognize as "safe, sane and consensual." The reiterated belief in violence perpetually on the verge of being out of control works to clearly depict participants as perpetrators and victims, rather than as people engaged in mutual and consensual pleasuring.

While a minority of voices in the Lords argued for allowing the appeal on a variety of grounds, neither did so on the basis that SM is a legitimate expression of erotic pleasure. They too expressed their repugnance of the activities, even while arguing to uphold the appeal:

> It is sufficient to say that whatever the outsider might feel about the subject matter of the prosecutions–perhaps horror, amazement or incomprehension, perhaps sadness–very few could read even a summary of the other activities without disgust. The House has been spared the video tapes, which must have been horrible. (Lord Mustill, R v Brown et al., 1993, 2 All ER 75)

The Lords invoked yet another paradigm to underline the socially dangerous quality of a conspiratorial pleasure in violence: "Society is entitled and bound to protect itself against a cult of violence. Pleasure derived from the infliction of pain is an evil thing. Cruelty is uncivilized" (R v Brown, 1993, 2 WLR 556). SM is here posited as a macabre, barbaric pseudo-religion, antithetical to the implied values of civilized behavior, and where even "safe words" are regarded as "code" words to protect against the recognized danger. "The dangers involved in administering violence must have been appreciated by the appellants because, so it was said by their counsel, each victim was given a code word which he could pronounce when excessive harm or pain was caused" (R v Brown, 1993, 2 WLR 556).

The use of safe words (or code words) by the Spanner defendants forms a key part of their practice of SM according to safe, sane and consensual principles, which represents a refusal to accept abusive qualities such as those ascribed by the House of Lords. The existence of a word or phrase that will bring an entire scene or a particular activity to an end simultaneously guarantees the mental and physical safety of the recipient, and also gives ultimate control over the scene to the recipient, who can call a halt at any time. But the House of Lords, while acknowledging the significance of safe words, throws doubt upon their existence ("so it was said") and replace "safe" with "code," thereby removing the connotations of responsibility and communication, and invoking a sinister frame of reference to condemn such practices.

THE ISSUE OF CONSENT

Although other charges were brought against the defendants, it is the issue of consent that has been at the centre of the activities of both the Spanner campaigners and the pressures to reform the law on assault and sexual offences.

The assault charges brought against the Spannermen took the form of aiding and abetting others to cause injury to self, aiding and abetting actual bodily harm, and actual bodily harm (ABH). In a restatement of definitions, the Crown Prosecution Service Code of June 1994 defines Actual Bodily Harm as "minor but not merely superficial cuts that require stitches." Regardless of the fact that the injuries in the Spanner Case were far less serious than the Code's definition, the men were charged and found guilty of ABH. However, it is the charges of aiding and abetting assault to self that are the most puzzling, since these charges had the effect of making the recipients of the dominants' attentions guilty of conspiring with others to assault themselves.

The charges of ABH were brought under the Offences Against the Person Act 1861, which is based on the premise that the injury is inflicted against the will of the victim. In consensual SM, there is, by definition, consent; therefore, as far as the defense lawyers were concerned, there was no crime. A plea of consent was put into court, with the expectation that the charges would not be upheld. When Judge Rant refused the defense of consent, he positioned the court as the arbiter of acceptable behavior within society. He stated:

> . . . much has been said about individual liberty and the rights people have to do what they want with their own bodies, but the courts must draw the line between what is acceptable in a civilized society and what is not. In this case, the practices clearly lie on the wrong side of that line. (Young, 1990, p. 5)

While maintaining that his ruling was neither a witch-hunt against homosexuals nor "a campaign to curtail the private sexual activities of citizens of this country," Rant determined that the prosecution's case was justified in documenting activities which went far beyond what the law allowed in claiming a defense of consent. For Mr. Michael Worsley, QC (i.e., Queen's Counsel, a member of the elite class of lawyers who can appear in Crown and Appeal Courts in England and Wales), for the Crown (i.e., the prosecution), the case involved "the violent and deliberate inflicting of injury and pain on human beings often to the point of real torture" and "brute homosexual activity in sinister circumstances about as far removed as can be imagined from the concept of human love" (R v Brown et al., 1993, 2 All ER 75; Young, 1990, p. 5). In light of the judge's decision disallowing the defense of consent, the defendants were left with no option other than to plead guilty.

Debate in the appeals courts focused on the nature of legitimate and illegitimate violence. The Court of Appeal, ruling on whether it was in the public interest to prosecute persons who had consented to acts of wounding performed for the victims' sexual pleasure, determined that the satisfying of sadomasochistic libido did not come within the category of good reason for causing bodily harm. They declared that the judge's ruling was correct, while giving leave to appeal to the House of Lords. It is this notion of "good reason" that preoccupied the House of Lords, as they sought to distinguish between bodily harm that can be consented to versus that that cannot. Their conclusion contends that, if the bodily harm is occasioned by a higher purpose in the public interest, it can be consented to. The "higher purposes" primarily considered were those of religion and sport. Amongst the precedents for the House of Lords' Spanner decision put forward was a 1980 Appeal Court case of two juveniles who had agreed to fight each other, where Lord Lane (then the Attorney General) said:

> It is not in the public interest that people should try to cause, or should cause, each other actual bodily harm for no good reason. . . . It is immaterial whether the act occurs in private or in public; it is an assault if actual bodily harm is intended and caused. . . . Nothing which we have said is intended to cast doubt upon the accepted legality of properly conducted games and sports, lawful chastisement or correction, reasonable surgical interference, dangerous exhibitions, etc. These apparent exceptions can be justified as involving the exercise of a legal right, in the case of chastisement or correction, or as needed in the public interest, in the other cases. (AGR, 1981, 719)

In this context, the Lords put forward a series of assertions and contentions that defined SM not as erotic pain-play, but as violence. This categorization was made by characterizing SM as a sinister and irresponsible activity. The Lords put forward an "inevitable" connection between homosexuality and paedophilia, and the potential for an unpredictable escalation of violence. They conjured horrific pictures of brutality, of genital torture, degradation and humiliation, beating,

wounding, bloodletting and the smearing of human blood, with a puta-
tive connection between gay SM and AIDS. Given that there was bloodletting, "there were obvious dangers of serious personal injury and
blood infection. Prosecuting counsel informed the trial judge against the
protests of defence counsel, that although the appellants had not contracted Aids, two members of the group had died from Aids and one
other had contracted an H.I.V. infection although not necessarily from
the practices of the group" (AGR, 1981, 715).

The Lords cite Lord Lane's statement in the Court of Appeal that:
"[Two of the defendants] were responsible in part for the corruption of a
youth K" and offer their comments on the situation:

> . . . It is some comfort at least to be told, as we were, that K. has
> now it seems settled into a normal heterosexual relationship. [One
> defendant] . . . introduced and encouraged K. in "bondage af-
> fairs". . . . One cannot overlook the danger that the gravity of the
> assaults and injuries in this type of case may escalate to even more
> unacceptable heights. (R v Brown et al., 1993, 2 All ER 75)

With such suggestions of the corruption of youth and the threat of
limitless violence, the House of Lords' judgment produced an image of
SM as uncivilized and dangerous, and in which consent was therefore of
no relevance.

The majority of the hearing was taken up with language that condemns and defines SM activity as socially destructive violence, which
frames it as profoundly anti-social, as a space and a ritual apart from
normative structures and practices:

> What the appellants are obliged to propose is that the deliberate
> and painful infliction of physical injury should be exempted from
> the operation of statutory provisions . . . the reason for the pro-
> posed exemption being that both those who will inflict and those
> who will suffer the injury wish to satisfy a perverted and depraved
> sexual desire. Sado-masochistic homosexual activity cannot be re-
> garded as conducive to the enhancement or enjoyment of family
> life or conducive to the welfare of society. A relaxation of the pro-
> hibitions . . . can only encourage the practice of homosexual
> sado-masochism, with the physical cruelty that it must involve
> (which can scarcely be regarded as a 'manly diversion'), by with-
> drawing the legal penalty and giving the activity a judicial impri-
> matur. (R v Brown, 1993, 2 WLR 556)

This contribution from Lord Lowry simultaneously condemns gay SM as antipathetic to family and state, as potentially attractive to those not yet doing it, and as distinct from boxing, that "manly diversion." Even though boxing necessarily involves causing injury to the opponent with that opponent's consent, Lord Mustill stated, "It is in my judgment best to regard [boxing] as another special situation which for the time being stands outside the ordinary law of violence because society chooses to tolerate it" (R v Brown, 1993, 2 WLR 556).

The misunderstanding or incomprehension of SM which underpins the spirit of the Lord's decision is summed up in the almost visceral response by Lord Slynn of Hadley (who nevertheless voted to uphold the appeal):

> Nor is it necessary to refer to other facts which are mentioned in the papers before the House which can only add to one's feeling of revulsion and bewilderment that anyone . . . should wish to do or to have done to him or her the acts so revealed. Some of those other facts, though no less revolting to most people than the facts set out in the charges, could not possibly have constituted an assault in any of the degrees to which I have referred. The determination of the appeal, however, does not depend on bewilderment or revulsion or whether the right approach for the House in the appeal ought to be liberal or otherwise. (R v Brown, 1993, 2 WLR 556)

In fact, the issue to be decided was whether "consent is relevant . . . or that the existence of consent . . . constitutes a defense for the person charged" (Lord Slynn, R v Brown, 1993, 2 WLR 556). However, the legal judgments repeatedly invoke notions of the rights of society, public interest, civilized values and public order, all of which are, in the view of the courts, in danger from the performance of consensual violence.

While the authenticity of consent can be damaged by elements of deception or duress or incompatible levels of power, there are other acts, "which the State ought not to allow, irrespective of whether the parties have given their fullest and most informed consent" (Furlong, 1991, p. 3). Given that there has never been "a comprehensive definition" of the concepts of consent or of public interest in British law, "it is for the judges to decide whether any particular class of acts is in the public interest" (Furlong, 1993, p. 4). As Judge Rant took it upon himself to define what was and what was not acceptable in a civilized society in ruling out a defense of consent, "there is no other guide available than the judge's own conscience" (Furlong, 1991, p. 8) to determine what the public interest is, other than what they may perceive to be the values of society. Lord Mustill's statement, cited above, that the legality of boxing is not against the public interest because "for the time being . . . society chooses to tolerate it" reveals the contingent nature of the standards of public interest. The implication is clear that if, at some time in the future, society chooses not to tolerate boxing, a defense of consent would equally be denied to boxers who had willingly engaged in a bout, as to those engaged in SM. Judge Rant, the Court of Appeal and the House of Lords all assume that SM acts are not tolerable or acceptable within society as it currently frames sexuality. Moreover, they presuppose that the conditions for constructing tolerance and acceptance should not be created by permitting the acts to continue. In this context, it is the responsibility of the law to curtail such activities and punish the perpetrators.

THE ISSUE OF PRIVACY

Hilary Benn MP was Under Secretary of State in the Home Office at the time and thus one of the ministers responsible for the Sexual Offenses Act (which includes references to a wide range of sexual offences, but does not include any references to sadomasochism). Responding to a letter from a Member of Parliament sympathetic to concerns raised over the proposed legislation, Benn wrote, "Under current law sadomasochistic activity which results in physical or mental harm to another could be charged under the Offences Against the Person Act 1861" (Benn, Personal Communication, January, 2003). However, Benn goes on to suggest that the use of a defense of consent where injury or serious injury has been caused during sadomasochistic acts is an aspect of the criminal law that rarely comes before court because it relates usually to activities that take place in private (Benn, 2003).

Although seeming to offer reassurance that the law is unlikely to be enforced very often because the acts take place in private, the UK Government claimed a right and responsibility in the Spanner case to intervene in private sadomasochistic practices. The Government took the view that it cannot condone acts, even consensual ones, involving injury, a position accepted by the European Court of Human Rights.

The claims of the British courts to regulate the private conduct of consenting adults on the basis of public interest were upheld by the ECHR. The Spannermen sought to overturn the UK courts' judgments on the grounds that they violated Article 8.1 of the European Human Rights Convention: "Everyone has the right to respect for his private and family life, his home and his correspondence." In 1997, the ECHR ruled that the UK Government had not breached the right to privacy as defined by Article 8 since it had legitimately intervened to defend the public health of UK society. This is consistent with the terms of Article 8.2, which states:

> There shall be no interference by a public authority with the exercise of this right except such as is in accordance with the law and is necessary in a democratic society in the interests of national security, public safety or the economic well-being of the country, for the prevention of disorder or crime, for the protection of health or morals, or for the protection of the rights and freedoms of others.

The ECHR ruled:

> It is evident from the facts established by the national courts that the applicants' sado-masochistic activities involved a significant degree of injury or wounding which could not be characterized as trifling or transient. . . . It is clear from the judgment of the House of Lords that the opinions of the majority were based on the extreme nature of the practices involved and not the sexual proclivities of the applicants. . . . In sum, the Court finds that the national authorities were entitled to consider that the prosecution and conviction of the applicants were necessary in a democratic society for the protection of health within the meaning of Article 8 § 2 of the Convention. In view of this conclusion the Court, like the Commission, does not find it necessary to determine whether the interference with the applicants' right to respect for private life could also be justified on the ground of the protection of morals. This finding, however, should not be understood as calling into question the prerogative of the State on moral grounds to seek to deter acts of the kind in question. (ECHR, 1997, ¶ 45, 47, 50 and 51)

This decision makes the actions of the government not only legal, but necessary on the grounds of health interests, while not questioning the rights of UK Courts to engage with and pronounce upon the moral aspects of SM that are nationally determined. The European Court of Human Rights has acknowledged in the past "it is impossible to find . . . a uniform European conception of morals" (Suarez, 1997).

From this stance of protection of health, the law and the Convention views SM as causing pain, bruises and wounds, and therefore should be stopped. Without consideration of consent, SM scene skills and structures, or the meaning of the acts to those practicing them, the ECHR chose to regard it as a matter of public health. The ECHR did not consider injury statistics (or lack thereof), hospital admissions, or any other measuring technique to determine the extent of the impact on public health or social services of SM activities.

PATHOLOGY AND THEATRICALITY

The legislative deliberations over SM and consent reflect a desire to and a claim to a right to regulate conduct in the interests of the social whole and to correct the misguided individual. Courts have successively prescribed and proscribed activities according to a continuum of violence, where the extent of injury and investment in the activities is used to determine what may come within the aegis of the control of the law. The appeals debates repeatedly struck notes on a theme of authentic pain and degradation. It is perhaps in consideration of the notion of the "real" quality of the violence and abuse that the regulatory paradigms and the SM paradigm encounter the most acute mutual incomprehension. While Lord Templeman suggested "sado-masochism is not only concerned with sex. Sado-masochism is also concerned with violence," an unnamed practitioner, in evidence to the 1995 Law Commission, contended "Sadomasochism is only violence by metaphor: a closer metaphor would be to view sadomasochism as theater" (British Law Commission, 1995, 10.32).

The evidence given by practitioners to the Commission emphasizes the crucial role of negotiation and consent, and repeatedly asserts the frequency of "switching" between dominant and submissive roles. This position seems designed to confront the beliefs, implicit and explicit, in the legal response to the Spannermen, that sadomasochism involves abuse and victimization in a fixed relationship of authentic violence and violation. "Switching," on the other hand, allows for a taking of turns at being the punisher and the punished, the giver and the receiver, undermining fixed categories of perpetrator and victim. It is the difference between SM as a "cult" and SM as theatre, between immanent identity and performative flexibility.

HETEROSEXISM AND HOMOPHOBIA

An aspect of the Spanner case which raised questions to many who followed it, but which was ignored by the European Commission as irrelevant, is the differential treatment of homosexual men and heterosexual married couples. In February 1996 the Court of Appeal, in adjudicating on the case of R v Wilson, overturned the conviction of a husband for branding his initials on the buttocks of his wife with her consent, declaring that "consensual activity in the privacy of the matrimonial home was not a matter for criminal prosecution" (*Times Law Report*, 1996, 2 Cr App R 241). The court believed that the defendant had been engaged in an activity which in principle was no more dangerous than professional tattooing, and that it was not in the public interest that his activities should amount to criminal behaviour. So, while no distinction was made between public and private environments in the Spanner hearings, and while the branding was more than a "transient and trifling" injury, the only, but crucial difference between R v Brown et al., and R v Wilson, is seemingly one of sexual orientation. While married heterosexuals seem to be permitted privacy and the right to consent, the same privileges were not granted by the Court of Appeal to homosexual men.

The Spanner Trust asked Ben Emerson and Rabhinder Singh, two human rights lawyers, to consider the ECHR's decision in light of the privacy provisions of Article 8 (and thus the state's right to intervene in actions that are "private"). According to Emmerson and Singh, proportionality and the extent of injuries are central to the arguments offered against the Spannermen's defense of consent. They offer a critique of the court's attempts to distinguish between R v Laskey and R v Wilson on the grounds of the severity of injuries inflicted:

> The emphasis which the Court placed in *Laskey* on the severity of the injuries inflicted drove it to distinguish the English Court of Appeal decision in *R v Wilson* [1996] 2 Cr. App. R. 241 on tenuous grounds. In *Wilson* the Court of Appeal held that a defense of consent was available to the defendant. . . . In an unconvincing response, the Court held that there was no evidence of a difference in the treatment of homosexuals, because it was the "extreme nature of the practices involved" in *Laskey* that distinguished it, rather than the sexual orientation of the participants. The facts of *Wilson* were, in the Court's view, "not at all comparable in seriousness"

with those of *Laskey* even though they amounted to assault occasioning actual bodily harm. (Emmerson and Singh, 2003: 3-4)

Although the courts insisted upon the severity of the injuries inflicted on and by the Spannermen, not one of them required medical treatment for those injuries, which were arguably less severe than might be caused by branding. The dismissal of R v Wilson and the upholding of R v Laskey seems illogical in this respect, based on the degree of injury.

The confusion and differential treatment represented by the Spanner case has led to anxiety, confusion and fear amongst SM practitioners, and is having an impact on the organization and practices of the SM scene, especially the gay SM scene. In correspondence with the Spanner Trust's Treasurer, Ian Gurnhill, a picture of fear and unwanted changes to the atmosphere and organization of the gay SM community emerges:

> Although SM Gays exists and holds monthly meetings, it has been advised NOT to create a membership list. This means it has no screening process . . . to filter inappropriate people from genuinely interested people who want more advanced education than the "Introduction to the Hard Scene" courses that SM Gays run several times a year. . . . The UK gay community has no such focus [as the US] and no equivalent of SM Gays outside London. (Ian Gurnhill, Personal communication, August 13, 2002)

The Treasurer of the Trust identifies a difference between straight and gay SMers, seeing a greater level of organization and opposition in the straight community than amongst gay practitioners.

> SM heterosexuals are now suffering discrimination like gays used to suffer. Social Services taking children into care because they find out a parent has a SM web site. Job termination because an employer finds out about an employee's SM activities. In fact like the Spanner case itself which galvanised interested parties into closer contact, these cases have stimulated greater contact between local groups and led to web pages and email lists. Something that the gay community still lack. (Ian Gurnhill, Personal communication, August 13, 2002)

Because the existing case law gives the appearance of distinguishing between heterosexual and homosexual sadomasochism, and because homosexuals still feel they are subject to persistent discrimination, gay sadomasochists feel they are doubly denied the possibility of organizing to defend themselves against future prosecutions.

LAW REFORM COMMISSION PROPOSALS–A RESPONSE?

As the Spanner case was working its way through the appeal process, there was public questioning of the role of consent and the criminality of SM activities in England. Perhaps as a result of the lack of clarity in the law, and of the lack of unanimity in the appeal process (with the House of Lords decision split: three to dismiss the appeal and two to uphold it) the British Law Commission initiated consultations and issued documents relevant to the case. In March1993 the Commission initiated consultation on the issue of consent in assault law. All interested parties were invited to make submissions to them, with some of the parties being invited to give evidence before the Commission. This process led to the publication of a consultation paper "Consent In The Criminal Law" (consultation paper 139). Almost two years later, in December 1995 the Commission issued a second consultation document on consent within SM activities.

As a Website on the Law Commission's report explained:

> The Law Commission is an official Government body that produces among other things Consultation Papers about particularly difficult or unclear areas of the Law. The Law Commission reports are intended to clarify the situation and are used by Politicians to help them draw up future Parliamentary Bills in the particular area of concern. When the Law is clarified by a change of Law it is usually in line with the recommendations of The Law Commission Consultation Papers. It therefore follows that The Law Commission recommendations are most important in the formulation of English Criminal Law. (*Revise* f65, page 1)

The Commission's second document (No 139 1995) contains "the most wide-ranging and detailed official survey ever conducted into SM activities" (Revise f65, p.1).

The objective of the second consultation document was described as "concerned solely with the question whether such acts should in themselves constitute criminal offences even if a valid consent is given to them" (Revise f65, page 5, Section 10.52). Having heard many submissions from SM practitioners and academics, the Commission concluded: ". . . nobody may give a valid consent to seriously disabling injury, but subject to this limitation the law ought not to prevent people from consenting to injuries caused for religious or sexual purposes" (British Law Commission, 1995, section 10.52). And further:

> We therefore provisionally propose that for the purpose of the proposals contained in paragraph 4.49 and 4.50 of this Paper any consent given by a person under 18 to injuries intentionally caused for sexual, religious or spiritual purposes should not be treated as valid consent. (section 10.55)

Effectively, the Law Commission proposed that consent to injury that is not "seriously disabling" would be legal, as long as the individual was over 18. While this proposal has not been made law, it does represent a change from the position taken by the judge, the Appeal Court, the House of Lords, and the European Court.

In January, 2003, the Sexual Offences Bill came into law. The Sexual Offences Act 2003 includes references to a wide range of sexual offences, including, among others, Rape, Assault, Child sex offences, Abuse of position of trust, Offences against persons with a mental disorder impeding choice, Abuse of children through prostitution and pornography, Exploitation of prostitution, Trafficking, etc., but does not include any references to sadomasochism. While it includes a definition of consent, and sections on evidential and conclusive presumptions of consent, it does not incorporate proposals from the Spanner Trust that:

- Sadomasochism be recognized as a sexual activity which may involve injury;
- The Law Commission's proposals for the definitions of consent and capacity to consent as laid out in "Consent in Sex Offences" should be adopted;
- A clause be added to any future Sex Offences Bill which decriminalizes SM which does not cause serious injury, whilst continuing the prohibition of activities which cause serious injury. (Spanner Trust, 2001 ¶8, 9, 10)

As a result, the Spanner Trust suggests that the Act "doesn't go far enough and still leaves the human rights of some adults infringed as far as their sex lives are concerned" (Spanner Trust, 2003).

PAST, PRESENT AND FUTURE

The conceptualization of SM as something to be regulated began with Krafft-Ebing in 1889, and, as the Spanner case demonstrated, it is still regarded with revulsion and horror by many. However, the potential criminalization of SM, and the vulnerability felt by many as the result of the Spanner decisions, has served to make SM less safe for its participants. As submissions to the Law Reform Commission pointed out:

> For private sadomasochists, Spanner has had a very negative effect. There is a clamp-down on sadomasochism. Sadomasochists have no ready access to safe sex literature or safe practice literature. It has also discouraged people from coming to our clubs and social spaces–the network of safety advice.

And again:

> Some activities are simply not safe to do alone. At least one person has died as a direct result of the "Brown" verdict. He was into breath restriction. . . . Following "Brown" he feared involving his partner in his activities and reverted to doing them alone. He was found dead. The current law endangers people rather than protects them. The best protection is sound safety information. (Law Reform Commission, 1995, section 10.39)

What the law seeks to control is the Theatre of Pleasure in which bodies, identities and pleasures are fluid, boundless and performative. As with homosexuality, SM has a self-aware and self-defining subculture, yet also standing in the way of political resistance is the fragmentation of that subculture, most notably between the "lifestylers" and those they dismissively term "players," full-time 24/7 masters and slaves set against the part-timers. It is, moreover, marked by a powerful individualism, simultaneously priding itself on having no part in 'normal' society, while, particularly amongst then lifestylers, regarding the precise forms of erotic power and pain play as emanating from the deepest truth of the individual. But such divisions should not be allowed to interfere with efforts to change the laws in order to prevent future Spanner-type persecutions. All those involved in SM–players and lifestylers, homosexuals and heterosexuals–are potentially affected, are potentially criminalized, unless the law is changed to explicitly permit consensual

SM activities which do not involved serious and lasting injury. If the means of removing SM from the purview of law is to adopt the tactics of the Gay Liberation Movement (we were born as we are and it is fruitless and against nature to try and change us), then what will be lost?

REFERENCES

AGR (1981). *Attorney-General's Reference* (No 6 of 1980) [1981] 2 All ER 1057.

AGR (1980) *Attorney-General's Reference* . No. 6, p. 719.

Asch, Stuart S. (1988). "The Analytic Concepts of Masochism: A Reevaluation." In Robert A. Glick and Donald I. Meyers, *Masochism: Contemporary Psychoanalytic Perspectives*. New Jersey: Analytic Press.

British Law Commission on Consent in the Criminal Law (1995). *2nd document No 139*. London: HMSO.

CAR: 498 E.(1991) Court of Appeal ruling in R v. Brown et al.

Crown Prosecution Service (1994). *Code*, 3rd edition, June 1994.

ECHR (1950). European Convention on Human Rights. Retrieved November 20, 2002, from Press for Change Website: http://www.pfc.org.uk/legal/echrtext.htm

ECHR (1997). *Reports of Judgments and Decisions*. Köln: Carl Heymanns Verlag KG.

Emmerson, Ben, QC and Rabinder Singh QC (2003). *In the Matter of the Spanner Trust: Joint Opinion*. Spanner Trust Website. Retrieved June 15th, 2003, from http://www.spannertrust.org.

Furlong, Anthony (1991). *Sado-Masochism and the Law: Consent versus Paternalism*. Legal Notes No. 12. London: The Libertarian Alliance.

Gibbs, Frances (1994). "Violent Sportsmen 'should be brought before the courts.'" *The Times*. February 24, 1994.

Jaggard, Richard (n.d.). *Spannerman*. Retrieved November 24, 2002, from http://www.bmezine.com/news/people/A10101/spanner/

Krafft-Ebing, Richard von (1893). *Psychopathia Sexualis, with especial reference to Contrary Sexual Instinct: a Medico-Legal Study*. (Authorized translation of the seventh enlarged and revised German edition by Charles Gilbert Craddock.) London: F. R Rebman.

Law Commission (1995). "Consent In The Criminal Law," consultation paper 139.

Revise f65, [nd] The Law Commission: the official text. Retreived August 5, 2004 from *http://www.revisef65.org/lawcomm2.html*

R v Brown, Laskey, Jaggard and others (1992). 2 WLR 441.

R v Brown et al. (1993). 2 WLR 556.

Spanner Trust (2001) Submission to the Home Office Sexual Offences Review Board Retrieved November 24, 2002 from Spanner Trust website: *http://www.spannertrust.org/documents/sexualoffencesreview.html*.

Spanner Trust (2003). Press Release "Sexual Law reform still leaves government open to HRA challenge" Retrieved August 5 2004 from Spanner Trust Website *http://www.spannertrust.org/press/sob29jan2003.asp*

Suarez, Ramon Prieto (1997). Report on "Article 10 of the European Convention for the Protection of Human Rights and Fundamental Freedoms: the Background of the Media in a Democratic Society." Brussels: Directorate of the Human Rights, Council of Europe.

The Times Law Report (1996). 2 Cr App R 241. March 5.

Young, David (1990). "Leaders of vicious and perverted sex gang jailed: Pornography ring." *The Times*, December 20 1990.

Negotiating Limits:
The Legal Status of SM in the United States

Robert B. Ridinger, MA, MLS

Northern Illinois University

SUMMARY. This paper reviews the origin of the concept of sadomasochism and its treatment by the American legal system. Relevant court cases and corollary issues such as the rights to privacy and sexual freedom, child custody, domestic violence, and employment discrimination are profiled. Organizations created by the gay, lesbian and heterosexual leather communities to create accurate public awareness of the SM subculture, and their programs of education and activism, are discussed and prospects for effective legislative change evaluated. *[Article copies available for a fee from The Haworth Document Delivery Service: 1-800-HAWORTH. E-mail address: <docdelivery@haworthpress.com> Website: <http://www. HaworthPress.com> © 2006 by The Haworth Press, Inc. All rights reserved.]*

KEYWORDS. Sadomasochism/SM, court cases and decisions, sex law and legislation, leather/levi community, civil rights law and legislation

---

Professor Robert B. Ridinger is Chair, Electronic Information Resources Management, 15E Founders Memorial Library, Northern Illinois University, De Kalb, IL 60115-2868 (E-mail: rridinger@niu.edu).

[Haworth co-indexing entry note]: "Negotiating Limits: The Legal Status of SM in the United States." Ridinger, Robert B. Co-published simultaneously in *Journal of Homosexuality* (Harrington Park Press, an imprint of The Haworth Press, Inc.) Vol. 50, No. 2/3, 2006, pp. 189-216; and: *Sadomasochism: Powerful Pleasures* (ed: Peggy J. Kleinplatz, and Charles Moser) Harrington Park Press, an imprint of The Haworth Press, Inc., 2006, pp. 189-216. Single or multiple copies of this article are available for a fee from The Haworth Document Delivery Service [1-800-HAWORTH, 9:00 a.m. - 5:00 p.m. (EST). E-mail address: docdelivery@haworthpress.com].

Available online at http://www.haworthpress.com/web/JH
© 2006 by The Haworth Press, Inc. All rights reserved.
doi:10.1300/J082v50n02_09

Attempted regulation of sexual behaviors engaged in by members of the gay and lesbian communities through specific pieces and categories of sex law and legislation within the United States has a lengthy history, beginning with the sodomy laws enacted by various colonies in the sixteenth and seventeenth centuries. However, the issue of legal control was rendered problematic by the reluctance of colonial lawmakers to be explicit in their description of precisely what sexual acts were considered to be objectionable, beyond utilizing, in many cases, already established terms borrowed from English and European culture, such as "buggery," referring to anal intercourse. Many of these sodomy laws have remained on the books (if infrequently enforced, depending on the jurisdiction involved) until the present time, and do not reflect well the changes in attitudes towards sexuality occurring in the larger American society. Their antiquated language became increasingly disconnected from the discussion of sexual subjects within the general population and set these laws up as the targets of many of the early gay liberation protest campaigns for legislative reform. As previously private and taboo aspects of homosexuality emerged into the light of discussion and acknowledged reality under the philosophy of "Gay Is Good," many legal strictures on sexual activity were seen to be irrelevant. They were either abolished outright or severely limited in authority and application. The present paper will examine the approaches taken by the American legal system to a particularly recognizable and distinctive variety of sexual behavior, sadomasochism (also known by the abbreviations SM and S/M), and the responses made to them from within the gay and lesbian communities.

MEDICAL, PSYCHIATRIC, AND LEGAL DEFINITIONS

Research into the subject of SM has historically been complicated by a supposition that the range of specific sexual practices and actions constituting sadomasochism is well defined and agreed upon by the culture as a whole and described precisely by the language of the fields of law and jurisprudence. This is somewhat inaccurate. An examination of the historical treatment of the subject within the scientific study of sexuality by Bullough notes that, "Until it became a diagnosis it received little attention and was not even classified as a sin" (Bullough, 1977, p. 210). Of the two terms, sadism is the older, being derived from the name of Louis Donatien Francois Alphonse de Sade (1740-1814), whose novels (chiefly written during his time in prisons) were intended to describe forms of sexual diversion. He believed that pain was more thrilling to the nerves than joy and that women possessed a greater capacity for cruelty than men due to the more sensitive nature of their genitalia. These themes were taken up and further elaborated by other French literary writers. They created a body of material from which the German psychiatrist Richard von Krafft-Ebing (1840-1902) drew in clinically defining sadism in his compilation *Psychopathia Sexualis* as the, "impulse to cruel and violent treatment of the opposite sex, and the coloring of the idea of such acts with lustful feelings" (Krafft-Ebing, 1894, p. 60).

Krafft-Ebing's approach to researching sexuality combined several nineteenth-century theoretical viewpoints regarding sexual perversion, the ideas that disease was caused by the nervous system, that hereditary physical defects in this system were known to occur, and the idea of degeneracy. This last equated genetic defects with the idea of atavism, the reemergence of primitive tendencies in otherwise civilized people, said tendencies including physical weakness and deviant behavior. This created the popular image of a, "sexual degenerate . . . an uncontrolled, primitive, animal-like person who might do anything" (Bullough, 1976, p. 640). The idea that a sexual orientation was inborn had been put forward by the German jurist Karl Heinrich Ulrichs (1825-1895). He proposed that homosexuals constituted a "third sex" and that their sexual behaviors should therefore not be penalized by the legal system, permitting them to enjoy the full civil rights open to any citizen (Kennedy, 1988, p. 50).

The first physician to study alternative forms of sexual expression was Carl Westphal (1833-1890), who in 1869 published the case study of a young woman who was drawn to her own gender and had historically dressed as a boy (Bullough, 1976, p. 639). His conclusions were similar to the arguments advanced by Ulrichs in that, while he considered there to be some elements of neurosis present, the patient's sanity was not in question (Bullough, 1967, p. 639). Westphal's work laid the foundation for a veritable explosion of publications on homosexuality in the late nineteenth century, with over a thousand appearing between 1898 and 1908 in German alone, thus legitimizing alternative forms of sexual activity as a proper subject for scientific investigation. The challenge to medicine was to find a cure for such inbred inversion of normal sexual instincts. This led to experimentation with hypnosis by the French neurologist Jean Martin Charcot (1825-1893) and his colleague Valentin Magnan (1835-1916), who met with only moderate success with their patients at the Salpetriere asylum. A comprehensive explanation of the causes of this hereditary degeneration was offered by physician Paul Moreau, who proposed that human beings possessed a sixth "genital sense" that could be damaged without affecting other normal sensory functions. Moreau cited environmental factors as creating "a sort of predisposition to perversion" (Bullough, 1976, p. 639), with factors ranging from climate, food and seasons of the year to age. The only option for persons suffering from these conditions (other than imprisoning them, which Moreau opposed) was their hospitalization, as, "this intermediate class . . . constituted a mixed class midway between reason and madness, forever being pulled close to madness" (Bullough, 1976, p. 640). Krafft-Ebing's encyclopedic work *Psychopathia Sexualis* can thus be seen in some ways as the culmination and distillation of a wide variety of prior research into the origin of nonstandard sexuality.

Krafft-Ebing also regarded the sole purpose of sexual activity to be procreation; other such activities were to be considered as a perversion of normal sexual instincts. This narrow focus led to the *Psychopathia Sexualis'* general categories of fetishism, homosexuality, sadism and masochism being augmented by a wide range of other topics such as cannibalism, collecting handkerchiefs, satyriasis, and nymphomania. The over 200 cases reviewed in *Psychopathia Sexualis* also served the function of bringing the full range of possible human sexual behavior before the public. This work was widely circulated (going through at least eleven editions), thus introducing sexual variation as an acceptable subject for social discussion outside the domain of medicine and the often exaggerated and lurid depictions provided by literature.

Krafft-Ebing coined the term "masochism," drawing his model from the novels of Austrian writer Leopold von Sacher-Masoch (1836-1895), where themes of being punished in an erotic context appeared. Sacher-Masoch was alive at the time and objected to Krafft-Ebing's use of his grandfather's surname in such a context. The terms sadism and masochism were in sufficiently widespread usage by 1888 and 1893 respectively to be noted in the *Oxford English Dictionary*. Both were intended to describe specific types of behavior within the category of sexual pathology, and their combination into the more widely circulated term "sadomasochism" provided the initial basis for the classification of such persons and their actions as deviant by public opinion. As applied to sexuality, a particular sexual behavior "is considered deviant . . . when a large or influential segment of society disapproves of it because it violates explicit or implicit social norms about 'normal' sexuality" (McAnulty, 1995, p. 239).

One would logically expect the terms to appear in all major legal reference works as guides to both police and members of the bar alike;

however an examination of standard dictionaries of law and legal terminology reveals that neither of these terms are well established within the
legal lexicon, appearing in only five sources. Sadism appears in the
third edition of *Ballentine's Law Dictionary* in 1969, although sadomasochism and masochism are not present. The second edition of the
Law Dictionary edited by Professor Max Radin of Berkeley issued in
1970 contains sadism only, while *West's Legal Thesaurus and Dictionary*, published in 1985, contains both sadism and sadomasochism.
Black's Law Dictionary, long considered to be the best reference available for interpreting the meanings assigned language by the field of law
to the general public, contains the term sadism in its sixth 1990 edition
but omits it in the seventh, issued in 1999, while masochism is not listed
at all.

The most revealing source of for the legal etymology of sadism and
words derived from it is the entries in the permanent edition of *Words
and Phrases,* which appeared in 2002. This tool provides a lexicon of
how specific terms have been defined in the judgments of individual
court cases, and notes the definition of sadism in Nevada in the 1910
case of *State v. Petty* as "a mental disease in which the sexual instinct is
abnormal or perverted" (Words and Phrases, volume 38, p. 4). The
other entries on sadistic purpose, sadistic or masochistic conduct,
sado-masochistic abuse and even sadomasochism itself all date from
1995 through 2000 and mirror the psychiatric definitions advanced by
Krafft- Ebing and his successors, emphasizing the infliction of pain for
the purpose of experiencing sexual pleasure. This relative absence of
definition is notable, as other sexual behaviors such as fellatio, bestiality and incest are explicitly mentioned and have been regularly
prohibited by American laws and legislation since colonial times.

Given the general practice within American culture until the early decades of the twentieth century of employing euphemisms when referring to sex in almost any context, the use of precise terminology for
sexual acts (often borrowed intact from the fields of psychiatry and psychology) was all the more shocking to the general public. It was in this
context that the term "sado-masochism" came into the awareness of
American lawmaking bodies in the nineteenth and twentieth centuries
as a sub-species of sexual behavior which should be regulated for the
protection of the common good and the possible "cure" of the individuals who practiced it. The initial definition of SM as a psychiatric phenomenon cast it as a type of disorder, which should be attended to by
practitioners of that field, and in the public mind made anyone who did
it "sick," and therefore not to be considered legally responsible. Police

and lawyers would thus have viewed it as something that was outside the moral norms of society, similar in that way to criminal behavior, and reacted to it within established categories of prohibited behaviors and defined crimes. Rather than taking it on themselves explicitly to police morality, they would have used other legal pretexts to shut down SM activities they had been taught were abhorrent to society.

LAW REFORMS, POLICIES, AND COURT CASES

The changes which occurred in the 1960s with regard to sex law and legislation at many levels of American society were stimulated in part by the younger generation's rejection of puritanical attitudes towards sexual experimentation in all forms, ranging from pre-marital sex to communal living, and a new openness regarding the acceptance of sexuality as a joyous and healthy facet of human psychology. One consequence of this social ferment was the replacement of the homophile movement of the 1950s (whose focus was the promotion of civil rights for homosexuals through education instead of confrontational activism) by the American gay liberation movement in 1969. Among its earliest stated aims was the repeal of specific pieces of state or local laws and ordinances, an example being the "victimless crime" laws of the state of California, which were widely employed by the police for the purposes of harassment. Yet even within the gay movement, those members of this new counterculture who engaged in SM behaviors (often as members of the leather/levi social and motorcycle organizations established in the 1950s) were seen as political liabilities to the philosophy of "Gay Is Good." Out of this philosophy came the attitude that gays and lesbians were just like their heterosexual friends and relatives, except for their sexual orientation.

Legal activism aimed at the elimination of sexuality as a proper category for government regulation, on the model of European legal systems based on the Napoleonic Code, received a substantial boost in 1953. At this time, the Rockefeller Foundation issued a grant to the American Law Institute for the purposes of exploring solutions to the need for a massive revision and unification of the penal codes of the United States. The resulting Model Penal Code was used by the State of Illinois as a referent when it became the first such jurisdiction to decriminalize private, consensual, homosexual behavior in 1961. Within the newly visible gay and lesbian communities, those whose sexuality found expression through the ritualized play of SM generally kept themselves apart in their own bars and organizations, a parallel and highly private social world which the more mainstream gay rights activism did not touch except occasionally. As a consequence, the philosophical priorities of gay and lesbian legal reform and the laws and ordinances, rooted in the activism that spawned them, did not acknowledge the civil rights of the sadomasochist or regard them as part of the spectrum of sexual activities that required legal protection.

This situation began to alter in the 1980s with the appearance of the AIDS pandemic and the frantic exploration of techniques of sexual expression that would not expose the participants to possible infection, a group of behaviors collectively labeled as "safe sex." The powerful rituals of sadomasochistic play, with their deep emotional satisfactions and freedom from the requirement that body fluids be exchanged, began to attract more attention from gays and lesbians and, as the fear of AIDS increasingly manifested in the heterosexual population, the mainstream media. Suddenly, discussion of this taboo subject became not only permissible but imperative. Longtime practitioners and novices alike (whether heterosexual or homosexual) found themselves the objects of intense scrutiny by a larger society. Up until that time, there had been little public interest in such matters outside the fields of medicine and psychiatry, and consequently there was no clear and ready response to fitting this newly revealed community into its established framework of legal regulations.

Spanner Case

The most notable involvement of SM practitioners with a legal system to date occurred not in the United States, but in Great Britain. This was the British police investigation of 1987 which became known as the Spanner case (after the name of the chief investigating officer), entered in the legal record as *Laskey, Jaggard and Brown v. United Kingdom*. In this proceeding, videotapes of private SM gatherings were utilized as evidence to prosecute several individuals on charges of assault and wounding over a period of ten years, under two provisions of the Offences Against the Person Act of 1861. The defendants attempted to argue that because the participants had given consent and had established agreed-upon safe words to end the play, their actions were not assault. The initial trial judge ruled this to be an inadmissible argument, obliging them to plead guilty, a decision later upheld on appeal and confirmed by the House of Lords. Three of the individuals, Colin Laskey, Roland Jaggard, and Tony Brown, were sentenced to prison but received reduced sentences on appeal. Following Laskey's death in 1996, Brown and Jaggard took their case to the European Court of Human Rights. The judgment in the case, delivered in Strasbourg on February 19, 1997, affirmed the right of government to regulate the infliction of harm through passage of criminal law. It was noted that domestic law could make SM behaviors a specific criminal offense without violating Article 8 of the European Convention of Human Rights, which covered the protection of private life from government interference. The Commission stated that the grounds of the original conviction under British law were the infliction of wounds upon the participants and the accompanying assault and violent behavior. These include prolonged whipping and genital torture. The judges stated that the interference with the applicants' right to respect for their private lives may be considered as necessary in a democratic society "for the aim of protecting health" (European Court of Human Rights. Report of the commission, section 63). No case on such a scale has as yet been adjudicated within the United States.

SM IN THE AMERICAN LEGAL SYSTEM

The range of sexual behaviors subject to regulation by the laws of the United States (as formally stated in both the U.S. Code and state law codes) is rape/sexual assault, violations of the age of consent, sodomy, transmission of disease, public nudity/indecency, fornication, adultery, the abuse of position of trust/authority, incest, bigamy, prostitution, the possession of obscene materials, obscene communications, necrophilia, bestiality and voyeurism (Posner, 1996). It is within this matrix of subjects that the legal attention paid to SM within American jurisdictions must be considered. An examination of the major databases in the field of law and criminology, *Legaltrac* and the *National Criminal Justice Research Service,* and the Uniform Crime Reports produced by Federal Bureau of Investigation conducted by the author in January 2003 revealed that no subject heading for sadomasochism exists, while a topical search retrieved very few citations.

The earliest involvement of sadomasochism with the law appears to have been as an element of the work of forensic pathologists. Articles appeared in the professional journals of forensic sciences detailing individual cases where SM practices such as breath control or bondage inadvertently resulted in conditions leading to death, or murder investigations which revealed that the event possessed an SM component. (The latter could be introduced either through deliberate misdirection by the perpetrator [such as the arrangement of the scene to indicate that sadómasochistic play had been occurring when this was in fact untrue], the dressing of the body in SM accouterments such as hoods, or placing physical signs on the body to be interpreted as caused by some type of SM activity.) This classification of SM as an activity which might occasionally affect technical questions in criminal investigations and the process of law enforcement appears in many of the articles written in American forensic and medical reviews of the subject in the last three decades of the twentieth century.

The codes and ordinances of American government at all levels lack clearly stated articles of law explicitly defining and prohibiting or limiting SM actions or practices, the type of measure noted as possible in the Spanner judgment. This leaves law enforcement personnel who, in the normal performance of their duties, encounter situations which appear to them to be SM-related with the sole option of defining them as violations of other provisions of the law. Law enforcement agencies could apply these categories provided under already extant sex laws to their efforts to prohibit both public and private events sponsored by SM social and educational groups. Zoning and public indecency laws might be construed to apply in this context. A review of the most important cases to date provides evidence of the sheer breadth of law which has been applied to this topic and the complexity of the simple term "consent."

People v. Samuels

The first significant appearance of SM as a primary element of a court case occurred in California in 1967. *People v. Samuels* centered on a San Francisco ophthalmologist who expressed his SM desires through the making of films depicting them, films in which he himself either acted, whipping a consenting individual who was bound, or served as director. He became acquainted with director Kenneth Anger, who had also made films showing SM, and Anger offered to send some of Samuels' films to the Kinsey Institute to assist in its study of SM behaviors. One of the films submitted for processing was sent to a different developer than Samuels' usual firm, and the new company notified the police. It is worth remembering that the appearance of this case is two years before the riot at New York's Stonewall Inn, which sparked the gay liberation movement. It thus falls during the very last years of the homophile movement, whose stress on achieving social change through education and acceptance via demonstrations of how similar to heterosexuals homosexuals were would likely have precluded any assistance from the Mattachine Society's San Francisco chapter to the plaintiff. From a purely legal viewpoint, it is valuable as the first case in which a United States court "refused to extend the idea of violent consent to an assault and battery within an S/M context" (Hanna, 2001, p. 257). The consenting partner in the offending film was not asked for testimony or even located, as Samuels had dropped him off at the bus station as prearranged. There was thus no physical plaintiff present during the deliberations, and the court did not require the prosecution to produce medical evidence of the extent of injuries actually inflicted on the victim. Despite this, the court noted that "it is a matter of common knowledge that a normal person in full possession of his mental faculties does not freely consent to the use, upon himself, of force likely to produce great bodily injury" (Lence, 1995, p. 10). Samuels was thus found guilty of cruelty to an unnamed person whose legal existence rested solely on an image and whose input was never sought or deemed necessary to the conduct of the case.

Mark IV Incident

California was also the site of one of the most widely publicized instances of a police force attempting to enforce existing law on an S/M-related event occurring in a public venue. On April 10, 1976, a fund raising event was scheduled to be held at the Mark IV bathhouse in Los Angeles by, as coverage printed in *The Advocate* described it, "the Leather Fraternity, an S/M club based in Los Angeles, and *Drummer* magazine" (*Advocate*, 190, p. 9), *Drummer* being the leading internationally circulated publication for gay men who practiced SM. A massive raid by the Los Angeles Police Department involving 30 metropolitan police officers, 30 vice officers, and a helicopter resulted in the arrest of 40 people; these ranged from auctioneers and buyers to the "slaves" themselves, all of whom were to be "sold" for the purpose of raising money for the Gay Community Services Center. Police cited the event as being in violation of section 181 of the penal code. The text of this section states:

> Every person who holds, or attempts to hold, any person in involuntary servitude, or assumes, or attempts to assume, rights of ownership over any person, or who sells, or attempts to sell, any person to another, or receive money or anything of value, in consideration

of having placed in his custody, or under his power and control, or who knowingly aids or assists in any manner anyone thus offending, is punishable by imprisonment in the state prison not less than one nor more than ten years. (Willmore, 1976, p. 13)

The statement issued to the press by the LAPD nowhere revealed the fact that all seven men had volunteered to take part in the event without coercion. A question posed in the reportage of the event and subsequent court actions, why, if the "slavery" was all voluntary, did police arrest everyone (including the slaves), seems never to have been answered. Neither the city attorney Burt Pines nor the District Attorney John Van De Kamp were informed of the police raid prior to the event. A group of Los Angeles city council members publicly attacked the action and called for an investigation. A later defense of this raid was a statement that the police acted on advance information that the event was somehow tied to a pandering conspiracy, a felony under California law. Protestors objecting to the violation of the accused's civil rights wore black buttons with white letters reading "LAPD Freed the Slaves, April 10, 1976." Charges against thirty-six of the accused were dropped, leaving only four defendants. One was the owner of *Drummer*, John Embry, and another, Jeanne Barney, editor of *News West*, was the only woman to be arrested. At their eventual hearing in November 1977 they pled guilty to the misdemeanor charge of soliciting an act of prostitution. Reaction from outside the Los Angeles area to this action was highly critical. Six letters of protest appeared in the April 16, 1976, issue of the *Los Angeles Times,* all decrying the raid as a waste of police resources which should have been applied to stemming the city's rising crime rate and objecting to Chief Ed Davis's longstanding vendetta against the gay community. Legal proceedings on the case took on the air of a carnival, with the prosecution exhibiting shackles, clamps and other equipment used in SM play.

Commonwealth v. Appleby

The next case establishing a precedent for the relationship of law and SM activities was *Commonwealth v. Appleby*, in 1980, the venue being the state of Massachusetts. In this instance, two men lived together for a period of two years and maintained a master-servant relationship. During this time, one of them was regularly subjected to physical punishment by the other, often at extreme levels, eventually resulting in a broken kneecap and causing Steven Cromer, the abused partner, to flee the house. In his testimony, Cromer stated that he possessed a low level of self-esteem and feared for himself and his family if he did not maintain the relationship. In upholding Appleby's conviction, the Massachusetts Judicial Superior Court created a judgment whose wording placed consensual SM in a context more akin to cases involving battered women. Their finding was that consent was inadmissible as a defense of sadomasochistic activities, even though undertaken with the object of achieving sexual satisfaction. The plaintiff in this case "was tried and convicted under a state law that implied, as a matter of public policy, that one could not consent to be the victim of an assault and battery within a sexual context" (Hanna, 2001, p. 260). This case differed from its predecessor in that there was an objecting victim and many of the same legal arguments seen in cases involving battered women were cited, bringing the idea of consent to SM activities a wholly new level of legal debate.

State v. Collier

The definition of SM activities within United States law continued in the next important case of this genre, *State v. Collier* in 1985 in Iowa. The point of law at issue here was not specifically consent but rather whether SM behaviors could be classified under the Iowa Code as a "social activity" and thus be exempt from prosecution as the crime of assault. While both persons involved were heterosexual, the final judgment (citing both *Samuels* and *Appleby* as precedents) was that the legislature never intended that sadomasochism be classified as a "sport or other social activity" (Hanna, 2001, p. 272). The court did not, however, formulate a definition of the social status of SM which could be used in other cases, preferring to examine each individual case on its own merits.

People v. Jovanovic

The widely publicized case of *People v. Jovanovic* in New York City in the late 1990s blended traditional SM practices with the complicating factor of interaction via the Internet and its capacities for entrapment. The case involved a Columbia University graduate student and a Barnard College undergraduate woman who met online and discussed a mutual interest in SM, eventually leading to a sexual encounter. During their time together, reportedly Oliver Jovanovic disregarded repeated pleas from his partner to stop and even ignored a "safe word" intended to signal that her limits had been reached. Following some twenty hours of activity, she released herself and several days later informed the authorities. Portions of the e-mail correspondence between the two highlighting the woman's experience with SM were refused admittance to the record by the presiding judge, who invoked the state's Rape Shield Law. The defendant was found guilty of kidnapping, assault and sexual abuse and sentenced to fifteen years to life. The Supreme Court of New York reversed the conviction and ordered a new trial, arguing that although Jovanovic had no constitutionally protected right to engage in SM activities, the excluded e-mails would have clarified the question of the victim having agreed to his actions. Cheryl Hanna, in her ground breaking review of the interrelationship between violence and consent in criminal law, notes that the key question in this case is not whether the jury believed the Barnard College student (whose injuries corroborated her story in full) but that, if she did consent, could the accused's actions still be classed as criminal? The Appellate Court's action in ordering a retrial "implies that Jovanovic committed no crime if the victim consented" (Hanna, 2002, p. 242). Said decision is the first to be rendered by an American court at the appellate level in a case involving SM. This judgment breaks with the prior approach of holding that one could not consent to any kind of activity that would cause death or severe bodily harm (with a few culturally sanctioned exceptions such as organized sports). It indicates that future trends in legal argument regarding sadomasochism may center on the formulation of a precise and workable definition of consent in such contexts. This process is being encouraged by dialogue between the bar, law enforcement, and practitioners of SM, who have become increasingly organized into formal bodies over the last three decades of the twentieth century. The nexus for this debate will center, as Hanna observes, in the fact that:

> Anglo-American law as to consensual violence is quite clear that consent is the exception and not the rule when one engages in activity that could cause serious bodily injury or death. The exceptions to that rule have been clearly defined, and S/M has never fallen within those exceptions. (Hanna, 2002, p. 268)

RELATED LEGAL ISSUES

In addition to the question of consent, several other legal issues have become involved in the debate regarding sadomasochism, these being sexual freedom, child custody, employment discrimination, the "rough sex" defense, and the right to privacy.

Sexual Freedom

The idea of freedom to explore different varieties of sexuality, or, indeed, to have sexual relations outside culturally sanctioned marriage in any fashion, has been consistently seen as a problematic area requiring regulation in the United States since colonial times. The general pattern of legislation in the seventeenth and eighteenth centuries centered on the safeguarding of the nuclear family and society as a whole by prohibiting a limited number of specifically named sexual acts, most frequent being sodomy, adultery and prostitution, or the more generic "crimes against nature." The very real threat of contracting syphilis or other venereal diseases also mitigated against active sexual exploration. The medical profession further complicated the matter. They shifted from a view of both sexes as sexually passionate beings to a more lopsided notion of women as chaste and emotionally involved with sex for procreation only. In contrast, males were viewed as lusty beings whose drives had to be kept under strict control lest they damage society. Medical mythologies about "normal" sexual activities such as masturbation proliferated during the nineteenth century, creating a situation in which sexual alternatives to procreation were widely written about in a clinical mode while the American public was enjoined from engaging in them except in their imaginations. Unrestrained sexuality was seen as a disruptive force that could threaten the stability of society if left unchecked.

Paradoxically, one of the more radical social reform movements of the era took the name of the Free Love Movement. It stressed that sexual matters were the concern only of the people involved and no one else, in much the same fashion as the Code Napoleon. Other social experiments carried out during the nineteenth century which challenged the prevailing social norms of sexual limits were the Oneida colony, the Shakers and Mormonism, representing the full range of sexual options from celibacy to polygamy.

The conquest of venereal disease by Paul Ehrlich and the development of penicillin and the sulfonamides in the mid-twentieth century placed the medical profession in the position of providing cures to remove some of the biological threats that had given their injunctions against promiscuous sexual behavior teeth. With the development of practical and effective safeguards (both medicinal and contraceptive) against sexually transmitted diseases, it was left to social sanctions (chiefly religion and law) to present the public with sufficient deterrents to performing such alternative sexual practices as sadomasochism. The addition of laws which could be used against easily spotted practitioners of non-mainstream sex (chiefly male homosexuals, some of whom were more easily found and entrapped due to their frequenting of specific geographical locations and business establishments) to the legal arsenal allowed police forces to act as the guardians of community morality, an example being California's "victimless crime" law. The drafting of the Model Penal Code and its adoption in whole or in part by many of the states marked the beginning of the erosion of absolute legal prohibitions of certain types of sexual activity. However, it was not until the "sexual revolution" of the 1960s and the emergence of a counterculture which praised sexuality in all its forms that sexual freedom in its contemporary sense entered the American social debate. The overturning of many of these restrictive laws became one of the early goals of the gay liberation movement, whose legal challenges laid the groundwork for the later activism of the NCSF. These challenges moved the discussion of alternative sexuality out of the context of procreation and towards the idea of sex as consensual play among adults, which is widely used among contemporary SM practitioners. The core issue of the legal argument for restricting personal sexual freedom to engage in SM can be clearly seen in Monica Pa's 2001 article, where she argues that SM should be seen as "consensual sex with potentially violent aspects" (Pa, 2001, p. 77); it should not be viewed as consensual assault with sexual aspects, as the courts have usually regarded it, thus rendering it an activity requiring legal limits. Until and unless this view becomes more widely accepted and encoded in legal precedent, the concept of sexual freedom will continue to be problematic as regards SM.

Child Custody

Writing in a review of then-extant decisions relating to the impact of changing sexual mores on family law, Phoenix superior court judge Robert L. Gottsfield (Gottsfield, 1984, p. 36) noted:

> Despite declarations that we live in an age of sexual liberation, the courts are in turmoil about the role a parent's sexual lifestyle plays in a custody or visitation dispute . . . sexual variation must be examined in view of what is best for the child. But it alone should not disqualify a parent from custody or normal visitation unless evi-

dence exists that it is detrimental to the child or somehow interferes with the parent-child relationship.

While his original subject was homosexuality, his remarks express with
equal validity a basic point of discussion in any custody case involving
SM identity, where exposure can lead to the removal of custody of minor children and can affect visitation rights in a divorce case. In the latter case, the usual occurrence is that one spouse or the other threatens to
play the SM card during divorce proceedings to influence the judge's
decision to grant them custody. Issues here are that judges are often very
ignorant of the SM lifestyle; this requires witnesses to be called from
within the community to present a balanced picture of its realities; the
question of what impact (if any) these practices have or are likely to
have on the welfare of the child who is or may be exposed to them in the
home environment; and the consequent question of the fitness of an
adult who engages in SM activity to be allowed to assume legal
responsibility for the welfare of a child.

Child custody also appears as an area of concern in the results of the
Violence and Discrimination Survey conducted by the National Coalition for Sexual Freedom (NCSF) in 1998 and 1999, with 3% of respondents stating that they had lost custody of a child on the grounds of their
alternative sexual practices, while 13% feared that they would lose custody rights if their identity as a "kinky" person were to become known.
The question of whether responses to this question would vary if the
parent or guardian in question were gay, lesbian or bisexual as opposed
to heterosexual remains to be explored in a more detailed, follow-up
study.

An example of the possible custodial consequences of being exposed
as an SM practitioner is provided by the Houghton case. In January
1996, a heterosexual couple in New York State who engaged in private
consensual SM behavior, Selina and Steven Houghton, had their two
children (a girl and boy ages twelve and six respectively) removed from
their custody and placed in foster care by a child protection agency. The
agency acted under pressure from a detective, Lieutenant Bernard,
known for his strong views against child abuse. He cited as evidence
photographs and a video showing the couple engaged in SM play stolen
from the Houghton's home by an acquaintance. The children did not appear in either photographs or the video. After viewing the tape, a case
worker at the agency found no evidence of child abuse and recommended that the children be returned to their parents, which the detective countered by threatening the agency with negative publicity. When

the couple went to court in March 1996 in an attempt to regain custody, they were arrested by Bernard in the courthouse on misdemeanor charges and bail set at four thousand dollars, paid by friends and supporters. Family court proceedings began in July 1996, with the proposal of a plea bargain whereunder the couple would plead guilty to neglect in order to have the children returned. In addition to this proceeding, the Houghtons also faced a criminal trial. Both lost their jobs and were forced to sell many of their possessions to meet defense costs, and were unable to remain in their home. The criminal case against the Houghtons ended on January 3, 1997. The couple accepted a plea bargain to counts of disorderly conduct and endangering the welfare of a minor and were ordered to pay fines and perform community service but did not receive jail terms. Their acceptance was intended to free them to pursue the family court case involving the custody of their children, which began February 13, 1997. On March 21, 1997, a New York State Appeals Court judge overturned a previous order and returned the children to their parents, on grounds that "the family court judge had ignored testimony of the children's law guardians, several psychologists, and Children's Protective Services representatives . . . that the children would be better off with their parents than in foster care" (Houghton Children Returned to Parents, 1997, pp. 1-2).

Employment Discrimination

The issue of employment discrimination is also tied in with one of the elements of fear that exist in child custody cases . . . the fear that revealing this aspect of personal identity may be taken as a reflection of one's character and thus, presumably, one's fitness to be trusted with information that must remain private in a business setting. Conversely, employers may fear to be attacked as condoning such practices if it becomes public knowledge that they employ someone known to be into SM and have not fired that person to express their moral outrage at such activities and their support for mainstream community values.

The National Coalition for Sexual Freedom (NCSF) conducted a four-question Violence and Discrimination Survey via both paper and electronic formats from April 1998 to February 1999. Five thousand surveys were printed and distributed at major leather subculture meetings and events occurring in the study period, including the Leather Leadership Conference in New York City, the International Mr. Leather (IML) contest in Chicago, and the Folsom Street Fair in San Francisco. In addition, the member organizations of the NCSF mailed 4,600 additional surveys to their membership. The specific aims of the questions were to gather demographic information on the SM-leather-fetish communities, to document the impact of social stigmatization on their members and provide data to justify a more detailed and professionally conducted inquiry. The second question asked whether the individual had ever "experienced discrimination due to your alternative sexual practices." The three most frequent types of discrimination affirmed by the respondents were persecution (40%), loss of job or contract (25%), and loss of promotion (17%). Respondents came from the homosexual, heterosexual and bisexual communities. One major problem with this survey is that the gay and lesbian leather communities were represented by only 22 percent of the surveys returned. This circumstance, while understandable, begs the question of whether gay and lesbian leatherfolk who are open about this aspect of their lives are being discriminated against on the basis of their sexual orientation or the sexual lifestyle they practice to express it.

The "Rough Sex" Defense

The "rough sex" defense, which has been widely discussed since its use in New York City's "Preppie Murder" case in 1986, in fact represents the invoking of SM practices in a context outside the community of regular practitioners for the purpose of shielding a defendant from prosecution. In this instance, the defendant, Robert Chambers, contended that the victim, Jennifer Levin, had died due to an accident during some rough sex play. This argument resulted in the jury being confused to the extent that the prosecution was obliged to plea bargain, resulting in Chambers receiving a reduced sentence. The rough sex defense was also used successfully to avoid murder convictions in the Dennis Bulloch case in Missouri and another New York case brought against Joseph Porto, both involving supposedly involuntary strangulation deaths. In his review of this strategy, George Buzash (1989, p. 558) observes:

> [It] is in fact a new twist on the old "she asked for it" defense. The "rough sex" defense to the charge of murder asserts that the victim literally "asked for" the conduct that led to the homicide and that the homicide was the result of sexual practices to which the victim consented, and may even have demanded.

The aim of this defense is to deny that the defendant possessed any intent to commit murder prior to engaging in the requested sexual behavior. American criminal law recognizes two types of bodily invasion. The first involves such things as offensive touching (which causes offense to the victim but does not inflict harm), while the second is more germane to sadomasochism. It covers types of bodily invasion which:

> . . . can be considered breaches of the peace, resulting in harm or serious injury to the victim. In this class of invasions, the state has a compelling interest to punish such conduct because it violates the state's own interest. For an invasion to qualify as a breach of the peace, it must create a disturbance in the public order or threaten a member of the citizenry with an injury so severe that the conduct is viewed as detrimental to the state. Because the state's interest in punishing those invasions that constitute breaches of the peace is so closely related to the preservation of its own well-being, the victim's personal consent is irrelevant. . . . The individual cannot subordinate the interest of the state by granting consent to conduct that is harmful to the state. (Buzash, 1989, pp. 564-565)

The most telling connection between this section of tort law and S/M was stated in the 1976 case of *State v. Brown*, where a New Jersey Superior Court rejected victim consent as a defense claim. The court opinion clarified the exact interest of the state in such matters, noting that "These acts, even if done in private, have an impingement . . . upon the community at large in that the very doing of them may tend to encourage their repetition and so to undermine public morals" (Buzash, 1989, p. 566). As noted above, the judgment rendered in the 1980 case of *Commonwealth v. Appleby* also rejected the idea that private sadomasochistic play could be protected by an individual's right to privacy.

The "rough sex" defense in cases involving consensual SM activities, whether or not the activity results in the death or unwanted injury of one of the participants, thus seems to be in collision with a widely accepted provision of criminal law and established legal precedent. A strict liability approach to rough sex, which would not accept accident as an defense but center attention on the actual cause of a victim's death or injury, has been proposed as a means of drafting legislation to cope with the use of the "rough sex" defense (Buzash, 1989, p. 569-570). Another application of rough sex as a mitigating factor appears in the context of cases of domestic violence and spouse abuse, although the term "rough sex defense" is not used. The specific link between these two subjects appears in the definition of possible types of abuse, which can include emotional and financial as well as actual physical force. In its report *Lesbian, Gay, Bisexual and Transgender Domestic Violence in 2000*, the National Coalition of Anti-Violence Programs (a network of 27 community-based organizations involved in responding to violence affecting persons who are gay, lesbian, bisexual, transgender or HIV- affected) noted several problems as unique to this type of abuse as distinct from its heterosexual manifestations. Among them is, "portraying the violence as mutual and even consensual" (Lesbian, Gay, Bisexual and Transgender Domestic Violence in 2000, p. 5); the same type of argument was vitiated by the finding in *Commonwealth v. Appleby* that a victim could not consent to be abused. The aim of the rough sex argument in domestic abuse cases appears to be one of redefining the actions of the perpetrator as requested sexual acts. This is a distinctly different approach than that taken in its more frequent usage in cases involving murder, where the goal is to eliminate any premeditated intent to kill. Determining the frequency of the use of this potential link to SM in domestic violence cases among gays and lesbians will require reanalysis of existing police and court records. Efforts to track the frequency of domestic abuse in the gay and lesbian community to date have not expressly addressed this issue.

An examination of the two major works on domestic battery among lesbians and gay men, *Naming the Violence* (Lobel, 1986) and *Men Who Beat the Men Who Love Them* (Island & Letellier, 1991), reveals that SM has also not been considered as an element of this problem in the analysis conducted within gay and lesbian studies to date. While the specific sexual behaviors involved and issues of consent have been the logical center of this defense, it also involves a third legal concept, the right to privacy.

The Right to Privacy

An example of the complex nature of privacy issues in relation to SM occurred in the state of Massachusetts on July 6, 2000. Police officers on the track of stolen guitars entered a warehouse in the town of Attleboro, only to find an "SM play party" with some 50 individuals in attendance engaging in SM activities. The host of the party, Benjamin Davis, was arrested on 14 charges ranging from possession of items of self-abuse (illegal in Massachusetts under the "Appleby Statute," the law cited in the 1980 case of *Commonwealth v. Appleby*) to maintaining a house of ill repute and assaulting a police officer. These last charges were the only ones later reviewed in court. A female participant was also charged with assault for paddling another woman. Quickly dubbed the "Paddleboro" case by the alternative media and supported by the National Coalition for Sexual Freedom, Davis appeared for a bench trial at the Attleboro District Courthouse on October 10, 2001. Twelve of the charges were dropped, and the judge ruled that Davis "was not guilty of the charge of keeping a house of ill fame" (Ben Davis not guilty, 2001, p.16) while the assault charge was continued without a finding. This latter meant that said charge would be dropped in six months, as the defendant had no criminal record.

The definition of a right to privacy within American jurisprudence originates with the Fourth Amendment to the Constitution of the United States. It provides for freedom from unreasonable search and seizure; the idea of unenumerated rights and liberties retained by the people recognized by the Ninth Amendment; the due process clause of the Fourteenth Amendment, and more specifically in the finding by the Supreme Court in the 1965 case of *Griswold v. Connecticut*. While the matter of this last case involved the right of a heterosexual married couple to use contraceptives, "it represented the first time that the right of privacy, a rather amorphous concept which had been expanding in civil, mainly tort, law, had been raised to the rank of a constitutionally protected right" (Barnett, 1973, p. 57), as well. It defines sexual intimacy as an area of private life into which the authority of the state may not enter. The idea of this right was further developed through a succession of court cases involving the possession of pornography (*Stanley v. Georgia*) and the extension of the right of privacy beyond the original framework of husband and wife (*Eisenstadt v. Baird*). The application of this extension to "deviate sexual conduct in civil cases" (Barnett, 1973, p. 63) began with the 1969 case of *Norton v. Macy*, which challenged the policy of the Civil Service Commission of dismissing any employee discovered to be homosexual. This last marked the inception of a continuing period of legal challenges to anti-homosexual laws across the United States, among them the longstanding sodomy laws of many jurisdictions. In the 1971 case of *In re Labady* (whose principal subject was the suitability of open homosexuals as immigrants), the court held that such behavior practiced only consensually in private was not sufficient basis for alleging that the defendant lacked good moral character. The court stated further that "it is now established that the official inquiry into a person's private sexual habits does violence to his constitutionally protected zone of privacy" (Barnett, 1973, p. 64). SM events taking place in private venues, such as the "Paddleboro" case in Massachusetts, have been the subject of police invasion. The element of privacy is interwoven with the issues of child custody (under the question of the degree, if any, to which the child is exposed to or aware of the SM activities engaged in by their parents and the parent's right to engage in such behavior in a household with children resident). Similar concerns arise with regards to employment discrimination, rooted in the fear of being fired if one's participation in SM activities became known to an employer.

The application of state sodomy laws to private consensual activities (attacked in the judgment of *In re Labady* noted above) received a substantial encouragement from the Supreme Court decision in the 1986 case of *Bowers v. Hardwick*. This case upheld the right of the state of Georgia to arrest two gay men for committing sodomy in the privacy of their own bedroom. The most recent evidence that the practice of consensual SM in private remains controversial are the remarks made on April 7, 2003, in an interview with the Associated Press by Republican Senator Rick Santorum of Pennsylvania. In his comments on the case of *Lawrence v. Texas* (a challenge to the sodomy law of the state of Texas brought by two gay men whose residence was invaded by police without a warrant), Senator Santorum stated that he did not believe a constitutional right to privacy existed. He added that such a right, if it did exist, contributed to the undermining of the family unit, with the right to consensual sex then allowing the right to commit bigamy, polygamy, incest and adultery.

On June 26, 2003, the United States Supreme Court handed down its decision in *Lawrence v. Texas*. As part of that decision, the court reexamined the logic of the ruling in *Bowers v. Hardwick*, pursuant to the complaint of the defendants that their right to certain types of intimate conduct was protected under the Due Process Clause of the Fourteenth Amendment. The defense argued that the sodomy law of the state of Texas violated said protection, a position with which the State Court of Appeals disagreed. In its finding, the Court overturned *Bowers v. Hardwick*, ruling that such private sexual actions were indeed constitutionally protected, thus rendering all sodomy laws then in force within the United States unconstitutional.

SM ACTIVIST/ACTIVISM

The establishment of organizations for both heterosexual and homosexual practitioners of consensual SM within the United States began in

1971 with the formation of the Eulenspiegel Society (TES) in New York City. Its stated goal was to "support sexual liberation as a basic requirement of a truly free society . . . freedom for sexual minorities and particularly the rights of those whose sexuality embraces any aspect of Dominant/submissive fantasies and urges" (TES: The Eulenspiegel Society http://www.tes.org/welcome.html retrieved January 5 2003: 1). In August 1974, a similar organization, the Society of Janus, was formed in San Francisco by Larry Olsen and the late Cynthia Slater, although its agenda emphasized educational programming more than legal activism. Its choice of name (taken from the two-faced Roman god of gateways) was intended to reflect the duality of dominance and submission present in most SM encounters, the passage from confusion to self-acceptance, and the struggle against stereotypes.

Within the homosexual communities, one of the more prominent organizations for gay male SM devotees was also formed in New York City in 1981, Gay Men's S/M Activists Association (GMSMA), whose statement of purpose called for greater community support and construction for gay sadomasochists. It notes, "we seek to establish a recognized political presence in the wider gay community in order to combat the prevailing stereotypes and misconceptions about S/M while working with others for the common goals of gay liberation" (GMSMA Statement of Purpose, http://www.gmsma.org/statement_of_purpose. html, retrieved January 5 2003).

In 1997, the evolution of this genre of sexual liberation organizing culminated in the formation of an umbrella organization of five American SM groups (which had expanded to twenty-seven by 2002). The NCSF, under the auspices of the New York SM Activists by a small group was led by Susan Wright and Len Dworkin. Wright had previously initiated the National Organization for Women's SM Policy Reform Project in November 1996 (Susan Wright, personal communication February 18, 2003). She was a member of the steering committee of the 1994 Leather Celebration in New York City, which raised funds for the Spanner defendants.

The language of the Coalition's statement of purpose marks a new politicization of the SM community. Its mandate was to combat the use of individual pieces of legislation by local law enforcement agencies, as it is dedicated to "altering the political, legal, and social environment in the United States in order to guarantee equal rights for consenting adults who practice forms of alternative sexual expression" (NCSF, http:// www.ncsfreedom.org/ retrieved January 22, 2003: 1). The NCSF further defines alternative sexual expression as meaning adults who are members of the SM-leather-fetish, polyamory and swinger communities. At the second Leather Leadership Conference, held in New York City in 1998, a policy document on "S/M vs. Abuse" was adopted. Its stated purpose was to "help law enforcement and social services professionals understand the difference between abusive relationship vs consensual sadomasochism" (SM vs. Abuse, http://www.leatherquest. com/law/smvabuse.htm retrieved January 10, 2003: 1).

An example of such a case is that of the "San Diego Six," initiated on October 29, 1999, with a raid by members of the police vice unit on a private play party being hosted by Club X in that city. Five men and one woman were cited for the misdemeanors of lewd behavior and nudity in a public place. The potential significance of convictions in this case for similar actions by other city vice squads across the United States was not lost on either the local or national SM communities, which quickly established a defense fund and publicized the circumstances of the arrests. On February 1, 2000, the deputy city attorney of San Diego informed the counsel for the defense that the charges pending against the five male accused would all be dropped. This followed a decision by the jury in the first trial in January 2000 to drop all charges of lewd acts against the woman involved, stating that they found the case made by the prosecution to be weak and the entire affair a waste of time.

At the national level, in the autumn of 2001, the NCSF brought suit in federal court as co-plaintiff with the photographer and artist Barbara Nitke of New York City (one of whose frequent subjects is intimacy between couples, including SM practices) against the remaining anti-obscenity provisions of the Communications Decency Act of 1996. This case is particularly noteworthy as the automatic right of appeal to the Supreme Court is provided in the Act. Therefore, this filing possesses the potential to place SM and other forms of alternative sexuality into mainstream media coverage of the ruling in a balanced light as well as clarifying regulatory limits on sexually clear materials on the Internet.

The NCSF was the first political activist group to become a member of the World Association for Sexology and also holds a seat on the National Policy Roundtable of the National Gay and Lesbian Task Force. To enhance its efforts, a lobbying office was opened in Washington, DC, in August 2001. It should be noted that none of the regional organizations of gay and lesbian leather and levi social and service groups, such as the Mid America Conference of Clubs or the chapters of the Trident International, was a signatory to the Coalition, although the Eulenspiegel Society, GMSMA and individual chapters of the National Leather Association (NLA) did take part.

A second response to the legal regulation of SM activities was initiated in at the eleventh Living In Leather conference (hosted by the local chapter of the NLA) held in Portland, Oregon, in October 1996 by attorney Spencer Bergstedt as part of the programming of the NLA-International. The Law Information Project sought to replace the frequently anecdotal stories of personal harassment and interactions with the police and courts with factual accounts given by participants. The announcement of the Project requested that the names, approximate date and location of the court case (including the case number if available), and a description of events for the record be sent to the NLA for compiling into a database. Profiles of individual laws, statutes, administrative codes and judicial opinions at the city, county and state level relating to some aspect of SM (for example, the wearing of uniforms or carrying handcuffs) were also to be assembled, with background on the governmental body which decreed the law and hard copy as available. By 2003, a dozen cases from Canada, Germany, England and New Zealand as well as the United States had been reported to the Project (Spencer Bergstedt, personal communication, January 24, 2003).

CONCLUSION

Resolution of the legal status of SM in the United States will not be achieved until a balance is attained between the legal concepts of consent, privacy, and protection in a process of redefinition through court cases. This will entail the successful construction and acceptance by American society of a definition of sadomasochism emphasizing its nature as sexual rather than criminal. It is hoped that the active pursuit of effective education of law enforcement personnel and members of the bar currently engaged in by SM activist organizations will lead to an increased awareness of the realities of the SM subculture and its forms of consensual sexual play within American society. The American legal system has yet to yield a comprehensive determination of sadomasochism's legal status at the national level on the order of the Spanner case in Great Britain. As such, it is likely that the observed pattern of exploration for methods of balancing individual rights of consent and social mandates of protection will continue for several decades.

REFERENCES

Associated Press. (2003, April 7). *Excerpts from the Santorum interview*. Retrieved June 7 2003 from http://www.post-gazette.com/nation/20030423santorumexcerpts0423p6.asp

Ballentine, J.A. and Anderson, W.S. (1969). *Ballentine's law dictionary with pronunciations*. 3rd ed. Rochester, NY: Lawyers Co-Op Publishing Co.

Barnett, W. (1973). *Sexual freedom and the Constitution: An inquiry into the constitutionality of repressive sex laws*. Albuquerque, New Mexico: University of New Mexico Press.

Ben Davis not guilty. (2001). *Leather Journal* 140, 16.

Bergstedt, S. *The Law, S/M and You*. Retrieved January 10, 2003, from http://www.io.com/~ambrosio/law/law.html.

Black's law dictionary. (1990). St .Paul, MN: West Group.

Black's law dictionary. (1999). St. Paul, MN: West Group.

Bowers v. Hardwick 478 U.S. 186 (1986)

Bullough, V. L. (1976). *Sexual variance in society and history*. New York; John Wiley.

Bullough, V. L., and B. (1977). *Sin, sickness and sanity: A history of sexual attitudes*. New York: Garland.

Buzash, G. E. (1989). The "rough sex" defense. *Journal of Criminal Law and Criminology 80* n.2, 557-584.

Chihara, M. (2000). Paddleboro, Mass. Sadomasochists fight for their right to a sex party. *Leather Journal 128*, 1, 6.

Communications Decency Act of 1996. Public Law 104-104, Title V.

Eisenstadt v. Baird 405 U.S. 438 (1972)

Ellis, H. (1942). Love and pain. In *Studies in the Psychology of Sex*. New York: Random House, 1942, volume 1, 66-188.

Eskridge, W. N, Jr. (1999). *Gaylaw: Challenging the apartheid of the closet*. Cambridge, MA: Harvard University Press.

European Court of Human Rights. *Case of Laskey, Jaggard and Brown v. The United Kingdom* Retrieved January 22, 2003 from http://perso.wanadoo.fr/paul.bailey/span.judg.txt

Gay Men's S/M Activists. Retrieved January 10, 2003 from http://www.gmsma.org/

Gottsfield, R.L. (1984) Private lives, public issues: Courts strive to strike a balance between a parent's sexual freedom and custody rights. *Family Advocate 6* (4), 36-38.

Griswold v. Connecticut, 381 U.S. 479 (1965)

Hanna, C.(2001). Sex is not a sport: Consent and violence in criminal law. *Boston College Law Review* 42 (2), 239-290.

Hazelwood, R.R., Dietz, P.E., & Burgess, A.A. (1982). Sexual fatalities: Behavioral reconstruction in equivocal cases. *Journal of Forensic Sciences 27*(4), 763-773.

Highleyman, L. Eye On Big Brother. Retrieved May 13, 2003 from http://www.black-rose.com/cuiru/archive/2-6/eyeonbb2-6.html

Incident Response Team. Retrieved January 22, 2003 from http://www.ncsfreedom.org/incident.htm

Island, D. & Letellier, P. (1991). *Men who beat the men who love them: battered gay men and domestic violence*. New York: Haworth Press.

In re Labady 326 F. Supp. 924 (SDNY, 1971)

Krafft-Ebing. R. von. (1894) *Psychopathia sexualis.* Philadelphia: F.A. Davis.

Lawrence v. Texas 02-102 41 S.W. 3d 349, revised and remanded

Leather Leadership Conference. (1998). SM vs. Abuse. Retrieved January 10, 2003 http://www.leatherquest.com/law/smvabuse.htm: 1.

Lence, D.E. (1995). Coding desire: Sadism, masochism and the law. *Legal Studies Forum* Spring 1995 v.19, n.1: 3-19.

Leonard, A.S. (Ed.). (1993). *Sexuality and the law: An encyclopedia of major legal cases.* New York: Garland.

Lobel, K. (1986). *Naming the violence: Speaking out about lesbian battering,* Seattle: Seal Press.

Lohr, B.. & Adams, H.E. (1995). Sexual sadism and masochism. In L. Diamant and R. McAnulty (Eds.) *The Psychology of Sexual Orientation, Behavior and Identity: A Handbook* (pp. 255-269). Westport, CT: Greenwood.

McAnulty, R.D.(1995). The paraphilias: Classification and theory. In L. Diamant and R. D. McAnulty. (Eds.) *The psychology of sexual orientation,behavior and identity: A handbook* (pp. 240-255). Westport, CT: Greenwood.

Murray, T.E. & Murrell, T.R. (1989). *The language of sadomasochism: A glossary and linguistic analysis.* Westport, CT: Greenwood.

National Coalition for Sexual Freedom. Retrieved January 22, 2003 from http://www.ncsfreedom.org/

National Coalition for Sexual Freedom. *Action Alert April 25, 2003.* Retrieved May 21, 2003 from http://www.ncsfreedom.org/news/bigotedsen.htm

National Coalition for Sexual Freedom. *Violence and discrimination survey (1998 and 1999).* Retrieved May 12 2003 from http://www.ncsfreedom.org/discrimination/viodiscrimsurvey.htm

National Coalition of Anti-Violence Programs. *Lesbian, gay, bisexual and transgender domestic violence in 2000.* Retrieved June 2, 2003 from http://www.qrd.org/qrd/www/orgs/avproject/2000ncavpdvrpt.pdf

Norton v. Macy 417 F 2d 1161 (D.C. Cir. 1969)

Odem, M.E. (1993). Sexual behavior and morality. In M.Cayton, E.J. Gorn, & P.W. Williams (Eds.), *Encyclopedia of American Social History* (pp. 1961-1980). New York: Charles Scribner's.

Pa, M. (2001). Beyond the pleasure principle: The criminalization of consensual sadomasochistic sex. *Texas Journal of Women and the Law 11*(1), 51-92.

Posner, R. A., & Silbaugh, K.B. (1996). *A guide to America's sex laws.* University of Chicago Press.

Radin, M. (1970). *Law dictionary.* Dobbs Ferry, New York, Oceana Publications.

Ridinger, R. (2002). Things visible and invisible: The Leather Archives and Museum. *Journal of Homosexuality 43*(1), 1-9.

San Diego Six. Retrieved January 12, 2003 from http://www.leatherquest.com/News/san.htm

San Diego updates. Retrieved January 14, 2003 from http://www.leatherquest.com/News/san1.htm

Selwyn, H.E. (1976, April 16). Police arrests at "slave auction" [letter to the editor]. *Los Angeles Times,* p. 46.

SM vs. Abuse. Retrieved January 10, 2003 from http://www.leatherquest.com/law/smvabuse.htm

Society of Janus. Retrieved February 10, 2003. http://www.soj.org/

Stanley v. Georgia 394 U.S. 557 (1969)

The Eulenspiegel Society. Retrieved January 5, 2003.from http://www.tes.org/

West's legal thesaurus/dictionary. (1985). St. Paul, MN: West Publishing Company.

Weinberg, M., Williams, C. J., & Moser, C. (1984). The social constituents of sado-masochism. *Social Problems 31*(4), 379-389.

Willmore. J. (1976, May 5). The great slave-market bust: A story only Los Angeles could produce. *Advocate*, 189, 13-14.

Words and phrases. Permanent edition. St. Paul, MN: West Group, 2002.

Where are the slave dollars going? (1976, May 19). *Advocate, 190,* 9.

Zugibe, F.T., Costello, J. T., & Berithaupt, M. K. (1987). The man in the mask. *Journal of Forensic Sciences*, 32(3), 810-817.

Discrimination
of SM-Identified Individuals

Susan Wright, MA

National Coalition for Sexual Freedom

SUMMARY. The belief that sadomasochism (SM) is violence or abusive behavior has resulted in harassment, physical attacks, and discrimination against SM-identified individuals. Historically, they were often opposed by self-identified feminists. One reason the women who practiced SM were targeted was the official opposition to sadomasochistic practices promulgated by the National Organization for Women (NOW). Current statistics of incidents of discrimination, harassment and physical attacks against SM-identified individuals and SM groups are compiled by the National Coalition for Sexual Freedom (NCSF). *[Article copies available for a fee from The Haworth Document Delivery Service: 1-800-HAWORTH. E-mail address: <docdelivery@haworthpress.com> Website: <http://www.HaworthPress.com> © 2006 by The Haworth Press, Inc. All rights reserved.]*

KEYWORDS. SM, BDSM, sadomasochism, social discrimination, sexual rights

---

Susan Wright is an unaffiliated author living in New York City. Disclaimers: Susan Wright coordinated the NOW SM Policy Reform Project, and is currently the Spokesperson for National Coalition for Sexual Freedom. Correspondence may be addressed: c/o NCSF, 822 Guilford Avenue, Box 127, Baltimore, MD 21202-3707 (E-mail: susanw@ncsfreedom.org).

[Haworth co-indexing entry note]: "Discrimination of SM-Identified Individuals." Wright, Susan. Co-published simultaneously in *Journal of Homosexuality* (Harrington Park Press, an imprint of The Haworth Press, Inc.) Vol. 50, No. 2/3, 2006, pp. 217-231; and: *Sadomasochism: Powerful Pleasures* (ed: Peggy J. Kleinplatz, and Charles Moser) Harrington Park Press, an imprint of The Haworth Press, Inc., 2006, pp. 217-231. Single or multiple copies of this article are available for a fee from The Haworth Document Delivery Service [1-800-HAWORTH, 9:00 a.m. - 5:00 p.m. (EST). E-mail address: docdelivery@haworthpress.com].

For the purposes of this article, sadomasochism or "SM" includes a wide range of alternative sexual practices including: consensual power exchange, body modification, role play (which highlights the power exchange), and intense physical and emotional stimulation in a sexual context. The term "SM groups" refers to non-profit membership organizations which provide social and educational opportunities for SM-identified individuals to learn about and practice SM in a safe and consensual manner.

I will use the term SM community to denote the over 500 SM groups that promote consensual SM behaviors in weekly, monthly and annual events in the United States alone (NCSF, retrieved 3/10/03). There are over 250 weekend SM events that are produced every year by SM groups and businesses in accordance with local, state and Federal laws (Rhodes, retrieved 2/26/03). These events include the following: (1) SM educational conferences that provide workshops on relationships, lifestyle issues, and sexual techniques as well as social opportunities such as parties, interactive role-playing games, charity fundraisers, entertainment, and banquets; (2) camps and retreats which take place in rustic settings and involve limited educational workshops as well as campfires, hiking and other outdoor activities; (3) "leather" contests, which are similar to beauty contests, that select "titleholders" for bars, cities, states, regions and international titles, i.e., International Mr. Leather and International Ms. Leather; (4) "runs" held by fraternal clubs in which members gather for a weekend of socializing; (5) street fairs which provide a venue for specialty vendors to reach SM practitioners.

In addition, the development of the Internet has enabled adults who are curious about SM to access educational forums and information, both in-person and online. Numerous businesses cater to the needs of the members of the SM community by selling books, clothing and equipment such as padded furniture, restraints, and implements that are used to stimulate the body.

The growth of this subculture can be seen in mainstream marketing strategies that target adults who have an interest in SM. In 2003, these included advertisements in major magazines by Dove Bars and Absolut vodka, as well as a Dannon Yogurt commercial featuring a couple with the wife dressed as a French maid, highlighting one common role-play scenario engaged in by SM-identified individuals.

Despite the growth of the SM community, the social stigma against SM is so pervasive that many individuals hide their sexual preferences from their partners, family, friends, medical doctors and/or mental health professionals. In one recent survey of adult SM group members, 70% of the respondents reported they were at least partially closeted (NCSF,1998, p. 2). The Violence & Discrimination survey was created by NCSF and was distributed electronically and in paper form from April 1998 to February 1999 to SM-identified individuals who were members of an SM group or attending a large SM conference or contest.

Because individuals conceal their SM practices, there are few accurate real-life representations that depict ordinary SM-identified individuals who are parents, neighbors and coworkers, rather than whip-wielding, latex-clad dominatrixes. Thus the stigma against SM is perpetuated by media stereotypes and religious-based moralistic opposition.

SM AND THE FEMINIST MOVEMENT

The early feminist movement, which supported political, economic and social equality of the sexes (NOW, retrieved 2/26/03), often had lesbian leaders. These women advocated for lesbian rights as part of larger struggle for women's rights and personal freedom. They felt that women could decide with whom and how to engage in sex. The National Organization for Women (NOW), which is the largest organization of feminist activists, passed a conference resolution in 1971 resolving to support lesbian rights through education and legislation (NOW, retrieved 2/26/03). However, this embrace of minority rights within the feminist movement specifically excluded SM-identified women.

Feminist Opposition to SM Practices

Feminists throughout the 1970s were caught up in the so-called "sex wars," a decades-long conflict carried out in both the media and legislatures to determine organized feminism's position on sex. Some vocal feminists rejected pornography and sadomasochistic practices, while other feminists supported them as issues of personal freedom (Vance, 1984).

Members of NOW passed a conference resolution entitled *The 1980 Delineation of Lesbian Rights Issues* (SM Policy Reform Project, retrieved 2/26/03). This resolution stated that NOW rejected sadomasochism along with pornography, public sex, and pederasty, because these issues, "violate the feminist principles" upon which NOW was founded.

In particular, *The 1980 Delineation of Lesbian Rights* stated, "Sado-masochism is an issue of exploitation and violence, not affectional/sex-ual preference/orientation." This position was further strengthened in NOW's 1982 "Concept Paper on 1980 Conference Resolution" which was attached to the original resolution (SM Policy Reform Project, retrieved 2/26/03):

> Sadomasochists seek to legitimize and provide a premeditated structure for violence. NOW opposes any repressive legislation concerning private consensual sexual activity between adults. Nevertheless, NOW opposes institutionalized violence as well as social structures which encourage or advocate the use of physical and psychological violence or domination among individuals. This opposition to violence precludes support or advocacy of sa-domasochism as a feminist issue.

This official stance against SM had a serious effect on women who engage in SM practices. NOW compared SM to the "social structures which encourage . . . violence or domination," meaning the patriarchal hierarchy. Anti-SM feminists claimed that the patriarchal society condi-tioned women to take on certain roles, and SM practitioners were con-demned for perpetuating those power relationships in their sexual behaviors (Linden, 1982, pp. 4-5). Some feminists tried to forcibly root out forms of patriarchal behavior by attacking and harassing SM-identi-fied women. As one contributor to *Against Sadomasochism*, a volume of essays by feminists who rejected SM practices, stated, "Isn't it time we stopped playing at power and especially time we stopped playing with the power of the rule of the fathers? Surely it is time we beginning to empower each other so we can become a force capable of success-fully *resisting* domination" (Hoagland, 1982, p.160, emphasis in origi-nal).

At the 1993 March on Washington, a nationwide survey was initiated by Female Trouble, a women's SM group in Philadelphia (Female Trouble, retrieved 2/26/03). This survey exclusively focused on the les-bian community and documented a pattern of abuse against SM-identi-fied women by other lesbians (Keres, 1994).

As documented in the results of the survey entitled *Violence Against SM Women Within the Lesbian Community* (Keres, 1994, p. 3):

> Reactionary lesbian feminism . . . created a confrontational atmo-sphere within our community that targets SM women and they

have duped and intimidated many women in the lesbian community into looking the other way when SM women are attacked. Touting themselves as the harbingers of "truth," they have sought to inflict their dogma upon a diverse and complex lesbian community, audaciously claiming the right to dictate and control the sexual expression of lesbian women.

Of the 539 SM-identified women who took part in the survey, over half reported they had experienced some form of physical assault or discrimination within the lesbian community because of their SM practices (Keres, 1994, p. 23). The surveys found twenty-five percent had suffered physical assault, including being hit, shoved, jabbed, chased, spat upon or objects thrown at them by women in the lesbian community. Another thirty percent were refused admittance or ejected from social, recreational, political, educational and spiritual groups within the lesbian community (Keres, 1994, p. 8).

It did not matter which SM role these women preferred; they were condemned as being violent simply because of the way they expressed their sexuality. The violence occurred against "bottoms" (those who preferred to receive stimulation), "tops" (those who preferred to give the stimulation), those who "switch" (play both top and bottom roles) (Keres, 1994, p. 36).Violence also occurred against the plurality of women who liked to "switch," meaning they played both top and bottom roles (Keres, 1994, p. 36).

As early as 1982, Vivienne Walker-Crawford, another contributor to *Against Sadomasochism*, acknowledged that some of her fellow feminists who opposed SM were actually attacking SM-identified women, and offered the following justification:

> Sadomasochism is a cancerous growth that has taken firm root in most wimmin [sic]. Sexual sadomasochism is exposure of that growth on very intimate terms. The proponents of sexual sadomasochism have turned themselves inside out to mirror our disease. This disease is frightening in its enormity. We immediately recoil, not wanting to recognize its vileness. Here we "beat the messenger with the bad news." We beat and badger these wimmin, throwing our internal fear and confusion onto them. (Walker-Crawford, 1982, p. 150)

It was ironic that some lesbians found it acceptable to act violently against an SM-identified woman because she was, by their definition, guilty of violence. This use of violence, ostensibly to end violence, was not questioned openly within the greater feminist community during the decades prior to the 1990s.

SM Compared to Violence

The proponents of NOW's anti-SM policy did not provide research documenting the problems that purportedly arose from SM behaviors. Instead, they quoted a few people who had encountered abuse during SM encounters, and generalized those accounts in order to condemn all SM practices (Linden, 1982, p. 16).

Some SM-identified individuals further confused the issue by claiming their sexual practices involved "violent" emotions. SM-identified author Tina Portillo (1991, p. 50) stated in the *Leatherfolk* anthology: "Instead of using violence to expel energy the way I did in my younger days, I choose SM as the vehicle for expressing the emotions that threaten to overwhelm me."

However when the practices themselves are considered, there are clear differences between SM versus abuse. The typical pattern of abuse includes the intentional intimidation of one partner to coerce or isolate the other. Abuse is unpredictable and out-of-control behavior. Abuse also tends to be cyclical in nature, escalating over time, and is characterized by calm periods between the episodes and promises that the behavior will never happen again (Abuse Counseling and Treatment, retrieved 2/26/03).

SM, on the other hand, is desired, consensual behavior. The participants consent freely to a power exchange, and can withdraw that consent and stop the interaction at any time (Houlberg, 1993). Limits and the level of desired stimulation are discussed, and communication takes place before, during, and after SM activities. SM participants seek out opportunities to engage in these activities and attempt to ensure their practices are as safe as possible.

Abusive individuals can be found in all groups, but SM itself is not inherently abusive. SM practitioners do not force or coerce their partners though SM behaviors may appear that way to casual observers. The goal of SM is to engage in mutually satisfying sex (Leather Leadership Conference, 1998, retrieved 3/10/03).

SM-Identified Feminists Protest Discrimination

In 1996, SM-identified members of NOW organized a campaign to remove the organization's anti-SM policy. An ad hoc project was formed and named the SM Policy Reform Project. These SM activists rejected attempts to police women's sexuality, claiming it was contrary to NOW's core belief that women have the right to chose for themselves, whether it concerned their careers, their lifestyles, or their sexual expression.

The SM Policy Reform Project sponsored a series of educational events at local NOW chapters to explain the differences between SM versus abuse. SM practitioners "came out" about their SM sexuality to fellow NOW members, and emphasized the importance of education about safe, sane and consensual SM practices. They demanded that NOW refrain from labeling SM as violence and help clarify the issues surrounding consent and abuse. NOW members were also made aware of the extent of violence and discrimination against women who practiced SM, which sprang in part from NOW's own anti-SM policy.

Many NOW members responded positively to the campaign to eliminate the anti-SM policy. At the July 1999 NOW National Conference in Beverly Hills, California, enough signatures were gathered to present an SM-positive statement along with other proposed NOW declarations. The Action Vice-President of NOW, Elizabeth Toledo, invited Susan Wright, the coordinator of the SM Policy Reform Project, to a breakfast meeting prior to the vote. Toledo stated that NOW leaders opposed the SM Policy Reform Statement because it contained language supportive of SM practices.

Toledo proposed a compromise that the original 1980 Delineation of Lesbian Rights be replaced with a statement of rights which would no longer oppose SM practices, nor would it openly support SM practices. It was understood by pro-SM feminists that the NOW leadership would be successful in opposing an SM-positive statement. Therefore, the NOW members representing the SM Policy Reform Project at the 1999 convention agreed to this compromise in order to remove the anti-SM policy.

With the support of NOW delegates and members at the July 1999 National Conference, NOW's official policy against SM was removed. *The 1999 Delineation of Lesbian Rights* replaced *The 1980 Delineation of Lesbian Rights Issues* that contained NOW's anti-SM policy (SM Policy Reform Project, retrieved 2/26/03). *The 1999 Delineation of Lesbian Rights* is straightforward and neither condemns nor supports any specific form of lesbian sexuality (SM Policy Reform Project, retrieved 2/26/03):

> **Whereas** NOW demonstrates a strong commitment to lesbian rights, and
>
> **Whereas** NOW's agenda embraces the rich diversity of issues and experiences that impact women's lives,
>
> **Therefore Be It Resolved,** that NOW reaffirms its commitment to a lesbian rights agenda that was a grassroots strategy to fight bigotry and discrimination based on real or perceived sexual orientation;
>
> **Be It Further Resolved,** that this resolution replaces the 1980 Delineation of Lesbian Rights.

Though still not openly supportive of SM practitioners, the feminist community is backing away from intolerance and antipathy. Women with differing viewpoints about sexuality are increasingly being listened to instead of censored and dismissed.

However without an SM-positive policy, NOW chapters are not likely to sponsor discussions about SM safer sex techniques. Educational discussions about sexual limits, consent, boundaries, relationships and desires would be a positive addition to NOW's wide range of feminist topics. NOW is unlikely to support anti-discrimination legislation or defend SM practitioners from discrimination, nor help women with SM interests find fellowship/sisterhood with women of similar interests.

MAINSTREAM PERCEPTIONS OF SM PRACTITIONERS

SM groups have assumed the responsibility to provide open discussions about sadomasochism. These SM groups create a safe environment for adults to talk about their sexuality and desires. Through this process, SM-identified individuals can learn how to recognize the differences between abuse and SM and how to engage safely in their activities.

The early SM groups marched in the footsteps of gay liberation groups formed in the 1960s (Rubin, 1981, pp. 196-197). The movement for sexual minority rights, including privacy rights and the right to sexual self-determination, was first known as the homosexual or "gay" movement. In the 1970s, due to the growing strength of feminists fighting for gender equality, this movement became identified as "lesbian and gay." Then individuals who had a sexual interest in both sexes, bisexuals, elucidated the special problems that they faced. Over time the movement became known as "lesbian, gay and bisexual." By the mid-1990s, transgendered individuals also delineated the special challenges that they faced, and the new umbrella term became "LGBT." Despite the problems SM practitioners faced, the presence of SM-identified individuals in the leadership of the LGBT movement, as well as the presence and support of SM organizations and businesses, SM has not been added officially to the movement.

The lack of commitment to fighting for SM rights by other sexual minority support groups led to the formation of SM advocacy groups. Currently there are a handful of SM groups that perform activism as well as provide educational forums. These include Gay Male S/M Activists (established in 1982), the National Leather Association–International (established in 1986), DC Sexual Minority Advocates (1998), and Baltimore AT-EASE (1999).

The National Coalition for Sexual Freedom (NCSF) was formed in 1997 to provide an advocacy umbrella for SM educational and social groups. Since 2002, NCSF has also included two other subculture groups in its advocacy program–swing and polyamory organizations (both of which involve non-monogamous relationships)–because they face similar legal and discrimination issues (NCSF, retrieved 12/12/03). NCSF is committed to creating a political, legal, and social environment in the United States which allows consenting adults to engage in alternative sexual expression without fear of discrimination or discrimination. The NCSF sponsors advocacy programs that directly combat the stigma against SM, such as the Media Outreach Project, Legal Education Outreach Program, Protect Your Privacy project and the Incident Response team.

The Woodhull Freedom Foundation is a new organization formed in early 2003 that addresses both international and national sexual freedom issues as well as a host of other health and human rights issues. The Woodhull foundation focuses on legislative reforms, and staff members do not engage in media advocacy or regularly assist individuals and SM groups who have been subject to discrimination.

Discrimination of SM-Identified Individuals

The 1998 Violence & Discrimination Survey by the NCSF documented a pattern of discrimination against SM practitioners. Of the 1017 SM-identified individuals surveyed, thirty-six percent had suffered some kind of violence or harassment because of their SM practices, while thirty percent had been victims of job discrimination (NCSF, retrieved 2/26/03).

NCSF annually tracks requests for assistance and compiles them in an Incident Response report. The 2002 report cites 81 separate cases with over 600 total contacts with NCSF staff as they attempted to resolve the incidents (NCSF, retrieved 12/15/03). NCSF assisted in 34 incidents involving individuals while the other 47 incidents involved groups, clubs or events (NCSF, retrieved 12/15/03).

The largest category of incidents concerning individuals involved parents who were engaged in child custody and divorce cases. SM-identified parents continue to experience difficulties in gaining or maintaining child custody through family court proceedings. NCSF worked with the attorneys who represented parents who are accused of being unfit because of their SM behaviors. In some cases, the courts decided that alternative sexual expression alone was not cause to deny child custody. In other cases, the sexual interests of the parent were a stated reason for denying custody or curtailment of visitation.

Job discrimination continues to be a problem for SM-identified individuals. In 2002, NCSF helped more than a dozen people draft and file formal complaints with their employers regarding employment discrimination (NCSF, retrieved 12/15/03). One high-profile incident concerned United Nations Weapons Inspector Jack McGeorge, who never concealed his involvement in SM. The propriety of McGeorge's participation as a weapons inspector in Iraq because of his sexual identity was questioned by the Washington Post (Grimaldi, 2002a; Rose, 2002). The scandal died out when Hans Blix, the Chief UN weapons inspector, stated that McGeorge would be retained as a member of the inspection team (Grimaldi, 2002b).

The Ombudsman of the Washington Post, Michael Getler, stated on December 8, 2002, that he did not find his newspaper's recent articles regarding the UN Weapons inspection team "up to the usual standard" and that James V. Grimaldi had "yielded to the titillation factor in featuring McGeorge so prominently" (Getler, 2002).

Individuals also consulted with NCSF on a variety of other issues including: the legality of obscene materials, guidelines for posting sexually frank information on Internet Websites, the laws and regulations pertaining to private SM parties, and dealing with personal media exposure (NCSF, retrieved 12/15/03).

Discrimination complaints were also made about two Internet companies in 2002 (NCSF, retrieved 12/15/03). In July, eBay pulled all of its SM-related material for sale, while Match.com deleted a psychotherapist's ad because it mentioned that the therapist had her own poly therapy practice.

Opposition to SM Events

The growing prevalence and visibility of SM events prompted a new trend in February-May 2002. Various conservative groups (Concerned Women for America [CWA], the American Family Association [AFA], and the American Decency Association [ADA]) mounted campaigns against five SM conferences in the Midwest (NCSF, retrieved 12/15/03). The campaigns were attempts to force each hotel to cancel the conference or to mobilize government regulatory agencies to find ordinances that would be violated.

The SM conferences provide workshops on safe sex techniques and relationship issues, and included charity functions, social activities, banquets, entertainment, vendors, and role-playing games. Each of these five Midwestern conferences worked with NCSF to counter sensationalized media claims made by the conservative advocacy groups, as well as resisting action by local authorities who attempted to shut down the SM conferences.

In April 2002, because of the media storm surrounding a St. Louis event, Missouri State Senator John Loudon introduced a resolution to prohibit all SM conferences from taking place in Missouri. The matter eventually was referred to the State Attorney General and Health Department who investigated (NCSF, retrieved 12/15/03). Ultimately, the event was held without incident.

The CWA pressured Cendant Corporation, the world's largest hotel franchiser with more than 6,400 hotels, into sending a letter to its franchisees threatening them with reprisals if they booked "controversial" guests or groups that "national interest groups find offensive" (Silverman, retrieved 12/16/03). This letter was sent in March 2002 to hotel franchisees from Henry R. Silverman, the Chairman Board of Directors of Cendant Corporation.

As a result of CWA pressure, Cendant hotels canceled their contracts with two of the SM conferences. Both conferences were able to relocate to new host hotels, but with obvious inconveniences and problems. The NCSF coordinated a successful media, petition and letter-writing campaign that convinced Cendant Corporation to clarify its position in September 2002, reaffirming the right of hotel franchisees to host the events of their choice (NCSF, retrieved 12/16/03). As of this date, a number of SM events are being hosted in hotels that are owned by Cendant franchisees.

Opposition to SM events based on moral and religious grounds continued in September 2003. One SM group planned to hold a conference in Ocean City, Maryland. Previously they had held their annual conference in New Carrollton, Maryland, without difficulty. However, two negative media reports about the upcoming SM conference were published in local newspapers in September 2003 (Carmean, 2003; Mook, 2003). These articles quoted two local churches, two Ocean City Councilmen, a parent with the Ocean City Elementary Parent-Teacher Association, and a local business owner who all questioned the appropriateness of the SM conference being held in their "family resort." Despite a statement by the Ocean City Police Chief that the activities at the conference were legal because they were being held in private (Mook, 2003), the local business association and church members continued to put pressure on the host hotel to cancel the SM conference.

The event was cancelled when City Solicitor claimed the conference would violate a rarely invoked provision in the Maryland Code relating to liquor license-holding establishments (Guy, 2003). Because the hotel had a liquor license and even though no alcohol was to be served at the annual conference, the activities would have technically violated the regulations. That interpretation makes it essentially impossible for these events to be held in counties covered by this provision; given their large size, no venue exists that does not hold a liquor license.

Another SM conference canceled in 2003 had been scheduled to occur in a suburb of New Orleans. The organizers contacted the local police precinct, as is standard practice to ensure that planned activities conformed to local regulations (Doster, 2003). The police chief responded by sending letters to 15 hotels, urging them to refuse to hold the event. In addition, the police chief authorized a press release bragging about his actions, though he quoted no laws or codes that the event would have violated (Doster, 2003). This SM conference was forced to relocate to New Orleans.

The Sexual Freedom Movement

The sexual freedom movement rests on the efforts of individuals, SM groups and SM businesses that actively support the right of adults to practice alternative sexual expression. This support is generated through letter-writing campaigns, fundraisers for legal defense funds, assistance during incidents, and media advocacy.

When a private party was raided in Attleboro, Massachusetts, in July 2000, SM groups raised over $30,000 for a legal defense fund. The host was charged with 13 counts, ranging from operating a business without a license, to assault and battery, and possession of a dangerous weapon: a wooden spoon (Pagnozzi, 2001). A party participant was arrested for performing consensual sadomasochism under the law that "consent is not a defense to assault" (Pagnozzi, 2001). After two years of legal proceedings, all charges were dismissed.

Many states still retain statutes that forbid the use of "consent as a defense to assault" during legal proceedings. These statutes were once used to arrest perpetrators of domestic violence before specific state legislation was enacted. "Consent is not a defense to assault" is now increasingly being used to target consensual SM activities which prosecutors deem to be too extreme (NCSF, retrieved 12/14/03).

CONCLUSION

The freedom issues facing SM-identified individuals are numerous. The list of protected classes in anti-discrimination legislature should be amended to specify that individuals cannot be fired or refused membership because of their consensual sexual practices with adults. People serving in the armed forces shouldn't be dishonorably discharged because of their SM practices. Judges in family courts need to be educated about consensual SM so that SM-identified individuals are not denied child custody nor receive unfair divorce settlements. Media outlets also must be educated so that negative stereotypes about sadomasochism are not perpetuated.

In addition, many SM activists believe that the American Psychiatric Association's *Diagnostic and Statistic Manual* should be revised, eliminating in their entirety the diagnoses for Sexual Sadism and Sexual Masochism (302.83 and 302.84). The stigma of mental illness now hangs over the head of every individual who practices SM because of these diagnoses. The APA's *DSM* is regularly used as justification for discriminating against SM-identified individuals; much as NOW's former anti-SM policy was used to justify discrimination against SM-identified women.

The wider goal of SM advocacy is to ensure that adults can choose freely the sexual practices that are best for them while being empowered to protect themselves from abuse and STDs. Thousands of SM-identified individuals have volunteered their time to assist SM groups in educating adults about safe and consensual sexual practices.

Currently, adult sexual education is hampered by the continuing stigma against SM. Groups and individuals are afraid to "come out" and make their presence known because of the pervasive legal and social discrimination that can ensue. Yet the best way to change the social perception of SM is for SM-identified individuals and SM groups to become more visible. Therefore the negative cycle is perpetuated.

REFERENCES

Abuse Counseling and Treatment (retrieved 2/26/03). Cycle of Violence. Available: http://www.actabuse.com/cycleviolence.html.

Carmean, J.E., Jr. (2003). "OC community objects to alternative sex convention: Some residents concerned for town's family-oriented image," Daily Times (September 22, 2003).

Doster, S. (2003). "Kenner sex fetish gathering hits kink: Organizer blames unconsenting chief," Times-Picayune (October 11, 2003).

Female Trouble (retrieved 2/26/03). Available: www.leathercares.com/History/Clubs/Female.htm

Getler, M. (2002). "Sexing it up," Washington Post (December 8, 2002).

Grimaldi, J.V. (2002a). "Weapons inspectors' experience questioned," Washington Post (November 28, 2002).

Grimaldi, J.V. (2002b). "Inspector's resignation rejected by U.N.'s Blix," Washington Post(November 30, 2002).

Guy, C. (2003). "Fetish, bondage group drops convention plan," Baltimore Sun (October 7, 2003).

Hoagland, S.L. (1982). "Sadism, masochism, and lesbian-feminism," Against Sadomasochism. San Francisco: Frog in the Well.

Houlberg, R. (1993). "The Magazine of a sadomasochism club: The tie that binds," Journal of Homosexuality (Vol. 21, pp. 167-83).

Keres, J. (1994) (retrieved 11/23/03). Violence against SM women within the lesbian community: A nationwide survey [Online]. Available: http://www.ncsfreedom org/library/femaletrouble.htm

Leather Leadership Conference (1998) (retrieved 3/10/03). "SM vs. abuse policy statement" [Online.] Available: http://www.leatherleadership.org/library/diffsmabuse.htm.

Linden, R.R. (1982). Against Sadomasochism. San Francisco: Frog in the Well Publishing.

Mook, B.L. (2003). "Sex expo in family resort?" The Maryland Coast Dispatch (September 19, 2003).

National Coalition for Sexual Freedom (1998) (retrieved 2/26/03). Violence & discrimination survey [Online]. Available: http://www.ncsfreedom.org/library/viodiscrimsurvey. htm.

National Coalition for Sexual Freedom. (2001) (retrieved 3/10/03). Media resources: Some quick facts [Online]. Available: http://www.ncsfreedom.org/media/media. htm.

National Coalition for Sexual Freedom (2002) (retrieved 12/12/03). NCSF mission statement [Online]. Available: http://www.ncsfreedom.org/index.htm.

National Coalition for Sexual Freedom (1999) (retrieved 12/14/03). Memorandum of law of Amicus Curiae [Online]. Available: http://www.ncsfreedom.org/ library/jovanovic/amicus3.htm

National Coalition for Sexual Freedom. (2002) (retrieved 12/15/03). NCSF supports your rights! [Online]. Available: http://www.ncsfreedom.org/overview.htm.

National Coalition for Sexual Freedom (2002) (retrieved 12/16/03). Cendant Corporation is urged by NCSF to drop "Controversial Guest" policy [Online]. Available: http://www.ncsfreedom.org/privacy/cendanturged.htm

National Organization for Women (retrieved 2/26/03). NOW history: Lesbian rights [Online]. Available: http://www.now.org/history/history.html#Lesbian.

Pagnozzi, A. (2001). "Kinky find a cause in 'Paddleboro'," The Hartford Courant, (March 9, 2001).

Portillo, T. (1991). "I get real: Celebrating my sadomasochistic soul," Leatherfolk Radical Sex, People, Politics and Practice. Boston: Alyson Publications.

Rhodes, D. (retrieved 2/26/03). The Leather Journal: Club directory [Online]. Available: http://www.theleatherjournal.com/directory.htm.

Rhodes, D. (retrieved 2/26/03). The Leather Journal: Calendar [Online]. Available: http://www.theleatherjournal.com/calendar.htm.

Rose, D. (2002). "World body not turned off by arms inspector's S&M," Washington Post (November 29, 2002).

Rubin, G. (1981). "The Leather menace: Comments on politics and SM," Coming to Power. Boston: Alyson Publications (pp. 194-229).

Silverman, H.R. (2002) (retrieved 12/16/03). Cendant letter to franchisees [Online]. Available: http://www.ncsfreedom.org/privacy/cendantsletter.htm

SM Policy Reform Project (retrieved 2/26/03). The 1980 delineation of lesbian rights issues [Online]. Available: http://members.aol.com/NOWSM/Delineation.html/#Delineation.

SM Policy Reform Project (retrived 2/26/03). The 1999 delineation of lesbian rights [Online]. Available: http://members.aol.com/NOWSM/Home.html.

Vance, C. (1984). Pleasure and danger: Exploring female sexuality. Routledge & Kegan Paul Books Ltd.

Walker-Crawford, V. (1982). "The saga of Sadie O. Massey," Against Sadomasochism. San Francisco: Frog in the Well.

SM (Sadomasochistic) Interests as an Issue in a Child Custody Proceeding

Marty Klein, PhD

Palo Alto, CA

Charles Moser, PhD, MD

Institute for Advanced Study of Human Sexuality

SUMMARY. This article describes a child custody case centered on the fitness of the mother, who was involved in an SM relationship with her live-in boyfriend. Although the investigation confirmed that no child abuse had occurred, that the child was unaware of the mother's sexual interests, that there were no incidents of inappropriate sexual activities in front of the minor, and that the child was doing well, the court severely limited the mother's visitation and custody arrangements and ended her alimony. Practitioners of alternative sexual lifestyles have not fared well in child custody hearings, and this case is no exception. The present case indicates how the family court system can be biased against sexual mi-

Marty Klein is a licensed marriage and family therapist in private practice. He also publishes "Sexual Intelligence," an electronic newsletter. Charles Moser is Professor and Chair of the Department of Sexual Medicine, Institute for Advanced Study of Human Sexuality, San Francisco, CA. Correspondence may be addressed: Charles Moser, PhD, MD, 45 Castro Street, #125, San Francisco, CA 94114 (E-mail: Docx2@ix.netcom.com).

[Haworth co-indexing entry note]: "SM (Sadomasochistic) Interests as an Issue in a Child Custody Proceeding." Klein, Marty, and Charles Moser. Co-published simultaneously in *Journal of Homosexuality* (Harrington Park Press, an imprint of The Haworth Press, Inc.) Vol. 50, No. 2/3, 2006, pp. 233-242; and: *Sadomasochism: Powerful Pleasures* (ed: Peggy J. Kleinplatz, and Charles Moser) Harrington Park Press, an imprint of The Haworth Press, Inc., 2006, pp. 233-242. Single or multiple copies of this article are available for a fee from The Haworth Document Delivery Service [1-800-HAWORTH, 9:00 a.m. - 5:00 p.m. (EST). E-mail address: docdelivery@haworthpress.com].

Available online at http://www.haworthpress.com/web/JH
doi:10.1300/J082v50n02_11

norities in general and SM practitioners in particular. In addition, the present case demonstrates how the *DSM* diagnostic criteria can be misused in dealing with alternative lifestyle practitioners. Recommendations for further education of the court and for future research are made. *[Article copies available for a fee from The Haworth Document Delivery Service: 1-800-HAWORTH. E-mail address: <docdelivery@haworthpress.com> Website: <http://www.HaworthPress.com> © 2006 by The Haworth Press, Inc. All rights reserved.]*

KEYWORDS. BDSM, child custody, paraphilia, psychotherapy bias, sadomasochism, sexual minorities

Divorce in this society is often contentious and, once divorced, partners often prefer to have no further contact with each other. Shared child-raising often forces the former partners to regularly interact with each other over an issue that engenders strong feelings: the rearing of their children. One partner may denigrate the other, in hopes of limiting contact, maintaining control of the childrearing process, and just to cause the other partner distress. Often the issues that divide the partners are real, honest disagreements that contributed to the dissolution of the marriage. At other times, of course, the opposite is true–partners cooperate, especially around child-rearing.

Each partner may try to discredit the other partner by exposing the other's sexual history in child custody cases. Parental fitness has been (and continues to be) questioned, for example, because someone has been a single mother, committed adultery, been "promiscuous," is homosexual, or participates in other "unusual" sexual activity. In such cases, the accusing partner suggests to the court that the child would be disadvantaged or endangered because the other parent has engaged in the suspect behavior.

The best-researched area in this regard is on the effect on a child of having a homosexual parent. The bulk of this research has shown that the sexual orientation of parents has little effect on parenting or on the child (Anderssen, Amlie, & Ytteroy, 2002; Dundas & Kaufman, 2000; Patterson, 1992; Tasker & Golombok, 1995). Nevertheless, other sexual interests (e.g., transvestitism, swinging, and sadomasochism) are still regularly contested in courts.

The present paper illustrates that parental sexual interests can be used to question one's fitness to parent without evidence that any harm has been done. We did not interview the principles in this case and take no position on whether the mother is fit or not. We do contend that the expert's report was prejudiced. We will analyze the appointed expert's report to the court, showing its inconsistencies and biases. This case is particularly compelling because all parties involved accepted the facts presented as true. Names and other identifying information have been changed to protect the confidentiality of the individuals. The court rendered its judgment in 2003.

THE CASE

The present case came to the attention of one of the authors (C.M.) when Sam Jones contacted him, seeking expert consultation in a custody hearing. Mr. Jones is the current SM (sadomasochistic) partner of Ms. Smith, the mother of Ed, an 11-year-old minor; the case involved custody of Ed. Mr. Jones and Ms. Smith live together in Ms. Smith's home; Ed lived with them part-time and with his father part-time

Mr. Jones and the author (C.M.) had met approximately 15 years earlier, when the author was involved in a research project involving SM participants. Mr. Jones facilitated distribution of questionnaires and helped arrange interviews from an SM social group in which he was involved. There was no subsequent contact after that, but that prior relationship precluded the author testifying in this case. The case was then referred to and accepted by the other author (M.K.). The psychological report and other court documents were reviewed and discussed by both authors.

This case concerns custody of Ed, the son of Ann and Bob Smith, born after 19 years of marriage. Ed was born with a congenital physical problem. His intellectual level is above average and his social functioning is appropriate for his age. The Smiths divorced after 27 years of marriage. Joint physical and legal custody of Ed was awarded to both parents; his primary residence was with his father. Ms. Smith received liberal visitation rights, and Ed resided with her during Mr. Smith's frequent business travel. One reason the couple divorced was their disagreements about Ms. Smith's interest in SM (sadomasochism), which she initially explored with her husband. After their separation, she eventually moved in with Mr. Jones, where they developed an ongoing, intense SM relationship.

The present court proceeding emerged after Ms. Smith informed Mr. Smith of a medical problem Ed experienced on his last visit. It was customary and expected for each parent to share any change in Ed's medical condition with the other. Ed's congenital problems had led to a fecal impaction, which caused him considerable pain. This problem had created difficulties for Ed and his family on several occasions. Mr. Jones had worked as a medical technician and knew how to disimpact someone. With Ms. Smith and Ed's permission, Mr. Jones inserted a gloved and lubricated finger into Ed's rectum and relieved the fecal impaction. Ms. Smith observed the entire procedure; Ed never complained of feeling violated during or after the procedure. In fact, Ed was grateful for relief from the pain, and thankful for the intervention. Nevertheless, Mr. Smith was furious that his ex-wife's boyfriend had penetrated his son with his finger. He felt this was child sexual abuse and petitioned the court to prevent Mr. Jones from having any further contact with Ed; a formal investigation ensued.

Dr. Blair, a forensic and clinical psychologist, was appointed by the court to evaluate Mr. and Ms. Smith, Mr. Jones, and Ed, and to render an opinion on whether the disimpaction constituted child abuse and on the parental fitness of all the adults. During that investigation, Dr. Blair was told about the SM relationship between Mr. Jones and Ms. Smith. Dr. Blair then shifted the focus of the investigation and pursued (1) the possibility that the SM interests of Ms. Smith and Mr. Jones posed a danger to Ed, and (2) the question of whether Ms. Smith was fit to parent Ed.

DR. BLAIR'S REPORT

Dr. Blair concluded that the fecal disimpaction, though perhaps ill-advised, was not "abuse." The court accepted this analysis, and the allegation that Mr. Jones sexually abused Ed was dropped as an issue in these proceedings.

Dr. Blair instead decided to focus on the SM interests of Ms. Smith and Mr. Jones. Although it is appropriate to explore any issue that may affect the welfare and development of the minor, Dr. Blair did not provide a rationale for focusing on the sexual relationship of Mr. Jones and Ms. Smith. He confirmed that the couple had successfully shielded Ed from any knowledge of the nature or specifics of their sexual relationship. He attempted to show that Mr. Jones had a sexual interest in children, but admitted that there was no evidence to support this belief. Additionally he admitted that Ed has good parent-child relationships with both his mother and Mr. Jones. He also determined that Ed is doing well in school, with his peers, and has no unusual social or psychological problems. All Dr. Blair's concerns focused on the possibility that something problematic could happen in the relationship between Mr. Jones and Ms. Smith.

From his interviews, Dr. Blair diagnosed Mr. Jones with Sexual Sadism and Ms. Smith with Sexual Masochism according to the *DSM-IV-TR* (APA, 2000). These diagnoses each have two criteria; both are necessary to make these diagnoses. The second criterion requires the person to experience significant distress or dysfunction as a result of his or her sexual interests. Dr. Blair did not indicate that Ms. Smith or Mr. Jones suffered from any distress or dysfunction; in fact, he indicated that they were happy and fulfilled in their chosen lifestyle. The *DSM-IV-TR* (2000) specifically warns against assuming that deviant behavior is indicative of a mental disorder: "Neither deviant behavior (e.g., political, religious, or sexual) nor conflicts between the individual and society are mental disorders . . ." (APA, 2000, p. xxxi).

Even if both Mr. Jones and Ms. Smith fulfilled the diagnostic criteria for their respective disorders, there is no indication that parenting deficits are associated with individuals so diagnosed. Considering that Dr. Blair should have known this, and that the court is unlikely to understand the finer points of these diagnoses, his report can be seen as deliberately misleading and prejudicial. Beyond simplistic speculation, the report did not describe how the health and welfare of the minor would be affected by the couple's involvement in SM.

Dr. Blair did not give any example of inappropriate behavior by Ms. Smith or Mr. Jones. Dr. Blair himself agreed that the incident which led to the proceeding was not inappropriate, though it did show questionable judgment. Thus, it is unclear on what basis, other than prejudice or lack of education, Dr. Blair decided that Ms. Smith and Mr. Jones's sexual relationship presented a danger to Ed's health and welfare. Dr. Blair argued that the *DSM* suggests that individuals diagnosed with Sexual Sadism or Sexual Masochism do present a danger. The DSM states, "Usually, however, the severity of the sadistic acts increases over time" (APA, 2000, p. 574) and, "Not uncommonly, individuals have more than one Paraphilia" (APA, 2000, p. 567). Dr. Blair used the first statement to justify his recommendation to limit Ms. Smith's custody of Ed as a mechanism to protect Ms. Smith from herself. He used the second statement to assert that Mr. Jones would likely develop Pedophilia and sexually molest Ed if the current custody arrangement remained in force, although he found no evidence of such an interest in Mr. Jones's history.

The problems with the logic, the lack of empiric literature to support the statements, the lack of internal consistency, inaccuracies, and other problems with the *DSM* in general and the Paraphilia section specifically have been discussed in detail elsewhere (Moser, 2001, 2002; Moser & Kleinplatz, 2002, in press). There is no empirical research suggesting that even those "appropriately" (according to the *DSM* criteria) diagnosed with Sexual Sadism or Sexual Masochism are likely to experience either a dangerous increase in the intensity of their SM interactions nor that Pedophilia is a likely outgrowth of these activities.

Accurate or not, the diagnoses given to Mr. Jones and Ms. Smith are contrary to the spirit of the cautionary notes in the *DSM* concerning its use in legal settings: "[T]here are significant risks that diagnostic information will be misused and misunderstood" (APA, 2000, p. xxxii-xxxiii). Additionally, the fact that individuals meet the diagnostic criteria for a mental disorder does not mean that these individuals will manifest every aspect of the diagnosed disorder, or that they will lack the ability to control their behavior (APA, 2000). It should be noted that impulse control disorders and compulsions are described elsewhere in the *DSM*, but are not mentioned in the definition or diagnostic criteria of a Paraphilia. Simply put, the diagnoses of Sexual Masochism and Sexual Sadism do not assume the individual will also have impulse control difficulties, obsessions, or compulsions.

Dr. Blair seemed to be overly concerned that Ms. Smith would be injured. But in fact, there was no history of Ms. Smith being injured or requiring medical attention. There is no indication that individuals with these diagnoses are clogging our hospital emergency rooms or that these individuals suffer an unusually high rate of serious injury from their sexual activity.

The following statements are from Dr. Blair's report and are illustrative of his attitude:

> I ponder the effects on the child if [Ms. Smith] were to die or become impaired during sexual activity, especially if the child was in the house.

> Although [Ms. Smith and Mr. Jones] describe their activities as a hobby or sport, I believe it is domestic violence. Although the child has not observed it, he is exposed to the after-effects. I don't have enough information to understand what the effects on the child might be at this time. However, it would obviously be cata-

strophic if a mother were injured or died as a result of her behavior and choices.

Dr. Blair also doubted that anyone could freely choose to be involved in SM; he also believed that everyone involved in the SM community is a potential child molester. The following are quotes from his report:

> I am not sure whether [Ms. Smith's] choice [of SM behavior] is reflective of self-gratification, or a desire to please Mr. Jones. I suspect, however, that she is so subservient and eager to please him that her thinking may be clouded or confused.

> I don't think it would be a good idea for [Ms. Smith] to use members of the [SM] scene for childcare; since they each have at least one paraphilia, which means they might have others, including pedophilia. Each member of the scene is an unknown quantity and possible risk factor.

The amount of sexually explicit material depicting SM and the large number of references to SM in the media argue that SM is not uncommon in the United States. If SM resulted in psychological or physical problems, they probably would be reported in the clinical literature. The clinical literature is lacking in any studies showing an association between these diagnoses and other clinical or social problems.

THE DECISION

The court's decision followed Dr. Blair's recommendations closely. It included new limitations on the liberal visitation rights with Ed that Ms. Smith had previously enjoyed. It also specified a complete ban on Mr. Jones having any contact with Ed. All parties involved acknowledged that Ed had a close relationship with Mr. Jones; Dr. Blair admitted that Ed's relationship with Mr. Jones was better than the relationship that Ed had with Mr. Smith. There appeared to be no concern for the effect of abruptly denying Ed access to Mr. Jones.

Ed's relatively frequent visits to his mother's home were severely limited for several reasons. His father was moving to another state, which limited the formerly easy accessibility to his mother's residence. In addition, the court's ban on contact with Mr. Jones limited the time Ed could realistically spend with his mother. The court order required that Mr. Jones vacate his own residence whenever Ed visited his mother. Not only is this problematic logistically, it added an additional note of cruelty to Mr. Jones's loss of contact with the boy he had been stepparenting. Ms. Smith also lost all spousal support, despite the fact that her husband made significantly more money than she did, and that their marriage lasted for 27 years. This loss of support limited Ms. Smith's ability to rent other lodgings for her visits with Ed.

It is also interesting that the court ordered that if Ms. Smith hired an attorney to represent Ed's rights in court, that attorney must have taken a domestic violence prevention training course. Ms. Smith was required to attend 30 psychotherapy sessions focused on her participation in "domestic violence." She was told to enroll in a domestic violence education program; refusal to do so would be held against her in any future court proceedings. It appears that the court was attempting to protect Ms. Smith from domestic partner abuse and her son from witnessing the tragic results of that abuse. One can only conclude that the court decided that Ms. Smith was a domestic violence victim and her reported interest in SM was a justification or denial of her abuse. It is true that without proper training someone might mistake SM for domestic violence. In this case, however, the court did hear testimony clearly differentiating domestic violence from SM, but chose to disregard it. Note that there is no record of any of the Smith/Jones's neighbors being concerned about domestic violence–no emergency room visits, no police calls, no child protective services reports. The only "evidence" supporting Dr. Blair's domestic violence accusations were Mr. Jones and Ms. Smith's own statements honestly describing their consensual sexual activities.

THE MEANING OF THIS CASE

It could be argued easily that this is a tragic situation in which a psychologist allowed his own prejudice to influence his opinion, encouraging the court, in its ignorance (or its own prejudice) of the situation, to disregard the testimony of another expert. Unfortunately, this is not an isolated case, and the results are regrettably similar to those of other cases in other family court systems across the United States. The authors have been consulted in other cases in which a parent's SM interests have been an issue. According to Susan Wright, Spokesperson for The National Coalition for Sexual Freedom, a sexual minority advocacy group, they receive many requests for assistance involving similar circumstances (personal communication, July 7, 2004). These cases generally result in the SM involved parent losing custody and other parenting privileges. We know of no cases where the parent admitting to SM interests obtained or retained custody of the minor.

In the Smith v. Smith case, it could be argued that the lack of evidence supporting the allegation of domestic violence and child abuse does not mean they did not happen. Similarly, one could argue that the likelihood of these occurring–despite the lack of evidence of their existence, or of statistical co-morbidity–was so great that the court acted preventatively, protectively and appropriately. Perhaps, but such reasoning is contrary to the philosophy and standards of the American judicial system.

Some might argue that the safety and well-being of the child is paramount, and the unknowns in this case support the court's actions. The argument is familiar, as it has been used for years by those opposed to custody by homosexual parents. The courts do not seem to have generalized the lessons provided by the contemporary discrediting of this common form of judicial discrimination. Because it is logically impossible to prove a negative, it will never be possible to prove that parenting by SM practitioners has no harmful consequences.

The court's decision to make Ms. Smith attend a domestic violence education program, participate in domestic violence psychotherapy, and hire an attorney trained in domestic violence cases implies that it believed Ms. Smith was a victim of domestic violence. It is important to recognize that the courts rarely punish domestic violence victims by limiting custody and visitation. If domestic violence victims fear that such an admission could result in the loss of custody of their children, this would be a powerful incentive for these individuals *not* to seek help to escape the violence. Obviously that is not in the best interests of these women, their children, or society.

This case has another important meaning. The content of Ms. Smith's private sex life led the court to limit severely custody of and visitation with her son, end her alimony, and ban Mr. Jones from having any contact with Ed. The decision is unequivocally about the couple's SM behavior alone. No other problem or obstacle to effective parenting was found to have any substance.

CONCLUSIONS

There is clearly a need to educate the courts and forensic professionals about SM, and how it differs from domestic violence. The present report may serve as an impetus to start such an education program; it also demonstrates the need to keep statistics about how SM-identified parents fare in child custody cases. We hope that this will attract future research.

The explicit mandate of the Family Courts is to act in the best interests of the children involved. In this case, the court chose to ignore its own expert's observation of the child's positive, emotional connections with Mr. Jones, as well as the child's own wishes. It decided that the positive relationship enjoyed by Ed and Mr. Jones was unimportant. It decided that decreasing the amount of time that Ed spent with his mother was appropriate because of her private sexual behavior.

This case is one example of many known to the authors that demonstrate how the *DSM* diagnoses are misused by forensic professionals. It should provide further impetus to the editors of the *DSM* to reevaluate its classification of atypical sexual behavior as pathological, and to strengthen its warnings against misuse.

REFERENCES

American Psychiatric Association. (1994). Diagnostic and Statistical Manual of Mental Disorders. (4th ed.). Washington, D.C.

Anderssen, N., Amlie, C., & Ytteroy, E.A. (2002). Outcomes for children with lesbian or gay parents. A review of studies from 1978 to 2000. *Scandinavian Journal of Psychology. 43*(4):335-351.

Dundas, S., & Kaufman, M. (2000). The Toronto Lesbian Family Study. *Journal of Homosexuality. 40*(2):65-79.

Moser, C. (2001). Paraphilia: Another confused sexological concept. In P. J. Kleinplatz (Ed.) *New directions in sex therapy: Innovations and alternatives* (pp. 91-108). Philadelphia: Brunner-Routledge.

Moser, C. (2002). Are any of the Paraphilias in the *DSM* mental disorders? *Archives of Sexual Behavior, 31*(6), 490-491.

Moser, C. & Kleinplatz, P.J. (2002). Transvestitic fetishism: Psychopathology or iatrogenic artifact? *New Jersey Psychologist, 52*(2) 16-17. [WWW document] URL *http://home.netcom.com/~docx2/tf.html*

Moser, C. & Kleinplatz, P.J. (in press). DSM-IV-TR and the Paraphilias: An Argument for_Removal. *Journal of Psychology and Human Sexuality.* [WWW document] URL *http://home.netcom.com/~docx2/mk.html*

Patterson, C.J. (1992). Children of lesbian and gay parents. *Child Development. 63*(5): 1025-1042.

Tasker, F. & Golombok, S. (1995). Adults raised as children in lesbian families. *American Journal of Orthopsychiatry. 65*(2):203-215.

The ICD Diagnoses
of Fetishism and Sadomasochism

Odd Reiersøl, PhD

Oslo, Norway

Svein Skeid

Oslo, Norway

SUMMARY. In this article we discuss psychiatric diagnoses of sexual deviation as they appear in the *International Classification of Diseases* (*ICD-10*), the internationally accepted classification and diagnostic system of the World Health Organization (WHO). Namely, we discuss the background of three diagnostic categories: Fetishism (F65.0), Fetishistic Transvestism (F65.1), and Sadomasochism (F65.5). Pertinent background issues regarding the above categories are followed by a critique of the usefulness of diagnosing these phenomena today. Specifically, we argue that Fetishism, Fetishistic Transvestism, and Sadomasochism, also labeled *Paraphilia* or *perversion*, should not be considered ill-

Author note: We thank Reidar Kjær, MD, for proposing changes in the manuscript, Jack Levinson, PhD, for helping with the language, and Lois Reiersøl, PhD, for various suggestions. This manuscript has not been published and is not under consideration elsewhere. But as the editors are aware, parts of this article can be considered a revised, condensed or expanded version of information already given at our Website (http://www.reviseF65.org). Correspondence may be addressed: Odd Reiersøl, Vækerøvn. 69a, N-0383 Oslo, Norway (E-mail: solverv@solverv.com).

[Haworth co-indexing entry note]: "The ICD Diagnoses of Fetishism and Sadomasochism." Reiersøl, Odd, and Svein Skeid. Co-published simultaneously in *Journal of Homosexuality* (Harrington Park Press, an imprint of The Haworth Press, Inc.) Vol. 50, No. 2/3, 2006, pp. 243-262; and: *Sadomasochism: Powerful Pleasures* (ed: Peggy J. Kleinplatz, and Charles Moser) Harrington Park Press, an imprint of The Haworth Press, Inc., 2006, pp. 243-262. Single or multiple copies of this article are available for a fee from The Haworth Document Delivery Service [1-800-HAWORTH, 9:00 a.m. - 5:00 p.m. (EST). E-mail address: docdelivery@haworthpress.com].

nesses. Finally, we present the efforts of an initiative known as *ReviseF65*, which was established in 1997, to abolish these diagnoses.

[Article copies available for a fee from The Haworth Document Delivery Service: 1-800-HAWORTH. E-mail address: <docdelivery@haworthpress.com> Website: <http://www.HaworthPress.com> © 2006 by The Haworth Press, Inc. All rights reserved.]

KEYWORDS. Fetishism, Sadomasochism, Transvestism, sexual deviation, Paraphilia

The first version of the *International Classification of Diseases (ICD)* appeared in 1900. It was intended to classify deadly somatic diseases. The *ICD* has undergone various revisions, and the list of diseases (deadly or not) has increased continuously. Today, the *ICD* also serves as a classification manual of mental and behavioral disorders and is widely used among mental health professionals in Europe. Sexual deviation was introduced as a general classification in *ICD-6* (1948). Subdivisions of that category first appeared in *ICD-8* (1965), and have barely changed since. The next paragraphs elaborate on the diagnostic criteria and the category of sexual deviation.

In the *ICD-10* Classification of Mental and Behavioral Disorders the sexual deviation category is called Disorders of Sexual Preference (DSP) and given the code F65. The heading of the sexual deviation category is described (World Health Organization [WHO], 1992, p. 217) as "Disorders of Sexual Preference, Includes: paraphilias, Excludes: problems associated with sexual orientation." The category includes the following sub-categories: Fetishism, Fetishistic Transvestism, Exhibitionism, Voyeurism, Pedophilia, Sadomasochism, Multiple disorders of sexual preference, Other disorders of sexual preference (including, for example sexual activity with animals).

According to The *ICD-10* Classification of Mental and Behavioural Disorders, Diagnostic Criteria for Research (WHO, 1993, p.135), the above disorders are characterized by the following general criteria:

1. The individual experiences recurrent sexual urges and fantasies involving unusual objects or activities.
2. The individual either acts on the urges or is markedly distressed by them.
3. The preference has been present for at least 6 months.

In this article we focus on the diagnoses of Fetishism (F65.0), Fetishistic Transvestism (F65.1), and Sadomasochism (F65.5). The argument for selecting these diagnoses will be addressed. The next section further elaborates on these diagnoses, which appear in the *ICD* (WHO, 1992).

Fetishism is described (WHO, 1992, p. 218) as:

> Reliance on some non-living object as a stimulus for sexual arousal and sexual gratification. Fetishism should be diagnosed only if the fetish is the most important source of sexual stimulation or essential for satisfactory sexual response. Fetishistic fantasies are common, but they do not amount to a disorder unless they lead to rituals that are so compelling and unacceptable that they interfere with sexual intercourse and cause the individual distress.

Similarly, Fetishistic Transvestism is described (WHO, 1992, p. 218) as:

> The wearing of clothes of the opposite sex principally to obtain sexual excitement. This disorder is to be distinguished from simple fetishism in that the fetishistic articles of clothing are not only worn, but worn also to create the appearance of the opposite sex.

According to the diagnostic manual (WHO, 1992, p. 220) Sadomasochism is considered to be "A preference for sexual activity that involves bondage or the infliction of pain or humiliation. This category should be used only if sadomasochistic activity is the most important source of stimulation or necessary for sexual gratification."

FORMING SEXUAL DEVIATION DIAGNOSES:
A HISTORICAL PERSPECTIVE

Influenced by psychiatric case studies as well as popular novels in the nineteenth century, early pioneers within the medical profession built a vocabulary and classification system of "unusual" sexual practices. On the one hand, the classification of sex practices was an innovative step forward. On the other hand, the use of diagnostic labeling established the persistent stigmatizing of individuals based on their sexual desires.

Given the scope of this article, we will not review the work of the early sexologists who made the first diagnoses during the period of approximately 1880-1930. In short, Krafft-Ebing (1903/1886), Ellis (1920), Stekel (1930), Hirschfeld (n.d.) and others originated the diagnostic terms of Fetishism, Transvestism, Sadism and Masochism. By the time Kinsey (1948) published *Sexual Behavior in the Human Male* these diagnoses were already well established. It was also in 1948 that the WHO assumed responsibility for the *ICD* and its further development. Although the exact inclusion process of these diagnoses in the *ICD* is not clear, it is well established that the American diagnostic system, the *Diagnostic and Statistical Manual of Mental Disorders (DSM)* published by the American Psychiatric Association, has influenced the *ICD* (and vice versa).

There have been few changes in the categories of sexual deviation in the last number of *ICD* revised manuals. For example, the spelling of "Transvestitism" in the *ICD-8* was changed to "Transvestism" in the *ICD-9* revision (WHO, 1978). Also, "Fetishistic Transvestism" was introduced in the *ICD-10* to distinguish that category from the Gender Identity Disorders (F64) diagnosis of "Dual role transvestism," categorized as F64.1 (WHO, p. 215). Despite these semantic changes to the categories, there seems to be no difference in the content of that diagnosis between *ICD-9* and *ICD-10*, and therefore no development. The same is true for Fetishism and Sadomasochism, which were originally classified in another subcategory (i.e., 302.8) in the *ICD-8* and 9 (WHO, 1978). In sum, there has been little development in the diagnostic criteria of sexual deviation disorders in the *ICD* over the past three revisions, and thus the impetus for the present article.

THE NEED TO REVISE F65

We propose that the diagnoses of Fetishism (F65.0), Fetishistic Transvestism (F65.1), and Sadomasochism (F65.5), which are included in the paraphilias, should be abolished. In this paper, we do not address other F65 diagnoses, although Moser (2001) has made a strong case for replacing the whole Paraphilia category of diagnoses in the *DSM*. In this article, we question the legitimacy of classifying sexual offences as sexual disorders.

Normative, Statistical and Empirical Reasons

There are several reasons for abolishing the diagnoses of Fetishism, Fetishistic Transvestism, and Sadomasochism. One reason is linked to statistical issues and normative issues, which influence inclusion/exclusion criteria in diagnoses. For example, the general criterion 1 is inaccurately referring to "unusual objects and activities." From a statistical standpoint, unusual refers to rare and uncommon. However, "unusual" can also be understood as "weird" or "bizarre." That is, statistical criteria are being confounded at times with moral judgments. Viewing unusual objects or activities as immoral is archaic; there is no scientific basis for diagnosing individuals' sexuality when diagnostic criteria merely mask moral indignation. Furthermore, a variety of sexual practices that were previously considered non-normative are not currently regarded as pathological (for example, homosexuality, fellatio and anal sex). It is interesting to note what Kinsey (1953) said about fetishism:

> Persons who respond only or primarily to objects which are remote from the sexual partner, or remote from the overt sexual activities with a partner, are not rare in the population. This is particularly true of individuals who are erotically aroused by high heels, by boots, by corsets, by tight clothing, by long gloves, by whips, or by other objects which suggest sado-masochistic relationships, and which may have been associated with the individual's previous sexual activity. (pp. 678-679)

Behavior should not be diagnosed just because it is unusual. It is not unreasonable to assume that stamp collectors have an unusual interest, in the statistical sense. Few would argue the unusual inclination to philately should be considered a diagnosis. If this hobby is practiced in an extreme way and causes distress, an individual might be diagnosed with something, but it would not be seen as originating in philately. Our main point here is that sexuality should not be pathologized just because it is unusual just as other unusual characteristics or interests are free of psychiatric scrutiny. The diagnoses of fetishism or sadomasochism also should not apply just because a person feels distressed about his or her own interest in that kind of behavior. When sexual behavior is safe and consensual, there is nothing wrong with it from a clinical point of view.

It is possible, however, that some individuals may feel that there is something "wrong" with their sexual practices. Nevertheless, the diagnoses of Fetishism or Sadomasochism should not apply in such cases just because a person feels distressed about his or her own sexual interest. This kind of distress is often associated with feelings of shame rather than with maladaptive behavior per se. In fact, individuals are more likely to experience shame if the kind of sex they prefer is frowned upon, stigmatized or subject to diagnosis.

The impact of social norms on diagnostic considerations is illustrated in the case of homosexuality. Homosexuality was withdrawn from the disorders of sexual preference (DSP) category in the *ICD-10* (it was still listed in *ICD-9*). The removal of homosexuality from the DSP can be mainly attributed to homosexual individuals who were organized and applied political pressure on the psychiatric profession. They argued that there was no scientific basis for the inclusion of homosexuality as a mental disorder. Although *ICD* revisions should not be based on popular opinion, it is important to recognize that many psychiatric diagnoses reflect, to some extent, social norms. Thus, diagnosing Fetishism and Sadomasochism is no longer in line with the norms of diverse multicultural societies that value acceptance and tolerance.

As stated earlier, when sexual acts are safe and consensual, they should not be considered immoral and pathological. Yet, nonconsensual acts with the intent to hurt others must be addressed. If a person has an uncontrollable urge to do something that violates a partner's personal boundaries, or has an uncontrollable urge to do something that causes harm to himself or herself, these are issues that must be addressed. There is no reason, though, to diagnose such urges as sexual problems. Unfortunately many people violate others' rights or their own integrity, in ways that seem uncontrollable. That can involve any type of behavior, and may or may not have anything to do with sexuality. It can involve "normal" heterosexual behavior inappropriately imposed upon someone or acted out compulsively in ways that are unsatisfying. If such behavior requires diagnosis, nonsexual categories are available, including the *Personality disorders* (F60) and the *Habit and impulse disorders* (F63).

However, addressing ethical issues does not imply that a specific behavior should be considered as a sexual problem. Rather, sexual assault should be viewed as a criminal act. Nonetheless, if the behavior in question requires diagnosis, nonsexual categories are available, including personality disorders (F60) and the habit and impulse disorders (F63).

Another consideration for revising the diagnostic criteria for sexual deviation is linked to anecdotal data, methodological shortcomings and empirical research findings. Before Kinsey, data on sexual deviation were derived almost exclusively from fictional literature or from psychiatric case histories. Despite the obvious methodological limitations of such sources, these data are still used in the psychiatric community. For example, many cases were referred to psychiatrists, because individuals were in conflict with the law. The generalization of findings from those cases to the general population is questionable, due to representability and generalizability limitations associated with external validity and sampling issues; it is impossible to generalize findings from the criminal population to the non-criminal population. Furthermore, Kinsey (1953) indicated that there is no reason to believe that fetishism leads to crime. Indeed, what do we know about law-abiding fetishists? In accordance with Kinsey (1953), demographic studies show that there are citizens in "good standing" who practice SM (Moser, 1995).

The psychoanalyst Robert Stoller (1991) conducted an extensive interview study of SM practitioners in the 1980s. His data indicated that there is no evidence for higher prevalence crime rates, psychoses or personality disorders among SM subjects in comparison to the general population. Stoller (1991, pp. 19-20) wrote:

> And these people, were one to try to apply character diagnoses to them, are as varied as I expect are the readers of this book. Most of my informants are stable in employment; most are college graduates or beyond, lively in conversation, with a good sense of humor, up-to-date on politics and world events, and not more or less depressed than my social acquaintances.

The fact that there are SM and fetish practitioners with psychiatric and/or criminal records does not warrant pathologizing these practices. One could pick any group with an arbitrary characteristic and, provided that the sample is big enough, find psychiatric and criminal cases among them. Thus, an arbitrary characteristic should not be used as a basis for psychiatric diagnosis. Correspondingly, sexual proclivities should not be used as the basis for psychiatric diagnosis.

Contemporary empirical research findings have had little impact on the diagnoses of Fetishism, Fetishistic Transvestism and Sadomasochism over the last 55 years in the *ICD*. The existing research over the past 60 years has not influenced the diagnostic thinking in the area of the Paraphilias. Nonetheless, there has been a substantial development in the diagnosis of other disorders. For example, the categories of neuroses and psychoses have been substantially refined over time. Surprisingly, the revision of *ICD-10* omitted *ICD-9*'s suggestion that "It is preferable not to include in this category individuals who perform deviant sexual acts when normal sexual outlets are not available to them" (WHO, 1978, p. 40). This omission in the *ICD-10* seems to be a step backwards in the classification system.

Organization, Clarity and Cohesiveness

The F65 diagnosis appears to be disorganized. It combines disparate, unrelated items, which are being perceived as unusual phenomena. For example, it combines consensual and nonconsensual sexual behaviors. Nevertheless, they are all being diagnosed as DSP; ergo, they share maladaptive qualities. This grouping is inappropriate, because abusers and perpetrators are being classified and diagnosed in the same general category as individuals with non-abusive interests. The rationale for clustering these sexual behaviors in one category (i.e., F65) is based on moral and "normative" issues. Hence, both professionals and the public view these behaviors as pathological sexual interests. Consensual games that are called SM or domination and submission are not abusive and therefore should not be diagnosed at all, let alone clumped together.

There is sometimes a concern that SM practices such as spanking and whipping can cause bodily harm. Indeed, people can be damaged from being hit in uncontrolled ways. However, there are ways to give and receive strong stimulation, including pain, that are safe. Both partners need to take responsibility in such acts. People have to learn what is safe and what is not safe, whether they practice SM or any other kind of sex. There are certainly safety issues concerning individuals who practice conventional heterosexual acts, which, once violated, are not diagnosed as sexual disorders. By the same token, individuals who practice SM acts should not be diagnosed based on occasional and naïve safety violations. Nonetheless, it is important to note that safety rules should be taken seriously. We encourage individuals with psychological problems around risk-taking to seek professional help, whether their interests revolve around sexual acts, sports, workplace hazards, etc.

The category of Paraphilia is also outdated. It does not reflect the descriptions of the paraphilic variations observed and classified in the 1950s and later by John Money (1986). Furthermore, most types of Paraphilia are not mentioned in the F65. Given that several kinds of sexual abuse are diagnosed as DSP, it seems strange that rape is not recognized as a diagnosis in the category. Similarly, the practice of unsafe sex does not appear as a sexual disorder diagnosis. A diagnostic category, like the F65, needs more consistency, clarity and empirical basis in order to be legitimate. However, adding more non-abusive categories to the classification system may be as pejorative as the present F65 category. Thus, the most suitable solution to this problem is simply to eliminate the Fetish and Sadomasochism subcategories from the F65.

Traditional Viewpoints

The *ICD-10* presumes the importance of intercourse: "Fetishistic fantasies are common, but they do not amount to a disorder unless they lead to rituals that are so compelling and unacceptable as to interfere with intercourse and cause the individual distress" (WHO, 1993, p. 218). This interference is one of the central arguments for labeling fetishism as pathological. The importance of intercourse reflects a traditional attitude towards all kinds of sexuality that do not have procreation as their purpose.

Ideas about sexual pleasure have changed radically in Western societies over the decades. For example, today, psychiatric perspectives largely regard non-procreative sex as a healthy pursuit. Furthermore, mental health professionals no longer assume that sex results in intercourse, or that sex and intercourse are synonymous. As such, it is unclear why fetishism, due to its alleged interference with intercourse, is singled out as a disorder. A possible argument for including fetishism as a diagnosis would be the involvement of emotional distress. Yet, "traditional" intercourse may result in emotional distress as well. However, in such cases, the individual is not diagnosed with fetishism (but maybe with sexual dysfunction, F52). Hence, there is no need to diagnose a consensual act that involves mutual pleasure as a maladaptive sexual behavior.

"Fetishistic transvestism is distinguished from transsexual transvestism by its clear association with sexual arousal and the strong desire to remove the clothing once orgasm occurs and sexual arousal declines" (WHO, 1993, p. 218). Interestingly, the guidelines do not comment on a situation in which there is no desire to remove one's clothing once orgasm occurred. Some individuals like to relax after orgasm and do not have the desire to remove their clothes. Does that make them Transsexual Transvestites? What if a person wants to continue sexual activity in anticipation of another wave of arousal? Let us consider an example of a man who identifies as male and likes to wear women's lingerie while masturbating. He reports enjoying the experience of wearing lingerie while masturbating. The appearance of a female in his own mind is being facilitated when he wears women's lingerie and focuses on it. Once orgasm occurred, he does not want to take the lingerie off. Instead, he wants to wear it because it feels good. Would this example qualify as a case of Transsexual Transvestism? Or, would it fit the case of simple fetishism? It appears that the diagnostic criteria are neither suitable nor clear in this case. In this example, the sexual act does not include distress; rather, it illustrates feelings of pleasure. Moser and Kleinplatz (2002) have an excellent discussion of the *DSM-IV-TR* (2000) diagnosis of Transvestic Fetishism (which is essentially the same as Fetishistic Transvestism). In a lengthy example of a man wearing female clothing and feeling good about doing it, they ask, "Should this behavior, which can be regarded as adaptive rather than distressing, be construed as psychopathological? The rationale for pathologizing a coping skill is questionable" (Moser & Kleinplatz, 2002, pp.16-17).

Another traditional view held by psychoanalysts and others (e.g., Grønner Hanssen, 1992; Money, 1986) proposes that Sadomasochism is caused by childhood trauma. This theory of etiology suggests that Sadomasochistic behavior is a manifestation of an underlying psychological problem and, hence, abnormal. However, there is no empirical evidence to support this commonly held etiological model. The occasional anecdotal finding, which suggests that there are individuals who seem to fit this kind of theory, is not sufficient to support a diagnostic category.

Diagnosing a phenomenon as an illness should not be based on a speculative theory. Some SM practitioners who incorporate spanking during their sexual acts were not spanked as children; at least we have not found any evidence of it. Others who clearly were traumatized as children have designed their SM games not only for pleasure but also as adaptive coping strategies. For example, a woman who practiced a masochistic game for many years stated that she had overcome her fear of sexual relationships with men by role-playing similar situations in the context of a safe setting with her husband, where she is in control. For her, the SM game has been adaptive, because she is no longer fearful of being abused, and because she is in complete control of her borders in sexual, erotic and intimate situations. Again, an effective healing strategy should not be diagnosed as a mental disorder.

SM and fetish interests are essentially normal variations. For example, some people are attracted to legs with stockings, others to feet with sexy shoes, etc. Similarly, the power dimension is usually present to some extent in "traditional" sexual activities, (e.g., who is on "top" and who is on the "bottom"). The interests are only suspect if there is a sense of "too much," but almost all behavior can be assessed as being "too much." If someone is compulsive about acting out his or her sexuality, no matter what kind of sexuality, he/she could be diagnosed with obsessive compulsive disorder (OCD). Hence, there is no more reason to single out "paraphilic OCDs" than to single out "philatelic OCDs" into special diagnostic categories. In other words, there is no reason to make a diagnosis based on the person's sexual preference or practice, per se.

Many SM practitioners are not aware of the fact that they are subject to diagnoses. One reason for this lack of awareness is that people with SM and fetish interests do not usually seek therapy to change their sexuality, and, therefore, they do not come into contact with the diagnostic system. Another reason is that many mental health professionals currently do not think it would be appropriate or necessary to make such diagnoses. Like other individuals, SM and fetish practitioners would first have to experience emotional distress before seeking psychological services of their own accord. Most of those individuals who actually receive diagnoses are probably referred by others (e.g., the legal system) and thus constitute a highly biased sample of the sub-population.

Human Rights Issues

The effort to change F65 is also a human rights issue. Diagnosing individuals based on types of sexuality is as unjust as discriminating against people based on race, ethnicity, or religion. It is as absurd as diagnosing people for being "blue-eyed" or "old." Individuals should not be diagnosed for who they are, for the tastes they have, for their beliefs or interests, nor for the kinds of sexuality they prefer.

There are different reasons for keeping diagnoses like Sadomasochism and Fetishism in our society. For example, there is still a lot of respect for and belief in the medical diagnoses. Thus, some may use the diagnoses to legitimize discrimination. There are numerous cases in which individuals have been fired from their jobs because their employers had heard that they were practicing SM. There have also been cases in which men have been harassed and physically threatened out in the streets, in Norway, for wearing effeminate clothing.

The "deviants" all too often look upon themselves as less valuable. The experience of stigma is not an argument in and of itself for abolishing the diagnoses in question, but it is a significant rationale given the lack of evidence to support the notion that practicing SM and fetishism is an illness. Labeling and stigmatizing individuals must be avoided when neither physical nor psychological difficulties are evident.

Some individuals have needed long-term psychotherapy to overcome the negative impact of stigma. For example, a male fetishist tells us that he would enjoy his practice of fondling his partner's boots more if the question "Is this sick?" was not present in the back of his mind. Another male fetishist suffered from the stigma and consequently felt inferior, because his wife regarded his preference to wear nylon stockings during intercourse as sick. She might be more comfortable with his wearing the stockings and enjoy the intercourse herself if she knew it was not an unhealthy practice.

Being Diagnosed and Its Aftermath

Individuals may believe they are ill because medical authorities said so; a diagnosis can often become a self-fulfilling prophecy. For example, a 52-year-old businessman had been distressed for many years because he was under the impression that he was sick. It started in adolescence when he felt an irresistible urge to wear a garter belt and sheer nylon stockings. After secretly masturbating while wearing his sister's nylons, he experienced feelings of shame. Soon thereafter he started reading about perversions in popular publications devoted to sexual education. He read that Transvestism and Fetishism were labeled perversions and were not normal behaviors, but rather were perceived as psychiatric illnesses. His feelings of shame were exacerbated after realizing that having that kind of illness was a psychiatric issue as well as a sexual disorder. Consequently, he tried to fight the recurrent urge to wear nylons as best as he could. He was popular with girls and when he reached the age of 17 he started having intercourse, which he enjoyed. He used to think that when he met the right girl, he would be so much in love with her that he would not think about wearing nylons anymore. That happened when he was 25 years old. He married and did not think about wearing stockings for a time. After a year of being married the urge came back and he could not resist doing it. So he resumed wearing stockings, but still in secret. He went for psychotherapy and was told that his urge to cross-dress was an illness to be treated. After 4 years in psychotherapy he was not "cured"; on the contrary, he felt even worse about himself. Finally, he decided to tell his wife about the reason he had sought therapy and about his "terribly sick" fetish. His wife accepted him and his urge to wear stockings as normal behavior. The couple incorporated his nylon stockings into their sex life together. That was the end of his psychotherapy and concluded many years of suffering. Previously, he had been distressed to the extent that he was on the verge of suicide a couple of times. Now he and his wife have a satisfactory sex life together and the distress is gone. The loving relationship between them has deepened. His pain would have been avoided if Fetishism and Fetishistic Transvestism had not been diagnosed as illnesses.

Negative self-image and low self-esteem from the stigma attached to the diagnoses can affect people severely. This may result in obsessions and compulsions, such as alcoholism, drug abuse or workaholism. Other possible results are suicide or suicidal gestures and other kinds of self-destructive behaviors (e.g., self-mutilation and passivity). For example, a middle-aged, gay man, with a rubber fetish and masochistic inclinations, has been looking down on himself for most of his adult life because of his "perversions." Currently, he is engaging in psychotherapy and is successfully overcoming his deep shame about himself and his sexuality. As in the previous example, in his youth he had read about "perversions" (including homosexuality) and therefore thought he was ill. The negative self-image led to severe, chronic, recurrent, major depression. He is now in a good relationship with his partner, who is also into SM and leather. Given that the impact of the stigma has been mitigated, he is living a much happier and more fulfilling life than before. His psychotherapist supported his belief that the rubber fetish and masochism are not sick. His therapist's encouraging words about his sexual choices have been essential for his recovery. Perhaps the most fulfilling aspect of his life is the love he shares with his partner. This satisfying relationship is worth commenting on, as intimacy problems are quite prevalent among both "normal" and paraphilic individuals. But, in the case of paraphilic individuals, psychiatry is quick to attribute such problems to deviant sexuality. It would be more appropriate to examine problems of intimacy in interpersonal relationships per se, rather than automatically conceptualizing the "paraphilic" behavior as a sexual deficit.

POLITICAL EFFORTS TO REVISE F65

In this section we will outline some of the incidents leading up to the establishment of the ReviseF65 group in 1997 (also known as "The Forum"). We also refer to some of the Forum's efforts inside and outside the lesbian and gay movement.

The organized gay and lesbian movement was established in 1950, and later called Landsforeningen for Lesbisk og Homofil frigjøring (LLH), the National Organization of Lesbian and Gay Liberation. Over the last fifty years in Norway, leaders in the gay movement have had SM interests. The gay community has always been a catalyst for gay leather men and women, galvanizing their self-expression and SM lifestyle. Yet due to prejudice, most gay leather and SM individuals had–and still have–to live closeted in the gay community, just as gays and lesbians in general have done in the rest of society. There have also been conflicts between gay leather individuals and other homosexuals about SM and fetish practices.

The group *Lesbians in Leather* founded in 1993, was a precursor of *Smia*, founded in 1995, a human-rights group for lesbian, bisexual, gay, and transgendered people. All these groups, namely Lesbians in Leather, Smia and ReviseF65 are subsidiaries of LLH, and were founded by Svein Skeid.

In 1997, the ReviseF65 Forum was formed by Smia, individual transgender people, and mental health professionals. The LLH gave the ReviseF65Forum a mandate to abolish Fetishism, Transvestism and Sadomasochism as psychiatric diagnoses from the *ICD*. The Norwegian gay leather men's organization Scandinavian Leather Men (SLM-Oslo), established in 1976, and the heterosexual SM organization "SMil," founded in 1988, joined the Forum in 1998; thus, the coalition continued to grow.

The impetus behind the F65 Repeal Movement was the flourishing of SM pride, with fetish men and women parading through the streets during Gay Pride week. Leather people were tired of being object of derision in the tabloids and being characterized by Norwegian psychiatrists as "violent" and anti-social individuals. The members of Smia also suffered from the effects of this prejudice. A celebratory attitude that started in a lighthearted way suddenly became deadly earnest, when everybody at a board meeting turned the palms of their hands upwards simultaneously. Scars on the wrists indicated that several of the people present had attempted suicide because of harassment or persecution within their own communities. As with other forms of assault, women were the chief victims; they were isolated because of their SM orientation or preference.

For several years, The Norwegian Board of Health (a part of the central health administration) has supported Smia's work financially to strengthen the self-esteem and identity of gay leather men as part of strategies to prevent sexually transmitted diseases including HIV. Stigmatizing fetish and SM practices amounts to an insult against healthy leather-people and, therefore, runs counter to effective public health and safer sex education efforts. It seemed like a paradox that the same official health authorities who grant money to LLH and Smia, who encourage a positive identity for fetishists and SM participants, also represent the agencies that employ discriminatory and stigmatizing diagnoses of these practices.

Another historic event that has had a great impact on the mobilization for SM human rights in general, and the F65 Repeal Movement in particular, is the British Spanner trial (1987-1997). During this trial process, several hundred gay leather men were questioned. Twenty-six men were cautioned and sixteen charged with mutual piercing, spanking and branding, that is, with consensual activities that are legal in other European countries, like Norway. Not only homosexual individuals were targeted, imprisoned and lost their jobs. The safer sex meeting places and magazines of straight SM people were also raided and shut down by police in the wake of the Spanner verdict (dissenting 3:2) by the House of Lords in 1993. The consenting SM men lost the Spanner case when it was appealed to the European Commission of Human Rights (dissenting 11:7). The Strasbourg human rights court affirmed the verdict in 1997.

Even though the case was lost, and the Spanner Verdict made some SM play illegal in the UK, it was inspiring for Smia and SLM-Oslo to be part of a worldwide movement in support of the Spanner defendants. For the growing SM human rights movements, the word "Spanner" attained as much significance as the Stonewall riot did in 1969 for the gay and lesbian movement. In Norway, a fund-raising campaign had the moral support of the lesbian and gay movement, human-rights groups, trade unions, women's organizations, and a variety of political organizations that included several hundred thousand members from both right and left political wings. In 1995 an official British law commission ("Consent in the Criminal Law," 1995) gave the fetish/SM/leather communities considerable support and argued that SM should no longer be considered a criminal offence in Great Britain.

The LLH-leader, Gro Lindstad, expressed strong support for SM human rights. In late June of 1994, her future, registered partner, Bente Vinæs, returned with good news from the International S/M-Leather-Fetish Celebration in New York City. The conference material she brought home stated: "For the first time, the leather-s/m-fetish community's style of sexuality is no longer considered necessarily pathological. . . . The new DSM-IV language means that we will no longer be considered sick unless our erotic play causes 'clinically significant distress or impairment in social, occupational or other important areas of functioning'" (Bannon, 1994). Project Coordinator Race Bannon (1994) described this as "a terrific development for the leather-s/m-fetish community!" Later, the ReviseF65 group contacted American mental health professionals who admitted that the *DSM-IV* (1994) was obviously an improvement, but by no means perfect.

Repeal of Sadomasochism Diagnoses in Denmark

In 1995, the Danish newspaper *"Politiken"* reported that "Sadomasochism is not a disease" in Denmark ("Sadomasochisme er ingen sygdom," 1995).

A letter from the SM organization "Det sorte Selskab" (The Black Society) demanded the removal of the diagnosis, and the Health Ministry issued a recommendation to remove the diagnosis of Sadomasochism from the Danish version of the ICD. "I agree with you that sexual preference is a completely private affair," wrote Yvonne Herlov Andersen, the Minister of Health, in her personal communication to the leader of The Black Society ("Sadomasochisme er ingen sygdom," 1995). "The acceptance of people with a different sexuality has increased, and in this area Denmark is a pioneer country," she wrote ("SM diagnosis withdrawal in Denmark," 1995).

These changes sparked debates in Norway. For example, psychologist Grønner Hanssen, author of a book on SM (see Grønner Hanssen, 1992), debated with health authorities on a radio show about the possibility of Norway following Denmark's lead. Grønner Hanssen reasoned that the stigma, prejudice, and misconceptions related to being diagnosed caused personal strain. Marit Kromberg, Department Manager of the Norwegian Board of Health, argued for retaining the diagnosis. She indicated that what people do in private is not the business of the Norwegian authorities, but if a person seeks treatment, it is the physician's responsibility to diagnose the problem correctly.

A 1994 national survey was conducted among the 2000 lesbian and gay members of LLH. Despite negatively slanted questions the respondents rejected discrimination against leather, SM and transgendered practitioners, and judged this diversity as a valuable resource. The September 1994 issue of *Blikk*, the Norwegian gay and lesbian newspaper, featured a spokesman of the Norwegian Board of Health, who asserted erroneously that Sadomasochism would be removed from *ICD* in 1996 ("SM-ere friskmeldt," 1994). In the January 1996 issue, readers were told that Fetishism and Sadomasochism were still classified as psychopathology in Norway ("SM-sex fremdeles en sykdom," 1996). The presence of Fetishism and Sadomasochism as diagnoses in 1996 created a great deal of confusion and frustration among gay rights activists. Following a proposal from LLH-Oslo, the biennial National Convention of LLH in May 1996 approved a long-term national and international project to remove Fetish and Sadomasochism diagnoses. LLH leader Gro Lindstad sent a letter to The Norwegian Board of

Health requesting copies of *ICD-10*, which at that time was being translated into Norwegian. LLH wanted to influence the translation process, so that Fetishism and SM would no longer be regarded as diseases. The request was rejected. Later it turned out that the Norwegian version contained the same F65 diagnoses as the international one.

The ReviseF65 group tried to follow Denmark's 1995 strategy. Unfortunately, the project was shelved soon after the Christian Conservative Government took over. The work of the Forum was resumed in 1998 with a new mandate from LLH that was renewed in 2000.

Surprisingly, prior to the National Convention of May 2002, LLH proposed to remove the ReviseF65 project from the organization's working plan, describing this worldwide endeavor as merely "a detail." After the vigorous intervention of the Forum and allies within LLH-Oslo, the convention decided to retain the mandate of the ReviseF65 project. This incident highlighted the importance of keeping steady contact with the mother organization. The work in favor of Fetish/SM human rights has to be fought continuously on different fronts, within as well as outside the gay/lesbian movement.

European Support

SM human rights leaders in SLM-Oslo have promoted the democratic revision of the rules and policies of the European Confederation of Motorcycle Clubs (ECMC) in order to address issues of sexual politics. In 2000, more than 50 ECMC member clubs, following a proposal by SLM-Oslo, decided to support the ReviseF65 effort. The European division of the International Lesbian and Gay Association (ILGA) issued a statement at its conference in Pisa, Italy (1999), supporting efforts to remove the diagnoses from the ICD.

During the lesbian and gay Europride 2002 in Cologne, more than one million people were confronted with the slogan "SM is healthy–Remove SM and fetish diagnoses!" during the parade. Conversations during Europride 2002 with representatives from German, heterosexual, SM organizations contributed to a change in strategic thinking. The ReviseF65 group has spent considerable time encouraging mental health professionals to address themselves directly to the WHO and initiate dialogue with WHO-collaboration centers.

Current efforts involve mobilizing support from the national professional organizations of sexologists, psychologists and psychiatrists. In this way, we are working to build a professional foundation for an initiative by the health authorities to remove the diagnoses. The ReviseF65 group is interested in participating in relevant, international, professional conferences to discuss the F65 Paraphilias. The Web site of the ICD project (ReviseF65, 2002), along with the corresponding mailing list, has facilitated national and international networks. The Web site, which is published in several languages (i.e., Norwegian, English, German and Portuguese), has given the Forum a good opportunity to disseminate a range of material about its work.

CONCLUSIONS

The ICD diagnoses of Fetishism, Transvestic fetishism and Sadomasochism are outdated and not up to the scientific standards of the *ICD* manual. Their contents have not undergone any significant changes for the last hundred years. They are at best completely unnecessary. At worst, they are stigmatizing to minority groups in society. There are people who are suffering from stigma and emotional distress because of the diagnoses.

The purpose of this article has been to get SM groups and kinky-friendly mental health professionals all over the world to join us in the effort to repeal the diagnoses. Specific strategies should be determined at the local and national levels, depending on the professional and political situation in each country. The support and work of leather men and women, SM community-leaders and organizations are crucial in order to reach this goal. The initiative of individuals is always welcome. Furthermore, formation of local and national working groups can be immensely effective, because they are able to approach the professionals in question. We encourage activists and kink-aware people of professional status everywhere to visit our Web site (www.reviseF65.org) and to join our discussion group (Yahoo! Groups, 2000).

REFERENCES

American Psychiatric Association (1994). *Diagnostic and statistical manual of mental disorders* (4th ed.). Washington DC: Author.
American Psychiatric Association (2000). *Diagnostic and statistical manual of mental disorders* (4th ed., Text Revised). Washington DC: Author.
Bannon, R. (1994). *The DSM Project*. New York: The International S/M-Leather-Fetish Celebration.

Bullough, V. L., & Bullough, B. (1977). *Sin, sickness & sanity*. New York: Garland Publishing.

Consent in the Criminal Law. Consultation paper no 139, pt. 10. (1995). London: Law Commission, the UK Home Office.

Consent in the Criminal Law. Consultation paper no 139, pt. 10. (1995). Law Commission. Retrieved February 15, 2003, from http://www.reviseF65.org/lawcomm1.html).

Ellis, H. (1920). *Studies in the psychology of sex*. Philadelphia: F.A. Davis Company.

Grønner Hanssen, S. (1992). *Den bakvendte erotikken. Sadisme og masochisme for nysgjerrige, begynnere og ille berørte* [Backwards eroticism. Sadism and masochism for the curious, beginners and offended]. Oslo, Norway: Sigma Forlag.

Hirschfeld, M. (n.d.). *Sexual anomalies and perversions*. London: Francis Aldor Publisher.

Kinsey, A., Pomeroy, W., & Martin, C. (1948). *Sexual behavior in the human male*. Philadelphia: W.B. Saunders Company.

Kinsey, A., Pomeroy, W., Martin, C., & Gebhard, P. (1953). *Sexual behavior in the human female*. Philadelphia: W.B. Saunders Company.

Krafft-Ebing, R. (1903/1886) *Psychopathia sexualis* Twelfth Edition. Stuttgart: Enke, trans. 1998). *Psychopathia sexualis* (Complete English-language Edition). New York: Arcade Publishing.

Money, J. (1986). *Lovemaps*. New York: Irvington Publishers, Inc.

Moser, C. (2001). Paraphilia: Another confused sexological concept. In: P. J. Kleinplatz (Ed.) *New directions in sex therapy: Innovations and alternatives* (pp. 91-108), Philadelphia: Brunner-Routledge.

Moser, C., & Kleinplatz, P.J. (2002). Transvestic fetishism: Psychopathology or iatrogenic artifact? *New Jersey Psychologist, 52*(2) 16-17.

Moser, C., & Levitt, E. (1995). An exploratory-descriptive study of a sadomasochistically oriented sample. In: Weinberg, Thomas (Ed.) *S&M—Studies in dominance and submission*. Amherst, New York: Prometheus Books.

ReviseF65: *SM and fetish human rights pages* (2002). Retrieved February 15, 2003, from http://www.reviseF65.org

Sadomasochisme er ingen sygdom [Sadomasochism is no disease]. (1995, April 1). *Politiken*, p. A7.

SM diagnosis withdrawal in Denmark (1995, April 1). Retrieved February 15, 2003, from *http://www.revisef65.org/denmark.html*

SM-ere friskmeldt av WHO fra 1996 [SM people labeled healthy by WHO in 1996]. (1994, September). *Blikk*, p. 15.

SM-sex fremdeles en sykdom [SM sex is still a disease]. (1996, January). *Blikk*, p. 12.

Stekel, W. (1930). *Sexual aberrations*. New York: Liveright Inc.

Stoller, R. (1991). *Pain and passion—a psychoanalyst explores the world of S&M*. New York: Plenum Press.

World Health Organization (1978). *Mental disorders. Glossary and guide to their classification in accordance with the Ninth Revision of the International Classification of Diseases*. Geneva, Switzerland: Author.

World Health Organization (1992). *The ICD-10 classification of mental and behavioural disorders. Clinical descriptions and diagnostic guidelines.* Geneva, Switzerland: Author.

World Health Organization (1993). *The ICD-10 classification of mental and behavioural disorders. Diagnostic criteria for research.* Geneva, Switzerland: Author.

Yahoo! Groups: reviseF65 (2000, August 28). *A list for discussion on the ongoing work to have ICD-10, ch. F65 "Disorders of sexual preference" revised.* Retrieved February 15, 2003, from *http://www.reviseF65.org/moderator.html*

SM International

Editors' Note: The recognition that most of the readily available, English information on SM tends to be American led the editors to put out a request on numerous listservs and Websites for information on SM Internationally. The request called for information on SM oriented social, educational, support and advocacy groups in the particular country, SM subculture(s), the social and legal status of SM, level of acceptance, tolerance or stigma, etc. Here are the authors' replies. We are grateful to them for contributing to this endeavor.

BDSM IN BRAZIL

Name of Group: A.N.T.R.O.
URL: http://br.groups.yahoo.com/group/antro_sm/ [for men only]

Until recently, BDSM in Brazil was restricted to a few, rare classified ad sections in some inexpressive erotic magazines. Brazilian sadomasochists spent much of the last decades oppressed by and scared of the censorship by a dictatorial government that settled in the country in 1964 and only loosened its garrote in the early eighties. BDSM practitioners only came, slowly, to awaken as a group or collective a few years ago, first with videotext and recently, with the Internet, when there was the boom of access to hundreds of foreign sites and to chatrooms.

Since then, the sexual life of middle and upper class Brazilian citizens has changed, allowing them to awake to new–and maybe ever de-

[Haworth co-indexing entry note]: "SM International." Co-published simultaneously in *Journal of Homosexuality* (Harrington Park Press, an imprint of The Haworth Press, Inc.) Vol. 50, No. 2/3, 2006, pp. 263-280; and: *Sadomasochism: Powerful Pleasures* (ed: Peggy J. Kleinplatz, and Charles Moser) Harrington Park Press, an imprint of The Haworth Press, Inc., 2006, pp. 263-280. Single or multiple copies of this article are available for a fee from The Haworth Document Delivery Service [1-800-HAWORTH, 9:00 a.m. - 5:00 p.m. (EST). E-mail address: docdelivery@haworthpress.com].

Available online at http://www.haworthpress.com/web/JH
doi:10.1300/J082v50n02_13

sired–ways of satisfying their libido. That which, for that part of the
population, had always been an unreachable fantasy suddenly became a
possible transgression.

The appearance of groups and discussion lists–many of them
dedicated to certain specific types of BDSM relationships–
ccelerated quickly. Society started to dialogue with BDSM, creating tangible responses and considerably broadening the scope of
such practice.

In the last two years, numerous sites in Portuguese appeared. One of
them, Desejo Secreto (Secret Desire) [http://www.desejosecreto.com.
br/], the only one so far with a clear educational purpose, offers a reasonable number of theoretical texts. As an extension of Desejo Secreto,
a new and small publishing house appeared in the market, dedicated to
BDSM themes, releasing as its first title a book with educational and
demystifying explanations on the subject. So, taking its first and hesitat-
ing steps, a Brazilian BDSM culture was born.

A first attempt to study this community is in the research. "The
So-Called Deviant Sexualities: Perversion or Right to Difference?"
by Martins and Ceccarelli was presented at the 16th World Congress
of Sexology in Cuba, in March 2003. In this study, 111 heterosexual
men and women, male bisexuals and male homosexuals were surveyed. The data indicated that 36% of respondents were involved in
BDSM practices with their partners and 25% without their partners'
knowledge; the last 39% were single and attempting to meet other
practitioners. All the respondents reported feeling comfortable about
their sexual preferences that were experienced as pleasurable and
claimed the right to choose how, when and with whom to express
their sexual fantasies.

Consensual S/M practitioners have been discriminated against in
Brazilian society due to misconceptions and myths surrounding
these kinds of behaviors such as being victims and/or perpetrators of
coercive acts of violence and sexual abuse. This study suggests that
unconventional sexual practices cannot be used as diagnostic criteria
of any kind, which means that the only aspect that distinguishes these
individuals from others is their sexual practices.

The doctrine of "Consent of the Offended" is accepted by the
country's law enforcement and allows people to conduct their lives
as they will, as long as they do not endanger life, health or physical
integrity. There is consensus, within the legal community, that there
would be no room for suits involving mentally competent adults who
consent to being dominated, imprisoned or in suffering lesions that

do not cause them major health damages. In fact, the only known case of an accusation was closed when evidence of consent between both parties was provided; this suggests that the law of Consent of the Offended is enough to serve as a defense in case of a public, formal charge.

Beatriz Kotek
Rodrigo Gurgel
Hélio Pachoal
Maria Cristina Martins

SM IN GERMANY

In 2002 there were approximately 100 predominantly heterosexual SM organizations in Germany, plus perhaps 20 exclusively homosexual organizations. The larger groups are found in the Rhein-Ruhr area, Hamburg, Berlin and Munich and range from 50 to several hundred active members. The smaller groups sometimes exist only for a short time (less than two years) and usually are organized as informal weekly, bi-weekly or monthly meetings with 5-30 participants. Most meetings offer opportunities for discussion and exchange of experiences, etc. Some groups offer only a meeting point (a pub or cafe) with no special subjects to be discussed, while some offer special interest groups (e.g., D/s, transgender, Goth), discussion groups or workshops.

A few groups organize parties as well, but most parties are commercial or semi-commercial. As many SM and fetish parties take place all over Germany there is no need to join a local SM group if one is more interested in fun and leisure than in activism. Most events are more or less open to the public, so there is no need to join any organization.

With few exceptions, all the heterosexual groups are less than five years old. About 10 organizations go back 5-10 years; beginning in the 1980s there were 2-5 groups with 10-50 participants each. Before that there were only small, private networks that were not easily accessible. Not much is known about these, but they should not be confused with the legendary "Secret Euro Houses of Domination"–which seem to be a myth that originated in the U.S. Homosexual SM organizations have been around since the early 1970s. Some of these already had several hundred members by the mid-70s. Most of them were gay bikers' clubs that seem to have gone a little out of fashion now and have been replaced primarily by more general Leather and Fetish organizations, mainly in Cologne, Hamburg and Berlin.

Only a few groups show an interest in political work beside their other activities (e.g., SMart Rhein-Ruhr e.V., BDSM Berlin e.V., Schlagwerk Hamburg e.V.) As far as we know, there is no homosexual SM organization with an interest in SM-specific political activities.

The gay and heterosexual scenes "sail mostly different oceans." Both scenes socialize separately. On the other hand there are no resentments. Heterosexual BDSM groups participated in several "Christopher Street Day" parades and were welcomed or at least met by indifference. Gay men have a well-organized community with many pubs and parties while lesbian sadomasochists are underrepresented because of discrimination by vanilla lesbian activists. Sadomasochism is often equated with violence in the lesbian community; therefore, sometimes SM practitioners face rejection. One of the biggest lesbian SM groups is Poison Ivy, a special interest group within SMart Rhein-Ruhr. It is still difficult for them to gain new members, but lesbian discrimination against SM practitioners seems to be on the decline.

The Internet was a very important factor in the SM subculture's development during the 1990s. There are many German-language BDSM Websites and chats. Many groups are started from mailing lists and chatrooms on the Internet. These sometimes evolve into regular meetings and finally into organized groups.

One of the oldest and largest groups from the "pre-Internet age" is SMart Rhein-Ruhr e.V. (www.smart-rhein-ruhr.de). SMart Rhein-Ruhr is an SM organization in the Northrhine-Westphalia region with more than 22 groups in 12 cities, with 200 members and roughly 1000 guests in 2002. Founded in 1992, its main goals are to provide support, education and social contact to SM practitioners as well as to decrease discrimination towards SM, thereby changing the social and political status of SM in society. The association is linked to many other groups all over the globe. It is a member of DGSS, Amnesty International and cooperates with Pro Familia and local AIDS networks. For further contacts and orders of the official publication, *SMart-Info*, write to SMart Rhein-Ruhr e.V. FAO: Vorstand P.O. Box 190532 42705 Solingen GERMANY (E-mail: Vorstand@SMart-Rhein-Ruhr.de).

Datenschlag (www.datenschlag.org) is a nationwide online group that provides data and texts for other groups and individuals. Datenschlag compiled the largest BDSM bibliography ("BISAM") on the Net with currently more than 3000 entries as well as a comprehensive BDSM history timeline ("DACHS") with about 1100 entries. The timeline has its main focus on BDSM in Germany but is currently being extended to European BDSM history. Both this and Datenschlag's large BDSM encyclopedia "Papiertiger" (about 1000 entries) will be translated into English over the course of the next couple of years.

SMJG (www.smjg.org) is a project for SM practitioners from 18-27 years of age. (People under 18 will not be admitted at most groups' meetings for fear of legal repercussions.)

"Berlin Leder und Fetisch e.V." (www.blf.de), founded in 1998, is a gay SM organization with 60 members from Germany and other countries such as the Netherlands and even the U.S. BLF have been holding the "German Mr. Leather" elections since 1998 and have taken over the organization of the Easter weekend gay SM festivities in Berlin, a tradition that drew thousands in the 1970s and is still going strong.

"Leder und Fetisch Community" (www.lfc-online.de), formerly known as SKvDC, is the association of German-speaking gay leather and fetish clubs. The LFC consists of 15 clubs and meets twice a year. LFC publishes the club magazine "Stiefel" ("Boot").

Schlagzeilen (www.schlagzeilen.com) is the only well-established BDSM magazine in Germany. It has been around since 1988, caters predominantly to heterosexual readers and today has a circulation of approximately 10.000 copies (bi-monthly). The "Schlagzeilen" Website provides the most comprehensive and up-to-date list of BDSM organizations in Germany, Austria and Switzerland.

The awareness that sadomasochism is not sick and therefore cannot or should not be "healed" is growing in Germany. But even if some persons are sent to BDSM organizations by professionals, there is room for improvement in mental health care. There is very little useful German literature on sadomasochism for mental health professionals. Sexological research in Germany has been much reduced since the Nazis destroyed this thriving field. Current scientific articles and books are few and far between and almost invariably written by psychoanalysts. There has been virtually no research on the Paraphilias in the last decades. However, recent contacts with organizations of sexual therapists are very promising and a survey on professionals' attitudes towards SM was conducted in 2003.

In the German penal code (Strafgesetzbuch, StGB), most SM practices constitute a form of "Körperverletzung" (battery/bodily harm). §§223-233 StGB as the relevant chapters distinguish three forms of battery where applicable to BDSM play: The first category, "simple" cases (§223), consists of spanking and mild whippings which leave no enduring marks. This is prosecuted only if the victim demands it. The second category is "dangerous" cases (§224) in which any kind of weapon is used or when two or more tops stage a scene that involves any potentially life-endangering techniques, e.g., breath control. The final category is grievous bodily harm (§226) which refers to any session that goes so wrong that a permanent disability results (e.g., castration, amputation).

The bottom can legally consent to any kind of battery that does not conflict with "good and just morals" (Einwilligung §228), a somewhat imprecise phrase. How far the consent can go and when exactly it goes "*contra bonos mores*" has not been tested in court. It is, however, safe to assume that any sane adult can legally consent to any play that falls under §223 but no one can consent to the cases ruled by §226. As prostitution (including SM parlours) is legal in Germany, most decisions regarding §224 come from cases where a pro-domme was later taken to court by a client. In recent years, judges usually took into account whether the extent of SM play was within the pre-negotiated limits.

Abduction, illegal restraint (Freiheitsberaubung, §239 StGB) and coercion (Nötigung, §240 StGB) are applicable to some forms of SM play, but it is likely that a court ruling would look at the context in which they happened and honor consent.

Indecency laws (§183a StGB) forbid public acts provoking offence among bystanders; this makes public sex play illegal. However, there are no legal restrictions on play parties other than the usual ones that apply at home as well. One can sell and drink alcohol as well as have sexual intercourse at play parties. At some parties the sale of alcoholic beverages is restricted voluntarily, though, and no hard drinks will be sold.

There have been several court rulings (the most recent in 1999 by a Berlin local labour court) that SM in itself is not a valid, legal reason to fire an employee. The court ruled that deviant sexual interests are not sufficient to suspect that a person is more likely to disrespect another person's sexual or other rights.

We have not yet heard of a case where the issue of one partner's SM orientation was raised successfully in a child custody battle. A family lawyer tells us that the courts are accustomed to ex-partners slandering each other and usually ignore such arguments; however, in a case where there are other problems with the partner practicing SM, the sexual proclivities might add to his or her disadvantage.

After the end of World War II, censorship was abolished by the German constitution. However, the constitution does not protect freedom of speech–only freedom of opinion and certain forms of artistic, religious and scientific expression, as long as they do not collide with the protection of youth from negative media influences. Descriptions or images of nudity and even sexual intercourse are legal as long as they constitute a form of art or are in a scientific context. Unfortunately, the criteria are quite vague and have in the past been used to discriminate against alternative sexualities, including homosexuality. Material is usually regarded as pornographic if its purpose is to arouse or to depict human sexuality in an offensive, stereotypical way.

"Hard" pornography is illegal. This prohibition pertains to child pornography, bestiality and rape/torture/violence in a sexual context, where consent is not completely clear from the context. It is legal to produce and own all kinds of pornography, including bestiality, for your own use except with child pornography, where even possession is illegal. Advertising pornography, mailing it and having it on display in public places is illegal. This means that while it is perfectly legal to buy pornography abroad and import it into Germany for personal use, when you mail-order it from abroad there is a fair chance of having it impounded by customs.

Anything that is deemed negative to the normal sexual and social development of children and adolescents can be restricted to adults. BDSM Webmasters have encountered trouble for publishing "how-to" texts on practices like breath control (Datenschlag 2002). This has not been contested in court and as there is no national legal defense board yet, a challenge is unlikely. Since 2000, many German BDSM Webmasters have been forced to hide all or parts of their content behind adult-check software and thus make it accessible only to paying customers because of expensive and unpleasant legal repercussions. Simply renting server space abroad would do them no good as the offense will be prosecuted regardless of the server's location as long as the domain holder is German and the content aimed at German readers.

There is a national institution called "Bundesprüfstelle für jugendgefährdende Medien" (BPjM) that lists Websites, books, videos and magazines (featuring sites such as rotten.com and bmezine.com) deemed inappropriate for minors. Any media included in this list must not be displayed in public. Many BDSM books (such as *Story of O*) and magazines were included on this list of banished media until the censors' attention turned to the Internet in the early 1990s. Since then, BDSM publications on paper have remained mostly unchallenged, but most authors and editors choose to censor their own texts because they cannot afford to risk confiscation. Descriptions and pictures of women dominating or hurting men seem to cause a lot less trouble than vice versa.

More restrictive laws regarding media came into effect in April 2003. Any kind of media that "glorifies war, depicts humans in a way that violates human dignity or portrays minors in poses that have a sexual appearance" have been banned. To date, it is unclear if this will have any impact on BDSM media but it could be applicable to pet play, heavy pain play or humiliating bondage scenes.

Private health insurance regulations require that all medical diagnoses be coded according to the *ICD-10*. The *ICD-10* still uses the old, diagnostic criteria for the Paraphilias from the *DSM-III*, so data on every sadomasochist who consults a physician or psychologist with SM-related problems will be recorded even if the practices per se cause no distress. This raises concerns about privacy and may lead to increasing difficulties for sadomasochists who want private medical insurance.

Tolerance of sadomasochism seems to be improving. It is difficult to tell how many people actually are "out," but most of those who are report positive or indifferent reactions. To date, no politicians or celebrities have come out publicly. SM has been shown on several sex-related TV shows (i.e., no pornography but rather a mixture of Dr. Westheimer and Playboy TV). Within these programs, many positive statements on SM can be found. SM and fetish themes feature heavily in music videos, movies and commercials. Most people have a fair understanding of what sadomasochism means. On the other hand, SM definitely has not reached the level of tolerance that homosexuality has attained in Germany, and in small towns, it may still be rather difficult to find acceptance.

Mark-A
Kathrin Passig
Johannes Jander

SM GROUPS IN CANADA

National Groups

- http://www.silverbirchbdsm.com/. This Website lists Canadian BDSM organizations throughout Canada from west to east and provides addresses for those not listed below.

- DominationSubmission_Canada@yahoogroups.com
- BDSMPersonals_Canada@yahoogroups.com
- BDSM_Canadians@yahoogroups.com
- BDSM-Canada@yahoogroups.com

Provincial Groups

British Columbia

- BC Bears Online, Vancouver
- bdsmbc.net Online Resource Services (online chat room, personal ad listings)
- Body Perve Social Club, Vancouver
- By Invitation Only, Vancouver
- Men in Boots Club International, Vancouver
- Sagacity, Victoria
- Vancouver Leather, Vancouver (listing site for West Coast links and events)
- Vancouver Women in Leather

Alberta

- Calgary Kink Society, Calgary
- Edmonton "O" Society, Edmonton
- Mythos Group, Calgary
- Northern Chaps, Edmonton

Manitoba

- Dominant/submissive Society of Manitoba, Winnipeg
- Prairie Caller, Winnipeg (magazine)

Ontario

- BDSMWindsorMunch@yahoogroups.com
- subsofwindsor@yahoogroups.com
- kitchenerwaterlooswingers@yahoogroups.com
- londonontariosexclub@yahoogroups.com
- Bdsm-London@yahoogroups.com
- hamiltonadultconnection@yahoogroups.com
- bdsmhamiltonontario@yahoogroups.com

- hamiltonsexclub@yahoogroups.com
- Mississaugasexy@yahoogroups.com
- brantfordandareafetishclub@yahoogroups.com
- BrantfordDominantsubmissivefetishgroup@yahoogroups.com
- thebrantfordsexclub@yahoogroups.com
- Barrie_Kinksters@yahoogroups.com
- BDSM_Newbies_Ontario@yahoogroups.com
- DSSG-org@yahoogroups.com
- DSSG-Toronto@yahoogroups.com,ehbc@ece.uwaterloo.ca
- BDSM_Toronto@yahoogroups.com
- bdsmtoronto@yahoogroups.com
- Toronto_Ds_Singles@yahoogroups.com
- Toronto_encounters@yahoogroups.com
- torontojewishkinksters@yahoogroups.com
- TorontoPets@yahoogroups.com
- Torontospank@yahoogroups.com
- torontosub@yahoogroups.com
- WhackingTO@yahoogroups.com
- BDSMQuinteWestONT@yahoogroups.com
- Ottawa_Kinky@yahoogroups.com
- OttawaBDSMCommunity@yahoogroups.com
- ThisGroupAnnounce@yahoogroups.com

Québec

- BDSM-MontrealAnnounce@yahoogroups.com
- BDSM-Montreal@yahoogroups.com
- fetishmontreal@yahoogroups.com
- Bad Boy Club, Montréal (gay/bi men)
- Club Les Cuirassés de Québec (gay men)
- The Dom-MS, Montréal (gay men)
- Le Club Fetish Montreal, Montréal
- Quebec Pantyhose Club, Montréal
- BDSM-in-and-around-Montreal@yahoogroups.com

Maritimes

- Club Halifax, Halifax
- Fredericton BDSM, New Brunswick (e-mail only)
- Newfoundland BDSM Club, Newfoundland (e-mail only–trying to set up a new group!)

- PALS, Halifax, NS
- NFLD_B_D_S_M@yahoogroups.com
- OTKGroup3@yahoogroups.com

SM IN TORONTO, CANADA

An SM Women's Discussion Group is found in Toronto. "Contact information" entails showing up at a meeting at the local community center located in the gay neighbourhood. There is also a leather grrls e-mail list. We also meet once a month at the local leather bar. The purpose is to meet other women, share information, organize play parties, socialize, organize other fun gatherings . . . with all things leading to building a social circle of SM dykes. SM remains a subculture because only a small percentage of any group are into SM.

SM is much more out and accepted/understood by health care professionals, especially in the big city and in the downtown core. That said, when looking for a health care professional, there is only one place recommended in Toronto, which is the queer counseling center. There, chances of being able to deal with personal issues and not SM as a problem are great. Toronto also has a sexual health care clinic that is excellent in that regard. In sum, there is one clinic for SM practitioners in the entire city for mental health, and one for sexual issues. More services would be welcome.

There is no such thing as consent to bodily harm in the Canadian criminal code. Flagellation is illegal in bars in Ontario. It goes on regularly at the 5 or so monthly fetish nights in downtown Toronto. This may one day be subject to legal challenge but not to date. SM is much more public in the last five years, much more accepted, but is now on the radar screen.

As for discrimination regarding child custody, etc., no problems have come to public attention, but they can certainly arise and parents are concerned.

The extent to which SM is accepted depends on one's location. In the core of downtown, in a big city, it is easier to be out. However, in suburbs or a small town, a conventional job with children, the situation parallels that of coming out as queer 20 years ago–not entirely safe! Most Canadians do, however, live in large cities.

Naughty Nancy

SM IN AUSTRIA

Austria, the homeland of Sigmund Freud–where some affinity to "neuroses," "perversions" and the dark sides of life seems to be omnipresent–activities and associations with SM can be traced far back in history, from Leopold von Sacher-Masoch to Richard von Krafft-Ebing. There is also a notable amount of Austrian SM-erotic literature from previous centuries, e.g., from Dolorosa, Edith Cadivec, Helene von Drudkowitz, Gertrud von Welck (known as "Ruth von der Weide"). It is no surprise that Austria has a very busy (noncommercial) SM scene at present.

"Libertine Vienna," the oldest and biggest noncommercial SM organization in Austria, was founded in 1986. Starting from a small bunch of activists and theoreticians, Libertine ignited almost all other activities in Austria. The "Libertine topic evenings"–open discussion groups for topics like "Feet and shoes," "How can S/M people be caring and responsible parents," "Erotic literature in former centuries" or "The role of rituals in S/M"–have continued for more than 15 years. The Libertine magazine, *Unter Druck*, has been published throughout this period. Other activities include a monthly open meeting, specialized groups for "Bondage," "D/s," etc., running a library and organizing many workshops about "Bondage Basics," "Bullwhip," "Serving with Style" and more. Libertine organizes SM parties with a special and playful atmosphere and takes part in cultural events like the famous exhibitions "Erotikreativ" in 1990 and 1992 or the "Long Night of Art and S/M" in 2001. Contact this organization at Libertine Vienna, PO box 63, 1011 Wien, Austria. www.libertine.at. contact@libertine.at. +43 664 488 31 12.

In the mid-1980s, a special group for gay leather and SM people called "LMC-Vienna" (i.e., "leather and motorbike community Vienna") was founded. Today they hold regular meetings, workshops, attend international ECMC activities, organize festivals like "Vienna in black," etc. They run many parties and cruising events for different flavors–once a month mixed with heterosexual folks (see pervs@ paradise). Contact information: LMC Vienna, PO box 34, 1011 Wien, Austria. www.lmc-vienna.at. info@lmc-vienna.at. fax: +43 1 796 61 43.

In connection with the gay leather community, the leather and fetish shop "Tiberius" evolved, not only offering fetish products for men and women, but also running the monthly party pervs@paradise and the famous "Pervienne," Vienna's biggest and most famous fetish party, which attracts some hundreds of people from all over Europe regularly. Contact information: Tiberius, Lindeng. 2,1070 Wien, Austria, +43 1 522 04 74, www.tiberius.at.

Today there are many more SM groups in Vienna:

- "Eat me Beat me" is an informal monthly munch, in existence since 1996, recommended for people who like to talk and for beginners Eat me Beat me, PO box 107, 1101 Wien, Austria, www.bdsm.at/ embm, embm@datenschlag.org.
- "Schlagfertig" is Vienna's oldest women-only SM group, running monthly meetings since 1998. www.bdsm.at/schlagfertig, helene@ bdsm.at.
- "TransX" takes care of the interests of all people trying to cross the gender barrier offering regular meetings, advice and more. TransX PO box 331, 1171 Wien, transx.transgender.at, transx@ transgender.at.
- "Schlagartig" tries to supplement the SM scene with regular meetings, seminars, discussion groups, a newcomer access and information point and other activities. Schlagartig, PO box 215, 1011 Wien, Austria, www.schlagartig.at, info@schlagartig.at, +43 664 174 88 47.

The description of Vienna's SM scene would not be complete without mentioning the famous Vienna "SMart Cafe" (which opened in 1999). A "Cafe" (Viennese style coffee house), restaurant, and meeting point where people with or without an interest in SM, with or without fetish outfits, can drop by at any time to talk, have some coffee or a beer, to meet people, relax or even to play at the playroom of the cafe. The SMart Cafe conducts many activities such as the monthly "SMart XTreme" party. It hosts many workshops and meetings of Libertine and other groups. With its relaxed, open and home-like atmosphere, the SMart cafe has developed into something like the living room of Vienna's SM scene. Contact information: SMart Cafe, Köstlergasse 9, 1060 Wien, Austria. www.smartcafe.at. +43 1 585 71 65. Open Tuesday to Thursday 4 p.m. to 2 a.m., Fr., Sa. 4 p.m. to 6 a.m.

However, the Austrian SM scene is not limited to Vienna; most of the capitols of the various Austrian districts have their own SM groups.

"Libertine Innsbruck" in Tirol was founded in 1995. Aside from their monthly meetings and their contacts with the Italian SM scene, they also run the yearly "SMash" party, which has developed into the main meeting point of the fetish scene in Western Austria and attracts many people from Austria, Germany and Italy. Contact information: Libertine Innsbruck, PO box 5, 6027 Innsbruck, Austria. www.bdsm. at/libk/, libertine.ibk@utanet.at.

Libertine Vorarlberg holds occasional meetings at the western end of Austria.

A group called "BDSM Linz" was founded in Linz (Upper Austria) in 2000 to take over from "Libertine Linz," which existed from 1995 to about 1999. Today BDSM Linz organizes regular meetings, parties about twice a year, and a separate women-only meeting. Contact information: mitglied. lycos.de/bdsmlinz/, bdsm-linz@gmx.at, +43 664 86 50 869.

In Graz (Styria) a group called "StamMtisch Graz" has met monthly since 1999 and regularly attracts some dozens of people. They also organize workshops. Additionally Graz now has its own new little fetish café called "Blackfantasie." The international festival "Graz 2003" contained exhibitions and events devoted to "Masochism" and L.v.Sacher-Masoch. Contact information: Blackfantasie, Griesg. 38, Graz, Austria, www.blackfantasie.at.

A very active group called "SMallTalk Salzburg" has held regular meetings in Salzburg since spring 2002. Contact information: smalltalk. salzburg@gmx.at.

Austria's SM scene sees itself as a part of the Austrian queer community. For example, in 2002, all the groups mentioned above were present at the major, annual "Christopher Street Day"parade, which is organized by CSD Vienna (www.pride.at) in central Vienna for gay, lesbian, transgender and queer folks and attracts thousands of people every year.

To sum up, at present the SM community in Austria is mostly accepted or at least ignored. There are many connections to SM-friendly health professionals, journalists and officials. More and more media report positively about the SM scene and about kinky erotics. There remains a threat of rejection and not every event can be advertised openly (particularly outside of Vienna). Still, many people cannot risk talking about their preferences in public. The situation improves every year and today most people in Austria can find ways to live their kinks and to contact like-minded people in Austria's SM, fetish and queer scene.

Robert

SM IN SWITZERLAND

IG BDSM, http://www.ig-bdsm.ch/

IG BDSM (IG is an abbreviation for "Interessengemeinschaft," "community of interests"). Our goals are BDSM/sex education and building public awareness. We are a social/political organization and a "behind the scenes" group to enable other groups and provide a minimal organizational infrastructure. There are about 10-15 active members and 20 sponsors. Gender-neutral. Address: IG BDSM, Postfach, 8021 Zürich, Phone: +41 79 738 01 40, Mail: info@ig-bdsm.ch.

sMalheur, http://www.smalheur.ch/

Local support groups in Olten (20-30 regular visitors), Zurich (20-30) and Basel (10-15). A gender-neutral group, but have mostly heterosexual visitors. Phone: (see IG BDSM), Mail: info@smalheur.ch

The first steps towards an "open" SM subculture occurred as recently as 1999. In the mid-1980s, there was an active organization, which dried out in the beginning of the 1990s. The most visible sign of the SM subculture at that time was the magazine *Sadanas*, which folded in the 1990s due to legal pressures.

Besides the local support groups provided by sMalheur, there are a few parties of varying sizes and orientation. The homosexual subculture there has mostly exclusive events, which are also SM specific; the heterosexual subculture mixes SM and fetish, especially in terms of parties.

The little feedback we have received to date about how mental health professionals regard SM has been encouraging; on the other hand, there might be a strong difference between urban and rural regions.

There are three texts in German on the Website of the IG BDSM that deal with legal issues (go to http://www.ig-bdsm.ch/-"Recht"). In essence, some (if not most) BDSM acitivities are regarded as bodily harm or assault by Swiss law; adults (i.e., from the age of 18) can give their verbal consent to these acts in a legally binding way.

There are strict regulations against some kinds of "hardcore pornography," which have been revised recently–sadly, in a even more restrictive way. sMalheur, the only organization active at that time, was able to contact the officials involved in the drafting of the law. Although no change to the wording of the law was possible, the Bundesrat (government) made the concerns part of their message to Parliament: "The notion of 'depiction of sexual violence' does, by perception of the

Bundesrat, not pertain to the depiction of consensual sado-masochistic practices, as far as no other elements of crime are present" (Source: "botschaft des bundesrates an das parlement," p. 38, http://www.smalheur.ch/[last visited: 31 Aug 2002]; our translation to English).

Except for the aformentioned problems regarding hardcore pornography, there are few restrictions on SM activity in Switzerland. The scene has become more open in the last few years, and a "noncommercial" scene is flourishing with no hindrance by federal or state agencies or private pressure groups.

The "do what you want as long as it does not affect others" mentality is widespread, but there are still gray areas on a more personal level. Outing in the families and in the workplace is still rather the exception than the rule, but this is in a process of change.

The Swiss S/M subculture has strong ties to Germany and Austria, mostly thanks to "Barde" (of Smart Rhein Ruhr and other organizations) and Kathrin Passig (of BDSM Berlin, Datenschlag, and many others).

Many people who come to sMalheur or IG BDSM are socialized to a strictly commercial style of SM, as professional dominatrices offer their services throughout Switzerland, and have been doing so for about a decade.

Since the "noncommercial," "open" scene in Switzerland started so late (lagging maybe 10 to 20 years behind the rest of German-speaking Europe), we have a long way to go in educating "the scene" that there indeed does exist something like a BDSM lifestyle or people doing "this sort of thing" of there own volition and with their own partners.

Contact between the homo- and heterosexual scenes definitively needs to be better, both socially and in terms of organization and politics, but improvements are underway. There is already a close relationship with the transgender subculture.

Matthias Leisi

SM IN NORWAY

Name of SM Group: SMil Norge

In Norway, some people with sadomasochistic interests have decided to cover it up and keep it a secret, because they feel that it is a personal matter that no one else should take interest in–and some because they are afraid of reactions. Others choose to be open about it.

In coming out, some fear negative reactions and although these do occur, they may be far less than expected. What really matters is how one reveals this side to others. Some people manage to make it a big sensation but one need not provoke anyone. And you don't have to leave your whips and dildos on the kitchen table, so that your kids find them and talk about them in the kindergarten or school.

There have been several cases of mothers subject to investigation by the children's protection department (Barnevernet). Discretion is key as a parent's sadomasochistic interests have been turned into a particular subject for investigation, as if such inclinations reflected on one's fitness as a mother.

Some have been subject to violence and filthy language because they wore leather outfits or PVC in public, out on the streets or in ordinary clubs/pubs.Others have lost jobs because of their openness. Even in the context of team-building activities which encourage self-disclosure, employees have been fired for acknowledging their SM interests and have learned to withhold such information from future employers.

Kelly

SM IN NEW YORK, U.S.A.

Names of Groups

- TES . . . (BDSM . . . largely heterosexual–social, educational–over 1000 members) www.tes.org
- DSF . . . (BDSM . . . largely heterosexual–social, educational–approximately 300 members) www.domsubfriends.com
- MAsT: Metro NY . . . (Master/slave support group–pansexual–about 25 members) www.mast.net and Yahoo! Groups
- MAsT: NYC . . . (Master/slave support group–men only–no membership) www.mast.net
- Le Cercle des Dommes (Dominant Women only–social and educational–no membership) [http://groups.yahoo.com/group/LeCercledes-Dommes/]
- Lesbian Sex Mafia (Women who engage in SM with other women–social and educational and support–approximately 500 members) [http://www.lesbiansexmafia.org/]
- GMSMA (Gay men only–support, educational and activist–approximately 500 members) [http://www.gmsma.org/]
- Hot Ash (Gay men only–approximately 100 members) [HotAshIntl@netscape.net]
- Bondage Club (Gay men only–approximately100 members)

There are more and this information is only a selection of groups in New York City. There are also parties and bars such as **THROB** (women only), The Lure, Manhole, Hellfire, and Paddles.

There IS an SM subculture/community. It is very, very divided, however. NYC is so large that each group is very separatist. Each group means . . . Gay men stay away from straight men and women. Lesbians stay away from all straights and most gay men too. Heterosexuals are typically homophobic. Bisexuals are somewhat fluid and are the only links–and likely the only people that wish for more cohesion.

People are very wary of mental health professionals regarding their SM–some because of their own lack of acceptance and some out of fear. I personally had a bad experience with a therapist and I try to steer people away from that particular therapist–even though he advertises in BDSM literature. I find that therapists may be ready to deal with SM, but not Ds (Dominant/submissive), dynamics.

It is not common for people into SM to be out. There is a lot of discrimination and child custody is certainly an issue. Most of it is behind people's backs that are out. There is no doubt in my mind that most of the population thinks negatively of SM. Or thinks SM is something to keep quiet about. Most of the population is uncomfortable talking about sex! It is very questionable whether or not SM is legal. SM may be considered assault or may be prosecuted under the sodomy laws. Certainly edge play falls under reckless endangerment. Sadly, consent is not a defense for these crimes. It's not a good thing to go into court with. I know a criminal judge that is into SM but says he'd rule against it. I know a prominent lawyer who fights for SM rights, but is afraid to be out himself and has distanced himself from the leather community because it lessens his credibility from his perspective. At my last job, the firm represented SM organizations and Web sites, but themselves considered SM sick and perverted.

SM is less accepted than homosexuality and that is not usually accepted by families and employers well. An SM orientation is not protected. Employment is at will in NY and an employer would likely fire you if you were "too out" for their tastes. In Manhattan, they might laugh it off, however, if it wasn't too "in their face."

American culture loves SM (sex too) images and uses them to sell everything, but is actually quite oppressed sexually and has very conservative hidden policies. Select individuals and groups of people are open-minded and even approving of personal expression and growth, but this is not true of the majority. Outside Manhattan, it is even more obvious that approval is based on conservative and religious moral standards.

Only putting our most palatable images forward will win us any approval and legal status.

Mistress Blair

Psychotherapeutic Issues
with "Kinky" Clients:
Clinical Problems, Yours and Theirs

Margaret Nichols, PhD

Institute for Personal Growth

SUMMARY. People whose sexual repertoire includes BDSM, fetish, or other "kinky" practices have become increasingly visible, on the Internet, in the real world, and in psychotherapists' offices. Unfortunately, the prevailing psychiatric view of BDSM remains a negative one: These sexual practices are usually considered paraphilias, i.e., de facto evidence of pathology. A different, affirming view of BDSM is taken in this paper. After defining BDSM and reviewing common misconceptions, a variety of issues the practitioner will face are described. These include problems of countertransference, of working with people with newly emerging sexual identities, working with spouses and partners, and discriminating between abuse and sexual "play." *[Article copies available for a fee from The Haworth Document Delivery Service: 1-800-HAWORTH. E-mail address: <docdelivery@haworthpress.com> Website: <http://www. HaworthPress.com> © 2006 by The Haworth Press, Inc. All rights reserved.]*

KEYWORDS. Sex therapy, BDSM, sexual minorities, SM, kinky sex, leather sex, queer psychotherapy

---

Margaret Nichols is affiliated with the Institute for Personal Growth, Highland Park, NJ.

[Haworth co-indexing entry note]: "Psychotherapeutic Issues with 'Kinky' Clients: Clinical Problems, Yours and Theirs." Nichols, Margaret. Co-published simultaneously in *Journal of Homosexuality* (Harrington Park Press, an imprint of The Haworth Press, Inc.) Vol. 50, No. 2/3, 2006, pp. 281-300; and: *Sadomasochism: Powerful Pleasures* (ed: Peggy J. Kleinplatz, and Charles Moser) Harrington Park Press, an imprint of The Haworth Press, Inc., 2006, pp. 281-300. Single or multiple copies of this article are available for a fee from The Haworth Document Delivery Service [1-800-HAWORTH, 9:00 a.m. - 5:00 p.m. (EST). E-mail address: docdelivery@haworthpress.com].

While recent decades have seen changes in the way in which gays, lesbians, and to a lesser extent bisexuals and transgendered people are regarded by psychologists and psychotherapists, this comparative enlightenment has not extended to the so-called "paraphilias." Moser (2001) has described in detail the inconsistencies and circular reasoning used in classifying atypical behavior and object preferences as paraphilic "disorders." I write from a perspective shared by a small but growing group of professionals (Kleinplatz, 2001, 2002; Morin, 1995; Moser, 2001, 2002; Weinberg & Levi-Kamel, 1983) who are challenging traditional psychiatric concepts of atypical sexual behaviors.

An underlying assumption of this particular paper is that certain "paraphilic" preferences are statistically abnormal but pathologically "neutral"; i.e., no more inherently healthy or unhealthy than mainstream sexual practices. Psychiatry has a rather shameful history of collusion with institutions of political power to marginalize certain subgroups of the population, particularly women and sexual minorities. Most psychological theories are unconsciously biased towards the preservation of prevalent social mores. Therefore, it is particularly critical, when evaluating behavior that has controversial social meaning, to base judgments of pathology strictly on factual evidence. At this time, the data do not exist to support the idea that BDSM activities are, by themselves, evidence of psychopathology, nor that their practitioners are more likely to be psychologically disturbed than the rest of the population.

Sexual behaviors included in the scope of this writing are variously described by practitioners as SM (sadism/masochism); D/s (dominance and submission); BDSM (bondage/discipline/dominance/submission/sadism/masochism) and fetishism. Collectively these practices and attractions are sometimes referred to as "kink." In general, "kinky" sexual activities include one or more of the following characteristics:

- A hierarchical power structure, i.e., one person dominates and the other obeys/submits
- Intense stimulation usually associated with physical or emotional pain, e.g., hitting, humiliation
- Forms of sexual stimulation involving sensory deprivation, sensory confusion, or restraint, e.g., bondage, use of blindfolds
- Role-playing of fantasy sexual scenarios, e.g., doctor-patient roles, abduction fantasies
- Use of certain preferred objects and materials as sexual enhancers, e.g., leather, latex, stiletto heels

- Other unusual sexual objects or practices often classified as a fetish or partialism, e.g., fixation with feet, sexual play with urine

The "kink community"–a loose network of advocacy and support groups, venues, activities and events–has itself promulgated guidelines for what is considered acceptable BDSM practice (Wiseman,1996): "Kinky" activities may be highly unusual, but they are always "safe, sane, and consensual." Kinky activities quite specifically do not include, for example, rape or sexual contact with children. Admittedly, these guidelines have blurry boundaries and these boundaries themselves can be a focus of controversy within the BDSM community, but the intent is for participants to be fully informed, fully able to consent and to avoid activities which incur medical or mental danger.

I am a psychologist and sex therapist who has worked primarily with "queer" clients for more than twenty years–in other words, with people who are gay, lesbian, bisexual, or transgendered, or who participate in "kinky" or polyamorous sexual activities. The agency I founded and direct in New Jersey employs two dozen therapists and has specialized in work with sexual minorities since 1983; the material in this paper derives from our collective experience. Over more than two decades, much of our work has amounted to "damage control": repairing egos battered by the judgmental attitudes of traditional psychotherapists. The focus of this paper, therefore, is education. First, I will address some of the most prevalent myths about BDSM, and then outline the most common clinical issues encountered in working with this population. Throughout, my goal is to give concrete, practical advice to clinicians who may find themselves working with clients engaged in BDSM activities. All cases used in this paper have been disguised to protect confidentiality.

BACKGROUND:
DEFINITIONS AND DESCRIPTIONS OF BDSM

Common Misconceptions About BDSM

Briefly, some of the most common misconceptions about BDSM are as follows:

1. *BDSM is mostly about the "dominant" partner getting his/her way with a passive, exploited "submissive."* In reality, BDSM

"scenes" (the name given for the often elaborate playing out of a sexual fantasy) are usually negotiated and scripted ahead of time, and the submissive partner sets the basic "limits." While the "dominant" is in charge, he or she acts within guidelines set by the "bottom." In theory, a submissive can be exploited in the same way any trusting sexual partner is vulnerable, and things can go wrong in BDSM sex just as in more traditional sex. The myth ignores the fact that the primary motive for the submissive partner to consent is pleasure–not fear of the dominant person.

2. *BDSM is about physical pain.* First, kinky preferences are highly variable, and even when they do include "pain," it is not pain as we typically think of it. Think "pain" as in biting your lover in a moment of sexual abandon–not "pain" as in root canal; visualize being pinched or scratched when you are highly aroused, as opposed to being punched in the nose.

3. *BDSM activities inevitably escalate to extremes and/or become addictive ("it's so good don't even try it once").* Some people who have suppressed their preferences for years may initially be consumed with "making up for lost time"; this is a phenomenon seen frequently when pleasurable desires have been repressed, e.g., married gay men who "come out" in middle age. Eventually, BDSM activity tends to level off, though that level may be different for different people and can range from a desire to occasionally incorporate kinky practices into a predominately "vanilla" script, to the wish to live a "24 by 7" BDSM lifestyle.

4. *BDSM is self-destructive.* There is no evidence that practitioners of "kink" use it self-destructively any more frequently than "vanilla" sex is used self-destructively. Anything pleasurable is subject to abuse; BDSM is no exception.

5. *BDSM stems from childhood abuse.* Again, there is no evidence that the incidence of childhood abuse is different within and outside the SM community (Moser, 2002).

6. *BDSM is an avoidance of intimacy.* In general, sex at times enhances intimacy, at times is an avoidance mechanism, and at times is irrelevant to intimacy. There is no evidence that BDSM is any more or less prone to intimacy amplification or aversion than more standard sexual practices. Many clinicians who practice psychotherapy within this community will tell you about long-term BDSM relationships that are not only intimate, but have "hot" sex years into the relationship, perhaps more frequently than their non-kinky counterparts.

7. *BDSM is separate from "vanilla" sex.* For most practitioners, BDSM activities and "regular" sex–intercourse, oral sex, etc., often called "vanilla" sex within the kink community–are combined some or all of the time, and "vanilla" sex can occur without BDSM.

The "Mysterious" Allure of BDSM: Towards a New Paradigm of Sexuality

Psychological theories, especially psychoanalytic ones, have an abundance of pathology-oriented explanations for the existence of "paraphilic" interests and behaviors. These unproven theories tend to get in the way of effective clinical work with "kinky" clients. It is helpful to remember that sex, by and large, is still a mystery even to those who study it professionally. In recent years attempts have been made to develop new paradigms of sexuality that can encompass the tremendous range of behavior found not only among humans but in all animal species (Bagemihl, 1999; Kaschak & Tiefer, 2001; Kleinplatz, 2001, 2002; Morin, 1995; Nichols, 2000). What these models share is a reluctance to assume pathology without evidence. Here are a few very straightforward, understandable, and healthy reasons why BDSM sexual activities may be appealing to kink aficionados:

1. BDSM can be a lot of fun, and it can make sex very hot. This is probably the most important factor.
2. Some people see BDSM sexuality as spiritual, not unlike Tantric sex.
3. Others feel it enhances intimacy in a committed relationship, and/or accomplishes healing of earlier psychic wounds in the context of a trusting partnership.
4. Some kinky practices explore the "shadow side" of sexuality. Just as risk makes activities like bungee jumping or rollercoaster riding fun for some people, the taboo or apparently risky nature of some BDSM can enhance pleasure. Moreover, as Jack Morin (1995) has pointed out, nearly every emotional state that can inhibit sex–shame, guilt, fear, for example–can also, under different conditions, enhance arousal.
5. Some BDSM practitioners feel that this form of sexuality is a non-chemical way of attaining pleasurable altered states of consciousness.

6. The tremendous variety of activities encompassed within kink mitigates against the tendency for sex to become routine and monotonous, especially in monogamous relationships.

It is probably clear by now that the appeal of BDSM sex is quite variable. In fact, it is possible that the only thing that people who engage in these forms of sexuality have in common is that they are sexual adventurers (Moser, 2002) and that sex is a high priority in their lives; they have high libido as a rule and get many needs met by their sexuality. Notice that none of these reasons for interest are necessarily "pathological."

CLINICAL ISSUES

Countertransference

The first and most common issue therapists confront when working with "kinky" clients is dealing with their own judgments, feelings, and reactions to this sexual behavior. The countertransferential feelings most commonly encountered by clinicians with comparatively little experience with BDSM are some combination of the following: shock, fear, anxiety, disgust, and revulsion. When this countertransference is intellectualized, the therapist may experience a deeply felt conviction that the client's behavior is self-destructive but have little more than vague abstractions to justify the firmness of the conviction. When counselors find themselves believing that their clients' pathology is "self-evident" despite no concrete evidence of harm, it is fairly certain that countertransference is present. For example, a client who reports picking up a stranger in a bar, going to an unknown location and allowing herself to be put in incapacitating bondage and experience penile penetration without a condom may alarm her therapist with this report–for very concrete reasons, and reasons having little to do with the "kinky" bondage activities. This client is putting herself in considerable physical danger, and it requires no abstract psychological theorizing to arrive at this conclusion. On the other hand, hearing a client describe sexual play that involves verbal humiliation may trigger feelings of alarm in the counselor as well. The therapist may conclude that this behavior is both evidence of low self-esteem and a reinforcer of poor self-image. The therapist's fears are based purely on psychological speculation–and, in all likelihood, upon countertransferential feelings of revulsion. It may occasionally be true that verbal humiliation play is associated with low self-esteem, but the therapist new to working with "kinky" clients is more likely to be jumping to this conclusion erroneously, through projection of his or her own reactions.

There are many reasons why this might occur. Often the therapist simply lacks information or experience. For example, the client may tell his or her therapist that he/she participates in "cutting" scenes and the therapist may assume danger when in fact the vast majority of all such activities involve superficial, easily healed wounds that are little more than well-placed scratches. Many sexual activities look strange to the uninitiated: consider children's usual reactions of disgust or disbelief when sexual intercourse is first described to them. It often helps to explore some of the "technical" information behind a practice. The clinician might want to read BDSM sex manuals such as those by Brame (2000), Miller and Devon (1995) or Wiseman (1996), or watch instructional videos such as *Whipsmart* (Good Vibrations/Sexpositive Productions, 2002). These books and videos often convey not just the technique, but something of the personal experience of BDSM. Besides gaining information, therapists can use these materials to identify their own "kink," even if it is a minor part of their sexuality. The more adventurous therapist might consider visiting an SM club or organization; this gives both a taste of the lifestyle and an appreciation of the attitude of warmth and community support found in these institutions.

At times, feelings of disgust or aversion may convey information about repressed or disowned parts of the therapist's own sexuality. In order to work successfully with kinky clients, the therapist should be able to handle unexpected sexual feelings arising in conjunction with his or her work–including feelings the therapist thinks are "wrong" or "dangerous" or "politically incorrect." In this situation, it is best to cultivate an attitude of slightly detached "observation" of the entire process, including the revulsion, the desire or arousal, and the defensive reaction to the arousal. This process might go something like this:

a. "I notice I feel disgusted when my client tells me about sexual scenarios in which her partner has humiliated her. What triggers this disgust in me–is it the humiliation, the specific method of humiliation, etc.?"

b. "Why is my reaction so strong and aversive? Might I secretly want to humiliate or be humiliated?"

c. "If so, why does that scare me? Why do I think it's 'bad' or 'wrong' for me to feel this way? Does it clash with other values? Does it trigger memories of past trauma or other experiences involving humiliation?" In the BDSM community, the term "squicked" refers to having a strong negative emotional reaction to an activity while knowing that you do not actually "judge" the activity as "wrong" or "bad." This is a helpful and neutral way to think of such countertransferential feelings.

This process not only can result in counselors learning invaluable information about their own sexuality; it may also mirror clients' internal experiences of self-hatred or shame. When therapists have analyzed their own negative reactions, they may also have enhanced abilities to be helpful to clients.

While this discussion has focus on countertransferential feelings of fear, disgust, or revulsion, the counselor may also experience being sexually aroused by activities described in session. Again, the therapist has to develop an accepting attitude of his or her own sexual arousal, or the countertransference around this will interfere with therapy.

Non-Disclosure of BDSM

Though we have no way of knowing how common this is, it is very clear that many people within the BDSM community go to counseling and never reveal their sexual preferences to their therapists. Sometimes this does not interfere with therapy, especially if the therapy is relatively short-term and problems are unrelated. When the client or clients' problems include sexual or relationship issues, however, therapy can be terribly compromised. Long-term individual work can be damaged as well, because the client is withholding information about a significant portion of his or her life. Clients themselves sometimes do not understand the therapy process well enough to predict that such secrecy may sabotage treatment, and so it may seem simpler to hide than to risk negative judgment. It is hard to blame people in the kink community for doing this, however misguided it may be; given the training most therapists receive about sexuality, many *would* judge a client negatively if the information were revealed.

How can the therapist avoid this and encourage self-disclosure? If the therapist or agency is not known for sexual openness, it can be communicated in indirect ways, with the literature, artwork, and books visible in the office. It is not necessary to have sexually explicit material on view to achieve this. A visitor to our offices sees a rainbow flag in one of the windows, literature on sexual minorities in the waiting room, and books like *S/M 101* on the bookshelf.

In addition, the questions asked on client questionnaires and in the initial interview with clients can establish a tone of acceptance. For example, clients who come for sex therapy at our clinic are asked to fill out a written survey that includes questions about bondage, fetishes, role playing, D/s, spanking, and so on, right next to the questions about oral, anal, vaginal, and manual stimulation. Other clients are asked less elaborate questions that nevertheless include items about sexual orientation and sexual interests. Over the course of therapy, a counselor might deliberately bring up BDSM in indirect ways. For example, when talking to presumed "vanilla" clients about sex, I regularly mention the excellent communication skills of people who practice BDSM–just in case the client needs permission to reveal a "secret."

Ignoring the Kink, Considering the Kink

It is important to understand that in all probability most clients involved in kink will be coming to therapy for reasons unrelated to their sex lives. For these clients, understanding of BDSM and empathy can be demonstrated by NOT prodding them to talk unnecessarily about their sexuality. In the early 1980s, my agency worked exclusively with gay and lesbian clients. Our clients often said they came to us in order to avoid talking about their gayness. Frequently they reported experiences with uninformed straight therapists who had focused on gay sexuality when the clients wanted to talk about depression, relationship issues, and family problems–in other words, the typical range of problems most people bring to therapy. Even if the desire to focus on a client's kinkiness is motivated by curiosity rather than by negativity, it is inappropriate to steer clients towards talking about issues that they do not consider important problems in their lives.

On the other hand, sometimes BDSM issues affect other apparently unrelated problems. For example, most people hide their BDSM activities from family, colleagues, and even from many friends. The fear of exposure is realistic: Kink practitioners have no protection in areas of employment or housing. Child custody and visitation can be threatened if BDSM activities are exposed, and the threat is as much as from state child welfare agencies as from angry spouses. Some states mandate that physicians report suspicious bruises as suspected domestic violence, and allow police to arrest the "abuser" even if the "victim" partner is not a complainant. These concrete hazards have an inhibiting or limiting effect on decisions and behaviors in areas like career, child-rearing, divorce, and family relationships. Moreover, hiding can compound fears or lead to a sense of isolation, thus contributing to anxiety or depression. It can be important for clinicians to recognize these connections, validate clients' experiences and help them overcome barriers imposed by unconventional lifestyles.

There can be more subtle interplay between BDSM and nonsexual issues as well. Roger, a man in his mid-thirties, became involved with a twenty-three-year-old woman with some limited exposure to BDSM practices, and through their relationship Roger came to develop and appreciate his dominant, powerful sexual nature for the first time. At the heights of romantic feeling, Roger and Julia decided to extend their master-slave sexual relationship beyond the bedroom; Julia proposed that she hand over her paycheck to Roger. Roger, however, had a history of being attracted to dependent younger women. He would at first be gratified by protecting and caring for each woman, but later he would tire of the responsibility of having an adult 'child' and end the relationship. He did not want to repeat this pattern with Julia, and I encouraged Roger to impose fairly strict boundaries around the BDSM sexual relationship in order to keep that power exchange in the realm of erotic fantasy. I felt, and Roger agreed, that this would help insure that the overall relationship remained egalitarian. It is beyond the scope of this paper to discuss the many subtle ways in which sexuality interacts with, mirrors, and affects other parts of a person's life, but it is clear that BDSM sex like other sexual practices can be rich with nonsexual meaning.

Problems of "Newbies"

If the therapist is not known within the "kink" community, it is possible that the most common kind of BDSM client who will request your services will be the "newbie": the person who is just "coming out" to self and/or others about kinky desires. Ironically, this is precisely the client for whom one must be most knowledgeable and positive about BDSM. People with "kinky" desires have grown up with the same judgmental, uninformed societal attitudes as has everyone else. Therefore, they are likely to have a good deal of internalized shame, fear, and self-hatred about their sexual preferences even if they have finally succeeded in admitting their identity to themselves or telling someone else. For such clients, providing acceptance and modeling positive attitudes is crucial and has intense therapeutic power.

"Newbies" look to therapists for a "seal of approval": The mental health professional can validate that they are "OK." Thus, with these clients one cannot assume a passive, "non-judgmental" stance; one must give feedback. "Newbies" are likely to assume that "no comment" equals negative judgment. Thus the therapist must emphatically reassure them their sexual preferences are not de facto "sick," or pathological. Moreover, the counselor needs to give information about the prevalence of BDSM behavior and the existence of BDSM educational and social organizations. It is comforting for clients in this stage of development to know that they are not alone. The therapist should be able to refer them to books, Internet URLs, and organizations where they can begin to develop support networks of people who can affirm their sexuality and guide them in exploration. The counselor can play an important role here and can be enormously beneficial with relatively simple comments and suggestions.

Some time may need to be spent helping clients understand how their own self-hatred (BDSM negativity) has been inculcated by societal prejudice, and in assisting them in improving self-image. Clients may have social problems related to their isolation; for example, some people avoid intimacy as a way of containing their desires, and therefore may have poor intimacy skills even after "coming out." Other clients may have built all their social relationships on lies, so to speak, and experience stress related to "fronting," fear of being "found out," and/or feelings of being "fakes" or "imposters." And indeed, the fear of being found out is not entirely paranoia. Because at present, few laws protect the rights of the BDSM community, people can and do lose jobs, friends, family, and children because of inappropriate disclosure or inadvertent "outing" (Wright, 2002). Advice about "coming out" to others must include information on realistic dangers. Treatment of "newbies" almost always involves validating them, psychoeducation, bibliotherapy, and guiding them to support groups. It is very gratifying and often not difficult work.

It is almost impossible to work with BDSM "newbies" without receiving requests from clients to eradicate their kinky desires. This can create conflict for the therapist, as clients who want to be "cured" report horrible psychic pain around their sexuality, and it is normal to want to help them attain their goals. In fact, such personal discomfort, coupled with BDSM desires, qualifies the client for a diagnosis of paraphilia, just as, in the 1970s, discomfort with homosexuals qualified an individual for the diagnosis of "ego-dystonic homosexuality" even after homosexuality per se had been removed from the nomenclature.

The category of "ego-dystonic homosexuality" was eventually removed as a diagnosis through the efforts of gay activists, who argued that the average gay person went through at least a stage, if not a lifetime, of introjecting societal values as self-hatred and rejection of the "offending" feelings and behavior. Activists called that phenomenon "internalized homophobia" (now called "homonegativity"), and insisted that appropriate treatment was to help the person eradicate the internalized homophobia–not the homosexuality.

In many ways the BDSM community of the early 21st century resembles the gay community of the 1970s, and individuals who struggle with BDSM desires experience a similar internalized shame about their sexuality (Nichols, 2000). When such clients ask to be "cured" of their kinky feelings, consider that the problem is not the BDSM, but rather clients' self-hatred and the desire to repress or obliterate their sexuality. In addition, it is important to be mindful that the history of attempts to eradicate particular sexual desires has been pretty dismal. Although clients can choose not to act upon their sexual feelings, they will probably never get rid of them, and not accepting these desires may very well inhibit the rest of their sexuality, as well. In most cases, when we–professionals who are "experts" on sexuality–validate the client's BDSM desires, the level of their self-hatred is immediately reduced and they quickly abandon their goals of repressing or eradicating their feelings. However, if clients continue to want help eradicating their desires, we refer them to local professional organizations who can connect them to counselors who will agree to work towards this goal. In addition to the fact that we think such "cure" oriented treatment has a poor prognosis, we also feel offering treatment like this would conflict with and compromise our stance of validation of BDSM.

This is not to say that clients always act on their BDSM desires in appropriate and healthy ways. Just as some people use "vanilla" sex in dysfunctional ways–they become "addicted," use sex to escape other problems, are irresponsible towards themselves and others in their sexual behavior–so can BDSM practitioners abuse their sexuality. Although we do not take a therapeutic "contract" to help someone eliminate "kinky" desires, we certainly help our clients modify all dysfunctional behavior, including sexually dysfunctional behavior. But we start from a position of assuming that BDSM behavior is psychologically "neutral" and is given positive or negative valence by the individual.

The Partner and Family

Many "kinky" individuals have been aware of BDSM sexual fantasies from an early age, although a large number will make enormous efforts to suppress behavior and repress desires because of the acute social disapproval of this form of sexuality. Therefore, many "kinky" people have chosen to hide their feelings, behavior and/or identities until mid-thirties and beyond. During their years of secrecy, they may have infrequent clandestine encounters, Internet contacts, or only allow themselves the outlet of masturbating to BDSM fantasies. By the time such individuals feel they can no longer contain their desires, they may have married long ago and perhaps had children in a (presumably) "vanilla" marriage. In addition to the issues experienced by most "newbies," the person with an unsuspecting partner has a whole host of other problems. In fact, some requests for help may come from the spouse who has just discovered the BDSM partner's sexuality. In other cases, it is disclosed by the BDSM partner in individual therapy, or both members of the couple may ask for couples counseling. The BDSM may have already been revealed before the person or couple comes for help, or it may be your job to facilitate disclosure.

Sooner or later, individuals in this position usually need to reveal their true interests to their partners. If you are called upon to aid in this process, consider fairness to the spouse as well as the individual desires of your client. While the reaction of the spouse who has been deceived ranges from surprise to horror–occasionally delight–there is almost always some anger about the deception. The therapist has some ethical responsibility to partners, however undefined that may be. Although confidentiality cannot be violated, try to steer the married BDSM client towards a resolution that is fairer to the partner, whether that be separation or disclosure. Aside from ethical concerns, there are practical therapeutic reasons to do this. This kind of deceptive lifestyle usually erodes the self-esteem of the deceiver, rarely works for long periods, tends to hinder growth for both partners, and often makes the situation worse when and if the truth finally becomes self-evident.

On the other hand, timing and readiness are crucial. As mentioned, the partner's reaction may vary widely. It is important to remember that one's first reaction is just that–a first reaction. Unless the partner is also unexpectedly kinky, the first reaction is unlikely to be a joyous one. So if your client is the "kinky" one, first prepare and help him or her assess readiness for an unpleasant interlude. When he or she is ready, the client can plan the disclosure for the most opportune time and setting, and can role-play in therapy to practice the actual situation.

Both the therapist and "kinky" client must be ready for the other partner to experience a grief process before he or she can think rationally about the marriage/relationship. Try to empathize with and validate the reactions of the partner, and provide referrals to support networks/ Internet groups. After the partner is able to consider options for the relationship, the therapist will assist the couple to integrate the new desires into their relationship, accommodate the partner's new interests, or separate. In this situation, success is contingent to a large degree upon factors beyond the therapist's control, namely, the partner's feelings, attitudes, and sexuality. In many cases separation or divorce will be the answer. In others, the partner may be willing to allow the kinky person to have some sexual outlets outside the relationship. In yet others, the vanilla partner will develop kinky desires. In fact, this is not at all an impossible goal. Keep in mind that BDSM practitioners usually enjoy vanilla sex as well, so there is already some compatibility in their sex lives. In addition, recognize that enjoyment of "kink" can sometimes be learned in adulthood: Not all kinky people fantasized about BDSM from childhood. Open, curious, flexible vanilla adults can develop quite strong kinky preferences over time; it helps if the vanilla partner has a strong libido.

The case of Gerry and Lisa exemplifies a situation where the vanilla "surprised" wife was able to adjust and accommodation is being negotiated. This suburban professional couple had two young children, an established home in a respectable, high-end community, and a strong and loving relationship. Gerry came for therapy when he was in his mid-thirties, about a year after the resurfacing of long buried, kinky urges. His fetishes included being dominated by a woman and forced to wear diapers or female undergarments. Gerry also enjoyed vanilla sex and many other forms of BDSM, however, and he was somewhat "switchable," meaning he was able to be either dominant or submissive in a sexual situation. Lisa, initially shocked that the man she thought she knew thoroughly could be hiding something of such import from her for so long, adjusted fairly quickly once assured that Gerry was most probably not a transsexual in early stages of transitioning, contrary to what she had been told adamantly by her last therapist. Lisa discovered she could get sexual enjoyment out of dominating Gerry and, in addition, she found she could get the housework done efficiently by ordering him to clean while diapered, and then end this "scene" with intercourse if she desired. This case is interesting in part because Gerry's primary fetishes are not "turn-ons" for Lisa, but neither do they "squick" her. Rather, what is happening is that the partners are evolving sexual scripts that satisfy his fetishes in a BDSM context while including elements that satisfy Lisa strongly.

Nick and Diane, on the other hand, have had a less happy outcome. Nick had gone through a period in his life where he decided he was a sex addict and had decided that kinky sex was inextricably linked to his addiction. During that period he not only repudiated BDSM, but he seemed to deliberately choose a rather asexual and prudish woman for his wife, perhaps in the hopes that she would help him repress his sexual preferences. Years later Nick began to secretly explore BDSM once again. This time, he found he could manage his desires without feeling compulsive, and began to want to manifest his fantasies in kinky sexual behavior with this wife. Diane, however, had not changed since their marriage. She not only refused to participate, she insisted upon Nick's abstinence from kink as a condition of marriage. The couple was see-sawing back and forth between periods when Nick controlled his urges to make his marriage work, and when he "acted out" sexually and the couple veered towards divorce. Ultimately, the latter seemed inevitable. As this case suggests, many kinky people attempt abstinence in order to keep a marriage and family together. Sometimes this works, depending upon many factors, including strength and quality of the relationship, presence of children, commitment to putting family life above individual needs, and, in all probability, factors like the "kinky" person's level of sex drive and self-control over sexuality.

Issues of Bleed-Through, Good and Bad

"Bleed-through" is a BDSM term used to describe situations when the boundaries between roles in the bedroom and roles in the rest of the relationship blur, or when relationship issues and sexual issues merge. Bleed-through occurs in "vanilla" relationships, too, of course: e.g., the male who feels powerless in his marriage develops erectile problems, or, on a more positive note, the partner who feels nurtured, protected, and connected during a sexual encounter behaves more compassionately to his or her partner in the rest of the relationship. In fact, it is probably unrealistic to think that any couple maintains strict boundaries between the bedroom and "real life." However, bleed-through can sometimes be more complex in BDSM relationships.

Pat and Claudia, a lesbian, self-designated D/s couple, are an example of how sexual and relationship roles blur so that each is a mirror of problems in the other. These women developed sexual dysfunction relating to their roles as submissive and dominant; Pat was having more and more of a problem being submissive during sexual encounters. Upon exploration, Pat realized she felt she was expected to be subservient to Claudia all the time, in and out of bed. Claudia denied wanting this, and it seemed apparent that both women valued egalitarianism in their day-to-day relationship. It took a few, traditional, couple counseling sessions to unravel the ways in which Claudia unconsciously generated cues that Pat interpreted as demands for subservient behavior. Once this happened Pat's comfort with sexual submissiveness began to increase again. In addition, I began to suspect that the couple's sexual issues were being exacerbated by the fact that the transition between "real life" and their sexual "scenes" tended to be gradual and indistinct. Claudia and Pat were encouraged to develop a special ritual to designate when "real life" was being left behind and "scene life" was being entered; this was all the treatment they needed.

Amy and Joanne, on the other hand, had a more serious kind of bleed-through issue, reflecting the more disturbed nature of at least one of the partners. In their sexual roles, Amy was Daddy to Joanne's little girl. Recently, Joanne had been asking to extend these roles outside of sex to many significant areas of everyday life; for example, Joanne wanted Amy to dress her in the morning for work. Amy felt frightened by her partner's behavior, and suffocated by the demands of the parental role. At the same time, her mild-mannered nature made it hard for her to say no to Joanne's demands. Therapy served to help Amy be assertive with Joanne. Moreover, Joanne was advised to return to her individual therapist to resolve her strongly felt urges to abdicate responsibility for herself and return to an infantile state. In this case, the bleed-through was emblematic of larger relationship issues, and especially of Joanne's psychological problems that were not particularly related to sex. Because sexual problems flagged deeper pathology in the larger relationship, most therapeutic interventions in this case had little to do with sexuality per se.

Diagnosing Domestic Violence or Self-Destructive Behavior

Domestic violence can occur in any type of relationship, including BDSM partnerships. Many BDSM organizations, mindful of the public perception of SM, make special efforts to educate "scene" participants about domestic violence and promulgate guidelines to help assess whether or not their relationships are abusive.

Occasionally domestic violence occurs during an actual sexual interaction, in the guise of SM, as this case illustrates. When Sarah married Dan, she had had submissive sexual fantasies for most of her life but had never participated in kinky activities with anyone. Dan claimed to be an experienced dominant who would teach her about BDSM. Dan, however, was merely an abusive spouse with a slightly different "spin" on abuse. Dan would immobilize Sarah in bondage and then, during sex, put a pillow over her face until she began to asphyxiate–an activity that terrified her. It is standard in BDSM "play" to use a "safe word"–a code word that the submissive partner can use to signify that he or she wants the kinky activity to stop. Dan convinced Sarah that to be a "good wife" she had to give up her safe word, leaving her truly afraid for her life. Sarah's behavior and psychology became that of a battered wife, as by degrees she became more and more passive about her abuse. Fortunately, eventually Sarah managed to assert herself with Dan and ultimately divorce him. Sarah was helped by the fact that her therapist, knowledgeable about BDSM, knew immediately that Dan's behavior was domestic violence, rather than kinky sex.

Sometimes BDSM activities, like other behaviors, are turned to a psychologically self-destructive use. Suzy was a young woman with borderline personality disorder who was a sexual masochist. At times her BDSM activities, which mostly revolved around getting heavily flogged, were pleasurable and she felt connected to herself and to her partners. But at other times she, by her own acknowledgement, got herself flogged because she was full of self-hatred. Although these floggings seemed to temporarily alleviate tension, both Suzy and I came to believe over time that they ultimately reinforced her self-loathing. Suzy eventually learned to distinguish when she wanted to be flogged for pleasure and when she was driven by the desire to punish herself. Once this happened, Suzy was able to stop the behavior that was motivated by self-hate without giving up her BDSM sexuality.

It is often difficult to detect when BDSM is being used in an abusive fashion, particularly if the activities involved are ones that "squick" the therapist. The client may accuse the therapist of bias or ignorance in a defensive attempt to cling to pathologically ingrained behavior; a victim of domestic violence may deny his or her partner's abuse. Consulting a colleague with a specialty in sexual minorities might be particularly helpful in these cases where real danger exists.

These cases illustrate situations in which BDSM is being used in an unhealthy way. Like all forms of sexual behavior, kinky sex can be enlisted in the service of neurotic or self-destructive forces, and it is not always easy to distinguish between positive and negative expressions of sex. When negative sexual behavior is suspected, it is of course important for the therapist to examine his or her countertransferential feelings, as described earlier in this paper. If, after doing so, concern about the client's behavior still remains, one can apply the same guidelines one would use in evaluating "vanilla" sexual behavior. Here are some questions the psychotherapist might consider:

1. How does the client feel about his or her behavior? If the client is worried, can this concern be accounted for by internalized sex-negative attitudes, or is there substance to the client's fears?
2. Is the behavior interfering with activities of daily life, such as work, family relationships, or friendships and social life? Caution is needed here; for example, isolation from friends may simply mean the kinky person needs to build a new support group that is accepting of his or her lifestyle.
3. Is the behavior compulsive? Does the client experience a loss of control over sexual impulses?
4. Is the client participating in genuinely risky behaviors, e.g., picking up strangers in unsavory places, engaging in unprotected sex, allowing alcohol and drug use to impair judgment?
5. Does the sexual behavior seem to be making the client feel worse–more depressed, anxious, guilty, self-hating–rather than better?

Recognizing situations in which BDSM is being used in an unhealthy way can take time because both client and therapist may have to counteract ingrained sex-negative feelings. However, a genuinely unbiased clinician neither automatically condemns nor automatically confers approval upon any behavior, but rather considers all evidence over time in the context of each client's particular life situation.

CONCLUSIONS

When "kinky" individuals and couples seek therapy, most of the time they are seeking help for the same reasons as other clients: depression or anxiety, family or relationship issues, and so on. However, there are some issues that are special to this population. Chief among them are problems related to "coming out," i.e., the recognition of "kinky" preferences after years of suppression of these desires. These problems include internalized shame and self-hatred, isolation from others with similar sexuality, and possible conflicts with existing marital or couple relationships.

Before therapists can help kinky clients with these problems, they must first examine their own beliefs about BDSM. The counselor must discard most pathology-oriented paradigms of sexuality; adopt new models that allow for neutrality and, at times, celebratory attitudes towards diverse sexuality. Therapists must also learn to analyze counter-transferential feelings that are based not only upon ignorance but sometimes on fears about their own "darker" sexual desires. In addition, therapists wishing to help "kinky" clients must undertake to educate themselves, not only about BDSM, but about all sexual minorities, because there is considerable overlap between the BDSM community and gay/lesbian/bisexual populations as well as with the polyamory movement.

Although considerable courage, effort, and honesty are required to attain a stance that will be helpful to clients in the BDSM community, the therapist is amply rewarded for his or her labor. First, this is a population that is truly under-served: The typical attitudes evinced by professionals towards BDSM are judgmentalism and condemnation. It is gratifying to know that one makes a difference, and supportive and validating therapy for "kinky" clients genuinely helps, perhaps even saving lives. But there are other benefits to the therapist as well. Working with sexual minorities keeps us constantly rethinking, questioning, and reformulating our own concepts of sexuality, and thus keeps our work in this area from becoming stagnant. And finally, working with people living "on the edge" helps bring us to our own edges, and this keeps us alive, growing and vibrant human beings.

REFERENCES

Bagemihl, B. (1999). *Biological exuberance: Animal homosexuality and natural diversity.* New York: St. Martin's Press.

Brame, G.G. (2000). *Come hither: A commonsense guide to kinky sex.* New York: Fireside.

Good Vibrations/Sexpositive Productions (Producer) (2002). *Whipsmart (video).* United States: Open Enterprises.

Kaschak, E., & Tiefer, L. (2001). *A new view of women's sexual problems.* New York: Haworth Press.

Kleinplatz, P.J. (2002, May). *Psychotherapy with kinky clients.* Workshop presented at the 34th conference of the *American Association of Sex Educators*, Miami, Fla.

Kleinplatz, P.J. (2001). A critique of the goals of sex therapy, or, the hazards of safer sex. In P.J. Kleinplatz (Ed.) *New directions in sex therapy: Innovations and alternatives*, (pp.109-132). Phila., Pa.: Brunner-Rutledge.

Laumann, E.O., Gagnon, J.H., Michael, R.T., & Michaels, S. (1994). *The social organization of sexuality: sexual practices in the United States*. Chicago: University of Chicago Press.

Miller, P. & Devon, M. (1995). *Screw the roses, send me the thorns*. Fairfield, Ct.: Mystic Rose Books.

Morin, J. (1995). *The erotic mind*. New York: Harper Collins.

Moser, C. (2002, May). *What do we really know about S/M: Myths and realities*. Paper presented at the 34th conference of the American Association of Sex Educators, Counselors, and Therapists, Miami, Fla.

Moser, C. (2001). Paraphilia: A critique of a confused concept. In P.J.Kleinplatz, (Ed). *New directions in sex therapy: innovations and alternatives* (pp.91-108). Phila., Pa.: Brunner-Rutledge.

Nichols, M. (2000). Therapy with sexual minorities. In S. Leiblum. & R. Rosen, (Eds.). *Principles and practice of sex therapy* (pp. 335-367). NewYork: Guilford.

Weinberg, T., & Levi Kamel, G.W. (1983). *S and M: Studies in sadomasochism*. Buffalo, N.Y.: Prometheus Press.

Wiseman, J. (1996). *SM 101: A realistic introduction*. San Francisco: Greenery Press.

Wright, S. (2002, May). *Sexual rights: The National Coalition for Sexual Freedom*. Workshop presented at the 34th conference of the American Association of Sex Educators, Counselors, and Therapists, Miami, Fla.

Investigating Bias in Psychotherapy with BDSM Clients

Keely Kolmes, PsyD

Stanford University

Wendy Stock, PhD

Alliant International University

Charles Moser, PhD, MD

Institute for Advanced Study of Human Sexuality

SUMMARY. There is a concern among consensual BDSM participants that they will receive biased care from mental health professionals. Results are presented of an anonymous Internet-based survey administered to both BDSM-identified individuals who have received psychological care and to mental health professionals. The survey included socio-demographic data and invited participants to write narrative accounts of biased or culturally sensitive care, from which common themes were

Keely Kolmes is Staff Psychologist, Counseling and Psychological Services, Vaden Health Center, Stanford University. Wendy Stock is affiliated with Alliant International University. Charles Moser is Professor and Chair of the Department of Sexual Medicine, Institute for Advanced Study of Human Sexuality. Correspondence may be addressed: Keely Kolmes, Vaden Health Center, Stanford University, 866 Campus Drive, Stanford, CA 94305-8580.

[Haworth co-indexing entry note]: "Investigating Bias in Psychotherapy with BDSM Clients." Kolmes, Keely, Wendy Stock, and Charles Moser. Co-published simultaneously in *Journal of Homosexuality* (Harrington Park Press, an imprint of The Haworth Press, Inc.) Vol. 50, No. 2/3, 2006, pp. 301-324; and: *Sadomasochism: Powerful Pleasures* (ed: Peggy J. Kleinplatz, and Charles Moser) Harrington Park Press, an imprint of The Haworth Press, Inc., 2006, pp. 301-324. Single or multiple copies of this article are available for a fee from The Haworth Document Delivery Service [1-800-HAWORTH, 9:00 a.m. - 5:00 p.m. (EST). E-mail address: docdelivery@haworthpress.com].

doi:10.1300/J082v50n02_15

identified. Mental health providers (N = 17) responded in fewer numbers than those who identified as BDSM-identified participants (N = 175). Descriptive characteristics of the sample will be discussed. Themes from the qualitative data may be useful in informing the future development of guidelines for practitioners to work more responsibly with clients who identify as members of this sexual minority group. *[Article copies available for a fee from The Haworth Document Delivery Service: 1-800-HAWORTH. E-mail address: <docdelivery@haworthpress.com> Website: <http://www.HaworthPress.com> © 2006 by The Haworth Press, Inc. All rights reserved.]*

KEYWORDS. Psychotherapy bias, paraphilia, cultural sensitivity, BDSM, sadomasochism, sexual minorities

Consensual sadomasochism (BDSM or SM) has both community-based and scientific definitions. By various definitions, sadomasochistic sexual behavior is not uncommon. Up to 14% of American males and 11% of American females have engaged in some form of sadomasochistic (BDSM or SM) sexual behavior defined as pleasure-in-pain practice, in which one inflicts harm and/or pain on another for sexual and/or psychological satisfaction or one achieves sexual gratification by anticipating or experiencing pain before or during sex (Janus & Janus, 1993). Other estimates indicate that up to 50% of the general population has experienced sexual arousal in response to being bitten (Kinsey, Pomeroy, Martin, & Gebhard, 1953), while 5% of the population has experienced sexual pleasure in inflicting or receiving pain (Hunt, 1974). It is likely that many more Americans experience sexual fantasies along the sadomasochistic spectrum, whether or not these fantasies are ever acted upon.

The community-based definition of BDSM is most commonly understood as the, "knowing use of psychological dominance and submission, and/or physical bondage, and/or pain, and/or related practices in a safe, legal, consensual manner in order for the participants to experience erotic arousal and/or personal growth" (Wiseman, 1996 p. 10). However, it is worth noting that Sexual Sadism has been described in the psychiatric literature as a pathological pattern of behavior that may be enacted with non-consenting victims (American Psychiatric Association [APA], 2000). This view of Sexual Sadism and Sexual Masochism does not allow for the healthy expression of BDSM, especially as a lifestyle as opposed to an isolated behavior. Similarly, it does not acknowledge that the experience and sensation of pain is subjective (Melzack, 1961). These discrepancies between the community-based and scientific definitions likely account for a wide range of experiences for the BDSM client in therapy.

It has been documented that the therapeutic process is influenced by the values and biases of the practitioner, in spite of aspirations of therapeutic neutrality (Lopez, 1989; Murray & Abramson, 1983). Mental health professionals have a long history of holding negative assumptions and stereotypes about the BDSM community, or of being otherwise ill-informed about the practices of this community. This has been demonstrated by the continued inclusion of Sexual Sadism and Sexual Masochism as Paraphilias in the *DSM-IV-TR* (APA, 2000). These diagnoses are listed under the category of sexual disorders or sexual dysfunctions. In our culture in which mental illness is stigmatized, the identification of any practice as pathological can result in related non-pathological behaviors being subjected to the same stigma by those who are unable to distinguish between them (Goffman, 1963). In fact, members of the leather (BDSM or SM) community may often be confused with individuals who are being physically or sexually abused, or may be perceived as acting out low self-esteem, interpersonal difficulties, or compulsive behaviors. Conceptually, the DSM may have led to the misinterpretation that those involved with BDSM were also suffering from various other personality disorders (APA, 1980). This is most likely due to historical writings in the psychological literature in which both sadism and masochism were described initially as personality disorders that might be manifested sexually (Freud, 1905/1957; Krafft-Ebing, 1886/1965). The shifts and changes in the diagnoses for Sexual Sadism and Sexual Masochism, beginning with their being listed as sexually deviant behaviors in the *DSM-II* (APA, 1968), along with the history of the provisional categories for Masochistic (Self-Defeating) Personality Disorder and Sadistic Personality Disorder (APA, 1987, Franklin, 1987) may have contributed to the confusion and pathologizing of these categories. While the diagnostic criteria for Sexual Sadism and Sexual Masochism continue to change in each new revision of the *DSM*, it may be assumed that these behaviors are pathological although there is no data to support this assumption.

The biases and misinformation borne from this history can result in unintentional harm being done to clients who identify sexually as "sadists" or "masochists." At its most extreme, such bias may lead mental health professionals to pathologize their SM identified clients when there is no associated disorder present. Therapists who are misinformed about the consensual SM community may assume physical or mental abuse in a client's history or current life, or judge a client as an unfit parent without other evidence, based solely on the client's BDSM practices. Other mental health professionals may conceptualize a personality disorder around the client's sexual role, assuming that a desire to explore pain or power dynamics sexually translates by default into a tendency to manifest these experiences consciously or unconsciously in non-BDSM relationships. At the lesser extremes, the consequences of such biases may lead to empathic failures and simple misunderstandings between clients and practitioners.

The goal of this research was to assess the cultural competence of mental health professionals when working with the consensual SM community. The intent of this study was to address this problem by surveying mental health professionals about their knowledge of treatment issues with SM identified clients. In addition, SM identified individuals received a similar survey asking them about their experiences (or knowledge of other BDSM participants' experiences) in mental health treatment. It is hoped that the results of this study might also be used to develop ethical guidelines for working competently with members of the consensual SM community.

DISTINCTIONS MADE BY THE BDSM SUBCULTURE

Some in the BDSM subculture make the distinction between B/D (bondage and discipline, which frequently involves physical restraint and/or the acting out of power dynamics without any pain-play) and SM (which sometimes includes more sensory experimentation involving pain or the threat of pain than traditional B/D). Others use the term D/S to signify that the interaction is primarily about dominance and submission (which, again, may or may not include B/D or SM types of activities). For the purposes of this study, however, SM and BDSM will be used interchangeably as an umbrella term meant to be inclusive of all types of play involving the conscious, safe, sane, and consensual use of power dynamics.

One position held by those who engage in BDSM is that SM is simply an alternative sexual identity. Others who practice BDSM argue that the term "sexual orientation" does not seem an appropriate descriptor of their BDSM interests. Clearly, referring to BDSM desires and activities as a "sexual orientation" remains controversial for those who practice SM and also for those who do not. However, in the interest of inclusivity, BDSM will be discussed in this paper as a practice, a lifestyle, an identity, and an orientation.

ETHICAL CONSIDERATIONS

The American Psychological Association's Ethics Code for Psychologists addresses the boundaries of professional competence in Ethical Standard 2. According to 2.01 (a), "Psychologists provide services . . . only within the boundaries of their competence, based on their education, training, supervised experience, consultation, study, or professional experience" (APA, 2002, p. 4). This standard holds that psychologists working outside of their area(s) of competence do pose a significant risk of harm to their clients. Therefore, no psychologist should be working on BDSM issues with BDSM identified clients without first obtaining the necessary skills or expertise to work with this population. It is also worth noting that having an "interest" in BDSM or even practicing BDSM does not necessarily qualify one to work in this area. The type of skills that would qualify one to work with BDSM issues with BDSM clients might include coursework and specialized training on working with BDSM clients, none of which are routinely available. In addition, those seeking supervision to work with BDSM clients should be supervised by one who is already competent in working with BDSM individuals. Often, students within training programs may be supervised by practitioners who are no more knowledgeable about SM practices than the students themselves. This can be particularly problematic, in that the supervisor may be unwittingly practicing outside of his/her area of competence, rather than modeling for the therapist-in-training how one seeks out appropriate training and supervision.

Standard 2.01(b) states:

> Where scientific or professional knowledge in the discipline of psychology establishes that an understanding of factors associated with age, gender, gender identity, race, ethnicity, culture, national origin, religion, sexual orientation, disability, language, or socioeconomic status is essential for effective implementation of their services or research, psychologists have or obtain the training, experience, consultation, or supervision necessary to ensure the competence of their services, or they make appropriate referrals. (APA, 2002, p. 5)

In addition, 2.01(c) states:

> Psychologists planning to provide services . . . involving popula-
> tions [and] areas . . . new to them . . . undertake relevant education,
> training, supervised experience, consultation, or study (APA,
> 2002, p. 5)

Until BDSM practices and lifestyles are included routinely as part of
the human sexuality component of training for all practitioners, and until the mental health profession begins to recognize BDSM individuals
as a subculture requiring special knowledge, skills, and sensitivity,
there remains the risk that therapists may be providing services to
BDSM individuals without ever having received appropriate study,
training, or supervision. It is worth noting that the Ethical Standards are
mandatory and may be accompanied by enforcement mechanisms.
Therefore, not only is there a risk of harm to clients by psychologists
who are not aware of BDSM practices and the other complex treatment
issues that can arise with these individuals, but mental health professionals are also putting themselves at risk. They may be opening themselves up to professional and legal sanctions by remaining ignorant of
SM practices.

Many mental health professionals may not recognize the need to seek
out training, or to make appropriate referrals for their SM clients. Other
mental health professionals may be working from a clinical orientation
that defines BDSM as pathological, *a priori*. For these practitioners, it
can be argued that implementing routine training about BDSM behaviors would provide them with alternative models with which to view
these practices. On this matter, an important component of training
might be a strong advisory to therapists to provide BDSM clients with
informed consent if their practices are viewed as pathological.

Without formal criteria for therapists who wish to work responsibly
with those who practice BDSM, clients in this lifestyle who are seeking
those with specialized knowledge of BDSM are left to rely on those professionals who self-identify as "kink aware" (Bannon, 2003). These are
professionals who consider themselves to be informed about the diversity of consensual, adult sexuality. While many "kink aware" professionals may have expertise in BDSM practices, many of them may *not*
possess the specialized knowledge required to work competently with
complex issues in the treatment of BDSM individuals. Meanwhile,
other mental health professionals with no training or knowledge of
BDSM practices may assume they are knowledgeable enough to work

with BDSM clients while working from the assumption that BDSM practices are pathological. Until training and education about BDSM lifestyles and practices are offered routinely, clients are left without reliable means to assess the expertise of "kink aware" professionals. It is apparent that there is a critical need to develop guidelines for psychotherapy with BDSM clients. This study is intended to begin the process, similar to that which was followed in the development of the guidelines for working with the lesbian, gay, and bisexual (GLB) communities (APA, 2000).

METHOD

A broad range of clients who self-identified as BDSM participants and who had sought psychotherapy were recruited through an announcement sent to various BDSM interest groups on the Internet as well as retail establishments and BDSM support groups. This announcement directed participants to a Web address which contained a consent form, along with details for eligibility of the study. This form outlined the procedures of the study, the potential benefits and risks of participating, and explained that participants should refrain from entering their names in any data field. Participants were also informed of how to contact the researchers if they should experience undue distress as a result of participation in the study, but were warned that contacting the researchers would compromise their anonymity. Those who were eligible were able to enter a code which took them directly to the questionnaire. Specific groups contacted included The Leathermen's Discussion Group, The Society of Janus, All Women of Leather, SAMOIS, The Lesbian Sex Mafia, and The Eulenspeigel Society. Internet lists that were contacted included ba-sappho, kinky-grrls, psych-bdsm, SM-ACT, ftmbdsm, leatherdykes, The Society of Janus, The Exiles, AWOL, The Lesbian Sex Mafia, and The Eulenspeigel Society. The announcement was sent to the following establishments: Mr. S. Leather, Ms. S. Leather, Stormy Leather, and Good Vibrations in San Francisco, California; Eve's Garden and Passion Flower in New York City; and Toys in Babeland in Seattle, Washington. All recipients were encouraged to post and/or forward the announcement to interested parties.

BDSM clients were considered eligible for this study provided they were (i) BDSM-identified individuals; (ii) 18 years of age or over; (iii) had actually participated in real life BDSM (as opposed to virtual BDSM on the Internet) for at least two years; (iv) maintained independent BDSM interests in their personal lives, for those who had also engaged in BDSM for money; and (v) previous or current consumers of mental health services. Participation was anonymous.

In addition, mental health professionals were also recruited for this study. However, there was not a high enough response from therapist participants to provide a meaningful analysis of the submitted data. Therefore, the therapist sample will not be discussed in this publication.

Materials and Procedure

The questionnaire began with 21 questions seeking to elicit demographic information and various distinctions among the terms people used to describe their BDSM behaviors. There were also questions asking participants to list the ages at which they first identified as interested in BDSM as well as the ages at which they became aware of their sexual and gender orientations. In addition, participants were asked to disclose their level of "outness" in various parts of their lives regarding these identities.

The questionnaire asked whether the participant had ever engaged in BDSM play for hire, and if so, whether the participant had maintained a personal interest in BDSM outside of his or her professional BDSM play. Items included the number of therapists seen, respective lengths of treatment, issues that brought the client into therapy, whether the BDSM interests were disclosed to the therapist(s) (and if so, when in the course of treatment the disclosure occurred), and whether the participant sought out the services of a "kink aware" professional. These questions were followed by essay questions using Garnets, Hancock, Cochran, Goodchilds, and Peplau's (1991) survey as a model. Participants were asked for any known incidents of "biased inadequate, or inappropriate care to a BDSM client in psychotherapy"; any known incidents of, "care demonstrating special sensitivity to a BDSM client in psychotherapy"; "what professional practices are especially harmful in psychotherapy with BDSM clients"; and "what professional practices are especially beneficial in psychotherapy with BDSM clients." A copy of the questionnaire is available from the first author upon request.

Sample Population

One hundred ninety-seven client participants responded to the BDSM client questionnaire and seventeen mental health professionals responded to the psychologist questionnaire. The current report focuses on the client data.

Of the 197 submitted client surveys, 22 did not meet the inclusion criteria for the study, as they had never received mental health services. The remaining 175 client responses were analyzed, and of these respondents, one chose not to provide an age. The mean age of participants was 38.63, with the youngest participant being 18 years old and the oldest being 62. Participants from 40 states in North America took the survey with the majority of participants (36) located in California. In order of response, the four next most frequent rates of response by states were from Washington (12), New York (13), North Carolina (11), and Massachusetts (11).

Of the 175 participants, when asked to indicate their biological sex, 136 (77.7%) were female, 33 (18.9%) were male, 4 (2.3%) identified as "other," and 2 (1.1%) were intersex. Again, a higher number of female respondents could be due to the fact that the announcement was sent to several lists for (bisexual and lesbian) women.

When asked to indicate their gender identity (how participants see themselves regardless of biological sex), 130 respondents (74.3%) listed female, 31 (17.7%) listed male, 7 (4%) listed bigendered, 6 (3.4%) reported other, and 1 individual (0.6%) listed intersex. As a subcomponent of gender identity, all participants were asked to identify themselves as butch, femme, androgynous, none, or other. On this item, 64 participants (36.6%) listed none, 47 (26.9%) were femme, 27 (15.4%) were other, 20 (11.4%) listed butch, 8 people (4.6%) did not respond to this item, and 9 people (5.1%) chose androgynous.

When specifically asked about sexual orientation, 42.3% considered themselves bisexual, 35.4% called themselves heterosexual, 18.9% called themselves lesbian, and 5.1% called themselves gay. For other ways of self-identifying, 4.6% identified as transgendered, 2.9% of participants considered themselves to be bigendered, 2.3% were FTM transitioning transsexuals, 1.1% were transsexual, and 0.6% were MTF transitioning transsexuals. Another 14.9% chose "other" for their sexual/gender orientation. These percentages contradict the numbers given in response to the gender identity question.

For ethnicity, 153 participants (87.4%) were Euro-American, 8 people (4.6%) listed themselves as bi/multi-racial, 6 people (3.4%) listed other, 3 people (1.7%) were Asian-American, 2 people (1.1%) failed to respond, 1 person (0.6%) identified as Native-American, 1 person (0.6%) as Latino, and 1 person (0.6%) African-American.

Participants were asked to disclose their current annual income. The three categories indicated most often were $30,000-39,000 (21.7%), followed by $40,000-49,000 (16%) and $20,000-29,000 (14.9%). At the upper and lower ranges, 8% selected "under $10,000" and 2.9% listed "over $150,000" as their annual income.

For geographical area, 46.9% live in the suburbs, 41.7% live in a city, 9.7% live in a rural area, 1.1% live on a farm, and 0.6% did not respond. In terms of the size of community, 41.7% said they lived in an area with a population over 500,000, 29.1% lived in a place with a population between 100,000 and 500,000, 27.4% lived in an area with a population under 100,000, while 1.7% did not respond to the question.

Respondents were given a list of BDSM terms and asked how they self-identified. Answers were not limited to one choice. "BDSM" was selected by 87.4% of respondents, "Kinky/bent/perverted," was chosen by 60% of participants, 37.1% selected "SM," as their identity, 35.4% chose "D/S," 22.3% of people selected "B/D," and 5.1% of participants called themselves "vanilla." Another 11.4% of participants said they used some "other" term to self-identify. The researchers assume that those who selected "vanilla" did so because they see this as part of their identity, along with other BDSM self-descriptor(s).

Participants were asked to report the ages at which they first became aware of their various identities and orientations. The responses are shown in Table 1.

Participants were also asked to check the settings in which their various identities and orientations were known to others. The responses are shown in Table 2.

RESULTS

Involvement in Professional BDSM Services

Participants were asked if they had ever engaged in BDSM play for hire, and, if they said yes, they were asked to describe these experiences. Ninety-four (53.7%) of the participants reported never engaging in BDSM for hire. Forty-four (25.1%) participants did not respond to this question. Another 22 (12.6%) participants said they had engaged in BDSM for pay, 3 (1.7%) said they had been paid once, another 3 participants (1.7%) said they had assisted others in their work (but had not received payment), 1 (0.6%) said they had done it two or three times, and another person (0.6%) had assisted someone several times without be-

TABLE 1. Age at Which Participants First Self-identified

Identity	Youngest Age	Oldest Age	*M* Age	*N*
BDSM[a]	0	58	26.45	506
Vanilla	0	32	15.39	18
Heterosexual	0	41	12.94	79
Lesbian	12	43	20.63	46
Gay	4	36	18.23	13
Bisexual	8	56	22.77	91
Bigendered	7	33	18.17	6
Transgendered	7	48	27.20	10
Transsexual	14	50	32.00	2
Transitioning	30	50	40.00	2

[a]Mean age for BDSM identity is a weighted mean for various responses including "kinky," "BDSM," "B/D," "D/S," and "SM." Number of responses for BDSM is the total of those who selected "kinky," "BDSM," "B/D," "D/S," and "SM," as their identity.

ing paid. There were two people (1.2%) who indicated that they had been paid for educational demonstrations on BDSM, while 1 person (0.6%) indicated that she seriously intends to begin providing professional BDSM services in the near future. Another four respondents (2.3%) stated that they had been paying customers in BDSM interactions. Those who responded yes to this question were asked if they had maintained a personal interest in BDSM play outside of their professional services. The 37 individuals who indicated that they had engaged in BDSM for hire all said that they had also maintained a personal interest in BDSM. One individual selected no for this item, but it was presumed to be an error because this individual wrote extensively about his personal interest in BDSM, and he also stated that he had not engaged in BDSM for hire.

Number of Therapists Seen

Participants were asked how many therapists they had seen over the years. Most of the sample had seen between one and five therapists. The

TABLE 2. Settings in Which "Kinky," "BDSM-Identified," "B/D," D/S," or "Vanilla-Identified" Identity Is Known to Others

Settings	N	P
Most friends	114	65.1
Primary partner	100	57.1
In home	96	54.9
All partners	94	53.7
In the community	72	41.1
Some friends	55	31.4
Most of nuclear family	45	25.7
At work	29	16.6
Some partner(s)	22	12.6
Extended family	11	6.3
Only to self[a]	5	2.9
To no one[b]	1	0.6

[a]All participants who indicated that they were only "out" to themselves listed other arenas in which they were "out." [b]The individual who indicated that she was "out" to no one listed other arenas in which she was "out." It is assumed that these responses are inaccurate.

most frequent response reported (21.7%) was one therapist. Another 20% of participants had seen two therapists, 19.4% had seen three therapists, 13.7% had seen four therapists, and 10.3% had seen five therapists. One individual (0.6%) reported seeing fourteen mental health professionals and another individual (0.6%) reported seeing as many as thirty. When totaled, the number of therapists seen by all clients was 633. The 17 therapists surveyed reported seeing at least 186 BDSM clients, or an average of 11 BDSM clients each.

Relationship of Mental Health Issues to Clients' BDSM Interests

Participants were asked to indicate those issues that had brought them into therapy and whether they were in any way related to their BDSM interests. Most participants (74.9%) said that the issues that brought them into therapy were not related to their BDSM interests in any way. A smaller percentage (12%) of the sample said that their BDSM interests were related to the issues that brought them into therapy. Another 11% said that their BDSM interests were tangentially related to the concerns that led them to seek psychological care. Two participants (1.1%) were not sure whether their BDSM interests were in any way related to the concerns that brought them into therapy.

Disclosure of BDSM Interests to Therapists

Participants were asked whether they had disclosed their BDSM interests to their therapist(s). Most participants (65.1%) had shared their BDSM interests with their therapist, while 28.6% had not told their therapists about their BDSM interests. There were seven participants (4%) who had specifically not told their therapists about their BDSM interests, indicating that this was because they were not yet aware of their BDSM orientation at the time that they were in therapy. Another three people (1.7%) did not respond to this question and one participant (0.6%) provided an uninterpretable response.

Most who disclosed their BDSM interests tended to do so early on in their treatment ("immediately," "right away," and "first or second visit," came up frequently in responses), explaining that it was their way of assessing whether they would feel comfortable in treatment. Others waited until the end of treatment. Those (32.6%) who did not disclose their BDSM interests indicated that this was because they were not yet aware of their BDSM interests (4%) or because their BDSM was not related to their treatment. Eight participants from both groups of those who had and had not disclosed their kink-orientation to their therapists reported being fearful at some point that it was too risky to "come out" to their therapists because the therapists would not understand or might think they were "crazy." A few individuals said that they had "come out" about other alternative sexual issues (multiple partners or same sex relationships) but not specifically about BDSM. Some stated that they had chosen to "come out" about these issues as a way of testing the waters about their therapist's attitudes towards BDSM, while others claimed that they had done so because these issues were more relevant to their treatment concerns than their BDSM identity.

Seeking Out Kink Aware Professionals

Participants were asked whether or not they had at any point sought out the services of a "kink aware" professional. The majority of the participants (59.4%) had not done so. Those who gave more information on why they did not seek one out listed reasons such as BDSM not being the primary treatment issue, not being aware that "kink aware" professionals exist, not yet being aware of their own BDSM interests, not having any "kink aware" professionals in their community, or having to accept therapists based upon health insurance rather than personal choice.

However, 33.7% of participants had sought out the services of kink aware professionals or had included questions about the therapist's BDSM knowledge when choosing a mental health professional. Many of those who sought out "kink aware" professionals said they would always do so. A number of people located "kink aware" professionals but found them to be inappropriate for a variety of reasons: three people found therapists who were too expensive; one person said the "kink aware" therapist was "unprofessional," but did not provide additional details; one located a male "kink aware" professional; however, finding a female therapist was of higher priority for her than seeing one who was "kink aware," and another participant said the therapist was "too far away." Of the two others who were dissatisfied in their search for a "kink aware" therapist, one offered that she had looked at a list and "did not find any who seemed to suit me," while another said that the therapist she found "seemed more interested in sharing stories about fun S/M stuff we'd both done than in acting as my therapist."

Of the remaining participants, 3.4% did not respond to the question, and 3.4% responded in a way that did not answer the question clearly.

Themes of Biased and Culturally Sensitive Care to BDSM Clients in Therapy as Reported by Sample

The researchers identified and coded the major themes that emerged in response to the answers given by participants. Regarding reports of "biased, inadequate, or inappropriate care to a BDSM client in psychotherapy," participants listed several major categories: (1) considering BDSM to be unhealthy, (2) requiring a client to give up BDSM activity in order to continue in treatment, (3) confusing BDSM with abuse, (4) having to educate the therapist about BDSM, (5) assuming that BDSM interests are indicative of past family/spousal abuse, and (6) therapists misrepresenting their expertise by stating that they are BDSM-positive when they are not actually knowledgeable about BDSM practices.

One participant responded: "A friend told me that her therapist told her that BDSM can never be done safely, is always abuse, and that the therapist could no longer see my friend if she would not stop." Another participant described the time she wasted in therapy: ". . . BDSM only came into play when I had to educate her therapist that it was not abuse, that it was not harmful to me, that I was not self-sabotaging with it, nor acting out past family/spousal abuse. It actually took quite a few sessions to get the therapist over their hang-ups and misconceptions about BDSM. Time that could (have) been better spent on the actual issues I was there for." Another respondent shared the following: "I disclosed my interest in SM to (my) therapist after seeing her for about 2 months. She told me that she believed BDSM to be aberrant and harmful to the people who practice it." This individual eventually decided that SM was not pertinent to the issues that brought her into therapy so they would have to "agree to disagree." But she mentioned that "the inability to freely discuss my sexuality has marred my therapy experience somewhat . . ."

In terms of the total number of incidents of "biased" or "inadequate" care reported by the sample, there were 118 reported incidents of therapists providing poor care to BDSM clients. Most participants listed the incidents clearly and each incident by an individual therapist was counted. If an individual reported several things that her or his therapist did that demonstrated bias, these were linked to one therapist and counted as one incident. However, when clients reported hearing of "some" cases, but did not indicate the number of incidents, these were coded as three incidents. This choice provided the most conservative estimate, assuming that "some" would refer to some unknown quantity that was more than two incidents.

Participants were asked to describe "any incidents where a therapist provided care demonstrating special sensitivity to a BDSM client in psychotherapy." Themes in the responses to this question included (1) therapist(s) being open to reading/learning more about BDSM, (2) therapist(s) showing comfort in talking about BDSM issues, (3) therapists who understand and promote "safe, sane, consensual" BDSM. A participant was pleased that her therapist "was both sensitive and interested in being educated when she (had) not (been previously) exposed to matters relating to my BDSM activities."

Similarly, therapists who responded to this question spoke about incidents in which they had let BDSM clients know that they were comfortable speaking about BDSM. They did this by being sensitive to when a client might be testing the waters about these issues, letting the client know that it was acceptable to talk about such things, having intake forms that reflected their awareness of alternative sexuality issues, and treating BDSM issues as part of the normal spectrum of human sexuality. One therapist also felt that making referrals when a therapist believed s/he was biased about BDSM showed sensitivity to BDSM clients.

The total number of incidents reported in which a therapist provided sensitive or culturally-aware care to a BDSM client was 113. Again, in cases in where the participant reported that "some" friends had shared positive experiences with them, these were coded as three incidents so as to provide the most conservative estimate of "some," with the assumption that the individual was referring to more than two incidents. In response to this question, nine individuals indicated that the therapist whom they were describing as demonstrating special sensitivity to them as a BDSM client was the same therapist whom they had previously described as providing biased care. Some of these individuals explained that after a therapist had made a particular blunder, he or she then showed a willingness to learn more about BDSM or came to better understand the role of BDSM in the client's life.

As for participants' ideas of those professional psychotherapy practices that can be especially harmful to BDSM clients, some of the themes that BDSM clients listed included: (1) not understanding that BDSM involves consensual interactions, (2) "kink aware" professionals who lack appropriate boundaries (e.g., "I find it frightening to see the lack of professional boundaries among those therapists who are specifically trolling for BDSM clients," says one participant, (3) assuming that "bottoms" are self-destructive, (4) therapists abandoning clients who engage in BDSM behavior, (5) trying to "fix" the BDSM client solely on the basis of the BDSM interests, (6) making reports/breaking confidentiality because the therapist assumes others are at risk solely due to the BDSM activities, (7) assuming past trauma is the cause of the BDSM interests, (8) expecting the client to teach the therapist about BDSM, and (9) having a prurient interest in the client's BDSM sexual lifestyle. One person was emphatic that "It is patently unfair of therapists to expect their clients to educate them on the subject of sexual variations."

Therapists also described practices that they considered harmful to BDSM clients: therapists who shame their BDSM clients or become judgmental, and therapists who adhere to theoretical perspectives that may give them pathological explanations for a client's BDSM interests. Therapists also acknowledged the dangers of assuming that all BDSM clients are healthy, emphasizing the need for therapists who can recognize the complexity and presence of both abuse and BDSM in some BDSM relationships.

BDSM clients were also asked what professional psychotherapy practices they would consider especially beneficial to a BDSM client. These themes included (1) asking questions about BDSM, (2) helping the client to overcome shame and stigma as related to the BDSM identity, (3) open-mindedness and acceptance, (4) not expecting the client to do all of the educating about BDSM, (5) understanding the distinction between BDSM and abuse, (6) being someone who practices BDSM and identifies with the BDSM lifestyle, and (7) the ability to appreciate the complexity of BDSM play and to realize that some clients need help to determine if they are using BDSM in a positive way in their lives. One participant wrote that she would appreciate a therapist who understood that "BDSM is not inherently a mental illness," but who also understood that "certain perceptions, behaviors, or practices (that can occur within a BDSM context) may be inappropriate, self-compromising, and/or self-destructive." Another offered: "I think that there are definitely aspects of BDSM that can be harmful when someone isn't mindful of their own limits, needs, and such . . . finding a therapist who would be open to helping me along that path in the healthiest way possible would be invaluable!"

Therapists agreed that beneficial therapy practices for BDSM clients include: the therapist being willing to raise questions about BDSM, normalizing BDSM interests for clients new to BDSM, open-minded acceptance, being well-informed about BDSM and the subculture (or even identifying as one who engages in BDSM practices), and not focusing on kinky behavior when it is not the client's focus of treatment. Therapists were also aware of the importance of appreciating the complexity of BDSM play and realizing that not all clients are engaging in it in a way that is healthy for them. Therapists discussed the need to sometimes acknowledge their own values and the willingness to refer when necessary. They talked about helping clients discuss safety issues in BDSM and helping them to set boundaries in their play (if the client struggles with setting such boundaries). Therapists also acknowledged that some BDSM-identified individuals might have issues of compulsivity in their sexual interactions that might need to be addressed and that knowing and being able to refer to other kink-friendly professionals is part of being able to provide culturally-sensitive care to BDSM clients.

DISCUSSION

One hundred seventy-five individuals from 40 U.S. states responded to the BDSM-identified client questionnaire. The response to the call for participants indicated that BDSM individuals exist nationwide, and that they are utilizing mental health treatment for both BDSM-related and non-BDSM-related issues. Although there were a higher number of BDSM participants located in California, the comparatively higher concentration of California participants is likely accounted for by the greater outreach to the San Francisco Bay Area. When totaled, the number of therapists seen by all clients was 633. We wondered how many of these therapists had knowledge or awareness of working with BDSM clients–especially considering the low response rate of therapists in this particular study.

It is of note that 65.1% of BDSM clients had disclosed their BDSM interests to their therapist(s). Considering that 74.9% did not feel that the issues bringing them into therapy were kink-related, one might assume that these clients would not be bringing the issue up in treatment–especially given that 59.4% had not actively sought out the services of a "kink aware" professional. However, it became clear that disclosure of BDSM interests early on in treatment is used as a screening process by some BDSM clients in order to assess whether a therapist is going to make them feel comfortable. Nevertheless, "coming out" in therapy was experienced as too risky by some individuals who feared that there might be dire consequences. This is important because these individuals are obtaining psychological services with therapists whom they do not trust to manage important information regarding their lives and relationships competently. Withholding any information from one's therapist out of fear of consequences certainly can have an impact on the quality of treatment and the therapeutic relationship.

In terms of seeking out a "kink aware" professional, 59.4% had not sought one out. Some of these individuals were unaware that "kink aware" professionals even exist. As consumers of mental health treatment, BDSM clients deserve to have easily accessible resources for finding culturally sensitive treatment. The lack of awareness by some BDSM-identified individuals of mental health treatment geared specifically to their special needs is further evidence of the marginalization of BDSM practices and lifestyles. About one-third of BDSM participants were interested in seeking mental health treatment from a "kink aware" professional.

Important information was gleaned by the responses of those who were disappointed when they sought out "kink aware" clinicians. Poor boundaries were mentioned by one individual when her therapist seemed more interested in exchanging fun personal stories about BDSM than maintaining a professional stance. This comment echoed another participant's response when asked for professional psychotherapy practices that can be harmful to BDSM clients. This individual worried about therapists who "troll" for BDSM clients. Although it was unclear whether the participant was referring to therapists who seek BDSM clients as a guise for finding BDSM play partners, the implication was that this might be the case. Comments of this nature highlight the significance of appropriate boundaries in treating sexual minority clients. Some inappropriate therapists may have voyeuristic interests in working with BDSM clients. Other "kink aware" professionals who are BDSM-identified themselves may also have other boundary issues to be aware of: the potential for running into clients when attending BDSM play parties or other community events, and the possibility of those who are both BDSM- and poly-identified to inadvertently find themselves (or their partners) engaging in BDSM play with a client's partner (or their own clients). These possible scenarios are not that uncommon when one considers the relative size of the BDSM population in some communities and the limited BDSM resources that may be available to these communities. Clearly, confidentiality issues can arise quickly. They must be anticipated and dealt with ethically by practitioners who wish to call themselves competent at working with BDSM clients.

There were many significant similarities between the client and therapist themes in the qualitative data collected. More than one individual mentioned incidents in which a client was required by a therapist to give up BDSM as a condition of treatment. These scenarios are extremely disturbing when compared to the imagined scenario of a client being told by a therapist that she must discontinue kissing her husband or stop having sexual relations with him in order to continue in treatment. Yet, abuses of this nature were among the more common themes described. Other responses made it very clear that therapists are in great need of resources to help them distinguish consensual BDSM from nonconsensual violence in a relationship. Many individuals were annoyed with having to serve as educators for lazy therapists who had not done their homework. The clients' annoyance over having to educate their therapists about BDSM or having therapists misrepresent their expertise about BDSM seems particularly significant when one considers that five out of the seventeen therapists in this study cited their clients as their primary source of information regarding BDSM.

In both the therapist and BDSM client group, the number of reported incidents of positive and negative care to BDSM clients in therapy was similar. The therapist group reported 12 cases of biased care and 12 cases of culturally-sensitive care. The client group reported 118 cases of biased care and 113 cases of culturally-sensitive care. The researchers note that the sample of BDSM clients recruited for this study already have access to BDSM resources, and are therefore more likely to be aware of both positive and negative experiences in treatment. Those who are most likely to have had more negative experiences are not likely to be represented by this sample. Also, participants were not asked to describe the consequences of biased care that they (or others) received. This question would be an important follow-up question in a future study. For example, some individuals who have sought treatment in the past may now avoid the therapy they need for fear of having another bad experience. Others may have tried to change or suppress their BDSM desires after being treated by therapists who believe BDSM is sick.

Several parallels exist between the experiences and needs of BDSM clients in psychotherapy and the experiences and needs of GLB clients in psychotherapy. These parallels include issues of disclosure, the need for a non-prejudiced, well-informed therapist, and the need for a therapist who is sensitive to the complex issues that can arise in BDSM relationships. In addition, as with GLB clients, BDSM clients need therapists who are able to differentiate diagnostically problems that are related to BDSM practices from those that are non-related. Furthermore, like GLB clients, BDSM clients who are already identified with the BDSM subculture may be more empowered in interacting with the mental health establishment because they may be better able to articulate their needs for a BDSM-sensitive or "kink aware" therapist and actively seek one out. Clients who have been traumatized by therapists who are ignorant about BDSM or who view it as pathological may fearfully steer clear of the treatment they need. Other clients may be new to BDSM, and these individuals may feel lost and in need of information. They may not know to pursue these resources without the help of a therapist who has access to them. Therefore, it is important for therapists to be aware of resources for their BDSM clients who are just "coming out" but who have not found the larger community. This is similar to how therapists working with GLB clients who are just "coming out" may also have to help these clients gain access to the GLB community.

The researchers hope that these findings will add to the creation of ethical guidelines for culturally-sensitive treatment with BDSM individuals similar to those created by the Division 44 Committee on Lesbian, Gay, and Bisexual Concerns Joint Task Force on Guidelines for Psychotherapy with Lesbian, Gay, and Bisexual Clients (APA, 2000). This Task Force was developed after the study by Garnets et al. (1991) which was the first step in identifying positive and negative experiences for GLB clients in psychotherapy. Suggested guidelines for psychotherapy with BDSM clients have been developed by Kleinplatz and Moser (2004) and are based upon the Guidelines for working with GLB clients. They also reflect many of the responses given by both the BDSM client and the therapist sample. Kleinplatz and Moser's guidelines for psychotherapy with BDSM clients address psychologists' attitudes towards BDSM, their knowledge about BDSM relationships and families, their awareness of issues of diversity for BDSM clients, and education for psychologists on BDSM issues and treatment. One recommendation is that Kleinplatz and Moser's guidelines should be expanded to reflect the needs of GLB and transgendered BDSM members. While GLB refers to gay, lesbian, and bisexual individuals, it should be acknowledged that the interests of transgendered individuals overlap considerably with those of the GLB community, and Division 44 currently includes a Transgender Task Force.

It appears that there is a great need for specific training in BDSM for mental health professionals. Such training would familiarize therapists with the BDSM subculture and the community codes and practices. It would help mental health professionals gain access to BDSM groups and literature. This training would also help practitioners understand the differences between the healthy expression of BDSM and abuse, and it would help therapists understand how to assess when something may be going awry in an otherwise healthy BDSM relationship. Mental health professionals need to understand how boundaries are established in BDSM relationships. In addition, there is a pressing need for an APA Division for those who are interested in the psychological study of sexuality. This Division would provide a home for practitioner groups, research, education, and policy. Therapists who want to work competently with BDSM clients also would benefit greatly from e-mail lists and consultation groups in which cases can be discussed and supervised by those who have developed expertise in working with BDSM clients.

A current challenge to both BDSM clients and those seeking supervision from "kink aware" professionals is that cultural competence is difficult to define given the current lack of formal training on working with the BDSM subculture. Even kink positive therapists will undoubtedly have their own biases and stereotypes and countertransferences to various BDSM behaviors, and they will need ongoing consultation with other "kink aware" professionals to address these issues as they arise. Creating professional literature will help both therapists and clients. Mental health professionals can share techniques and problems that are specific to this population. Unique challenges may exist when working with BDSM clients. Some clients may have multiple partners or roles. For example, a practitioner's standard model of couples therapy would have to be expanded upon when working with a BDSM individual who presents with a Master/slave lifestyle and wants to resolve a relationship conflict while maintaining the power differential in this relationship. Other issues that are specific to this population include "coming out" and countering BDSM negativity that can exist for a client internally as well as in his or her relationships with friends, family, partners, or work environment.

Given the findings of this study, it is apparent that mental health professionals are needed who are prepared to work with BDSM-identified clients on the issues they present in therapy without attempting to refocus the treatment on BDSM issues when this is not the client's desire. As some BDSM-identified clients may also be in abusive relationships concurrent with their BDSM interests, therapists need to be able to help a client distinguish between BDSM and abuse.

CONCLUSIONS

It is clear that BDSM interests span various ages, genders and sexual orientations, and there are BDSM participants nationwide who are utilizing mental health treatment for both BDSM-related and non-BDSM-related issues. BDSM interests are not in and of themselves pathological interests and there is no study that demonstrates that BDSM is pathological. There are times when BDSM fantasies and behavior may become symptoms of pathology whether acted out in a non-consensual fashion or when a participant is unable to make distinctions about his or her own boundaries. Therapists treating BDSM clients must be able to differentiate between BDSM and abuse.

It is hoped that these results will contribute to the contemporary development of ethical guidelines for culturally-sensitive treatment with BDSM individuals similar to those developed by the Division 44 Committee on Lesbian, Gay, and Bisexual Concerns Joint Task Force on Guidelines for Psychotherapy with Lesbian, Gay, and Bisexual Clients (APA, 2000). Suggested guidelines for psychotherapy with BDSM clients would look very similar to those created for working with GLB clients, and they would reflect many of the suggestions made by both the BDSM participants and the therapist participants regarding what would constitute culturally-sensitive care to BDSM clients.

It is incumbent upon the field of psychology to recognize the need for specific training to help mental health providers to better meet the particular needs of BDSM clients in therapy. This would include training based on more accurate information about this population, awareness of the effects of cultural bias and stigma, and sensitivity to the complexities that BDSM-identified individuals present in therapy.

REFERENCES

American Psychiatric Association. (1968). *Diagnostic and statistical manual of mental disorders* (2nd ed.). Washington, DC: American Psychiatric Association.

American Psychiatric Association. (1980). *Diagnostic and statistical manual of mental disorders* (3rd ed.). Washington, DC: American Psychiatric Association.

American Psychiatric Association. (1987). *Diagnostic and statistical manual of mental disorders* (3rd ed., rev.). Washington, DC: American Psychiatric Association.

American Psychiatric Association. (2000). *Diagnostic and statistical manual of mental disorders* (4th ed. rev.). Washington, DC: American Psychiatric Association.

American Psychological Association (2000). Guidelines for psychotherapy with lesbian, gay, and bisexual clients. *American Psychologist.* 55, 1440-1451.

American Psychological Association (2002). *Ethical principles of psychologists and code of conduct.* [Electronic version]. Retrieved March 22, 2003, from http://www.apa.org/ethics/code2002.html

Bannon, R. (2003). Kink aware professions. Retrieved March 16, 2003, from http://www.bannon.com/kap/

Franklin, D. (January, 1987). The politics of masochism. *Psychology Today, 21* (1) 52-57.

Freud, S. (1957). *Three Essays on the Theory of Sexuality.* Standard Edition 7: pp. 125-245. London: Hogarth Press. (Originally published in 1905).

Garnets, L., Hancock, K. A., Cochran, S. D., Goodchilds, J., Peplau, L. A. (1991). Issues in psychotherapy with lesbians and gay men. *American Psychologist, 46,* 964-972.

Goffman, E. (1963) *Stigma.* New Jersey: Prentice-Hall.

Hunt, M. (1974). *Sexual behavior in the 1970's.* Playboy Press, Chicago.

Janus, Samuel S., & Janus, Cynthia L. (1994). *Janus Report On Sexual Behavior.* John Wiley & Sons, Inc.

Kinsey A. C., Pomeroy, W.B., Martin. C.E., & Gebhard, P.H. (1953). *Sexual behavior in the human female.* Philadelphia: W.B. Saunders.

Kleinplatz, P.J. & Moser, C. (2004, June). Towards clinical guidelines for working with BDSM clients. *Contemporary Sexuality, 38*(6), 1, 4. [WWW document] URL *http://home.netcom.com/com/~docx2/AASECT.mht.*

Krafft-Ebing, R. von (1965). *Psychopathia sexualis.* (F.S. Klaf, Trans.). New York: Bell Publishing Company. (Original work published 1886).

Lopez, S.R. (1989). Patient variable biases in clinical judgment: Conceptual overview and methodological consideration. *Psychological Bulletin, 106,* 184-203.

Melzack, R. (1961). The perception of pain. *Scientific American.*

Murray, J., Abramson, P.R. (1983). *Bias in psychotherapy.* New York: Praeger.

Weinberg, M.S., Williams, C.J., Moser, C. (1984). The social constituents of sadomasochism. *Social Problems, 31,* 379-389.

Wiseman, J. (1996). *SM 101.* San Francisco: Greenery Press.

Learning from Extraordinary Lovers: Lessons from the Edge

Peggy J. Kleinplatz, PhD

University of Ottawa

SUMMARY. This paper discusses lessons about sexuality and eroticism gleaned from those who engage in extraordinary sex, even though such relationships have typically been classified as pathological. What can clinicians learn from those who seek and attain uncommon sexual relations? Such individuals' sexual epistemology, goals, understanding of the nature and spectrum of sexual and erotic relations, communication strategies and "outcome" criteria can provide valuable lessons for those who treat sexual problems or aim to overcome sexual mediocrity. For example, while traditional sex therapy often focuses on what is on the surface, some SM participants are interested in the meanings that lie at a deeper level. Whereas conventional clinicians may focus on enabling particular sexual acts (especially heterosexual intercourse), SM participants are more apt to be concerned with the varied spectrum of underlying purposes motivating these acts. Whereas many couples are willing to settle for merely functional sex, SM practitioners may be more interested in contact that necessitates intense, erotic connection; sophisti-

---

Peggy J. Kleinplatz is affiliated with the Faculty of Medicine and School of Psychology, University of Ottawa. Correspondence may be addressed: 161 Frank St., Ottawa, ON K2P 0X4, Canada. The author would like to thank Ronald E. Fox, PhD, for his constructive comments and suggestions on earlier drafts of this article.

[Haworth co-indexing entry note]: "Learning from Extraordinary Lovers: Lessons from the Edge." Kleinplatz, Peggy J. Co-published simultaneously in *Journal of Homosexuality* (Harrington Park Press, an imprint of The Haworth Press, Inc.) Vol. 50, No. 2/3, 2006, pp. 325-348; and: *Sadomasochism: Powerful Pleasures* (ed: Peggy J. Kleinplatz, and Charles Moser) Harrington Park Press, an imprint of The Haworth Press, Inc., 2006, pp. 325-348. Single or multiple copies of this article are available for a fee from The Haworth Document Delivery Service [1-800-HAWORTH, 9:00 a.m. - 5:00 p.m. (EST). E-mail address: docdelivery@haworthpress.com].

cated communication of subtle differences in intent; and eventuates in profound self-knowledge and transcendent levels of intimacy. Illustrative case examples are provided. *[Article copies available for a fee from The Haworth Document Delivery Service: 1-800-HAWORTH. E-mail address: <docdelivery@haworthpress.com> Website: <http://www.HaworthPress.com> © 2006 by The Haworth Press, Inc. All rights reserved.]*

KEYWORDS. Sexual sadomasochism, BDSM or SM, sexual dysfunction, eroticism, sex therapy

UNCOMMON SEX: LEARNING FROM EXTRAORDINARY LOVERS

The purpose of this paper is to explore what clinicians can learn from those who seek and attain uncommon sexual relations. Specifically, what can we learn about the farther reaches of human erotic potential by studying self-identified, consensual SM practitioners?

The idea of studying those we deem as "other" to learn about sexuality is not original but remains uncommon. In 1979, Masters and Johnson studied the sexual behavior patterns of gay and lesbian individuals. They concluded that gay men and lesbians were more sensitive and effective lovers than their heterosexual counterparts (Masters & Johnson, 1979). Gay and lesbian couples devoted more time to lingering over the various stages of erotic arousal, spent more time talking with each other, were more empathic and had more effective communication strategies (Masters & Johnson, 1979). These findings, unfortunately, did not garner much attention. The import of these findings goes beyond what they reveal about a particular group of individuals; rather, Masters and Johnson's work demonstrates the benefits that can accrue from a shift in perspectives and methodology in sexology. The over-arching contribution of their research is that there is a great deal that "we" can learn from "them," if only we attempt to study those we consider different. Much can be gleaned from studying all kinds of individuals, even when there seem to be superficial or even significant differences between "us" and "them." Divergent groups have much more to teach us than the workings of a particular brand of sexuality; they also can teach us about sexuality per se and how to improve it (Kleinplatz, 2001).

The mental health professions and society have marginalized SM practitioners. Sexual Sadism and Sexual Masochism are still classified as mental disorders in the *Diagnostic and Statistical Manual* of the American Psychiatric Association (APA, 2000). Society has discriminated again SM practitioners. But there is another way of thinking about the margin: What if we conceive of it as the cutting edge of human sexuality? The intent here is to turn our thinking about human sexuality on its head. Instead of simply pathologizing sadomasochism, we might ask what lessons can be learned about human erotic potential by learning from those who engage in uncommon sex. We may have a great deal to learn if we quit pathologizing whatever seems alien and, instead, examine and perhaps embrace the possibilities and potentials that may be revealed (Kleinplatz, 2001).

This is neither a plea for inclusiveness nor for recognizing sexual diversity but rather to acknowledge and study the erotic lives of individuals we have marginalized, from the elderly, to the disabled, the polyamorous and those diagnosed as Paraphilic. In this particular paper, the focus will be on individuals who practice SM. The goal is not to advocate that everyone practice some particular variety of sex–let alone SM. The intent here is to see what can be discovered about the range of healthy or even optimal sexuality by exploring and examining divergent modes of sexual expression.

Below are two case illustrations. The first couple identified as SM practitioners when they came for therapy. The other couple did not practice SM initially but by the time therapy terminated, their erotic horizons had expanded. Having already stepped outside the bounds of traditional sexuality, that is, having already violated the norms of conventional sexual definitions, identities, preferences and orientations, SM practitioners are well situated to chart their own paths. They are free to ask themselves, "How high can we fly?" "How far can we take each other via erotic play?" Clearly, they have something to teach us about the farther reaches of human erotic potential. The next section describes these two couples and is followed by ten lessons from the edge.

What brings SM individuals/couples into therapy? In my clinical practice, which is limited to sex therapy, the presenting complaints among SM practitioners resemble the concerns of other patients seeking sex therapy, such as erectile dysfunction, lack of sexual desire, vaginismus, etc. So it was with these clients. My approach, however, tends to differ from the norm in the field of sex therapy (Kleinplatz, 2001, 2004) which often aims at treatment of symptoms of sexual dysfunctions. In my practice, when clients are so inclined, we use the presenting complaint as an avenue towards substantive change (Mahrer, 1996/2004) and optimal erotic fulfilment.

Both cases are discussed with informed consent and identifying details have been disguised to protect the couples' identities (Clifft, 1986).

CLINICAL ILLUSTRATION: JOHN AND MARIE

The first couple is John and Marie. I have described the first few sessions with this couple previously (Kleinplatz, 2001, 2004). The surprise for me was that after their initial problems had been resolved, this couple chose to remain in therapy to fulfill an entirely different agenda. The couple were referred to me because of his erectile dysfunction. They had spent so many years prior to the outset of therapy literally watching his penis going up and down that they had lost interest in sex.

During the second session, I asked her about the last time that she had felt sexually excited. She said she could barely remember. I asked her to find a moment where something was happening inside of her. It did not matter if it was "sexual" or not. She said, "Actually, it was just the other night. I was starring in *Carmen*. I got up there on stage and I started singing." She described what it was like to have all the members of the cast at this rehearsal with their eyes upon her. I pictured her there at the center of the village square strutting her stuff–being so ravishing that she was daring all the men around her to look. Marie was really blushing as she realized that what she wanted was not only to be ravishing but to be ravished. She wanted every man in the room to be unable to take his eyes off of her. She wanted to capture her partner with her raw aesthetic and to have him unravel her. This was not acceptable to them but there was no denying that the room was heating up as the session progressed. She felt flustered until she turned to him and found that he was "ready to eat [her] alive." She liked that. Within a week after the conclusion of the session, his erectile dysfunction vanished as did her lack of sexual desire because they had discovered something they had never dared to discuss: She wanted to be dominated and he was eager to get out of politically correct mode with her and to own her.

By the next session their presenting problems had evaporated, yet, surprisingly, they returned for 40 more sessions. It was no longer to deal with problems but in order to attain higher levels of erotic intimacy. They chose to deal with what they named initially "our submerged fear of sexual demons," that is, their intense guilt and shame upon discovering that they were very excited by SM. For him in particular, this did not fit intellectually, given his "pro-feminist values." It was quite a discovery that male aggression could be a life-affirming force when it was carefully marshaled in the context of nicely challenging, mutually consensual dominance and submission

At the next session, as they were in the first thrall of discovering that the erectile dysfunction had dissipated, they said, "It may have been lousy SM but it was the best lovemaking we've ever had. It's funny that by playing the role that's not who you really are, you can come close to becoming who you really are . . . And that's why it's so scary."

As they began to explore tentatively in foreign territory, they said, "What's lurking there? Is it a monster? It's hard to know what to do with a part of oneself you don't know." I asked them if they really wanted to know: "How far into this voyage of self-discovery are you willing to take each other?" She would say to him, "What scares me is needing too much and you being overwhelmed by my needs so that you can't find out what you want." She would pull back from expressing her wishes so as not to impose upon him with her erotic desires. She would become silent and then resent being silent. Over the course of several months, both during psychotherapy sessions and in their time alone, they developed better communication and negotiation strategies. They then used these new skills to ask for what they wanted and to have those needs fulfilled without feeling that they were pushing each other beyond tolerance. Instead, they began pushing each other's limits in ways that were mutually beneficial.

Both began realizing the importance of owning their own fantasies instead of placing the origins and responsibilities for their fantasies someplace else. She would say, "I realize that I've been in my head sexually rather than in my body. . . . Now it will take some work to bridge the faceless men I've always fantasized about with this actual man whom I love and who loves me and who could reject me by discovering who I really am." He reported, "I'm very excited to be tapping into something outside my usual evaluative mode–to be discovering my own capacity for exploration, openness and creativity." And with that, they both commented on innocence in a new form: unselfconscious sexual experience and the lifting off of the adult perceptual imprint from experience, thereby exposing raw sensation. They revelled in pure sensuality, in pre-verbal, fully embodied touch, unadulterated, uncorrupted, and undiluted by assessment, judgment and beliefs.

They also began violating various other kinds of norms that most do not even notice or detect such as the belief that sex was supposed to be "natural and spontaneous" (Klein, 2002). It did not seem romantic to them–as they had previously defined romantic–when they had to *plan* carefully to spend three, four or five hours or perhaps even an entire Sunday in bed together. It took them a while to consider the possibility that the incontrovertible, sexual rules they had taken for granted were, in fact, subject to change. Once they grasped the advantages of arranging time for slow, sensuous, erotic intimacy, they grew to like it. "Spontaneity" was replaced by anticipation and playfulness as well as a willingness to enter into the unknown.

Each had regarded their fantasies as a prison, never once sharing them with one another; these prisons had prevented them from communicating for fear of being understood–not misunderstood, but understood accurately. Now that they recognized fantasies as potential–as possibility–they grew less afraid of being seen, of being known, and being utterly naked to each other. In one of our last sessions, she commented, "To be really free would be to say, 'I like SM'–period. Not to say, 'We're doing it to *be* free, eventually' so that we can ultimately drop it when we are free but just because I like it. I used to think that the day I was free would be the day I would be rid of my SM fantasies. Instead I discover that the day I *am* free is the day I *claim* all this." She began to laugh. Then she began to cry. Then he joined her in crying.

They discovered their mutual love of high levels of erotic intensity. They engaged in all kinds of role-playing, from Sleeping Beauty to vampire scenes, in which they explored their own shadows.

At the outset, they had been a very conventional, politically correct couple; by the time of our last session they were experimenting with sharing a "24/7," dominant-submissive relationship.

CLINICAL ILLUSTRATION:
CAROL AND DANA

Dana and Carol were a couple who had been together for twelve years and who referred to themselves as Leather Dykes, with Dana primarily topping Carol. They came to therapy for a multitude of reasons. Carol was a survivor of physical and sexual abuse. She had been referred for treatment of lack of sexual desire and anorgasmia. She would "freeze" during sex, shutting down to the point where she would hyperventilate and faint. Notwithstanding her unorthodox sexual behavior, she held many "conventional" attitudes about sex. She was emotionally inhibited and disembodied. She was also exceptionally intelligent.

Dana, also, was a survivor of physical and sexual abuse brutal enough to require plastic surgery to remove scar tissue. Previously, she had been diagnosed with obsessive-compulsive disorder and panic disorder. She had numerous somatic problems including arthritis, cardiovascular disease and genital pain. She was on a large regimen of medications and was seeing gynecologists, psychiatrists and cardiologists, among others.

Carol and Dana reported that for five years before commencing therapy, neither one of them had had sex, let alone with each other. Both had a history of flashbacks every time they did have sex. They had constructed a relationship very carefully in which one had lack of desire or arousal problems only to be alleviated as the other developed similar problems. It was as if they had decided to take turns having difficulties with desire and initiation. In systemic terms, they had manoeuvered to keep the absolute distance between them constant, even if this distance occasionally shifted locations.

They had sought my help primarily because of my work with the sexual concerns of sexual abuse survivors. In our first session, as they catalogued the drugs that might be affecting them sexually, I suggested they discuss their medications with their physicians. They responded that both were terrified of seeing health-care professionals, especially physicians. In the past, every time either would be examined by a physician, there were numerous questions about the various, readily visible marks on their bodies. Given that Dana had a myriad of serious physical problems, requiring continuing medical attention, she could not afford to go too long without receiving appropriate health care. I recommended *Health Care Without Shame* (Moser, 1999) to help them deal with their quite legitimate suspicions of conventional health care and to provide useful information about how to obtain the medical attention that Dana required.

During our second session, one week after I had recommended this reading material, they announced, much to my surprise, that the book had been arousing. The book is intended to provide health-care information rather than be a source of erotic material. I asked them to describe what they had found arousing. They answered vaguely that it had been, ". . . a bunch of stuff . . . like about piercing." This had led them to begin having sex, ". . . but of course, it led to pain so we stopped." I asked about what got them going and about what exactly made them stop. Carol said, ". . . an orgasm equals fears of loss of control." Nonetheless, they had spent some time playing together erotically, which is more than they had done in five years.

After the second session, Dana tied Carol up and penetrated her anally. Carol had felt very embarrassed about being aroused. She said, "I couldn't protect myself." These words provided fuel for our work together. From what did she need protection? She explained that every time she shut down, it was not because of lack of desire: "I dissociated but it wasn't only around leather–it was around losing any kind of control." Dana intervened, saying, "That's OK. You can lose control. I know how to bring you back." They considered this carefully and both agreed that they were willing to let Dana exercise this emotional power in their explorations.

At the following session, Dana said, "Well I wanted to take her further but I hesitated to come up against Carol's mental walls." Carol responded, "Having my clit stimulated makes me feel like a puppet on a string." As these words clarified Carol's dilemma, their solution began to crystallize: Could Carol control Dana's hand while Dana controlled Carol's clitoris, even though Dana had already secured Carol in bondage? Given their sincere willingness to work together and to put their entire trust in one another, they were able to devise ways of doing this. They were inspired and creative in their use of cues. They used "safe words" (i.e., code words popular in SM communities) which spelled out what each could or could not do, plus "Let's try this," "Let's not try that," "I don't know if I'm into that but I'd like to find out," and especially, "No, I'm not into that but please take me further anyhow, if you can." That "cured" the anorgasmia.

Specifically, in the next session, Carol reported that as she had approached orgasm, she had felt afraid of how she looked and of being laughed at. While bound by Dana, she had begun to cry and went into a fetal position. Nonetheless, she expressed her fears, remained present and connected with Dana. Dana's response had been "to keep stroking Carol and talking to her, reassuring her." The safety Carol had felt during this process had allowed her to reach orgasm. Carol expressed a willingness to venture still further: "I'm willing to let go and give you more control." Dana responded, "Funny, my agenda is to help you find your limits and then to push them." Carol said, "I need the freedom to let my censor leave the room." The love and faith that allowed them to experience this freedom via bondage were palpable in the session.

As their explorations continued, their activities involved nipple clips, extreme bondage, renewed experimentation with Carol's pain-pleasure threshold and flogging. The flashbacks had ceased. The sexual dysfunction had been eliminated. Their level of intimacy had increased.

Both of them, but especially Dana, had brought a lot of baggage to therapy. Dana had come out as an SM activist twenty years ago and had had to contend with being called a bad lesbian and a bad feminist because of her SM activities. She had shut down the leather parts of her identity out of fear of doing further damage to her reputation as a feminist and because of the judgment and rejection she had already received. In so doing, she, "had lost [her] adult autonomy." Thus, when she entered into her current explorations, it was not merely to help Carol to become more orgasmic; rather, along the way, Dana was reclaiming parts of herself that she had disowned in the past. In the process, Carol helped Dana to demystify the desires that their own community had pathologized.

As they delved deeper, Dana expressed a readiness to deal with her history of abuse. She described the contours of the scene she envisioned to help transcend her suffering. It involved switching roles with Carol and allowing her to assume control. Dana turned to Carol saying, "Tie me up so it's safe for me to go back there and remember it and work through it and get my own power back from it." Carol was touched by this request and replied, "I am honoured by the opportunity and challenge." Then Dana added, "I want to be swept off my feet . . . I want someone to get inside me and tune into what turns me on . . . Except for my abusers, no one could ever tune into me on that level . . ." To which Carol responded playfully, "I volunteer to penetrate and turn you inside out." Carol's glee at the prospect brought Dana to tears of joy. She described her senses as suddenly very acute.

The notion that survivors of childhood sexual abuse can endeavour to resolve their pain via erotic explorations is bound to make many therapists recoil. Yet I have come to respect the power of (what some therapists might call) such "corrective emotional experiences" to transform one's relations with the past. Carol and Dana did not undertake this challenge lightly but cautiously and respectfully, despite the impish tone. This work requires skill and care on the part of the therapist to help navigate through the numerous minefields involved in any such process. Furthermore, it involved tremendous skill and courage on the part of these clients; they were playing as lovers with early childhood memories as well as with family of origin issues and adolescent sexual assaults. They were deliberately, consciously, knowingly rewriting the horrors of the past and re-integrating missing parts of themselves in the process. Although I do not advocate the routine use of their approach by others, their experiences invite further exploration and thinking regarding the healing processes that may be at play.

Their effectiveness was evident in their outcomes: Previously, they were haunted by the ghosts of childhood sexual abuse and the ghosts of politically correct, lesbian feminism whispering, "You are really sick." Now, the accusatory monologues were being replaced by an inner dialogue fostered by our therapy as well as by the work these women engaged in as lovers. They were enabled to thumb their noses at the demons and to say in essence, "But it turns me on and it's life affirming." Or as Dana exclaimed after a particularly intense fisting scene, "I'm a pervert, a slut and loving it." A core of solidity, vitality and authenticity emerged from years and layers of deadness.

They flourished as they continued to use SM sex in the process of self-definition. In our final session, they commented about what an enormous gift they had bestowed upon one another. Both asked, "How far am I willing to go . . . and what does that say about me?" They were enjoying their intimate union, on the verge of transformation and headed towards the unimaginable. Their parting words as they left their last session were, "If we keep doing this, we win."

TEN LESSONS FROM THE EDGE

I would like to honor these four, very courageous individuals by recounting what I have learned from them. The following are 10 lessons from the edge, that is, what ordinary clinicians and ordinary lovers can learn from extraordinary couples who are at the farther reaches of human erotic potential. These lessons do not pertain only to SM practitioners; on the contrary, the value of these insights is their relevance for sexuality in general. The 10 categories overlap in some instances but are separated in order to emphasize differing nuances of meaning.

Lesson 1. The power of intense eroticism lies within.

Talk of keeping sexual relations vibrant often focusses upon increasing variety (e.g., varying routines, trying new positions, adding sex toys). However, such simple "solutions" risk missing the point: The power of intense eroticism is not to be found in clever, skilled or expert stimulation and manipulation of the partner's genitals but in penetrating the person within. Too many people, including too many therapists, are focused on partners' bodies. One must reach inside the partner's inner world to find his or her secret places and to appreciate his/her uniqueness.

Unfortunately, in the last few years, our discourse around sexuality has been dominated by the pharmaceutical industry (Tiefer, 2000) which encourages us to think in terms of a "fit-tab-A-into-slot-B" model of human sexuality (McCormick, 1994). What my clients (above) teach is that in order to become a great lover, one must first enter into the partner's phenomenal world and find the other's secret places. It was very difficult for John and Marie to acknowledge to each other what they really wanted. Although it was anxiety-provoking, it was even more life affirming to uncover and discover themselves in each other–to see themselves reflected in each other's eyes and to know that even when they were utterly naked, they were accepted for exactly who they were.

Eroticism can potentially go beyond the sensory to involve the entire range of intrapsychic and interpersonal elements. The passion of eroticism may perhaps be most profound when both partners sense the metaphoric penetration of one another's deeper, inner, hidden selves (Kleinplatz, 1996a). Such intrapsychic penetration can be scary. Most pull back from it. But what makes it frightening is also what makes it embarrassing, exhilarating, compelling, remarkable and unforgettable.

How can we come to know one another in bed? One answer may be through heightened empathy and by continuing to uncover and discover the other, long after the most expedient routes to orgasm have been mastered. Sex goes awry when people touch without feeling; clients report how dismal it feels to be touched as if they were pieces of wood rather than embodied beings, alive in their flesh. That kind of disaster is relatively easy to detect. The more interesting problem occurs when two people have ceased to explore one another precisely because they have confused the goals of erotic intimacy with the goals of sexual performance or release. One involves emotional safety and tension reduction while the other entails heightening of erotic tension and, often, raising the emotional stakes. There is a shift in epistemology from a focus on knowledge of the partner's bodily responses per se, by perfecting the manipulation of the partner's genitalia, to using the partner's responses as a way to penetrate and enter the person within. In conventional sexual relations, the epistemology is unclear. In extraordinary sex, the objective of coming to know each other–particularly the secrets that one is ambivalent about sharing or even that one senses only dimly oneself–is made explicit. This intricate level of self-revelation and knowledge is essential if partners are to "push the limits" in SM interactions.

Lesson 2. The devil is in the details. Aim for better, more finely tuned, intricate, specific phenomenology.

We are missing the boat by not looking carefully enough at the details of what erotic arousal is about. Combinations of subjective, sexual/erotic meanings are as distinctive as fingerprints. While traditional sex therapy often focuses on what is on the surface, many SM participants are interested in the meanings that lie at a deeper level.

If a patient walks into a therapist's office and states that he has intense, long-standing fantasies of being bound and beaten and has uneasy feelings about it, the therapist now has sufficient information, based on the *DSM*, to diagnose him with a paraphilia, specifically Sexual Masochism (Kleinplatz, 2001). In contrast, if he were to present himself to a professional dominatrix with the same opening remarks, she would be out of business very quickly if she decided on that basis to simply restrain and flog him. Instead, she would be interviewing her client very carefully to discover precisely what he was seeking.

The clients described above paid a great deal of attention to the cues coming from each other. The "top"/Dom/Domme/Master/Mistress needs to know the precise nature of the partner's desires and must use sophisticated communication skills to discover subtle differences in intent and meaning.

The devil is in the details. Describing a person as dominant or submissive does not begin to capture it. Four dominant individuals may bring distinctively different intentions to superficially similar acts: The first wants dominion, rule, to stake claim, to possess, to mark his territory; a second wants a target for her aggression, her pent-up, uncivilized, pre-verbal, wild energy; a third seeks freedom, abandon, unrestrained license to do as he pleases without having to account for his choices; and a fourth is deliberate, calculating, methodical, proceeding sometimes with scientific detachment and other times with scientific zeal, in search of knowledge and absolute control. Similarly, here are four submissive individuals: The first wants to belong, the security of knowing his place, to be part of something bigger than himself, to be possessed. The second longs to be known and exposed, no escape from her own secrets, to be penetrated and plundered, to have no way out, no deceiving, misleading or concealment possible. The third seeks adventure, to go on a ride with no known destination, time line and no built-in safety net, and once she signs on, all right to back out is forfeited. The fourth is compelled by losing control, by being overwhelmed, by being penetrated, invaded and intruded upon, until he surrenders, body and soul, until there is no will of his own remaining, only the capacity to respond fully and without question.

As a field we spend too much time focused on labels and not enough on unique, individual phenomena. In fact, our diagnostic labels may obscure further exploration of the distinctive individual present in the office. We can learn a lot from extraordinary clients. They do not stop at the peripherals or at the superficial level but aim to access the level of underlying meanings.

If we develop and employ more sensitive epistemologies, we may begin to understand the vast array of ways of being, sexually and otherwise, that have been lumped together. In order to become more effective therapists, we will need to strip away the pretense of clinical understanding implicit in our diagnostic processes and to discover the particular erotic meanings that reside in the details.

Lesson 3. Do not engage in "sex" (whatever that means) until your level of arousal is through the roof. Otherwise, you invite and incur the risk of developing sexual dysfunctions, pain or desire disorders.

The model of sexual relations that predominates in our culture is one of heterosexual intercourse as the defining act and ultimate end of sex. For most heterosexual couples, intercourse remains *the* sex act. Everything else is relegated to "foreplay." As soon as she has begun to lubricate and he has an erection, they are seen as "ready" for "sex." However, engaging in sexual intercourse when the necessary physical conditions have been barely attained may not be sufficient for ensuring long-term sexual/erotic satisfaction. Thus, paradoxically, settling for sexual functioning as the primary indicator of readiness for sex may risk eventual sexual dysfunction.

Some regard this line of reasoning as nonsense and would reply that people can withstand all kinds of tolerable or even miserable sex without it causing them sexual dysfunctions, pain or desire disorders. Whereas that may be true of one-night stands and of very short-term relationships, if one is going to have a long-term relationship, then "sex" had better be exciting, or else why bother?

There is a reason that the most common sexual problem is lack of sexual desire: It may be that couples settle for mediocre sex until their bodies finally begin to protest at the death of their dreams. John presented with erectile dysfunction. Typically, they had initiated coitus while at fairly low levels of arousal. What they discovered was that if they attempted to engage in intercourse when they had barely reached the threshold for minimal sexual functioning, that choice would sometimes result in "sexual dysfunction" and sometimes not. On the other hand, if they refrained from intromission until their arousal levels soared, then they could not go wrong. Then, not only was John going to be erect and Marie well-lubricated and both of them very desirous, but the focus of the sex was no longer to revolve around whether or not they managed to "function" well enough/adequately to get through intercourse. Their lovemaking began to sizzle and, more importantly, the rest of their relationship became passionate, too. Thus, they were no longer worrying about whether or not he would be able to attain "an erection sufficient for penetration."

Lesson 4. Relationship factors require continuing attention. The levels of trust, communication and negotiation skills required for extraordinary, erotic intimacy far exceed those common in ordinary sexual relations.

This "lesson" seems obvious. This is sex therapy 101 and yet perhaps we sometimes forget it. None of these principles is unique to SM couples. On the contrary, the point is that these principles can and do apply to all of us. We may sometimes overlook them because the focus of our work can be terribly mundane. When looking at extraordinary couples, we see that in order to attain their calibre of sex, one has to (or both have to) expend considerable effort to achieve the required level of trust. For example, the level of trust typically required for a woman to allow a man to insert his penis into her vagina cannot compare to the level typically required for a man to allow his partner to insert his or her fist into his rectum. The latter requires communication and negotiation skills, exercised in advance. It will not "just happen" unless it has been worked out, that is, discussed, planned, organized and consented to beforehand.

Even the level of trust and communication required to accomplish the physical aspects of fisting is distinct from the trust required to share feelings of emptiness and fullness/completeness, of wanting intense bonding, to be known and touched and felt from the inside out, so fully and profoundly that one or both are changed by virtue of the encounter and the knowledge that they have entered the transgressive realm together.

Obviously, the submissive must trust that the dominant's motives are honorable and respectful–that all exploitation will be mutually advantageous, desired, consensual and beneficial. Perhaps less obviously, the dominant must trust that the submissive has enough self-knowledge and awareness of the risks and benefits to enter into their encounter giving fully informed consent. No dominant–at least in a successful, ongoing, erotic relationship–can function effectively without knowing that he or she is truly free to act as he or she deems best; he or she must trust the submissive's judgment which allows him or her to "top": the submissive without fear of actually damaging (or even of being accused of damaging) the "bottom" or their relationship. The required dialogue is not easy but can be a deeply rewarding means of ensuring that the other's needs are met.

Many individuals want others to be mind-readers so as to evade responsibility for their own desires. Disputes about even relatively simple matters, such as sexual initiation, are common. Lovers have difficulty saying, "How about if we switch positions this time?" or even ". . . a little to the left, dear." When sex therapists coach couples in sexual communication skills, we are typically aiming towards relatively low levels of request and refusal behaviors. If even that is difficult, it is infinitely more risky to share the deep desires that put one's joys, sorrows, unresolved wounds and temptations on display before a beloved partner. If we probe extensively enough and deeply enough, most of our clients and most of our lovers have little or not so little desires that haunt them in the dark, that niggle at them and yet cannot be denied, commanding attention while simultaneously demanding relief. The challenge in sharing such desires is not merely a matter of technical difficulty. It is not a matter of finding the words to communicate the unspeakable. It is choosing to reveal one's inner self so openly, without pretense or guile, that there is no going back.

This means a willingness to go beyond truthfulness or even honesty to authenticity and transparency, to allowing oneself to be vulnerable and naked, whether as "top" or "bottom," to allow one's deepest desires, fears, hopes and sources of joy to be touched, explored in the trust that they will be handled with care. The very act of establishing a safe-word is a shared acknowledgment that protests in moments of extreme intensity may be fraught with ambivalence–or outright play-acting–but are created in the spirit of mutuality and goodwill.

This level of vulnerability is not only implied by the "Safe, Sane and Consensual" SM credo but is the essence of the underlying principles. The notion is of entering into the erotic encounter with enough presence of mind, integrity, trust and fortitude to divulge one's most exciting, stimulating, titillating, threatening, joyful, anxiety-provoking fantasies with the expectation of respect for self and other(s) to make that mutual consent knowing, informed and meaningful.

Lesson 5. Sex has as many purposes as there are people having sex. "Sex" is about "nonsexual" purposes, also.

Men and women who practise SM are often judged as mentally ill on the basis of their motives. Admittedly, they may engage in SM for goals, objectives, purposes and reasons other than "sex." Some sex therapists regard it as pathological when individuals become sexually aroused by stimuli or associations "that are not inherently about sex" (Hastings, 1998, p. 110). One of the criteria listed in the sexual addiction movement for diagnosing pathology is when individuals use sex for nonsexual purposes (Carnes, 1983, 1991; Schwartz & Brasted, 1985). But even the authors who advocate this position rarely define what a "sexual purpose" is. It seems implicit that there is a correct purpose for sex.

What is this purpose? Is it reproduction, sexual intercourse or orgasm? How is this determination to be made? When the goal of treatment for the Paraphilias is to have clients become aroused only in the presence of the correct stimuli and for the correct purpose(s), there must be someone authorized to assess which kinds of arousal are acceptable and which are to be diagnosed and treated as pathological. The problem is that this determination is not about the well being of the clients; this may say more about the values of the therapist (and/or the society that he or she has been designated to represent). This pernicious process is about a particular set of social mores being disguised in scientific jargon and harnessed to further sexual oppression.

The notion that sex has a correct purpose is equivalent to saying that the only purpose for going for a walk in the woods is to get exercise. There are many good reasons for going for a walk in the woods. Maybe one just likes the scenery. It is dangerous to allow "experts" to dictate what the right reason is for having sex, let alone that the right reason ought to be reproduction or orgasm.

It is claimed that participants engage in SM as a means of affect regulation and/or that they are unable to maintain intimacy (APA, 2000; Levine, Althof & Risen, 1990; Schwartz & Masters, 1983). My clients demonstrate that the capacity for intimacy, even though expressed unconventionally, runs deep indeed. It is further argued that the evidence for SM as pathology, specifically sexual addiction, is that the dependence/withdrawal process is progressive and degenerative (Carnes, 1991). But under which circumstances is affect regulation perceived as problematic? How are we to distinguish when attempts to intensify or modulate one's emotions signify a pathological process and when they are healthy or life-affirming? All too often such judgments are moral– not scientific in nature. Do we express concern for the mental health of the person who progresses from sailing a boat down a river to circum- navigating the globe? Do we speak of dependence when individuals feel uneasy because they missed their morning workout? Vague criteria and scare-mongering tactics keep us afraid of the dark unknown. Maybe all that is proven by virtue of increasing SM intensity is that its participants are seeking increased growth.

Erotic sex often serves nonsexual purposes. To think otherwise seems to be foolish and to sell sex short. The irony is that the definition of pathological sex is also the marker of multidimensional sex. To use sex for only one purpose, tension release, is to deny all the manifold purposes that every human connection can attain/contain. What the cli- ents (above) illustrate is that as they finely tuned the purpose of their sexual relations to fit their own inner needs, they had more and more fulfilling sex.

Here is the paradox: Engaging in sex for nonsexual purposes is con- sidered pathological. Mediocre sex often fulfills the goal of tension re- lease. Great sex has to tap into much more; it has to touch our cores. Very often, in conventional sexual relations, people are reluctant to ac- knowledge what they are really seeking or hoping to attain via their sex- ual contacts. Among some SM practitioners, emotional and erotic transparency is valued so that at least in theory, particular motives and goals are to be divulged and shared rather than hidden obliquely.

Lesson 6. Sex can accomplish more than tension release and orgasm. It can bring about feelings of aliveness, expansion, self-knowledge, joy, a sense of peace, harmony, ecstasy, wholeness and of "coming home."

Conventional models of sexuality, whether held by sexologists or or- dinary lovers, stand in stark contrast with the actual experiences of some SM practitioners. Whereas many couples are willing to settle for merely functional sex, SM practitioners seek erotic contact that necessi- tates intense, erotic connection and eventuates in profound self-knowl- edge and transcendent levels of intimacy.

Although some sexologists are interested in multidimensional per- spectives on sexuality (Helminiak, 1998; Ogden, 1999), much of the discourse around sexuality has robbed our field of an understanding of just how all-encompassing human sexuality can be. Sex can involve our very souls. This is the kind of sex the clients cited above are having. The power of the deep erotic connection they attain is such that it is often described as "coming home."

Whenever partners share in extraordinary sexual relations of whatever kind, one of the characteristics reported is a sense of synchronicity, of high levels of mutual attunement which typically stems from and inevitably creates an intense mutual bond. Such partners know each other so intimately that they can almost predict the other's responses while also aware that if they play just the right notes at precisely the right moments, the chords they strike will create an entirely new melody–never heard before and never to be repeated in quite the same fashion. This combination of expectancy, unpredictability and heightened empathy provides the elements necessary for intensifying their erotic bond/intimacy. It is a high wire act, albeit with a net underneath.

The sexual relations found among the clients cited above are not about people who are running away from intimacy, notwithstanding the unusual nature of their sex lives; it is about choosing an extraordinary level of intense, erotic intimacy and of mutual trust. Once one enters the power exchange with a trusted partner, there is no going back, literally or figuratively. To put oneself in another's hands is not about escapism but rather about being uncovered, exposure and discovery. To be held, appreciated, embraced and loved despite being (or because of having the courage to be) vulnerable and known intimately can lead to self-discovery and acceptance that is transforming. This is living on the edge. It may entail placing oneself in suspended animation, changing one's pain threshold and intensely focused concentration.

What the clinical illustrations above demonstrate is that unfettered erotic expression can be an important avenue for emotional release and psychic freedom. Access to one's deepest inner needs and wishes enables greater self-knowledge which in turn facilitates authenticity (Mahrer, 1996/2004).

Lesson 7. Sex can be profoundly transformative. It can be therapeutic, healing and/or transcending not only sexual wounds but various kinds of psychological injuries.

The transformative power of the erotic (Kleinplatz, 1996a, 1996b, 2001, 2004; Leonard, 1989; Morin, 1995; Ogden, 1999; Rofes, 1996; Schnarch, 1991) has been largely absent from our discourse in sex therapy. However, the couples above and others like them have discovered that sex can serve as a vehicle for intrapsychic, interpersonal, erotic and spiritual growth occurring on multiple dimensions simultaneously.

In fact, for the individuals described above, their erotic encounters were designed specifically to create transformative moments. Although their choices may be controversial, Dana and Carol choreographed their erotic play in order to enable Dana to confront and exorcise the ghosts that had haunted her ever since her childhood sexual abuse. In particular, they employed the consensual power exchange of SM to recreate the childhood moments when much of Dana's inner self had been prematurely and forcefully shut down. Their work/play together (as planned and rehearsed in therapy) allowed Dana to access hidden parts of her self and to reclaim them on her own terms.

Dana's cardiovascular disease remained present but her need for medication decreased dramatically, and, certainly, her genital pain was eliminated. Her anger about the incredibly violent abuse that she had suffered had dissipated. Dana was not only fully alive but later chose to volunteer with an organization serving other survivors of sexual abuse. She wanted to share with others the knowledge that sex need not be the enemy but could instead provide the road to healing when one enters into one's own eroticism with nothing held back.

Some have suggested that SM desires are not only pathological but are symptomatic of a history of sexual abuse (Maltz & Boss, 1997). Similarly, others argue that SM activity indicates attempts at escape from self (Baumeister, 1989, 1997). On the contrary, Dana and Carol's experiences indicate that SM may be a powerful tool in self-discovery. I am not advocating SM as a "treatment" for incest survivors but I am suggesting that those who are drawn to power exchange should not automatically be "treated" with elimination of these desires set a priori as the therapy goal. At least in some instances, individuals can use consensual SM play as a vehicle to change their relations with the past and to re-integrate the potentials that have been hidden within.

For both couples above, living out their fantasies meant putting their ambivalence, conflict and even torment on display. They had deliberately laid out the strictures in which they could discover what they were capable of–providing one another with the permission, security and parameters wherein to test limits. (The theme of freedom in bondage is common among bondage enthusiasts.)

Lesson 8. Aim high. Learn from those who refuse to settle for merely, incredibly pleasureful and thoroughly satisfying sex.

Sexologists focus primarily on the abnormal and pathological despite the lack of a clear reference point; there is little knowledge of what constitutes normal sexuality, let alone the nature of optimal sexuality or how to attain it.

Correspondingly, most clients come to sex therapy because they are having little sex, little desire for sex or because of sexual dysfunctions. Therapists often terminate treatment when we have helped clients to achieve mediocre levels of sex (Schnarch, 1991). Their sexual problems may have been treated to the point where they have attained normative performance standards. However, the clients' sex lives may not be especially fulfilling, either. The quality of their sexual relations often remains disappointing and dissatisfying. Mechanical, quick-fix treatments for sexual performance problems (e.g., erectile dysfunctions, vaginismus) may eventuate in infrequent sex and future problems of low sexual desire.

Instead, we may need to learn from those who aspire much, much higher than even merely incredibly pleasureful and thoroughly satisfying sex. My clients reveal a great deal about the farther reaches of human erotic potential by virtue of how high they aim. If we want to know something about fitness, there are obvious advantages in studying Olympic athletes rather than couch potatoes. Similarly, sex therapists will need to focus more attention on erotic adventurers who refuse to settle for merely satisfying sex but who seek transformation. This kind of sex does not just "happen," let alone spontaneously–it requires attention, forethought and devotion. It presupposes a mindset in which participants aim for growth and in which erotic intimacy provides a vehicle for expanding one's boundaries and stretching one's limits.

Whereas many people conceal themselves during sex, extraordinary lovers deliberately seek out the anxiety provoking. That which creates embarrassment, trepidation, a sense of foreboding, or provokes uneasy nervous laughter, curiosity, a titillating sense of risk and/or a compelling hint of arousal (Mahrer, 1996/2004) may suggest the potential for growth resides there. Rather than trying to dampen, modulate, contain and ignore (i.e., "bypass") the anxiety that interferes with "functioning," such lovers explore and exploit sensitive areas and use them as an avenue towards personal development and erotic intimacy. They may not know what lurks in their own shadows but the attitude is of welcoming unknowns.

Lesson 9. Keep going deeper, higher and further. The eroticism is in the continuing exploration, uncovering and discovery of possibilities and potentials (especially key in long-term relationships).

Very often, couples who report low frequency of sexual relations and little excitement during sex (the ones who are just ripe for having affairs) say, "The mystery is gone. I look back so fondly to that first year, to the honeymoon phase of our relationship and . . . it's over. I don't know what happened. . . ." It is often because they spent the early part of their relationship trying to get to know each other but stopped exploring once they found the formula to help reach orgasm as expediently as possible. Knowing the formula, they then repeated it, not noticing that nothing kills sexual desire as much as doing what works–relentlessly. The message from my clients is that in a long-term relationship, despite sure knowledge of the partner's body, it is essential that one continue to explore the person within–and then explore deeper, higher and further. The consequences of participating in sex over a prolonged period without intimate, sexual connection, even when the mechanical aspects of sex are satisfactory, may be the loss of sexual desire or the ability to become aroused (Kleinplatz, 1996b, 2001).

The need for continuing sexual exploration, even or particularly when it feels risky to pursue further, is particularly important in light of the common belief in the sex therapy literature (cf., Carnes, 1991; Johnston, Ward & Hudson, 1997; Schwartz and Brasted, 1985) that it is important to contain (what we perceive to be) deviant impulses. Paradoxically, the attempt to contain impulses, in effect, is making those impulses increasingly ego alien or ego dystonic. My "paraphilic" clients often initially try to hold their desires at bay. It seems safer that way. John and Marie worked very hard never to acknowledge to themselves or each other what really excited them. The more they tried to make their inner selves opaque, the more energy was required to dissimulate. On the other hand, once they began the process of self-revelation, things shifted. The elements she had always thought were erotic proved to be so at first, but soon began to evolve. Even the greatest of fantasies tends to shift in character once fulfilled, or as some would say, once it is no longer ego alien and becomes ego syntonic.

Clients often fear that once they acknowledge their desires–or even more dangerously, attempt to fulfill them, no matter how minimally– they will never be able to deny them again; they will be drawn to living out their fantasies endlessly, becoming "addicted." Yet the opposite is often the reality. Those who attempt to foreclose on their deepest desires often find secrecy and isolation only fuel fantasies. The effect of disclosure, in contrast, brings relief. Fantasies seems less crazy, lose their intensity and the power to menace. The effect of actualizing fantasies, even a little bit, serves as a reality check and provides the realignment that comes with finding out precisely what one really wants. When the ultimate fantasy, the simultaneous fear of and desire to be known surfaces, the possibility for self-knowledge and erotic intimacy grows.

Those who presuppose the need to contain impulses may have it backwards: They may be colluding with their clients' fears of what lies within. If on the other hand we as therapists stop being afraid of the things we are afraid of and if as lovers we are willing to go deeper and higher in penetrating one another's souls, then we can have long-term relationships with the potential for long-term joy.

Lesson 10. Being on the edge is scary but then so are the alternatives. Erotic adventures are genuinely risky but then the risks of erotic stagnation are no less dangerous.

Others, including other sex therapists, question the wisdom in validating and perhaps even encouraging individuals and couples to explore erotic alternatives, asking me, "Don't you understand what you are advocating is scary?" Yes, of course it is scary. Being on the edge is scary but then so are the alternatives. Erotic adventures are genuinely risky but then the hazards of erotic stagnation are no less risky. That is the part we are not talking about as a field and that we need to discuss. Sometimes, when our clients present with complaints of arousal problems or lack of desire, there is no pathology. There is nothing wrong with either of them. There may be nothing wrong with them as a couple but if I had their sex life, I would be bored, too. As summarized by Moser, "Enjoyable sex is not a substitute for hot or passionate sex" (1992, p. 69).

Teetering over the edge may involve remaining present while exposed, being raw and emotionally unprotected. It means opening oneself up and surrendering to being known with no guarantee of safety. There will be no assurance that feeling intensely means feeling only joy and pleasure; when one is fully engaged, pain can really hurt. Is that a good thing or a bad thing? The answer requires a value judgment.

Perhaps it is time to consider the alternative. Of course erotic adventures are risky. My clients' sexual activities may seem disconcerting to many people. But the hazards of erotic stagnation are what bring many clients into our offices. Instead of searching for psychopathology, why not acknowledge the lackluster nature of their sex lives and learn from those who have extraordinary sex even when it is extraordinarily kinky sex? We can tell clients, "Look, you can stay where you are, but there is a cost to doing that. There is a cost to engaging in risky sexual behaviors as well. Pick one."

CONCLUSIONS

Two couples were referred for sex therapy for treatment of sexual dysfunctions including erectile dysfunction, low sexual desire and anorgasmia. Both couples resolved their sexual difficulties as they became increasingly intimate in the context of consensual SM relationships. Although Sexual Sadism and Sexual Masochism are still classified as pathological (APA, 2000), sexologists may have much to learn by studying those we have marginalized. Instead of merely treating patients for sexual dysfunctions or Paraphilias, we may use both their "disorders" and their solutions to teach us about the farther reaches of human erotic potential. Having transgressed outside the realm of conventional sexuality, these clients were enabled to experience extraordinary levels of arousal, desire, self- and mutual knowledge, authenticity, trust and eroticism. The lessons they teach are not specific to SM; on the contrary, they demonstrate that those on the edge can reveal much about extraordinary sex per se for individual/couples in general. We can either continue to dismiss/condemn transgressive individuals/couples or we can study their sexual relations in an attempt to discover the transformative potential of intense erotic intimacy.

REFERENCES

American Psychiatric Association (2000). *Diagnostic and statistical manual of mental disorders*, 4th edition-text revised. Washington, DC: APA Press.

Baumeister, R. (1997). The enigmatic appeal of sexual masochism: Why people desire pain, bondage, and humiliation in sex. *Journal of Social & Clinical Psychology. 16*(2), 133-150.

Baumeister, R. F. (1989). *Masochism and the self.* Hillsdale, NJ: Erlbaum.

Carnes, P. (1983). *Out of the shadows: Understanding sexual addiction.* Minneapolis: Comp Care.

Carnes, P. (1991). *Don't call it love.* New York: Bantam.

Clifft, M. A. (1986). Writing about psychiatric patients: Guidelines for disguising case material. *Bulletin of the Menninger Clinic, 50*(6), 511-524.

Hastings, A. S. (1998). *Treating sexual shame: A new map for overcoming dysfunction, abuse, and addiction.* Northvale, NJ: Jason Aronson Inc.

Helminiak, D.A. (1998). Sexuality and spirituality: A humanist account. *Pastoral Psychology. 47*(2), 119-126.

Johnston, L., Ward, T., & Hudson, S.M. (1997). Deviant sexual thoughts: Mental control and the treatment of sexual offenders. *Journal of Sex Research, 34*(2), 121-130.

Klein, M. (2002). *Beyond orgasm: Dare to be honest about the sex you really want.* Ten Speed Press.

Kleinplatz, P. J. (1996a). The erotic encounter. *Journal of Humanistic Psychology*, *36*(3), 105-123.

Kleinplatz, P.J. (1996b). Transforming sex therapy: Integrating erotic potential. *The Humanistic Psychologist*, *24* (2), 190-202.

Kleinplatz, P.J. (2001). A critique of the goals of sex therapy or the hazards of safer sex. In P.J. Kleinplatz (Ed.) *New Directions in Sex Therapy: Innovations and Alternatives* (pp. 109-131). Philadelphia: Brunner-Routledge.

Kleinplatz, P. J. (2004). Beyond sexual mechanics and hydraulics: Humanizing the discourse surrounding erectile dysfunction. *Journal of Humanistic Psychology*, *44*(2), 215-242 .

Leonard, G. (1989). Erotic love as surrender. In G. Feuerstein (Ed.), *Enlightened sexuality: Essays on body-positive spirituality*. Freedom, CA: Crossing Press.

Levine, S. B., Risen, C. B., & Althof, S. E. (1990). Essay on the diagnosis and nature of paraphilia. *Journal of Sex & Marital Therapy, 16*(2), 89-102.

Mahrer, A. R. (1996/2004). *The complete guide to experiential psychotherapy*. Boulder, CO: Bull Press.

Maltz, W., & Boss, S. (1997). *In the garden of desire: The intimate world of women's sexual fantasies*. New York: Broadway Books.

Masters, W. H., & Johnson, V. E. (1979) *Homosexuality in perspective*. Boston: Little, Brown.

McCormick, N.B. (1994). *Sexual salvation: Affirming women's sexual rights and pleasures*. Connecticut: Praeger.

Morin, J. (1995). *The erotic mind*. New York: HarperCollins.

Moser, C. (1992). Lust, lack of desire, and paraphilias: Some thoughts and possible connections. *Journal of Sex & Marital Therapy, 18*(1), 65-69.

Moser, C. (1999). *Health care without shame*. Greenery Press: San Francisco.

Ogden, G. (1999). *Women who love sex: An inquiry into the expanding spirit of women's erotic experience*. Cambridge, MA: Womanspirit Press.

Rofes, E. (1996). *Reviving the tribe: Regenerating gay men's sexuality and culture in the ongoing epidemic*. New York: Haworth Press.

Schnarch, D. (1991). *Constructing the sexual crucible: An integration of sexual and marital therapy*. New York: Norton.

Schwartz, M.F., & Brasted, W.S. (1985). Sexual addiction: Self-hatred, guilt, and passive rage contribute to this deviant behavior. *Medical Aspects of Human Sexuality, 19* (10), 103-107.

Schwartz, M.F., & Masters, W.H. (1983). Conceptual factors in the treatment of paraphilias: A preliminary report. *Journal of Sex & Marital Therapy, 9* (1), 3-18.

Tiefer, L. (2000). Sexology and the pharmaceutical industry: The threat of co-optation. *Journal of Sex Research, 37* (3), 273-283.

Index

ABH. *See* Actual Bodily Harm (ABH)
Ability to leave, in 24/7 SM slavery,
    92
Absolut vodka ad, 218
Abuse
    child, SM practices resulting from,
        44
    sexual
        in children, sexual orientation
            effects of, 53-54
        defined, 53
Access Hollywood, 110
Activism, SM, 210-213. *See also*
        Sadomasochism (SM)
        activist/activism
Actual bodily harm (ABH),
        169-170,174
ADA. *See* American Decency
        Association (ADA)
AFA. *See* American Family
        Association (AFA)
Against Sadomasochism, 220,221
Alison, L., 7,20,22,23,41,51
All Women of Leather, 307
Altoids breath mint ad, 123
American Decency Association
        (ADA), 227
American Family Association (AFA),
        227
American Gay Liberation Movement
        (1969), 194
American Psychiatric Association
        (APA), 12,29,229,246,327
American Psychological Association,
        Ethics Code for
        Psychologists of, 305
Amnesty International, 266

Andersen, Y.H., 258
Anger, K., 197
ANOVA, 145-147
Anthony, E., 76
Antisocial personality disorder, 141
A.N.T.R.O., 263-265
APA. *See* American Psychiatric
        Association (APA)
APEX. *See* Arizona Power Exchange
        (APEX)
Appeal Court, 170
Appellate Court, 201
"Appleby Statute," 208-209
Arizona Power Exchange (APEX), 33
Arsenio Hall Show, 74
Associated Press, 210
Asylum(s), Salpetriere, 191
Attention, continuing, for relationship
        factors, 338-339
Attleboro District Courthouse, 208,209
Austria, SM in, 274-276
Authoritarianism subscale, of DPQ,
        141
AWOL, 307

B & D. *See* Bondage and discipline (B
        & D)
Ballantine's Law Dictionary, 193
Baltimore AT-EASE, 225
Bannon, R., 257
"Barde," 278
Barnard College, 200,201
Barney, J., 199
ba-sappho, 307
Bass Ale beer print campaign, 108,123
Baumeister, R.F., 48,136-137,142,147

349

practitioners of, mainstream
    perceptions of, 224-229
prevalence of, 302
preview of, 6-15
process of, 35
progressive stages in, 35
research on, 62
social sciences and, 17-40
    challenge to *DSM* nosology, 30
    content analyses, 25-27
    critical essays, 29-32
    ethnographic research, 27-29
    legal decisions related to,
        critiques of, 30-32
    survey research and
        questionnaire studies, 20-25
    social/context-based perceptions of,
        135-137
spanking in, 61-64
state of our knowledge of, 1-15
subcultures in. *See*
    Sachomasochistic subcultures
in Switzerland, 277-278
in United Kingdom
    changing law on, 167-188
    facts related to, 168-171
    past, present, and future,
        185-186
in U.S., legal status of, 189-216
    Commonwealth v Appleby,
        199-200
    described, 196-197
    law reforms, policies, and court
        cases, 194-196
    Mark IV Incident, 198-199
    People v Jovanovic, 200-201
    People v Samuels, 197-198
    related legal issues, 201-210. *See
        also* Legal issues,
        SM–related, in U.S.
    State v Collier, 200
violence *vs.,* 222
what we know about, 32-37
Sadomasochism (SM)
    activist/activism, 210-213

Sadomasochistic events, opposition to,
    227-228
Sadomasochistic interests, as issue in
    child custody proceeding,
    233-242
    case example, 235-242
    conclusions, 241-242
    decision, 239-240
    described, 235-236
    Dr. Blair's report, 236-239
    meaning in, 240-241
Sadomasochistic organizations,
    historical background of,
    36
Sadomasochistic practices, feminist
    opposition to, 219-222
Sadomasochistic slavery, 24/7,
    81-101. *See also* 24/7 SM
    slavery
Sadomasochistic subcultures, gay *vs.*
    straight persons in, 41-57
demographic features, 45-46
"Safe, Sane and Consensual"
    SM credo, 339
Safewords, in 24/7 SM slavery, 90-91,
    90t
Salpetriere asylum, 191
SAMOIS, 307
"San Diego Six," 212
Sandnabba, N.K., 7,20-22,27,41
Santorum, R., 210
Santtila, P., 7,20,41,52
Satisfaction, in 24/7 SM slavery, 92
SBI. *See* Sexual Behavior Inventory
    (SBI)
Scandinavian Leather Men (SLM),
    256,257
Scat, 52
"Schlagartig," 275
"Schlagfertig," 275
Schlagzeilen, 267
SCL-90-R subscale, 144
Script(s), sexual, 64
"Secret Euro Houses of Domination,"
    265

BOOK ORDER FORM!

Order a copy of this book with this form or online at:
http://www.haworthpress.com/store/product.asp?sku= 5794

Sadomasochism
Powerful Pleasures

_____ in softbound at $29.95 ISBN-13: 978-1-56023-640-5 / ISBN-10: 1-56023-640-X.
_____ in hardbound at $59.95 ISBN-13: 978-1-56023-639-9 / ISBN-10: 1-56023-639-6.

COST OF BOOKS _____

POSTAGE & HANDLING _____
US: $4.00 for first book & $1.50
for each additional book
Outside US: $5.00 for first book
& $2.00 for each additional book.

SUBTOTAL _____

In Canada: add 7% GST. _____

STATE TAX _____
CA, IL, IN, MN, NJ, NY, OH, PA & SD residents
please add appropriate local sales tax.

FINAL TOTAL _____
If paying in Canadian funds, convert
using the current exchange rate.
UNESCO coupons welcome.

❑**BILL ME LATER:**
Bill-me option is good on US/Canada/
Mexico orders only; not good to jobbers,
wholesalers, or subscription agencies.

❑**Signature** _____

Payment Enclosed: $ _____

❑ **PLEASE CHARGE TO MY CREDIT CARD:**

❑Visa ❑MasterCard ❑AmEx ❑Discover
❑Diner's Club ❑Eurocard ❑JCB

Account # _____

Exp Date _____

Signature _____
(Prices in US dollars and subject to change without notice.)

PLEASE PRINT ALL INFORMATION OR ATTACH YOUR BUSINESS CARD

Name

Address

City   State/Province   Zip/Postal Code

Country

Tel   Fax

May we use your e-mail address for confirmations and other types of information? ❑Yes ❑No We appreciate receiving
your e-mail address. Haworth would like to e-mail special discount offers to you, as a preferred customer.
We will never share, rent, or exchange your e-mail address. We regard such actions as an invasion of your privacy.

Order from your **local bookstore** or directly from
The Haworth Press, Inc. 10 Alice Street, Binghamton, New York 13904-1580 • USA
Call our toll-free number (1-800-429-6784) / Outside US/Canada: (607) 722-5857
Fax: 1-800-895-0582 / Outside US/Canada: (607) 771-0012
E-mail your order to us: orders@haworthpress.com

For orders outside US and Canada, you may wish to order through your local
sales representative, distributor, or bookseller.
For information, see http://haworthpress.com/distributors

(Discounts are available for individual orders in US and Canada only, not booksellers/distributors.)

The **Haworth Press** Inc.

Please photocopy this form for your personal use.
www.HaworthPress.com

BOF06